Civil War

CAMPAIGNS *in the* HEARTLAND

STEVEN E. WOODWORTH
AND CHARLES D. GREAR
SERIES EDITORS

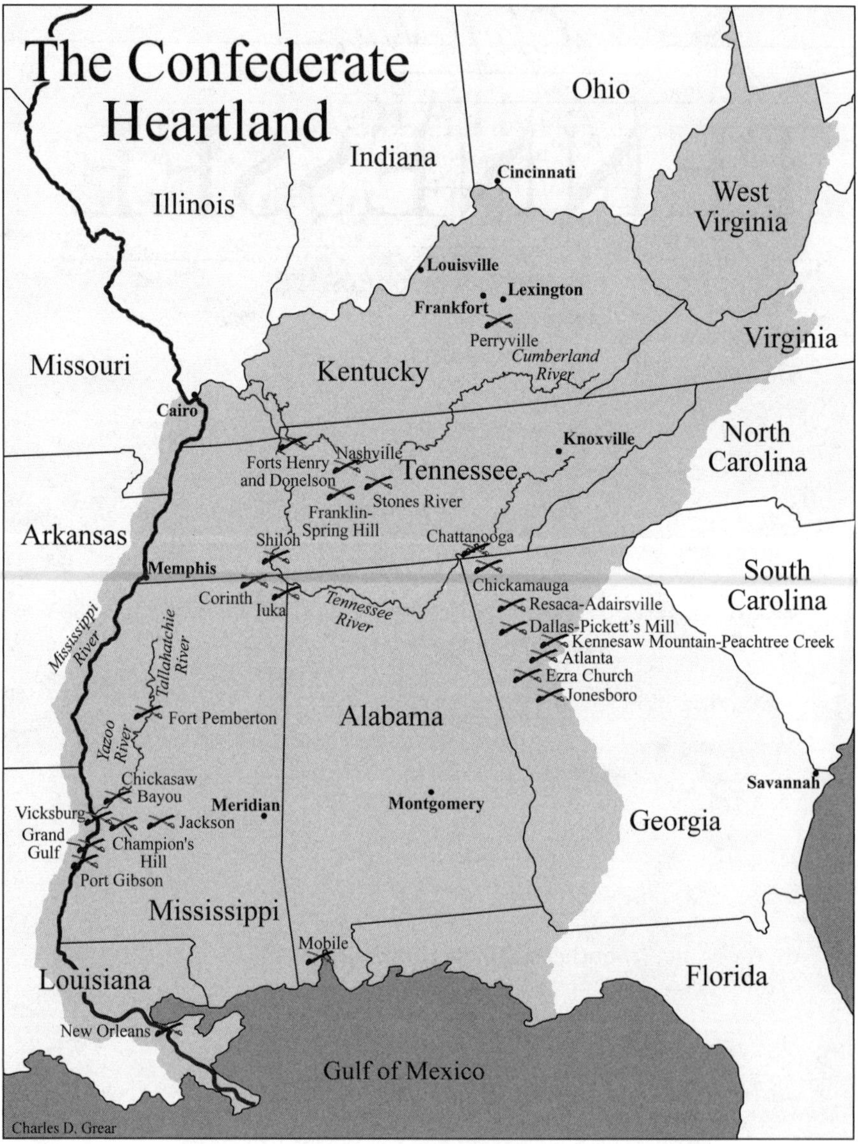

The Confederate Heartland
Ohio
Indiana
Illinois
Cincinnati
West Virginia
Louisville
Lexington
Frankfort
Perryville
Cumberland River
Virginia
Missouri
Kentucky
Cairo
Knoxville
North Carolina
Forts Henry and Donelson
Nashville
Tennessee
Stones River
Franklin-Spring Hill
Arkansas
Shiloh
Chattanooga
Memphis
South Carolina
Chickamauga
Corinth
Iuka
Tennessee River
Resaca-Adairsville
Dallas-Pickett's Mill
Kennesaw Mountain-Peachtree Creek
Atlanta
Ezra Church
Jonesboro
Mississippi River
Tallahatchie River
Yazoo River
Fort Pemberton
Alabama
Chickasaw Bayou
Savannah
Vicksburg
Meridian
Montgomery
Jackson
Grand Gulf
Champion's Hill
Georgia
Port Gibson
Mississippi
Mobile
Louisiana
Florida
New Orleans
Gulf of Mexico
Charles D. Grear

The TENNESSEE *Campaign* OF 1864

Edited by Steven E. Woodworth
and Charles D. Grear

Southern Illinois University Press
Carbondale

Printed in the United States of America

19 18 17 16 4 3 2 1

Jacket illustration: *Battle of Allatoona Pass* (lightened in color), chromolithograph by Thure de Thulstrup (Boston: L. Prang, 1887). Library of Congress Prints and Photographs Division; LC-USZC2-497.

Library of Congress Cataloging-in-Publication Data
The Tennessee Campaign of 1864 / edited by Steven E. Woodworth and Charles D. Grear.
pages cm. — (Civil War campaigns in the heartland)
Includes bibliographical references and index.
ISBN 978-0-8093-3452-0 (cloth : alk. paper)
ISBN 978-0-8093-3453-7 (e-book)
1. Tennessee—History—Civil War, 1861–1865—Campaigns. 2. Franklin, Battle of, Franklin, Tenn., 1864. 3. Nashville, Battle of, Nashville, Tenn., 1864. I. Woodworth, Steven E., editor, author. II. Grear, Charles D., [date] editor, author.
E477.52.T46 2016
973.7'359—dc23 2015016937

Printed on recycled paper. ♻

The paper used in this publication meets the minimum requirements of American National Standard for Information Sciences—Permanence of Paper for Printed Library Materials, ANSI Z39.48-1992. ∞

To my lovely stepdaughter, Haley Marie Martinez
I am proud of your achievements
and the young woman you have become.

Again, for Leah

CONTENTS

ILLUSTRATIONS

Maps

Figures (beginning on page 123)

ACKNOWLEDGMENTS

Books cannot be developed without the help of many people. We, the editors, only serve a small role in creating this volume. The staff of Southern Illinois University Press has invested countless hours throughout every step of the publishing process; from designing the book to printing and marketing. Thank you. We owe our deepest gratitude to all the contributors. Their cooperation and dedication to this book made it a joy to work on—more importantly, it would not exist without them. Thank you all. As always, Southern Illinois University Press editor Sylvia Frank Rodrigue deserves distinct recognition for all her efforts. Sylvia campaigns for our books and goes above and beyond what is expected of any editor. Lastly, we would like to express our deepest appreciation to our families for their constant support. They inspire us in all our endeavors.

The Tennessee Campaign

OF 1864

INTRODUCTION

Steven E. Woodworth

The fall of Atlanta to the forces of Union general William Tecumseh Sherman on September 1, 1864, leading as it did to the reelection of President Abraham Lincoln two months later, probably extinguished the last remotely realistic chance of Confederate success in the Civil War. It's possible that Lincoln might have been reelected even if the Confederates had held Atlanta. It's possible that the Union might have won its final triumphs during the winter and early spring of 1865 even under a lame-duck Lincoln and then a newly inaugurated President George B. McClellan. But it's almost unimaginable that the Confederacy could have maintained its independence through another four years of Lincoln presidency or even through another two under the staunchly Republican Congress northern voters had elected when they returned the great Illinoisan to the White House. After the fall of Atlanta, then, Confederate soldiers were truly fighting for a lost cause, a fact that makes all the more tragic the campaign that followed in North Georgia and Middle Tennessee.

That realization, however, is the product of hindsight. It was true, but the participants, from generals to private soldiers, could hardly be expected to have known it. The Confederates might have had their qualms from time to time and with growing frequency and intensity as defeat followed defeat and southern prospects deteriorated, but those who struggle in great conflicts must be familiar with such feelings—and must learn to dismiss them. History was full of causes that had looked lost and then somehow prevailed. Many Rebels no doubt called to mind their Revolutionary forebearers in the dark days of Valley Forge and hoped that with similar fortitude and perseverance their own cause also might triumph. Some men deserted the gray and butternut ranks. Most soldiered on.

The Confederate general who lost Atlanta was John B. Hood. He had performed tolerably well in defense of the city. Elevated to command of the Army of Tennessee after his predecessor had retreated literally into the outskirts of the city, Hood had fought three battles in nine days in an effort to fend off another of the turning movements with which Sherman had maneuvered the Army of Tennessee back over the ninety miles from Dalton to Atlanta. With no more miles to give up, Hood had no choice but to fight. His battle plans were good, in one case very good, and his audacity enabled him to surprise Sherman twice in the space of a week. Sherman's subordinates knew Hood better. They included Hood's 1853 West Point classmates James B. McPherson and John M. Schofield as well as Oliver O. Howard, who had been in the class of '54. McPherson and Howard anticipated two of Hood's attacks, and their troops, as well as those of Sherman's senior subordinate, Major General George H. Thomas, fought tenaciously, handing Hood three defeats in as many battles.

If Hood was open to criticism for his performance in these fights, it was that he had not done well enough in preparing, coordinating, and controlling his attacks. Throughout the war, Confederate generals struggled to direct their armies with inadequate staffs. A defect of Confederate law allowed army commanders too few staff officers for all the work that was required to direct an army's operations.[1] In trying to compensate for that lack, among other numerous reasons including proving their leadership and courage, a number of Confederate army commanders had chosen to direct at least some of their battles from positions dangerously near the front. Notable among these were Joseph E. Johnston, who had been badly wounded at Fair Oaks; Albert Sidney Johnston, who had been killed at Shiloh; and Robert E. Lee, who could easily have been killed at any one of the Seven Days' Battles. As a subordinate, Hood too had led from the front. It had cost him a leg at Chickamauga and the permanent crippling of an arm at Gettysburg. He now rode strapped in the saddle, with his crutch strapped on behind. There would be no more vaulting onto a horse and galloping off to survey and direct events at far ends of a battlefield. During the fighting around Atlanta, Hood stayed at his headquarters and tasked subordinates with directing the battles from horseback. It had not worked out particularly well.

Yet despite the three defeats Hood managed to stretch his lines far enough to prevent Sherman from cutting the railroad supply lines into Atlanta. For five more weeks he thwarted the skillful Union general, until at the end of August Sherman launched a bolder and wider turning movement aimed at the railroads south of Atlanta. Hood dispatched a subordinate to strike at Sherman with two-thirds of the army but again suffered defeat and this time had to abandon Atlanta or face encirclement and capture there.

With Atlanta gone, Hood undertook a new campaign, which is the subject of this volume. Seeking to force Sherman to abandon Atlanta and fall

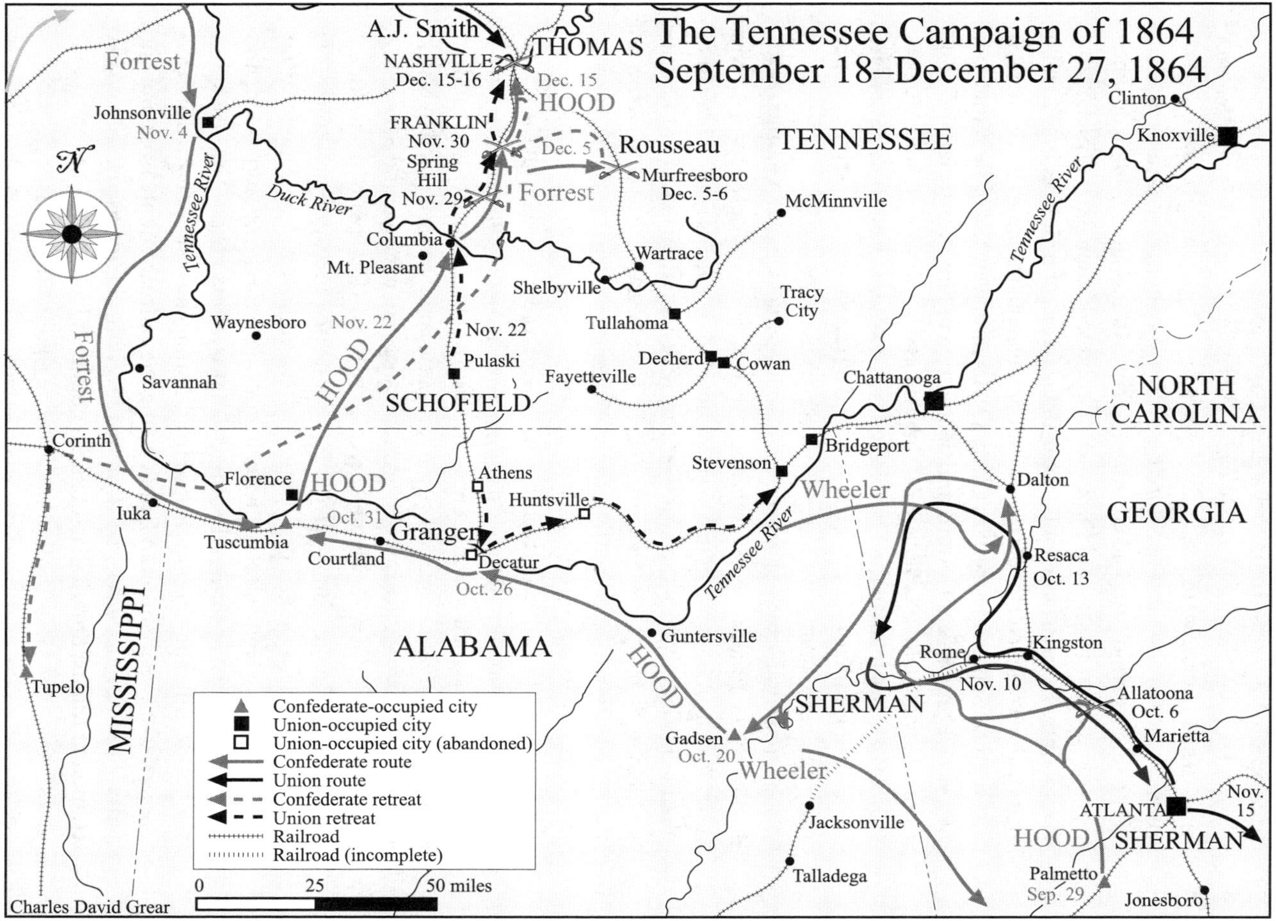

The Tennessee Campaign of 1864
September 18–December 27, 1864
A.J. Smith
THOMAS
NASHVILLE
Dec. 15-16
Dec. 15
HOOD
FRANKLIN
Nov. 30
Spring
Hill
Nov. 29
Dec. 5
Rousseau
Murfreesboro
Dec. 5-6
Forrest
TENNESSEE
Clinton
Knoxville
Johnsonville
Nov. 4
Tennessee River
Duck River
Columbia
Mt. Pleasant
McMinnville
Wartrace
Shelbyville
Tracy
City
Tullahoma
Waynesboro
Nov. 22
HOOD
Nov. 22
Pulaski
Decherd
Cowan
Fayetteville
Savannah
SCHOFIELD
Chattanooga
NORTH
CAROLINA
Corinth
Bridgeport
Stevenson
Athens
Florence
HOOD
Dalton
Wheeler
GEORGIA
Iuka
Huntsville
Oct. 31
Granger
Tuscumbia
Courtland
Decatur
Resaca
Oct. 13
Oct. 26
Guntersville
Kingston
ALABAMA
Rome
Nov. 10
MISSISSIPPI
Tupelo
Allatoona
Oct. 6
SHERMAN
Gadsen
Oct. 20
Marietta
Wheeler
Jacksonville
ATLANTA
Nov.
15
HOOD
SHERMAN
Palmetto
Sep. 29
Talladega
Jonesboro
Confederate-occupied city
Union-occupied city
Union-occupied city (abandoned)
Confederate route
Union route
Confederate retreat
Union retreat
Railroad
Railroad (incomplete)
0
25
50 miles
Charles David Grear

back on Chattanooga, Hood threatened the Union's vulnerable single-track railroad supply line in North Georgia. Sherman left a garrison in Atlanta and turned back toward Dalton with a force adequate to deal with Hood. For several weeks in early autumn the rival armies maneuvered across some of the same terrain they had traversed during the summer's Union advance toward Atlanta. Hood could not form a solid lodgment astride Sherman's supply line, and Sherman could not bring Hood to open battle, in which he was confident of defeating the Army of Tennessee.

Two chapters in the present volume deal with this phase of the campaign. Lee White presents a previously little-known portion of the diary of Confederate major general Patrick R. Cleburne from this period, and Stewart Bennett gives a detailed account of the small but intense Battle of Allatoona Pass, during which a Union garrison held the pass as well as the supply depot there against an entire division of Hood's army.

After several weeks of indecisive maneuvering in North Georgia, both of the rival commanding generals became frustrated and opted for radically different plans of campaign. Sherman decided to cut his own supply line, abandon Atlanta, and set out for the coast with sixty thousand men. To deal with Hood, Sherman detached Thomas with the Fourth Corps of his Army of the Cumberland together with Schofield's Twenty-Third Corps of the Army of the Ohio, directing Thomas to collect additional troops from Union garrisons in Tennessee. These forces, together with reinforcements then on the way to Nashville, would give Thomas an army more than sufficient to defeat Hood.

Thomas assigned Schofield with the Fourth and Twenty-third Corps to delay Hood's advance until the rest of the army could be assembled in Nashville. Hood moved quickly and with surprising skill to go around Schofield's small army at Columbia, Tennessee, and by the late afternoon of November 29 was near Spring Hill, twelve miles to the north, in position to cut off Schofield's retreat. Somehow he failed to accomplish that goal, and during the night, while Hood slept, Schofield's contingent marched north along the turnpike only a few hundred yards in front of Hood's army, thus escaping the threat of being trapped. The Spring Hill incident immediately became the subject of intense controversy, as first the participants and then in later years the historians strove to assign blame for the Confederate fiasco. In his chapter in this volume, John R. Lundberg takes a fresh look at the affair and gives a balanced assessment of its probable significance.

The following morning, November 30, Hood was furious to discover that his enemy had escaped. After scolding several of his subordinates for allowing that to happen, Hood ordered the available portion of his army into immediate pursuit of Schofield's Federals. One of his three corps, along with most of his artillery, was some miles behind, still catching up after having served as the holding force for the turning movement that had allowed Hood to go around Schofield at Columbia. So Hood pursued with the other two corps and only a couple of batteries. That afternoon his force caught up with Schofield at Franklin, another twelve miles to the north, where the latter had turned at bay while his engineers scrambled to repair the bridge over the Harpeth River so that his two corps, having now bought enough time for Thomas's consolidation at Nashville, could continue their march to join him there.

Hood rashly ordered an immediate frontal assault by his two available corps. The resulting battle was one of the two major actions of the campaign, and it is the subject of two chapters within this volume. Drew Bledsoe looks at the unusually high mortality the battle produced among Confederate generals, while Jonathan Steplyk examines the attitudes of soldiers at Franklin toward the act of killing their enemies, something the battle featured in unusually close and intense form.

After repulsing Hood's attacks with great slaughter, Schofield marched his army across the by now repaired bridge and continued his progress toward Nashville, another fifteen miles or so to the north, where he arrived the next day. Hood followed and encamped in front of Thomas's entrenchments. Lacking sufficient numbers either to attack Thomas in his earthworks or to deploy a line that could stretch to confront Thomas's position from the banks of the Cumberland River above Nashville to the same river's banks below the city, Hood placed his army in a defensive position a couple of miles south of the center of Thomas's line. He had his men entrench, and he bent back, or refused, both ends of his line in hopes of fending off the Union flanking attacks that his short line almost invited. In this somewhat pathetic suggestion of a siege, Hood gave up the initiative and sat down to wait for something to turn up.

Due to various circumstances, Thomas waited until December 15 to launch his attack on Hood, inaugurating the climactic battle of the campaign. During the two weeks of delay, Union general in chief Ulysses S. Grant became increasingly dissatisfied with Thomas. Brooks Simpson examines this strained relationship in his chapter of this volume, while in a separate chapter Paul Schmelzer analyzes Thomas's approach to warfare.

When the fighting did open, some of the troops who played a conspicuously courageous role were those of the U.S. Colored Troops, most of them former slaves freed by the Emancipation Proclamation. Scott Stabler and Dannette Turner look at these men's struggle.

The most successful Federal unit in the Battle of Nashville was a three-division detachment of the Army of the Tennessee commanded by Major

General Andrew J. Smith. Steven E. Woodworth's chapter deals with this unit and seeks the reasons for its unusual success. John Gaines adds a chapter on the experience of civilians during the weeks in which the armies were marching, camping, and fighting around Franklin and Nashville, and Charles D. Grear assesses the reactions of Texans to the outcome of the 1864 Tennessee Campaign.

Finally, Timothy B. Smith provides a chapter on efforts toward the preservation of the Franklin battlefield, and Jennifer Murray rounds out the volume with a chapter on preservation attempts for the Nashville battlefield.

Note

1. R. Steven Jones, *The Right Hand of Command: Use and Disuse of Personal Staffs in the Civil War* (Mechanicsburg, PA: Stackpole, 2000), throughout.

1

THE LONG LOST DIARY OF MAJOR GENERAL PATRICK R. CLEBURNE

Edited by William Lee White

Major General Patrick R. Cleburne has become one of the most popular commanders of the Army of Tennessee, but very little in the way of personal writings is known to still exist. Cleburne was known to have kept a diary, and it is assumed that at the time of his death at Franklin it was sent along with other personal belongings to his fiancée, Susan Tarleton in Mobile, Alabama. Unfortunately the diary has not surfaced despite rumors that it survives. It thus came as a great surprise for me to stumble upon *The Walker County Messenger*, my hometown newspaper in LaFayette, Georgia, that published the manuscript, titled "Diary of One of Hood's Generals," as a serial in three parts, July 26, August 2 and 9, 1894.[1] As I read, it became clear that this was a diary of Patrick Cleburne. Apparently the general began a new diary at the beginning of what would prove to be his final campaign, and kept daily entries in it until he lost it on October 17 at LaFayette, where it was found by a local boy who went through the camps before the arrival of Union soldiers. The diary does not reveal anything earth shattering about the general, but it does confirm things that have been assumed about him and provides some insight into the man who was known as "The Stonewall of the West."

Patrick Ronayne Cleburne was born on March 16, 1828, the third child of Dr. Joseph and Mary Cleburne, in County Cork, Ireland. The Cleburnes were a respected middle-class family of the Protestant faith, and Patrick received a good education, excelling at history, geography, and literature. In 1843, after his father's death, he failed the entrance exam for medical school, and instead enlisted in the 41st Regiment of Foot in the British Army rather than face the humiliation of returning home. He hoped to be sent to India; however, that did not happen. The 41st was assigned to stay in Ireland for civil duties as the country endured the potato famine. His service was uneventful and full of the daily drudgery of a soldier's life, and though he was promoted to the rank of corporal, he was demoted after prisoners in his charge escaped. The prisoners, members of the Young Ireland movement, were most likely released on purpose by the young Cleburne, who shared sympathies with their cause.

In 1849, after three years' service, Cleburne decided it was time to leave, and purchased his discharge. The situation in Ireland was grim, even for the middle class, and Cleburne, along with his two oldest brothers and a sister, decided to leave for America. They arrived in the bustling port city of New Orleans on Christmas Day, 1849. The siblings did not stay long in the city, instead making their way north in search of employment, a quest that landed them in Cincinnati, Ohio, in early 1850. Patrick's future, however, lay elsewhere. Because he had some medical knowledge, Patrick was hired as a druggist in the little riverboat town of Helena, Arkansas, and he arrived there in April to begin his new job.[2]

Cleburne embraced his new community, joining social clubs and other affiliations that quickly made him a known and respected citizen of his adopted home. He joined the local Episcopal church and entered into politics initially as a Whig, but with the death of that party in the early 1850s and the rise of the anti-immigrant Know Nothings, he became a member of the Democratic Party in 1855. Cleburne signed on with the local militia company, the Yell Rifles, and by 1860 he was elected captain of the company. As the secession crisis loomed he stood "with the South in life or in death, in victory or defeat. I never owned a Negro and care nothing for them, but these people have been my friends and have stood up to me on all occasions."[3]

Captain Cleburne was at the forefront as his state began its slide from the Union: in February he led the Yell Rifles to Little Rock after word came from the governor's office calling for the surrender of the U.S. arsenal there. When Arkansas finally left the Union in May 1861, the Yell Rifles, like many other similar groups, stepped forward to offer their services to the Confederacy. As regiments were formed, the men elected Cleburne to the colonelcy of what became the 15th Arkansas Infantry Regiment. Cleburne led his regiment for the first months of the war before being elevated to command a brigade, and then receiving promotion to brigadier general in March of 1862.

Cleburne led his brigade into its first real battle at Shiloh, Tennessee, on April 6, 1862. There Cleburne's command lost heavily in the engagement, but he emerged much lauded for his conduct on the field. Cleburne's star continued to rise—he was given temporary command of a division in the late-summer campaign into Kentucky, where he was wounded at both the battles of Richmond and Perryville. He received promotion to major general and permanent command of a division in early December 1862, and led his command into the battle of Stones River a few weeks later, again achieving praise for his actions.

In the lull that followed in the spring of 1863, Cleburne set about molding his division into a more effective fighting force, increasing drill and training of his officers. In his spare time he read a favorite book of poetry and a two-volume set of *Chambers Information for the People*, a collection of scientific articles. When campaigning finally began in late June, Cleburne's division took to the field better prepared; however, it was not enough. The following campaign was disastrous for the Confederates and led to the abandonment of Middle Tennessee and retreat to Chattanooga, the Gateway to the Deep South. In the last days of summer Cleburne led his men through the first battle for control of that city, the Battle of Chickamauga, a three-day struggle that resulted in a costly Confederate victory, with the Union Army, in its defeat, occupying Chattanooga.

The Confederates placed the city under siege, but Union victories on the slopes of Lookout Mountain and Missionary Ridge ensured the failure of the campaign. Still, Cleburne and his command shone in defeat at what would become known as Tunnel Hill, holding their position on the northern end of Missionary Ridge even though they were greatly outnumbered. During the Confederate retreat, Cleburne was ordered to buy time for the retreating army. On November 27, at Ringgold Gap, Georgia, he once again faced off against great odds and managed to end the disastrous Chattanooga Campaign with a small battlefield victory for the Confederates.

With Cleburne's success at Ringgold Gap, the battered Army of Tennessee managed to complete its retreat to Dalton, Georgia, and went into winter quarters for the season. At Dalton, General Bragg resigned from command of the army and was replaced by General Joseph E. Johnston. Cleburne and his division encamped near Tunnel Hill, Georgia, a short distance west of Dalton. There he examined in his mind the disastrous course the war was taking and came to the conclusion that the war was lost unless drastic action was taken. Cleburne, probably with the influence of his old friend and now fellow division commander, Major General Thomas C. Hindman, drew up a proposal to enlist slaves into the ranks of the Confederate army in return for their freedom after faithful service. When Cleburne made the formal proposal to General Johnston and the senior leadership, he was met with a storm of criticism. In the aftermath he saw what he considered the Confederacy's last hope squashed and silenced when its president, Jefferson Davis, ordered the destruction of all copies of the proposal and declared there should be no further talk on the matter.

However, he didn't give up—he continued to train his men and officers at Dalton, and as a result, his division moved into the field at the peak of its combat effectiveness when the Atlanta Campaign began in May of 1864. During the weeks that followed, Cleburne and his command endured conditions unlike anything they had seen before: they fought almost constantly, slowly yielding ground in North Georgia to General Sherman's armies as they pushed the Confederates from position to position.

On May 27, Cleburne once again fought a battle that saved the Confederate army at Pickett's Mill near Dallas, Georgia. Finally the army ended up on the Kennesaw Line—a line of mountains and hills on the north side of Marietta, Georgia—where they halted Sherman for almost a month, but by early July they were retreating again to the outskirts of Atlanta. There Johnston was relieved of command and General John Bell Hood took command of to try to save Atlanta. However, it was too little and too late—by late August the city was lost, and Hood cast about for what to do next. With few prospects that didn't all but admit defeat, Hood decided on a desperate effort to try to reclaim the ground that was lost and maybe even turn the tide of the war. He would move into Sherman's rear and try to force him to give up what he had gained that spring. In this new campaign, Cleburne would play an important role, and it is here that he would note the events in his diary.

Sept. 28th—Informed by Hood we would leave in the morning and cross the Chattahoochee [River].[4]

Sept. 29th—Left our works at 8:30 o'clock this morning. Marched within two miles of River. Delayed in consequence of being behind the corps. Only traveled nine miles yet did not get into bivouac before sunset.[5] Men in high spirits.

Sept. 30th—Started at 7 o'clock A.M. Crossed on pontoon at Phillip's Ferry [Georgia].[6] Ran into rear of [Major General William Brimage] Bates'[7] on the side of the River. Delayed by them all day. Did not camp before dark, although we had not made more than 9 or 10 miles. Began early part of night to be very rainy. Road very hilly. Camped just south of Dog River.

Oct. 1st—Started at 8 A.M. so as to let [Major General Benjamin Franklin] Cheatham, who was 4 miles in front get well out of way. Took new, shorter and better route for wagons. Ran into Bates' division before it had started. Got to camp at 4 P.M., at Flat Rock Church.[8] Hood sent for me. Wished me to explain to officers and men the position of affairs and what he intended to do and what the men might be called on to endure. Had my brigade commanders together tonight and gave them instructions.[9]

Oct. 2nd—We remained at Flat Rock until 4:30 P.M., and then as I suggested to Cheatham we ran into Bates' division. It was just dark when I went into bivouac beyond Dark Corner. Meat was just issued before we left and I had to leave cooking details which did not catch up till very late. The enemy's cavalry have crossed Sweet Water Creek are coming in this direction. I have one regiment, Tyus'[10] picketing at Skinned Chestnut.[11]

Oct. 3rd—I had no marching orders, but started at 8:30 o'clock to catch up with Bate. We continued to march till near 4 P.M., in a perfect flood of rain, when we halted on the right of the line we have since fortified. Cannon at intervals all through the evening. My headquarters at a house on Dallas and Burnt Hickory Road. No room for me at the house. Loaned me a trundle bed four feet long. I had to pitch it out during the night, it was freighted with bed bugs.

Oct. 4th—We are ordered to fortify the line we were placed on last night. A dispatch from headquarters says [Lieutenant General Alexander] Stewart's Corps[12] struck the Rail Road in enemy's rear at Big Shanty at 3:30 o'clock P.M., on yesterday and is tearing it up in direction of Altoona. News that [Major General Nathan Bedford] Forest has torn up one of the enemy's Rail Road lines of communication for forty-five miles. Strong threats and small attempts at rain all day. Rode round my lines all except [Brigadier General Mark P.] Lowry's.[13] He was yesterday left at Gray's Burnt Mill[14] the picket on same place though farther in our rear. Just ordered to withdraw Lowry, leaving a regiment to do the picketing. He is to go to work continuing our line to the left in the morning. All very quiet. Rain still threatening.

Oct. 5th—Still threatening rain. All still quiet. I was out most of the morning examining the front. Rode to and through Powder Springs with Gen'l John C. Brown.[15] Received among other letters, one from Col. [Robert Bogardus] Snowden of Virginia,[16] thanking me for recommending him for brigadier general and telling me how high I stood with his troops.

Just at dark Brown and Cheatham called on me and announced that we would march at daylight in the morning for

Parson's. Start my wagons so that my troops can follow and yet get off at day light. I am to order the regiment on picket at Gray's Mill to a point on the Powder Springs road to catch some stragglers or deserters. To cook what rations we have on hand. Mine and Gen'l Brown's Pioneers[17] to start in front of everything and put the road in good order. I must move sufficiently far ahead to enable Cheatham's left to rest at Parson's.

Large body of enemy's cavalry moving north parallel to our line. Stewart captured three or four hundred infantry being the garrison of Ackworth.[18]

Oct. 6th—Started this morning at daylight and before 11 A.M. commenced camping on Van Wert road, about two miles west of Parson's and 9 miles west of Alman's. My headquarters at Mr. Busby's[19] on said road. It rained on us nearly the whole way. Roads very badly cut up. Heard that Stewart or rather [Major General Samuel G.] French's Division of Stewart's Corps made an attack I suppose on the Etowah Bridge with a loss of 120 men. Should have been at least 500.[20] A marrying widow here entertained us by talking of her better days and showing us her gaudy party-colored quilts.

Oct. 7th—Started at daylight, Cheatham looking for a better road. Found a longer and worse one. Pioneers reinforced by a fatigue party of a hundred. Had to bridge a branch of Pumpkin Vine.[21] Also the head waters of the Tallapoosa [River]. Our artillery crossed the latter at a deep ford but came through, I think, without any injury to the ammunition. Sent ordinance round. Halted near 18 miles from Busby's in the region called the Mountain. It was chiefly a pine forest boldly diversified.

Camped the men 4 miles west of Tallapoosa [Georgia]. Went a mile or two further myself. Cleaned out a beautiful little spring that trickled out of a rock and fell into a pure looking little basin of disintegrated quartz.

How tall the pines looked by the fire light. How grand looked the smoke looked curling up—up, among the bare lofty stems.

Slept in my tent on a little hill. This country would look beautiful if one could disassociate it from ticks.

Oct. 8th—Up by clear star light that peeped down through the openings in the pines. Saw one [wagon] train pass by before day. The heavy pine tops made the road dark and each wagon was accompanied by a soldier bearing a pine torch. It looked like some strange, grand procession. This morning clear and cold, almost biting winter showing his teeth. Caught a crawfish in our little spring. Had him cooked and ate him. Could not kill the thing by sticking it in the head. My flesh almost creeps when I think the cook had to drop it into boiling water to kill it. I will not trouble the genus craw again.

Arrived and camped at Cedartown[, Georgia,] about noon. It is a little place in a broad rich country where the phenomenon of men begging us to buy farm produce is again exhibited. The air though keen was pure as ice and without a speck of cloud. I felt exhilarated, enjoyed vitality and felt thankful for another moment of glad existence.

Hood overtook me on the road. He made the impression on me that instead of going to or via Jacksonville to any place we would again strike the railroad above the Etowah river and try to force the enemy back to Chattanooga. We will take with us nothing that can be done without, but one battery to a division, and a limited supply of ammunition and transportation, leaving all else at our depots near here. All these we are to find here (when having accomplished our work we return to move into Tennessee) in improved order. I did not gather whether we were to go through Rome[, Georgia]. I am informed there is a corps there. If so we will have work before us. He told me what he would do at Resaca[, Georgia].[22]

We are camped on Cedar Creek and I am in a house near by. We gave up our cows today for beef.[23] On the march they lost their value to us.

Oct. 9th—Reducing our transportation to the lowest possible standard. 1st. Enough for the smallest supply of cooking utensils. 2nd. One forge to division.[24] 3rd. One forage wagon to each brigade. 4th. Transportation for 40 rounds over and above what we carry in boxes.[25] 5th. Limited supply of ambulance and medical wagons and only one ambulance each to brigade and division headquarters. 6th. One battery with full supply of ammunition. Two forage wagons and forge. 7th. Tool wagons.[26] I brought only my blankets and one change of underclothing.

We cooked three days' rations and started at 1:30 o'clock P.M. I was delayed by Stewart's corps which somehow was in my road and traveled for two or three miles in my front. I got excited once thinking [Major General Edward C.] Walthall's division[27] was trying to get the road from me. It was one to those pure cold autumn evenings. The country open, the scenery grand. I made one and half miles beyond Cave Spring on the Coosaville road with but one halt. [Brigadier General Hiram Granbury] Granberry[28] told me the general opinion of me was that then duty was concerned I was severe and ignored all friendships. He thought it the secret of my success, but would not make me popular.

Camped in some old lady's parlor near my division. Cooked another day's rations. [General Pierre Gustave Toutant] Beauregard has just passed into Cave Spring.[29] His arrival creates unusual enthusiasm among the troops.

Oct. 10th—Crossed the Coosa at Quinn's Ferry[30] and bivouacked for the night within a miles of Berry Hills, 3 ½ miles east of Coosaville[, Georgia,] on the Alabama road, known as the old Alabama road. Enemy pickets out two or three miles in front of Rome and within less distance of us. They could be seen coming on this road from the fortified hills near Rome. A negro carried information of our movement across the Coosa to the Yankees early this morning.

The people here seem friendly to us, true to the cause. Two young girls met us on the roadside waving green boughs and singing a patriotic song urging us to fight on. The rough verse was their own or some other rustic poet's composition. The sight was rousing and touching.

My headquarters at a Mr. Blank's, a man evidently governed by his wife. He is a big, fat, silent man; she as thin as a witch.

Rode over a bridge hurriedly made of loose rails for the infantry to cross; rails laid side by side. My horse fell through and came near killing me and himself. When he was assured of his danger, he lay still as death till extricated.

Crossed the river at Quinn's Ferry. Some mistake in the roads again this evening.

Oct. 11th—We have to thank our good God for another beautiful morning. The spring mornings may be beautiful, but I admire most these misty autumn mornings when the outline of the trees and the distant mountains is indefinite and the proportions of everything are magnified; when the cobwebs are seen upon the sedge grass and the fences; when the grass is sprinkled with liquid diamonds and the sun himself walks up from the horizon with a veil before his ardent beams. The song and perfume of spring are missing, but the flowers are insignificant when compared to the grand coloring of the autumn woods.

We started at day light east of Alabama road. Turned to the left on a dim, pine straw covered road a few yards beyond Berry hill's. Two miles brought us to the Summerville road in which we found Cheatham's and Bate's divisions passing. They will delay us some time.

Col. [John] O'Neil, 10th Tenn., Irish, called on me this morning.[31] Said the Irish prisoners taken from the enemy were very indignant because they were not being exchanged. A lot of them offered to Sherman was by spilled their blood now that their times is out, has basely abandoned them. They are willing to take the oath of allegiance and enlist in my division. Bate wants to get them, but O'Neil has permission from the Secretary of war to enlist them and starts today for that purpose. He expects at least 1500. I spoke to Cheatham of it and he will see Hood today and have his consent.[32]

We are flanking around Rome today at an apparent distance of 6 or 8 miles.

Hood has ordered the pressing of all cattle. This is a painful necessity on true Southern families such as we meet here. I hope at least we will leave them the milch [milk] cows.

When I went first I kept out of the way of the divisions behind, but now I am going to have plenty of time for writing up journals.

One o'clock, P.M. We are traveling the Rome and Daniel's Gap road and are about to go through Daniel's Gap of Lavender Mountain. Got through the Gap at 4:30 P.M. Marched northeast through the Texas Valley. When within 3 ½ miles of Armuchee Creek one of Bate's couriers, breathless and pale, informed me Gen. Bate had sent him to inform me the enemy was advancing in force on the Summerville road towards the bridge over Armuchee Creek which I had to cross; that he had sent out Smith's brigade[33] on the road. Presently Captain [Charles] Hill,[34] unusually alarmed, came up to say the enemy were trying to destroy the bridge. I cross questioned both and satisfied myself it was a small matter and that the bridge was not in much danger. And so it proved. I, however, marched forward rapidly and without halting till within a mile of the bridge, sending one regiment forward. It proved to be a small party of the enemy's cavalry who had descended on some of our stragglers who had wandered off on our right flank. They captured one soldier, three nigs, and some horses. Another fatal result of straggling is shown here. It may reveal to the enemy our positions and plans.

Got into bivouac north of the River by 8 P.M. I camped on Summerville road at a Mr. Williamson's[35] a refugee from home. His house and place seemed to be in charge of some negro women.

Oct. 12th—Started north on Resaca and Dalton road at 7:30 o'clock. I have ordered a company of skirmishers kept constantly in front and rear of each brigade.

12 m. We have now turned to the right, taking a road to Calhoun or Resaca or rather to both. We are being delayed almost as provokingly as on yesterday by the troops in front and have to rest long and frequently. Gen. Granberry and I scratched a draft board[36] on the road. Marked the black squares with green leaves. I took red dogwood berries for men. Gen. Granberry took puff balls. Played two games, both drawn. Had a jumping match. I won at a running jump, he at a standing.

The people are all overjoyed. The women look like some terrible incubus had been lifted from their hearts.

Passed Bate and moved forward and camped at Widow Gins[37] on Sugar Valley road, close to Snake Creek Gap. Lee is in front of Resaca, Stewart breaking railroad above there.

Oct. 13th—Moved at light. Passed by my old works near Snake Creek Gap.[38] Took right hand road just beyond there and am now moving across to railroad. At 11:30 o'clock struck railroad 7 ½ miles south of Dalton. Sent two regiments in front, one on dirt and the other on railroad. Covered well my front with skirmishers, but did not halt moving up towards Dalton, where at 2 o'clock P.M., I commenced tearing up the track. This was a far more exciting business than I had supposed. I can hardly understand the effect on my mind of the scene that followed. The men would lift shear up one hundred yards of the track at once and then pitch the immense grating of wood and iron over on its back. The heavy fall would break rails and cross ties loose. The shouting of the long line of lifters, the ringing of pick and ax heads against the iron pins fastening the rails to the wood, the interminable line of fires as the cross-ties were given to the flames, the thousand columns of smoke, the scene so suddenly and completely changed, it bewildered me as I have been by the roar and sights of a great city and a few minutes before this road was still as death.

I soon heard the Block House at Tilton[, Georgia,] had surrendered;[39] next that Dalton had surrendered.[40] This and the news of an issue of flour satisfied most of the men and they worked on with a will till 11 o'clock, P.M., at night. I went to town to see about rations. Hood told me Bate was engaged trying to take a little Block House in Mill Creek Gap which his cannon had no effect on. He was going to plug the port holes and then burn it. The party in it, supposed to consist of sixty men, fired on our flag of truce sent to demand the surrender. Got some hard bread[41] for my men. Ate supper at Cheatham's.

The men destroyed effectually over ten miles of track.

Oct. 14th—Started through Dalton a few minutes after 4 o'clock, A.M. and commenced destroying the Cleveland railroad at 9 A.M. Had destroyed as far as the stone bridge north of Dalton when I moved through Mill Creek Gap for Villanow. The Block House had surrendered and was in flames. The flames were pouring out of the entrance and port holes. It was a formidable looking place, but determined men could take one without much loss. I noticed that three of the angles could bring but one piece to bear at a time when within fifty yards of it.[42]

Saw the captured negroes and whites taken at Dalton and in the Block Houses.[43] Our men were very bitter on the negroes and the officers hollering to the latter to kiss their brothers. A great many of the men think that negroes ought not to be taken prisoner and in case of a fight I think they will catch it. I told several if the universally acknowledged principle that to a higher scale of intelligence was attached a heavier weight of responsibility be true when the whites, who employ, incite and almost drive these poor creatures into their armies, are a thousand times more guilty than they.[44]

Camped at Villanow[, Georgia,] after a day's march of 18 miles. Slept under a China tree.

Oct. 15th—Received orders to move to LaFayette and take charge of the stores there. Moved at daylight. Got to LaFayette, 11 miles, early. This once pretty village is a wreck now. The Court House, roughly pierced with port holes and spattered all over with bullet marks, is doorless and windowless.[45] All the adjacent houses torn to shreds—irregular conglomerations of plank shelters—half finished, half ruined intrenchments—deserted houses—all the fencing and paling gone. I put up at Church. It had evidently been used and misused by the enemy. A platform for theatricals was at one end. Its walls were defaced all over with yankee names. Horse dung was on its floor. But latterly it must have been deserted by the yanks, for dead butterflies and half devoured birds lay about on the floor and spiders had built their webs across the entrance.

I took my headquarters at an empty, but picturesque cottage half a mile out on the Chattanooga road. The little gate was open, but creeping rose bushes almost barred entrance to the open rooms. Doves were roosting (for it was after sunset,) in the apple trees that darkened the windows. The vines on the supports could be seen above the luxuriant weeds. The flowers were hidden or choked out by them. But there was a pretty little silent greensward in front, carpeted with withering leaves and planted with cedars and other ornamental trees, some of which were circled with wood bine with here and there an evergreen bush, showing here and there a scentless flower. Its desolate beauty attracted me and I made my headquarters here, although it was far in advance of my troops and therefore by no means a safe place. In front of the gate was still visible a dried up dark red patch. [John P.] Gatewood's guerillas had shot a yankee dead on this spot three days before.[46]

Major Moon[47] sent me a small share of captured delicacies, viz: a couple of cans of cove oysters, a couple of bottles of wine, two of stomach bitters and some pepper. We had a feast tonight on the oysters.

Oct. 16th—We have had delightful weather ever since leaving the neighborhood of Parsons. Yesterday it threatened rain but only threatened. Today, Sunday, Cheatham called on me: ordered me to move on the Summerville road 2 ½ miles this evening, leaving one brigade here and a section of artillery. Guillotined one of my bottles of captured bitters (we had no cork screw) and the company drank of its rosy, exhilarating blood. Enemy said to be advancing through Snake Creek Gap and already beyond Villanow. I suppose we will hear from them today.

Cleburne evidently lost his diary that day or the next in the shuffle to get his division on the move again. When he started his next volume, or if he tried to fill in the gaps from his lost book, is unknown at this time. Cleburne and his division would continue on with Hood's desperate gamble, moving into North Alabama and eventually into Tennessee. He was struck by melancholy as the army neared Columbia; he remarked to Captain Hill as they marched past St. John's Episcopal Church, near Columbia, Tennessee, that "Its [*sic*] almost worth dying to be buried in such a place." A few days later, after his death at Franklin, his body would be returned there for burial.

Notes

1. *Walker County Messenger*, LaFayette, Georgia, July 26, August 2, and August 9, 1894.

2. William Lee White, *A Meteor Shining Brightly: Essays on Major General Patrick R. Cleburne* (Milledgeville, GA: Terrell House Publishers, 1997), 30.

3. *Pat Cleburne: Confederate General* (Gaithersburg, MD: Olde Soldier Books, Inc., 1987), 74–75.

4. The news of this came as an unpleasant surprise to Cleburne, who had gone to Hood's headquarters to ask for a furlough to visit his fiancée, Susan Tarleton, in Mobile.

5. Captain Samuel T. Foster of the 24th Texas Infantry notes, "At 8 O'Clock A.M. we move. Pass through Palmetto and down the West Point R.R. a few miles—left it and turn to the right towards the river, and camp two miles from the river. Before we left our camp . . . Genl Hood sent for all the regimental commanders to come to his HdQurs. As he had something to say to them of great importance." Norman D. Brown, ed., *One of Cleburne's Command: The Civil War Reminiscences and Diary of Capt. Samuel T. Foster, Granbury's Texas Brigade, CSA* (Austin: University of Texas Press, 1980), 135.

6. Crossing of the Chattahoochee River near Campbellton, Georgia.

7. The division of Major General William Brimage Bate. Bate was seriously wounded in fighting near Utoy Creek in August and command of the division went to Brigadier General John C. Brown. At Palmetto, Brown received permanent command of Cheatham's division after his promotion to corps command, thus relinquishing the command of Bate's division. I have been unable to find any evidence as to who took command of Bate's division, but I can speculate that it was Brigadier General Henry Rootes Jackson, the senior brigade commander of the division. Jackson's lack of experience could account for the problems that Cleburne notes.

8. A few miles south of the town of Villa Rica, Georgia.

9. The following morning the regimental commanders would relay the information to the men. "That we were going to flank Sherman out of Atlanta, and in maneuvering we might be short of rations occasionally, but that he (Gen. Hood) would do his best on that point. That he expected to have some fighting and some hard marching, and wanted an expression of the men upon it. Of course every man said go." Brown, *One of Cleburne's Command*, 136.

10. Captain Benjamin R. Tyus commanded the consolidated 6th and 15th Texas Infantry Regiment in Granbury's brigade.

11. Although he doesn't mention it, Cleburne delivers a speech to his men, as General Hood had requested of him. Lieutenant John L. McKinnon recalled,

> He spoke to us at some length, explaining to us the purpose of the rear move—the forced march—the result, if it succeeded, the consequences if it failed. He urged every man to do his whole duty, to stand firm by the righteous cause they had espoused. He pictured to us Ireland in its downfallen and trampled condition and told us if we failed our condition would be much worse than that of Ireland's, as long as that spirit of hate and revenge lived in the North. In closing his address that night he turned his face towards the skies and with all the fervency of his soul he exclaimed, "If this cause that is so dear to my heart is doomed to fail, I pray heaven may let me fall with it, while my 'face is toward the enemy and my arm battling for that which I know to be right.' It was one of the most stirring patriotic speeches I ever listened to."

John L. McKinnon, *History of Walton County* (Atlanta: n.p., 1911), 299–300.

12. Stewart's corps made the first moves of the campaign, striking the railroad at Big Shanty, Acworth, and Moon Station, Georgia, capturing the small garrisons there, and destroying the Western and Atlantic Railroad at those locations.

13. Brigadier General Mark Perrin Lowrey was known as the "Preacher General," as he was a Baptist minister before the war in Kossuth, Mississippi.

14. Located on Sweet Water Creek a short distance to the east of Flat Rock Church and west of Powder Springs.

15. Major General John Calvin Brown commanded the division formerly commanded by Major General Benjamin Franklin Cheatham.

16. Lieutenant Colonel Robert Bogardus Snowden of the 25th Tennessee Infantry. The 25th Tennessee had originally been part of Cleburne's brigade, and later his division as part of General Bushrod Johnson's brigade. They served under his leadership until it was detached to reinforce James Longstreet's corps in his failed attempt to take Knoxville in November 1863. With the failure of Longstreet and the simultaneous fall of Chattanooga, the Tennesseans were cut off from returning to the Army of Tennessee; they would go to Virginia with Longstreet in 1864.

17. Pioneers were troops detailed to help clear roads, build or repair bridges, and construct fortifications.

18. Stewart's corps struck the railroad and Big Shanty, Acworth, and Moon Station, capturing the garrisons in all three after small but severe engagements. The troops destroyed the railroad for several miles.

19. Elias Busby, a sixty-two-year-old farmer and Methodist minister.

20. French attacked the Union garrison at Allatoona Pass on October 5, and was defeated by an obstinate Federal stand there.

21. Pumpkinvine Creek; it was along the banks of this creek that Cleburne won the Battle of Pickett's Mill on May 27, 1864.

22. Resaca, scene of the largest battle of the Atlanta Campaign, now had a large Union garrison there to protect the railroad and bridge across the Oostanaula River.

23. Cleburne had a cow to provide milk for himself and his staff.

24. Every artillery battery was supposed to have a traveling forge, a vehicle housing a portable blacksmith shop to make replacement iron parts for cannons, make horseshoes, and do other repairs.

25. Rifle or musket ammunition. Soldiers typically carried forty rounds in their cartridge boxes.

26. Tool wagons were a fairly recent addition to the army's mule-drawn vehicles, used to carry shovels, picks, axes, spades, and other items that were necessary for the construction of fortifications.

27. Major General Edward C. Walthall commanded a division in Stewart's corps.

28. Brigadier General Hiram Granbury commanded Cleburne's Texas brigade.

29. General P. G. T. Beauregard took command of the newly created Department of the West, consisting of Hood's army and the forces of General Richard Taylor's Department of Alabama and Mississippi. Beauregard's main concern was to oversee and work with Hood's operation.

30. Ferry located a few miles west of Rome, Georgia.

31. Colonel John G. O'Neil, born in County Kerry, Ireland, who became a prosperous farmer in Humphreys County, Tennessee. O'Neil rose from captain to colonel of the 10th Tennessee Infantry, a regiment made up mostly of Irish immigrants from the Nashville area. In 1864 O'Neil was assigned the duty of recruiting Irish-born Union prisoners from the POW camps at Andersonville and Millen for Confederate service.

32. No details of what happened are known, though the unit was not assigned to Cleburne. Instead they became Burke's battalion of the 10th Tennessee Infantry, numbering a little over 250 men, far less than the 1,500 Cleburne was told. They did not serve with the rest of the 10th, however, and were assigned instead to guard the Mobile and Ohio Railroad in Mississippi where most of them were captured in December 1864 in the Battle of Egypt's Station.

33. Brigadier General Thomas Benton Smith of Bate's division.

34. Captain Charles Hill, Cleburne's ordinance officer and long-time member of his staff.

35. Probably Thomas Williamson, a wealthy Floyd County farmer and slave owner.

36. A "draft board" is the game board for chess.

37. Most likely Sarah Gian, a 52-year-old widow living with her children.

38. Snake Creek Gap is a narrow defile through part of Rocky Face Ridge that provided a backdoor to General Joseph Johnston's seemingly impregnable position at Dalton, Georgia, in the opening of the Atlanta Campaign. The infiltration led to Johnston's retreat and the Battle of Resaca, Georgia, in May 1864.

39. Stewart's division captured the blockhouse at Tilton after a short but severe engagement.

40. Dalton surrendered its garrison after Hood surrounded it and threatened that he would take no prisoners in an assault. A large force of men from the 44th U.S. Colored Troops Regiment made up the Union defense at the garrison.

41. Hard bread, also known as "hardtack" or "crackers," was the standard bread source for Union soldiers, and it occasionally made its way into the hands of Confederate soldiers. It was a cracker of biscuit made of flour and water, generally bland to the taste and at best incredibly hard; at worst it was also infested with weevils that led soldiers to nickname the crackers "worm castles."

42. Smith's brigade and the 5th Company Washington Artillery of Bate's division attacked the blockhouse. It was defended by a company of the 115th Illinois Infantry, who put up a spirited defense until artillery caught it on fire.

43. Although the officers of the 44th USCT would be exchanged, the men were carried along with the army. At Villanow it was announced that any runaway slaves in the unit could be reclaimed, and many were returned to slavery. Those who were not continued along with the army, and while some managed to escape, very few others would remain by the time the army reached North Alabama a few weeks later, their fates still unknown.

44. Cleburne demonstrates a common racist view here that the formerly enslaved men of the USCT must have been impelled to join, and that their white officers were guilty of inciting slave insurrection by those efforts, ignoring the idea that the men wanted their freedom and were willing to fight for it. It is a rather ironic statement since Cleburne had earlier advocated the enlistment of slaves into the Confederate armies. See White, *A Meteor Shining Brightly*, 142–66.

45. Union troops turned the Walker County Courthouse into a makeshift fort during the Battle of LaFayette on June 24, 1864, and withstood several attacks by Confederate cavalry. Then the courthouse was used as a base by Union cavalry who were trying to clear the area of guerillas. Finally, guerillas operating in the area commandeered it.

46. John P. Gatewood, a noted and brutal guerilla, led a band of so-called "Scouts" that tormented Northwest Georgia and Southeast Tennessee.

47. Major Moon was an officer in the quartermaster department.

2

"THE STORM BROKE IN ALL ITS FURY"

THE STRUGGLE FOR ALLATOONA PASS

Stewart Bennett

Private Charles Senior of the 7th Iowa Infantry arrived on the Allatoona Pass battlefield too late to take part in the horrible slaughter. "The sight of the battleground was shocking, worse than anything I ever saw before. . . . The ground was literally thick with killed and wounded in many places, so that a man could step from one to another . . . the groaning of the wounded could be heard all around us. I went to a spring for water to make coffee and nearly tumbled many times over the bodies of men in the dark. I took a stroll next morning as soon as day and the sight was horrid."[1] The locals called the place Allatoona Pass but one commander recalled it as "a needless effusion of blood."[2] The Battle of Allatoona Pass, and the days of maneuvering that led up to it, were a microcosm of an ill-fated Confederate campaign that was marked with problems from its inception.

Hood was determined to maneuver around General William Tecumseh Sherman's armies, "turn the enemy's right flank and attempt to destroy his communications and force him to retire from Atlanta."[3] Lieutenant General Alexander P. Stewart's corps struck the railroad north of Atlanta on October 3. Two divisions from Stewart's corps attacked the stretch from Big Shanty five miles north to Acworth. Major General William W. Loring's division captured a small Union garrison at the Big Shanty depot, and the next morning it moved to Acworth, taking more prisoners. Major General Edward C. Walthall's division attacked Moon's Station, capturing its small garrison. Stewart reported that by the afternoon of October 4 "ten or twelve miles" of the Western and Atlantic Railroad, Sherman's supply line, was "effectually torn up, the ties burned."[4]

A message from Hood that day directed Stewart to send his third division, commanded by Major General Samuel G. French, five miles beyond Acworth to the pass at Allatoona, "and fill up the deep cut at Allatoona with

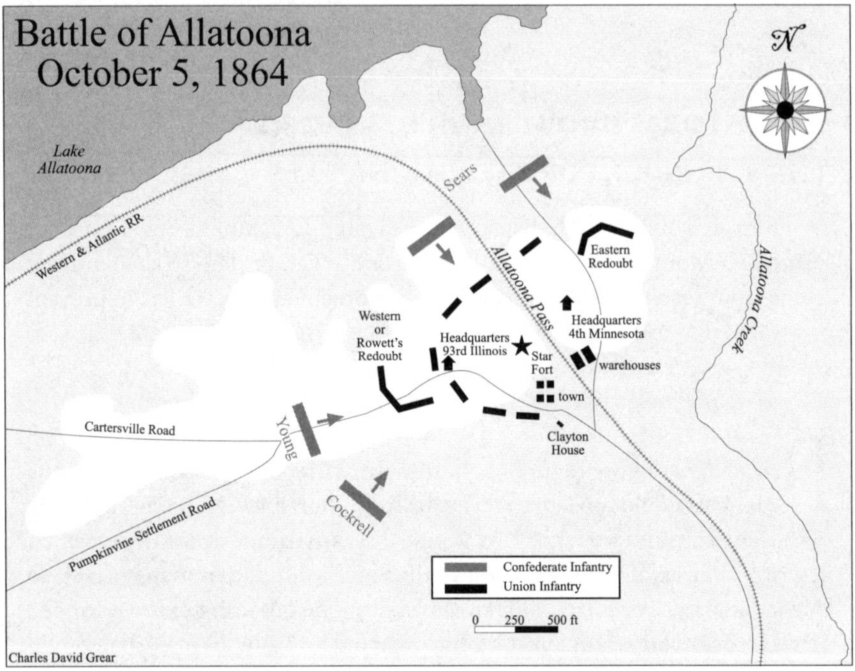

logs, brush, rails, dirt, &c.,."[5] French, a New Jersey native, was a West Point graduate and Mexican-American War veteran who had settled on his wife's Mississippi plantation and sided with the Confederacy. A second message from Hood added that it was "of the greatest importance" that French burn the bridge across the Etowah River. Taking Allatoona Pass, filling the gap, and destroying the Etowah Bridge—all before Sherman's army could interfere—would be challenging. Reassuringly, Hood mentioned that based on the best intelligence he then had, "the enemy cannot disturb us before to-morrow, and by that time your main body will be near the remainder of our army."[6]

That same day citizens warned French that Union troops had fortified and garrisoned Allatoona Pass and set up a supply depot there. Stewart and French discussed Hood's order and, as French explained after the war, "were convinced that Hood did not know the condition of affairs at Allatoona." At French's request, Stewart assigned some additional artillery to accompany his division in the attack on Allatoona, Major John D. Myrick's four guns, bringing French's total to twelve.[7] Historian Joseph M. Brown, son of Georgia's Civil War governor, claimed that Stewart gave the matter little concern, stating to French, "Hood does not appear to know that Allatoona has been fortified. You now have an independent command, and I hope you will be successful."[8] French recalled Stewart's words much the same: "General Hood does not seem to be aware that the place is fortified, and now, French, here is a fine opportunity for you."[9] In any case, Hood should have expected that Allatoona would be held by Union troops and that its natural strengths would be difficult to overcome. Regardless, French moved his division on the afternoon of October 4 and arrived at Acworth before sundown.[10]

From Acworth French dispatched a cavalry detachment under Captain James R. Taylor to tear up the railroad near Etowah Bridge "so as to prevent trains from reaching Allatoona with re-enforcements, as well as to prevent any trains that might be there from escaping." This was important. The success of French's mission would depend on the success of Taylor's.[11]

Local citizens told French that there were two redoubts with outer works along with four artillery pieces at Allatoona Pass and that about three and a half Union infantry regiments manned this area. When rations finally arrived, French moved out of Acworth. He soon realized that Union forces were watching his command. The Rebels could see night signals from Union troops on Kennesaw Mountain signaling to Allatoona. To the east, campfires from a large encampment of Union soldiers dotted the countryside. French's small division moved out along poor roads and into a night remembered for its darkness. "And so I went all alone," remembered French, "into the land occupied by the enemy, and Gen. Hood moved farther and farther away, leaving me isolated beyond all support or assistance."[12]

Knowing its strength, Sherman had bypassed Allatoona in his drive toward Atlanta that spring.[13] Once it was in Union hands he inspected it. "I have been to Allatoona Pass, and I find it admirable for our purposes," wrote Sherman on June 7. "It now becomes as useful to us as it was to the enemy, being easily defended from either direction." He also noted, "I regard Allatoona of the first importance in our future plans. It is a second Chattanooga; its front and rear are susceptible of easy defense and its flanks are strong."[14]

Thus Allatoona became an important Union supply depot. Unknown to Hood, Stewart, and French, it held around 1 million rations, not counting at least nine thousand head of cattle Union soldiers were protecting about five miles north of the pass.[15] Such a gain for the Confederate army could boost morale and help supply needed rations for Hood's Tennessee Campaign. It had the potential to be an incredible *coup* for French and his men if they could take Allatoona Pass and its stockpiles.

Union forces had accomplished a great deal in fortifying Allatoona. On July 20, George Hanson of the 4th Minnesota wrote, "Allatoona is well fortified, our camp being on a high hill. . . . This morning we commenced digging more rifle pits around our camp, which will do good service in case of an attack."[16] The topography around Allatoona made it a formidable obstacle, and the work of the Union soldiers made the position even stronger.

After leaving Cartersville, the Western and Atlantic Railroad made its tortuous route south toward Atlanta, winding its way near Allatoona Creek, cutting through the Allatoona ridges, ravines, and gorges. The railroad cut through the ridge was roughly 175 feet deep and about sixty feet wide, leaving a hill on either side. On these two hills Union troops built forts to control and protect the area and especially the supplies in the small town of Allatoona. The town was little more than six or seven houses just south of the pass and west of the cut. Two large sheds on the east side of the railroad housed the large quantity of rations.[17]

On the ridge about 220 yards east of the railroad stood the eastern redoubt. Lieutenant Harvey Trimble of the 93rd Illinois recalled that this redoubt was "nearly square, and averaged about sixty feet long and fifty feet wide." The walls were twelve feet thick at the top, with six openings for artillery. A deep ditch surrounded it. East of this redoubt was a footpath Union soldiers used to get to their crow's nest or signaling station. Allatoona Creek gave added protection northeast of the redoubt. A mill dam raised the water level from six feet to fourteen, thus flooding the ravine. In the opposite direction Union breastworks extended west from the redoubt toward the railroad cut. These works helped protect the area near both forts and provided cover for communications. They continued along the ridge to a steep bluff seventy feet high and began again on the opposite side of the ridge. The line stopped at the gap caused by the railroad. These breastworks also allowed the western portion of the line to deliver enfilading fire on attackers advancing against other parts of the defenses.[18]

About sixty feet west of the railroad gap was the Star Fort redoubt. This redoubt had "six sides and six angles," being "about seventy-five feet long and sixty feet wide." It was octagonal in shape with earthen walls that averaged ten feet thick at its base. In front of the fort was a ditch, five feet deep and six feet wide. The top of the fort's parapet rose at least ten feet above the bottom of the ditch and boasted eight artillery emplacements. A soldier could follow one of two routes in order to get from one redoubt to the other. One path descended from the ridge, crossed the railroad, and ascended the other side of the cut. The other path led across a footbridge twenty-five yards north of a direct line between the two redoubts. However, it was four feet wide and spanned the cut about ninety feet above the rails, making it a precarious route, especially in battle.[19]

About 125 yards west of the Star Fort two lines of entrenchments followed the ridge facing south and parallel to the Cartersville Road. This road ran along the top of the ridge. The entrenchments cut across the road and angled north while still facing west. The angle of these entrenchments was about 275 yards from the Star Fort. At this angle stood a "bastioned redoubt," with one gun and four-foot-high earthen walls topped with a head log. Although not as impressive in height and strength as the Star Fort or eastern redoubt, this redoubt was "finished with timber facings on the inside, which held together for years after the battle."[20] From this redoubt, works continued for about fifty yards down the spur of the ridge north while a traverse ran back to the east about ten yards to the apex of another steep ravine. This configuration allowed a crossfire on any attacker advancing by the ridge or the ravine. In front of this line of works were abatis described as three rows of three-foot-long stakes, sharpened, eighteen inches apart, slanted toward the enemy, and firmly settled into the ground. In front of these obstacles were trees that were felled for about two hundred yards in order to form an entanglement.[21]

North of the far western redoubt, rifle pits continued to the east to the next ravine not far from the Star Fort. On the next spur of the ridge east and just north of the Star Fort, breastworks and a ditch continued to the railroad cut, commanding the area. If enemy troops managed to fight their way past this area, a line of detached rifle pits faced them from the top of the bluff on the east side of the ravine and south of the works. Union troops positioned in these rifle pits would have the advantage of crossfire on attackers storming the ditch and breastworks below. The Cartersville and Pumpkinvine Settlement Roads met just before reaching the far western redoubt, with the Cartersville Road continuing toward the Star Fort but curving near the Star Fort and proceeding south into the small town of Allatoona. Here, along the curve, the road cut into the land about four to five feet making it an excellent breastwork for Union soldiers to watch over the town and Union supplies stored there. Those who studied the area and examined its defensive strengths, natural and man-made, could understand why Sherman, earlier that summer, was "resolved not even to attempt [an assault], but to turn the position."[22]

Lieutenant Colonel John E. Tourtellotte of the 4th Minnesota commanded the post at Allatoona Pass. He and his men "had for several days previous to the attack seen the heavens to the south shining with the glare of the burning railroad."[23] Tourtellotte's garrison consisted of the 290 men of the 93rd Illinois, seven companies of the 18th Wisconsin numbering 150 men, the 4th Minnesota with 450 men (of whom 185 were new recruits), and the six guns of the 12th Wisconsin Battery, as well as fifteen men of the 5th Ohio Cavalry.[24] Holding Allatoona Pass with such small numbers would be a great feat even with all its advantages.

Lieutenant Charles H. Fish of the U.S. Army Signal Corps was stationed on top of Kennesaw Mountain eighteen miles south of Allatoona Pass. This summit afforded a great view of Atlanta to the south and Allatoona to the north. On October 3 Fish's signalmen observed Stewart's Corps moving on the Western and Atlantic Railroad between Kennesaw and the village of Big Shanty, about three miles away. Weather and landscape partially obstructed Fish's view of the column's movements, but at the corresponding signal station at Allatoona, Signalman John Q. Adams could see the Confederates clearly. "From our signal station we could see fires and volumes of smoke all along the line of railroad to the south of us," recalled Adams, "from within two or three miles of Allatoona to the base of Kennesaw Mountain. It was evident that the enemy were in strong force on the railroad destroying it." By October 4 the Signal Corps stations were abuzz with news of the Confederate movement from Atlanta to Allatoona. Around 3:00 P.M. Fish again spotted the Confederates but lost them. "The night brought with it a dense fog," he recalled, "which precluded the sending of all messages, no matter how important they were."[25]

Sherman believed Hood's next move would be against Allatoona. He wrote Tourtellotte, "If he [Hood] goes for Allatoona I want him delayed only long enough for me to reach his rear. . . . his infantry would try to capture stores, without which Hood cannot stay where he is. If he moves up toward Allatoona I will surely come in force." Once Sherman realized the telegraph wires had been cut above Marietta, he used the Signal Corps to make contact with Union forces at Rome, Georgia, "over the heads of the enemy." Sherman needed reinforcements for Allatoona quickly, and he knew whom he could count on.[26]

Brigadier General John M. Corse had seen combat at Corinth, Vicksburg, Chattanooga, and during the Atlanta Campaign. In early October he commanded a division of the Army of the Tennessee stationed at Rome. He received Sherman's flag signal around noon on October 4. The dispatch directed Corse to move his division immediately to the support of the small garrison at the pass.[27]

Corse realized it would be difficult to get his men to Allatoona before the Confederates. Recent rains had reduced even the railroad's efficiency, and moving the division through the night in time to reach Allatoona posed a challenge. By 7:00 P.M. an engine and twenty cars were ready for boarding in Rome.[28] Corse took what troops he could on the first of what would be a series of trips to transport his men. The first trainload included Colonel Richard Rowett's brigade consisting of eight companies of the 39th Iowa (280 men), nine companies of the 7th Illinois (267 men), eight companies of the

50th Illinois (267 men), two companies of the 57th Illinois (61 men) and a 155-man detachment of the 12th Illinois. Corse's first contingent would add 1,054 to the defenders of Allatoona Pass. Also on board were 165,000 rounds of ammunition.[29]

The train rolled out of Rome around 8:30 P.M. Though he had been over the tracks a few hours before, Captain Hill worried about their reliability: "I had observed as I went over the road that the rails were very light and many of them loose, and I feared there might be a disaster, without the utmost care in running with so heavy a train."[30] The greater peril for Corse's troops was not the tracks but the Confederate destruction of the bridge over the Etowah north of Allatoona. If Captain Taylor's cavalry did its duty, the bridge would be destroyed before the train carrying Corse's men could cross. If so, Corse's troops would likely be too late to help Tourtellotte defend Allatoona. Instead, Taylor's men failed in their mission, allowing Corse and his soldiers to arrive safely at Allatoona around 1:00 A.M. on October 5.[31] No other troops from Rome made it in time for the battle. Spreading of the tracks caused a train accident and many hours of delay. Corse would have to defend Allatoona with what he had. Fortunately for Corse, French was still unaware of the early morning Union reinforcements.

While Corse's men made their way along the railroad, French had his own problems marching to Allatoona that night. "All was darkness," recalled French. He realized that although he had no knowledge of the area, he had to be ready to assault the Union forces by daybreak. "At last a young man, or rather a boy, was found," recalled French, "who knew the roads and had seen the position of the fortifications at Allatoona, he being a member of a cavalry company." After the division crossed the bridge at Allatoona Creek, French detached the 4th Mississippi to surround the blockhouse guarding the span, capture its Union garrison, and destroy the bridge while the rest of his division continued toward Allatoona.[32]

Although Corse recalled "a brisk fire" along the skirmish line as early as 2:00 A.M., French remembered his division arriving at Allatoona around 3:00 A.M. "Nothing could be seen but one or two twinkling lights on the opposite heights," wrote the Confederate general, "nothing was heard except the occasional interchange of shots between our advanced guards and the pickets of the garrison in the valley below."[33] Sergeant Major William Pitt Chambers stumbled through the night in the ranks of the 46th Mississippi. "Our route was so crooked and our progress so slow that we were practically all night in traversing the distances," Chambers wrote. "We arrived in the vicinity of Allatoona an hour or two before day on Wednesday 5th, and lay down in the mud and slept a little."[34]

Undeterred, French deployed his artillery on hills south and east of the railroad, leaving two infantry regiments in support. This task completed, French, the guide, and the rest of the division moved forward in search of the Union works. Finding the enemy proved difficult in dense woods and absolute darkness. After about an hour French and his men had managed to cross the railroad, climb and descend various densely timbered mountain spurs, and end directly in front of the Union works instead of on the main ridge. The guide tried a second time to find his way by gaining the ridge, but this effort also failed. A frustrated French "therefore determined to rest where we were and await daylight."[35]

It was 7:30 A.M. on October 5 before French and his men saw the Union fortifications, just 600 yards east of his position. Lieutenant G. W. Warren of the Missouri Brigade recalled, "After marching all night for over twelve miles, and at a rapid pace, the head of our column emerged from a sheltering ravine just as the first faint gleams of daylight appeared, displaying to our eyes, as we deployed along the ridge, the 'work' that was before us. Three forts, guarding Allatoona pass, stood out in bold relief on the opposite hill, within musket shot."[36]

With the artillery in place, French sent Brigadier General Claudius W. Sears and his Mississippi brigade to the northeast side of the Union works. Brigadier General Francis M. Cockrell and his brigade of Missourians were to move on the center or the northwest end of the ridge occupied by Corse's men, and Brigadier General William H. Young's brigade of four Texas regiments formed to the rear of Cockrell's line. The plan was for Myrick's artillery to bombard the defenders until the advancing Confederate infantry was almost in the gunners' line of fire. Then Sears and his men would attack from the northeast, striking the Union rear. On hearing the firing of Sears's men, Cockrell was to "move down the ridge" with the support of Young and his troops, thus carrying the Union line by flank attack. It was a good plan, but the topography would not cooperate. "So rugged and abrupt were the hills," recalled French, "that the troops could not be got in position until about 9 A.M., when I sent in a summons to surrender." French was still unaware of the Union reinforcements.[37]

The crackle of picket firing in the predawn darkness had alerted the Federals at Allatoona. Tourtellotte reinforced the Union outposts with the 18th Wisconsin and before dawn added the 7th Illinois. By daylight, Corse began pulling his forces back from the town to the ridge on both sides of the railroad cut. By 6:00 A.M. Corse had positioned the 7th Illinois along with the 39th Iowa facing west along a spur that overlooked the railroad cut and covered the Star Fort. A battalion of the 93rd Illinois formed a skirmish line along the ridge running west from there to guard the Union right flank. The

4th Minnesota along with the 50th and 12th Illinois occupied the works on the hill east of the railroad cut.[38]

First light revealed to the men of the 12th Wisconsin Battery a Rebel gun in one of the new Confederate artillery positions. The Union artillerymen carefully aimed and fired one of their pieces. "Flash! Crash! went the gun, and into the air went the ball," recalled John Shearer of the battery. "We watched it until hurrahs, yells, and cheers announced the effect of one of the best shots of the war. It struck the gun, dismounting it, crushing the carriage, and killing or wounding every gunner." The Confederates now sprang into action. "We saw the flash, flash, flash then the jets of smoke, and heard the bomb, bomb, bomb, and on came their shots. Rising into the air like rockets, they made their arch and few around us. Some buried themselves in the embankment and earth, some over-reached their mark and some made us dodge under shelter." For nearly two hours, Corse and his men felt the unrelenting fire of Confederate artillery as both sides dueled. It was, according to Shearer, "a continuous thunder and roar of cannon, shrieking and bursting of shot and shell, keeping the air filled with deadly missiles. It presented a grand but dangerous spectacle." Peter Daniel Anderson of the 4th Minnesota remembered, "We started our bombardment against them. It was not long before we received answer from them with thunderous cannon bombardment and the shells were flying in the air around us until nine o'clock when the rebel cannon became quiet again." Once the assaults began, Confederate artillery hit the far Union right where Eason of the 4th Minnesota admitted, "We were being furiously shelled from the opposite direction."[39] Meanwhile, skirmishers kept up a brisk fire on both sides of the Union position.[40]

It was about 8:30 A.M., according to Corse, when a flag of truce came into the Union lines.[41] French addressed his summons to the "Commanding Officer U.S. forces" and explained, "I have placed the forces under my command in such position that you are surrounded, and to avoid a needless effusion of blood, I call on you to surrender your forces at once and unconditionally. Five minutes will be allowed you to decide. Should you accede to this, you will be treated in the most honorable manner as prisoners of war."[42]

Major D. W. Sanders of French's staff had accompanied the flag of truce and handed the message to Lieutenant O. C. Ayers of Corse's staff, who carried it to his commander. Corse read the summons and penned a reply: "Your communication demanding surrender of my command I acknowledge receipt of, and would respectfully reply that we are prepared for the 'needless effusion of blood' whenever it is agreeable to you."[43]

Ayers reached the Union breastworks on his way back from the picket line when he saw the Rebel formations advancing to attack. Sanders later told

French he had waited seventeen minutes at the picket lines before he had given up and left without a response from the Union commander. Either way, French had his answer, but had Sanders been a little more patient, Corse's message might have told him something else. It was signed, "Jno. M. Corse, Brigadier General Commanding U.S. Forces." A reply from such a relatively senior officer, rather than the more junior Tourtellotte, might have tipped off French that Allatoona had been reinforced.[44]

While Sanders stewed on the Union picket line, the rest of French's division had time to contemplate their situation. "As I looked across the intervening space to the bristling forts, and viewed the rugged mountain side, with the interminable *abatis* that lay between, and then cast my eye along our slender line," wrote the Missouri Brigade's Lieutenant Warren. "I thought to myself, 'there will be hot work here if those regiments are made up of resolute men.'"[45]

Corse hurried to his regiments, explaining the nature of the flag, his answer, and the need for all to prepare for a hard fight. Colonel Rowett, with the 39th Iowa and 7th Illinois, was to hold the spur on the left of the Union line. Colonel Tourtellotte oversaw the eastern redoubt with instructions to hold the area to the last man. Two companies of the 93rd Illinois lay parallel with the railroad and the cut with orders to hold the north side as long as possible. Three more companies of the 93rd Illinois readied themselves in the ditch south of the redoubt. These men were to watch the town along with the depot, which contained more than a million rations. What was left of the 93rd was positioned between the redoubt and the line Rowett's men had held, ready to reinforce where needed. Corse had hardly finished giving his instructions before, as he put it, "the storm broke in all its fury."[46]

French wasted no time in beginning the assault. The idea that Sherman's army could pounce without warning while the rest of Hood's army was miles away made the situation urgent. Besides, French was relying on past communications that there were only about 900 Union soldiers in his way.

By the time Sanders had returned from his flag-of-truce mission, all the elements of French's planned attack had reached their jumping-off points. Sears and his Mississippians had had a particularly hard time as they made their way around to the north side of the Union outpost. Sears reported to French that his path was obstructed by what he believed was a "bayou," and his men were compelled to move single file between the bayou and a steep ridge. The bayou was in reality the millpond the Federals had created for just that purpose.[47]

Around mid-morning, French ordered Cockrell's brigade to advance from the woods toward the abatis of felled timber, launching the first phase of the Confederate assault.[48] Cockrell had the 1st and 3rd Missouri Cavalry (dismounted) on the right with the 3rd and 5th Missouri on the right-center. The 1st and 4th Missouri formed the left-center alongside the 2nd and 6th Missouri on the left.[49] "Forward men!" shouted Cockrell. His Missourians responded with a yell and strode toward the Union works.

Their target was the Union breastworks along the Cartersville Road, defended by the 7th and 93rd Illinois and the 39th Iowa. The latter two regiments carried standard Springfield single-shot, muzzle-loading rifles, but the men of the 7th, at their own expense, had reequipped with the popular lever-action, sixteen-shot, Henry Repeating Rifles. Charles Van Gorder of the 39th Iowa recalled, "We have always felt that the day was saved at Allatoona, from the fact that the 7th Ill. was armed with the Henry rifle. . . . Had the 7th Ill. been armed with the Springfield as we were, it would have been impossible to have held our ground."[50]

The Missourians were impressed. "The enemy fought like men," wrote 4th Missouri's Private James Bradley, who went on to note that when he and his comrades were "within twenty yards of the entrenchment, so deadly was their fire, that the line halted and the contest seemed doubtful. Here many of [our] brave men, officers and privates, fell to do battle no more." The defenders also had a cannon on this line, having shifted the gun from Rowett's redoubt. Firing double canister, it staggered the Confederate advance.[51]

Once Cockrell's Missourians had begun their advance, Young's Texans joined the fight. Young advanced with the 14th Texas Calvary (dismounted) in the center of the Texan line flanked by the 9th Texas to their right and the 10th Texas Cavalry (dismounted) to their left. The 29th North Carolina formed the far left of the brigade line.[52] Young's and Cockrell's men found that the fight was playing havoc with their formations. "When we reached the *abatis*," recalled Missourian Robert Bevier, "our advance was momentarily checked. By the time our line had made its way through the network of fallen timber all our organization was gone. Companies and regiments were thoroughly mixed up."[53] In Young's brigade, Lieutenant Colonel Abram Harris recalled, "We moved forward to within twenty steps of the first works of the enemy and formed again, having our lines broken by the brush and fallen timber which covered the ground."[54]

Advancing on the left where the woods were thicker, the 29th North Carolina fared even worse, and the regiment soon became separated from Young's brigade. When it finally reached the abatis, Major Ezekiel H. Hampton realized his regiment was not only separated from the brigade but possibly behind the other regiments. Hampton ordered his men to the double-quick to within forty feet of the Union entrenchments, then to "lie down, rest, and reload."[55]

The 7th Illinois held the rifle pits on the left of the Union line near the Cartersville Road with the right of the regiment resting on the road and connecting with the 39th Iowa.[56] While these regiments managed to hold the line temporarily, Confederates continued to make their way around the line's right flank. From this position, the Rebels were able to unleash an enfilading fire. "The right of the line gave way before a vastly superior force," admitted Lieutenant Colonel Hector Perrin of the 7th Illinois, "which movement compelled my command to abandon their rifle-pits and retreat to the fort."[57] Though fighting with tenacity, the 39th Iowa was being cut to pieces from front and flank. "The enemy was in such force as to be irresistible," recalled the 39th's Major Joseph M. Griffiths, "and the remainder of our regiment fell back contesting every foot of ground to the fort."[58]

What Griffiths called a fort was Rowett's redoubt, the next Union strongpoint in the rear of the Cartersville Road. Having crossed the road, the Confederates quickly pressed home their assault against the redoubt. The 29th North Carolina's Major Hampton reported that his men "moved into the enemy's works, where they had a hand-to-hand encounter with sword, bayonet, butt of muskets, rocks, &c., killing a good many and capturing 25 or 30 prisoners." It was the same for Harris and the 14th Texas Cavalry (dismounted). "We moved forward with a yell and carried the works in front of us in less than five minutes, driving the enemy out of their intrenchments with the butts of our guns and rocks, as we did not have any bayonets, pursuing them to within twenty steps of their last and only work." Sergeant John M. Ragland of the 1st and 4th Missouri captured the flag of the 39th Iowa regiment and "waved it in defiance at the enemy and carried it safely away," recalled fellow soldier R. S. Bevier. Rowett's redoubt had fallen—at a great cost for both armies. As the Rebels continued driving on the Union left, those Federals who could made their way toward their last bastion of hope, the Star Fort and Corse.[59]

As Cockrell's and Young's brigades assaulted the Union left and center, Sears and his Mississippians moved against the Union center and right. Tourtellotte commanded the Union right, with Corse in the center at the Star Fort. Sears had four Mississippi regiments—the 39th Mississippi on the left, then the 35th with its right flank on the railroad. Just across the tracks were the 36th, then the 46th, and the 7th on the right.[60] "I felt assured all the morning that it was a more serious undertaking than many seemed to think it was," believed William Pitt Chambers of the 46th Mississippi, "and when an officer remarked that taking the place was only 'a breakfast task,' I assured him that anybody was welcome to *my* share of *that* breakfast."[61]

The Mississippians moved down the hillside toward the Union position on the ridge. Like the Missourians and Texans, Sears's men faced the web of felled trees along with palisades of sharp pointed stakes protruding from the earth toward the assaulting column. Bullets flew thick and fast around them, and the obstructions caused the brigade to lose all semblance of formation. Hastily reforming his line, Chambers realized what he had to do. "Inwardly, commending my soul to my Savior, I mounted the crest of the hill, and turning and waving my hat I shouted at the top of my voice, 'Come on boys! The 46th goes ahead!'" About twenty-five men followed Chambers. "Oh! What a devastating hailstorm of bullets met us! In thirty seconds or less only two of us were left." Then Chambers received a wound in the shoulder, and his friend was shot dead. "Finding I could not use my arm, I lay down behind the body of my friend," recalled Chambers, "I could hear and feel the balls as they struck the corpse."[62] Sears and his men hit the flank of the 39th Iowa hard, but the Mississippians were taking a murderous enfilading fire from the Star Fort and the eastern redoubt. The men of the 93rd Illinois laid down a hail of gunfire while the 12th Illinois created a deadly enfilading fire from the opposite side of the railroad.[63]

Around 10:00 A.M. Lieutenant Colonel William Hanna positioned the 12th Illinois to the right of the 50th Illinois, which was just east of the railroad. Soon, Hanna received an order to move one of his regiments to the bank of the railroad cut. He sent the 12th, which faced west and fired on the Confederates attacking the Star Fort.[64]

Soon after this move, Hanna ordered Captain Robert Koehler and the 12th Illinois to move closer to the Star Fort, where they found hot work.[65] Hanna then moved the 50th Illinois into a new position with its right resting in the rear and to the right of Tourtellotte's redoubt and the left on the road running between the redoubt and the Star Fort. Hanna reported that his line repulsed three Confederate assaults. Then Tourtellotte later recalled, "By some error in communicating the order, both the Twelfth and the Fiftieth Illinois Regiments moved to the other side of the railroad, leaving the Fourth Minnesota to contend against the troops advancing directly upon us from the north." Worse, as the 4th's Major James C. Edson reported, "About 160 men of my regiment were recruits who had received their arms only three days before."[66]

The 39th and 35th Mississippi regiments faced the same difficult obstructions and withering rifle and cannon fire that confronted the other Confederate regiments. Since Sears's men were a greater distance from the Union line than Cockrell's, the Mississippians found themselves assaulting several minutes after Cockrell's attack. Despite these disadvantages, Confederate cannoneers kept a constant and deadly fire on Tourtellotte's redoubt as Confederate troops continued their crossfire. As the two Mississippi regiments moved forward, they had to climb a steep ridge that was cut by a deep ravine. A number of the Mississippians struggled through the morass of tangled brush while moving toward the north side of the ridge only to find their movements blocked by a steep bluff. The Mississippians were in a quandary. "But now an ordeal presented itself that had not been contemplated," admitted Lieutenant Colonel Reuben H. Shotwell of the 35th. "In withdrawing, the moment we left the position we then occupied we came in full view of the enemy and were exposed to the same terrific fire to which we were subjected while advancing. . . . So great was the danger of withdrawing, that many of the men were inclined to remain and surrender, rather than take the risk of getting away." Although Shotwell managed to make his escape, more than eighty Mississippians were captured by the end of the fighting, along with the flags of both regiments.[67]

As the fighting continued, Lieutenant Colonel Charles E. Jackson arrived with four companies of the 18th Wisconsin to reinforce the hard-fighting Minnesotans. The 4th Minnesota with its new recruits had passed the test, at least for the moment. By 12:30 P.M., Sears reported that his men were "fighting bravely. Will get up a charge as soon as the men rest a little. We will take this work, if possible. Men are greatly fatigued." Regardless, the fighting around Tourtellotte's redoubt was mostly over. Many of the Union troops moved from there to reinforce Corse and the Star Fort while other Federals ran from capture around Rowett's redoubt for safety in the Star Fort. All was moving toward a climatic final fury near the middle of Allatoona Pass and within the Star Fort.[68]

While Cockrell, Young, and Sears moved their brigades against the Federal line; two other Confederate forces made their presence known. The Confederate artillery French had placed to the south of the pass continued to fire upon Corse's line. Although his 39th North Carolina was detailed to support the Confederate artillery, Colonel David Coleman led about forty men out as skirmishers from the south of Allatoona. With Confederate forces attacking from the west and north, troops coming from the south would add to the confusion for Union troops and act as a diversion for the Confederates. The 39th moved quickly with a cheer and fired rapidly on the Federal line. The sudden fire of these North Carolinians had the desired effect. Union skirmishers, numbering about 200 were, according to Colonel Coleman, "observed on the side of the hill in our front in the act of halting, apparently confused and undecided what to do. These by a sharp fire from us were driven into the shelter of their works on the summit." The shelter of the railroad worked in Coleman's favor. His men kept a constant fire on the Union troops in and near the Star Fort until around 2:45 P.M.[69]

"October 5th dawned upon us in all the glory of an immense fog bank that hung around the brow of Kennesaw like a funeral pall," recalled Captain Fish, "Nothing could be seen, not even twenty feet down the mountain side. We were a little above the fog bank, and could see along the crest of the mountain a short distance. All objects around us were as invisible as though they had been blotted out of existence." Sherman paced along the path behind the station hoping for the moment when the fog would burn off and positive news could be gathered concerning Corse and Allatoona. Inside the beleaguered outpost Captain Adams of the Signal Corps moved his station from near Tourtellotte's redoubt to the Star Fort shortly after daybreak. Around 10:00 A.M. Adams could finally see Kennesaw Mountain and signaled, "Corse was here with one brigade," then, "Where is General Sherman?" The reply merely stated, "Near you."[70]

Sherman recalled, "The signal-officer on Kenesaw reported that since daylight he had failed to obtain any answer to his call for Allatoona; but, while I was with him, he caught a faint glimpse of the tell-tale flag through an embrasure, and after much time he made out these letters—'C.,' 'R.,' 'S.,' 'E.,' 'H.,' 'E.,' 'R.,' and translated the message—'Corse is here.'" This was a great source of relief for Sherman, as he stated, "It gave me the first assurance that General Corse had received his orders, and that the place was adequately garrisoned." This was false relief. While it was true that Corse was at Allatoona, his entire division never made it. If Sherman had known this information, he might have hurried reinforcements more quickly to Allatoona Pass, and a different outcome might have transpired.[71] Instead, Corse continued the fight with what men he had and most of them were scrambling for the Star Fort.

Confederate forces under Cockrell and Young readied themselves for the assault on the Star Fort while Sears's Mississippians, on the west side of the railroad, continued to fire at the Union troops trying to make their way into the fort. Around 12:30 P.M. Sears reported to French, "Our men are fighting bravely. Will get up a grand charge as soon as the men rest a little. We will take this work, if possible. Men are greatly fatigued." Sears then added, "We are in enemy's works, but have not the fort yet. The yells of your men do us great good."[72] As the Confederates readied for the assault Corse recalled how they filled "every hollow and take every advantage of the rough ground surrounding the fort, filling every hole and trench, seeking shelter behind every stump and log that lay within musket-range of the fort."[73]

Federal troops continued to pour into the Star Fort. The 93rd Illinois' Trimble recalled, "Men standing in the embrasure, over the cannon, and on the parapet, seized the extended hands of those outside, and, with the aid of those in the rifle-pits at the base of the wall, literally lifted them into the fort." Cotton bales that were used to secure the gateway into the fort were now impediments to many of the Union troops trying to get in. The men within the fort seized the bales, and "there was one great surge, and that mass of men swept through the gate into the fort. The weight and strength of their movement carried that brass cannon in with them." Soon after, the cotton bales were set in place closing the fort from the Confederates.[74] Corse also organized what was left of his command and placed them in the trenches and parapets around the Star Fort. Only the 4th Minnesota, four companies of the 18th Wisconsin, and four cannon of the 12th Wisconsin Battery continued their stand around Tourtellotte's redoubt.[75]

Cockrell's and Young's men advanced on the Star Fort, but the 12th Wisconsin Battery fired so effectively that it became, in Corse's words, "impossible for a column to live within 100 yards of the works." The Confederates took cover and poured rifle fire on the fort. One defender after another was hit.[76] The fort was not sufficiently excavated, and the center was higher than the parapets. It was "crowded, and as bloody as a slaughter pen," recalled Corse's aide Lieutenant William Ludlow. With scant cover from the heavy incoming fire, the wounded "in some cases were shot over and over again." As for the dead, "the ground became covered with them [and] they were let lie as they fell, and were stood or sat upon by the fighters."[77]

Around 1:00 P.M. a bullet struck Corse in the face along the left malar bone passing out and to the ear. This wound, Corse recalled, "rendered me insensible for some thirty or forty minutes."[78] The fight continued. "A battle was waged there, for four hours, in which every Union soldier was his own commander," according to Trimble of the 93rd Illinois. "There was not even a lull in the musketry firing from the beginning to the end. It was all the time as rapid and intense as the number of men and guns engaged could make it." The battle continued as "the gabions in the two embrasures were literally gnawed off by the enemy's bullets, so that the dirt caved in, and caused much inconvenience in working the guns." Two of the cannon in the fort were rendered useless and ammunition was running out for both artillery and rifles.[79]

Rumors of surrender moved throughout the fort shortly after the wounding of Corse. As Corse heard the words "cease firing," he struggled to come to his senses and encouraged the men to continue the fight, reminding them that Sherman was on his way. The Federals fired what ammunition they could find. The artillery, however, was depleted. A volunteer sprinted toward Tourtellotte's redoubt via the footbridge in order to keep the artillery roaring. Fortunately for the Federals, the volunteer arrived back at the Star Fort with his hands loaded with case shot and canister. Corse described what followed: "A few shots from the gun threw the enemy's column into great confusion, which being observed by our men, caused them to rush to the parapet and open such a heavy and continuous musketry fire that it was impossible for the enemy to rally."[80]

French was preparing for the final attack when new intelligence arrived. Earlier, cavalry general Frank C. Armstrong had reported Union forces encamped north of Kennesaw and east of the railroad. Now, Armstrong warned of Union infantry entering Big Shanty. French realized those Federals could cut him off from getting back to the safety of the Army of Tennessee. Further Confederate assaults might have won the battle, but the time this would have taken could have led to the capture of French's entire division. Also, Confederate ammunition was running low. Ammunition would need to be carried about a mile from the wagons and distributed among the forces before a final assault could be accomplished. This would require two more hours before the attack could take place. French realized that his men had been pushed to their physical limits from severe fighting and a lack of rest over the past few days. "Under these circumstances," he admitted, "I determined to withdraw, however depressing the idea of not capturing the place after so many had fallen, and when in all probability we could force a surrender before night. . . . I deemed it of more importance not to permit the enemy to cut my division off from the army."[81]

Cockrell's and Young's brigades withdrew at 1:30 P.M. Sears and his men were next but had to find their way back through the ravines—a treacherous journey. The Confederates loaded some of their wounded into ambulances, but had to leave many behind due to the difficulty of the terrain and dense woods. By 3:30 P.M. the attacking forces met with their artillery on the south side of the battlefield and made their way toward New Hope.

Although the fighting on the battlefield ended, there was still unfinished business near Allatoona Creek. Colonel T. N. Adaire and the 4th Mississippi had destroyed the bridge, but they had not accomplished their objective of taking the blockhouse. With an increase of men and artillery, French was able to gain the surrender of around eighty-five Union prisoners.[82] This hardly made up for the frustration and losses earlier in the day.

At Allatoona Pass the firing had been so intense in and around the Star Fort that the Union troops found it difficult to raise their heads above the parapets without being shot at. Around 3:00 P.M. the firing had finally slackened. Some held their hats above the parapets on ramrods to ascertain any signs of the enemy. When all seemed quiet, men began to look out at the area around the fort.[83] The ground before them was carpeted with the dead of both armies. "Silence, like the pall of death, rests over Allatoona;" recalled French, "it is as lifeless as a grave-yard at midnight."[84]

The losses at Allatoona Pass were staggering for the numbers involved. Of the scarcely more than 2,000 troops French committed to battle, 799 were killed, wounded, missing, or captured. Sears's brigade had the highest losses at 425, including 256 missing. Corse brought 1,944 men into the battle, losing 706 in killed, wounded, or missing. Of the 299 men of the 7th Illinois, 141 were casualties, or 47 percent. Even greater were the losses of the 39th Iowa, which lost 170 of 284, or 59 percent.[85]

Sherman had planned to use Jacob Cox's Twenty-Third Corps and "to interpose this corps between Hood's main army at Dallas and the detachment then assailing Allatoona. The rest of the army was directed straight for Allatoona." Soon after Sherman realized Corse was at Allatoona he admitted that he watched "with painful suspense the indications of the battle raging there, and was dreadfully impatient at the slow progress of the relieving column." Around 2:00 P.M. Sherman noticed the smoke around Allatoona starting to clear, and by 4:00 P.M. it had dissipated. At first Sherman believed that the relieving column had finally arrived. He later learned that Corse and his men had withstood the Confederate assault on their own.[86]

Numerically, the forces engaged were nearly evenly matched. Had Corse and his men not made it to Allatoona, French might have taken the Union positions quickly. Also, since Federals were at Allatoona, Hood's orders to fill the pass and focus on destroying the Etowah Bridge were impossible.

Although French was aware of a Union presence at Allatoona, he was unaware of Corse and the Union reinforcements that made their way to the pass. Communications from Taylor concerning the failure to destroy the Etowah Bridge should have been communicated to French. In his report on the fight at Allatoona Pass, French believed that it was the fault of the cavalry officer "who was sent to cut the railroad and failed to perform that duty . . . had he taken up the rails—and there was nothing to prevent it—re-enforcements could not have been thrown in the works, and the result would have been different."[87]

Not only was French unaware of the Union reinforcements, he was also forced to move to the battlefield in darkness without knowledge of the topography. This hampered Sears and his Mississippians on the Confederate left. Sears was late to start the attack and during the assault lost men captured due to the terrain. Sears also lost precious time when withdrawing from the battlefield. The environment also delayed any possible transport of ammunition to Confederate troops for a last assault and served as an impediment to helping the wounded off the field.

Many Union soldiers believed the Confederates were attacking Allatoona for the rations stored there. Hood never mentioned this as part of French's directive for the attack. According to his report, French was unaware of such rations at the time of the assault, yet in his memoirs he mentioned knowing of "commissary stores there." French admitted that the stores were captured but not at first set on fire since the men wanted them. French did not realize the large accumulation of stores until Cockrell and Young had withdrawn, for it was while waiting on Sears's brigade that French learned from the soldiers of the vast supplies. Since French could not carry off such an abundance of stores, he sent a party of men to set them on fire. Supposedly, among all of those in attendance, they could only find three matches. All three failed to ignite.[88]

The main reason French decided to leave the battlefield was that he received the two reports from Armstrong of Union activity, especially that Union infantry were entering Big Shanty with a cavalry force east of the railroad. Sherman wanted to combine his forces, explaining on the evening of October 4, "To-morrow I will concentrate the whole army at Kenesaw and move upon the enemy wherever he may be." This would be more difficult than expected. Sherman sent General Jacob Cox with the Twenty-Third Corps toward Kennesaw; however, the rains had washed out bridges along their march hampering any quick movement by these troops. Cox camped the night of October 5 only a mile beyond Kennesaw Mountain on the Marietta and Acworth Road and too far away to help Corse when he needed it most. Anderson may have been mistaken when he thought Union infantry were moving toward French. Instead, according to Cox, the forces Armstrong most likely viewed were those of a cavalry reconnaissance in the front of General David S. Stanley's Fourth Army Corps. It was also possible that Armstrong could have seen what might have been the head of Stanley's corps. Stanley had reported to Sherman from near Pine Mountain, "Will halt head of column here, and send a brigade on reconnaissance to Pine Top." This occurred on October 5 at 12:30 P.M., well after the time French mentioned hearing from Armstrong.[89] Regardless, there was enough Union movement to worry Armstrong and Corse concerning their getting back to Hood's army and relative safety. Sherman consolidated his forces in order to possibly move upon French's division, but poor weather and bad roads worked against Union plans.

In the following months, major battles at Franklin and Nashville would bring great losses and calamity to the Army of Tennessee. In comparison, Allatoona would be regarded as a skirmish. The struggle that took place along the ridges and ravines of Allatoona Pass may have become a footnote to many, but this heroic struggle became a microcosm of a greater problem for the Army of Tennessee. Communication breakdown between commanders, lack of advanced planning, little understanding of the battlefield terrain, and a tenacious Union army precipitated another failure for the Confederacy. The Confederate soldiers fought with determination and tenacity under difficult circumstances, but this was not enough to turn the tide of the outcome. Losses for both armies were great in proportion to the numbers engaged, but—as the Southerners would see in coming months—the Confederacy could ill afford such setbacks.

Notes

1. Charles Berry Sr., letter from Charles Berry Sr. to his father, October 22, 1864, Electronic Text Center, University of Virginia Library.

2. U.S. War Department, *The War of the Rebellion: A Compilation of the Official Records of the Union and Confederate Armies*, 128 vols. (Washington, DC: Government Printing Office, 1880–1901), ser. 1, vol. 39, pt. 1: 763 (hereinafter cited as *OR*; all references are to series 1 unless otherwise indicated).

3. Ibid., 801.

4. Ibid., 812.

5. Ibid., 814.

6. Ezra J. Warner, *Generals in Gray: Lives of the Confederate Commanders* (Baton Rouge: Louisiana State University Press, 1959), 93–94.

7. Samuel G. French, *Two Wars: An Autobiography of Gen. Samuel G. French* (Nashville, TN: Confederate Veteran, 1901), 272; Fred E. Brown, "The Battle of Allatoona," *Civil War History* (September 1960): 282; *OR*, vol. 39, pt. 1: 812, 814–15.

8. Joseph M. Brown, *The Battle of Allatoona, October 5, 1864: One of the Gamest and Bloodiest Fights of the War; Some Facts Never Before Published* (Atlanta: Record Publishing Company, 1890), 1.

9. D. W. Sanders, "Hood's Tennessee Campaign," *Southern Bivouac* 3 (1884–85), 147; *OR*, vol. 39, pt. 1: 815.

10. Hood made no mention of being in or near Allatoona during May of 1864 in his memoir. *OR*, vol. 38, pt. 4: 735; Joseph E. Johnston, *Narrative of Military Operations, Directed, During the Late War Between the States* (New York: D. Appleton and Company, 1874), 326; Craig L. Symonds, *Joseph E. Johnston: A Civil War Biography* (New York: W. W. Norton and Company, 1992), 295–96.

11. *OR*, vol. 39, pt. 1: 815.

12. Ibid.; French, *Two Wars*, 272; Sanders, "Hood's Tennessee Campaign," 147–48.

13. William Tecumseh Sherman, *Memoirs of General W. T. Sherman: By Himself* (New York: Charles L. Webster and Company, 1890), 2:42, Johnston, *Narrative*, 334–35.

14. *OR*, vol. 38, pt. 4: 428; *OR*, vol. 38, pt. 5: 141.

15. Phil Gottschalk, "'Is It Surrender or Fight?' The Battle of Allatoona, October 5, 1864," *The Campaign for Atlanta and Sherman's March to the Sea* 1(1992): 104.

16. George Hanson, "From the Fourth Regiment," *The St. Cloud Democrat*, August 11, 1864, 1.

17. Harvey M. Trimble, *History of the Ninety-Third Regiment, Illinois Volunteer Infantry, from Organization to Muster Out* (Chicago: The Blakely Printing Co., 1898), 103, 106; Alonzo L. Brown, *History of the Fourth Regiment of Minnesota Infantry Volunteers during the Great Rebellion 1861–1865* (St. Paul, MN: Pioneer Press Company, 1892), 307.

18. Trimble, *History of the Ninety-Third*, 103, 106; Brown, *Battle of Allatoona*, 2, 4, 6.

19. Trimble, *History of the Ninety-Third*, 103, 106; Brown, *Battle of Allatoona*, 4.

20. Brown, *Battle of Allatoona*, 4.

21. Ibid.; William C. Winter, ed., *Captain Joseph Boyce and the 1st Missouri Infantry, C.S.A.* (St. Louis: University of Missouri Press, 2011), 180.

22. Brown, *Battle of Allatoona*, 4, 6; Sherman, *Memoirs*, 2:42.

23. Alonzo Brown, *Minnesota in the Civil and Indian Wars 1861–1865* (St. Paul, MN: The Pioneer Press Company, 1890), 215.

24. *OR*, vol. 39, pt. 1: 748.

25. Charles H. Fish, "The Signal Corps: The Confederate Movement against Allatoona," *National Tribune*, April 19, 1883.

26. Sherman, *Memoirs*, 2:146; *OR*, vol. 39, pt. 3: 53.

27. Ezra J. Warner, *Generals in Blue: Lives of the Union Commanders* (Baton Rouge: Louisiana State University Press, 1964), 94–95; William Ludlow, "The Battle of Allatoona: October 5th 1864," in *Papers of the Military Order of the Loyal Legion of the United States* (Detroit: Winn and Hammond, Printers and Binders, 1891), 15.

28. George W. Hill, *From Memphis to Allatoona, and the Battle of Allatoona, October 5, 1864* (Providence, RI: Published by the Society, 1891), 26–30; *OR*, vol. 39, 1: 762.

29. *OR*, vol. 39, pt. 1: 762–63; Hill, *From Memphis to Allatoona*, 31–32.

30. *OR*, vol. 39, pt. 1: 762–63; Hill, *From Memphis to Allatoona*, 31–32.

31. *OR*, vol. 39, pt. 1: 762, 819.

32. Ibid., 815.

33. Ibid., 763, 815.

34. William Pitt Chambers, *Blood and Sacrifice: The Civil War Journal of a Confederate Soldier*, ed. Richard A. Baumgartner (Huntington, WV: Blue Acorn Press, 1994), 172–73.

35. *OR*, vol. 39, pt. 1: 815–16.

36. Ibid.; R. S. Bevier, *History of the First and Second Missouri Confederate Brigades: 1861–1865 and From Wakarusa to Appomattox, A Military Anagraph* (St. Louis: Bryan, Brand and Company, 1879), 244.

37. Mathew D. Ector had his left leg shattered when a shell fragment tore through his lower left thigh. The wound made it necessary to amputate the leg between the knee and hip. This put an end to his active field service yet he was able to take part in the defense of Mobile toward the final days of the war. R. Todhunter, "Ector's Texas Brigade at the Battle of Allatoona," *Confederate Veteran* (1900; repr., Wilmington, NC: Broadfoot Publishing Company, 1987–88), 26:340–41; Jack D. Welsh, *Medical Histories of Confederate Generals* (Kent, OH: Kent State University Press, 1995), 60; *OR*, vol. 39, pt. 1: 816; Ephraim McD. Anderson, *Memoirs: Historical and Personal; Including the Campaigns of the First Missouri Confederate Brigade* (St. Louis: Times Printing Company, 1868), 392.

38. *OR*, vol. 39, pt. 1: 763.

39. Kenneth Carley, *Minnesota in the Civil War* (St. Paul: Minnesota Historical Society Press, 2000), 134; *OR*, vol. 39, pt. 1: 751.

40. *OR*, vol. 39, pt. 1: 751; John Shearer, "Hand-To-Hand: The Valiant 12th Wis. Battery at the Battle of Allatoona," *National Tribune*, October 18, 1894, 3.

41. *OR*, vol. 39, pt. 1: 763.

42. Ibid., 763, 816.

43. Ibid., 763.

44. Elisha Starbuck of Company "K," 39th Iowa later wrote of what he witnessed of the Union message from Corse that never made its way to French. He recalled,

> Standing near headquarters in the field, I saw Corse write his reply to Gen. French's summons for surrender. Lieutenant O. C. Ayers carried this answer to the enemy, who were in waiting at our picket line. The five minutes French gave for deliberation and reply had more than expired. The enemy were advancing rapidly before Ayers reached our outer works on his return. En route Ayers passed the 39th Iowa, a part of whom were on a ridge, and two companies (K and E) partly entrenched. I went to this regiment, of which I was an enlisted member, and there awaited Ayers's return.

E. Starbuck, "Hold the Fort: Recollections of the Battle of Allatoona," *National Tribune,* October 1, 1903, 2; *OR,* vol. 39, pt. 1: 763, 816; Sanders, "Hood's Tennessee Campaign," 149.

45. Bevier, *History of the First and Second Missouri Confederate Brigades,* 244.

46. *OR,* vol. 39, pt. 1: 763–64.

47. French, *Two Wars,* 226; *OR,* vol. 39, pt. 1: 824; Brown, *Battle of Allatoona,* 6.

48. Times for the actual assault vary. French mentioned in his report that he sent a summons of surrender at about 9:00 A.M. and waited seventeen minutes. He also stated in his memoirs that the summons took place at 8:00 A.M., and that the assault took place at 10:20 A.M. Corse reported that the time of the truce was 8:30 A.M. Therefore it is safe to believe that the assault occurred sometime during the mid-morning of October 5. *OR,* vol. 39, pt. 1: 816, 763; French, *Two Wars,* 226.

49. Winter, *Captain Joseph Boyce,* 180.

50. Charles Van Gorder, "Allatoona: A Short Statement from One Who Was in the Fight," *National Tribune,* April 28, 1887, 3.

51. James Bradley, *The Confederate Mail Carrier or From Missouri to Arkansas through Mississippi, Alabama, Georgia, and Tennessee: An Unwritten Leaf of the Civil War* (Mexico, MO: James Bradley, 1894), 217; Trimble, *History of the Ninety-Third,* 112; J. A. Watrous, "Incidents and Anecdotes of the War," *Valentine Democrat,* August 29, 1907, n.p.; Subscriber, "Assault on Allatoona: The Fierce Struggle for the Possession of the Pass," *National Tribune,* July 12, 1883, 7; Van Gorder, "Allatoona," 3.

52. *OR,* vol. 39, pt. 1: 820–24.

53. Bevier, *History of the First and Second Missouri Confederate Brigades,* 245.

54. *OR,* vol. 39, pt. 1: 823.

55. Ibid., 820–21.

56. Company D of the 7th Illinois Infantry had been left in Rome on duty. *OR,* vol. 39, pt. 1: 777–78.

57. Ibid.; Trimble, *History of the Ninety-Third,* 113.

58. *OR,* vol. 39, pt. 1: 785.

59. Ibid., 821–23; Bevier, *History of the First and Second Missouri Confederate Brigades,* 245–46.

60. The smaller 7th Mississippi, having fewer companies than the others, was designated a battalion rather than a regiment. *OR,* vol. 38, pt. 3: 908; *OR,* vol. 39, pt. 2: 855; Brown, *Battle of Allatoona,* 7; R. H. Shotwell, "Hood's Campaign through

North Georgia," *Confederate Veteran* (1900; Wilmington, NC: Broadfoot Publishing Company, 1987–88), 1:311.

61. Chambers, *Blood and Sacrifice*, 174–75.

62. Ibid., 175–76, 178.

63. Brown, *Battle of Allatoona*, 7.

64. *OR*, vol. 39, pt. 1: 779–80, 773–74.

65. Ibid.

66. Ibid., 780–81, 750–51.

67. Ibid., 751; Brown, *Battle of Allatoona*, 7; Shotwell, "Hood's Campaign through North Georgia," 311.

68. *OR*, vol. 39, pt. 1: 825.

69. Ibid., 821–22.

70. Charles H. Fish recalled that the first contact with Kennesaw Mountain was around 10:50 A.M. Fish, "The Signal Corps," 1; John Q. Adams, "Hold the Fort!" in *Papers of the Military Order of the Loyal Legion of the United States* (Des Moines, IA: n.p., 1898), 167.

71. Sherman, *Memoirs*, 2:147.

72. *OR*, vol. 39, pt. 1: 825.

73. Ibid., 764.

74. Trimble, *History of the Ninety-Third*, 115.

75. Tourtellotte would later explain to Corse, "The guns of the 12th Wisconsin Battery were equally divided in the two forts. A Lieutenant of that Battery assures me that they had eight guns, four on a side, that day. They had been ordered to turn in their three-inch rifled guns and to draw 12-pounder Napoleons. They had drawn the Napoleons, but not yet turned in the rifled guns." Lieutenant Colonel J. E. Tourtellotte to General Course, Washington, D.C., May 25, 1886, in *The Annals of Iowa: A Historical Quarterly, Volume Two Third Series*, ed. Charles Aldrich, A.M. (Des Moines: The Historical Department of Iowa, 1895–97), 287.

76. *OR*, vol. 39, pt. 1: 765.

77. Ludlow, "The Battle of Allatoona," 33; *OR*, vol. 39, pt. 1: 761.

78. *OR*, vol. 39, pt. 1: 765; Jack D. Welsh, *Medical Histories of Union Generals* (Kent, OH: Kent State University Press, 1996), 78–79.

79. Trimble, *History of the Ninety-Third*, 116; Mortimer R. Flint, "The Battle of Allatoona," in *Papers of the Military Order of the Loyal Legion of the United States* (St. Paul, MN: Review Publishing Co., 1903; repr., Wilmington, NC: Broadfoot Publishing Company, 1992), 198–99; Ludlow, "The Battle of Allatoona," 33.

80. *OR*, vol. 39, pt. 1: 765.

81. Ibid., 816–17.

82. Ibid., 817; Brown, *Battle of Allatoona*, 11, 14.

83. Trimble, *History of the Ninety-Third*, 124.

84. French, *Two Wars*, 257.

85. *OR*, vol. 39, pt. 1: 766, 777–78, 785, 818, 820.

86. Ibid., 766; Sherman, *Memoirs*, 2:147.

87. *OR*, vol. 39, pt. 1: 819–20.

88. Ibid., 813–20; French, *Two Wars*, 225.

89. *OR*, vol. 39, pt. 3: 67, 89; *OR*, vol. 39, pt. 1: 790; Jacob D. Cox, *Atlanta* (Dayton, OH: Morningside House, 1987), 231.

3

ERRANT MOVES ON THE CHESSBOARD OF WAR

THE BATTLE OF SPRING HILL, NOVEMBER 29, 1864

John R. Lundberg

At 3 A.M. on November 29, 1864, the Confederates sleeping in and around the Warfield house near Columbia, Tennessee, began to stir. General John Bell Hood himself, using the house as his headquarters, awoke at that hour and had his staff strap him into his saddle. Hood had grand plans for that day. It was, he wrote later, an opportunity "for one of those beautiful moves upon the chess-board of war," to crush the enemy in front of him and, in his mind, change the complexion of the whole war. When Hood bid good-bye to his chaplain, Dr. Charles Quintard, the doctor "prayed God's blessing, guidance and direction upon him. 'Thank you, Doctor,' he replied, 'That is my hope and trust,' and as he turned away, he remarked 'the enemy must give me fight, or I will be at Nashville before tomorrow night.'" With this remark, Hood set in motion one of the most controversial chapters of the Civil War.[1]

The Battle of Spring Hill has come to occupy a unique place in Civil War history. Most historians have interpreted Spring Hill as a lost opportunity for the Confederacy to change the tide of the 1864 Tennessee Campaign, and the war in the western theater. Hood and his army did lose a possible opportunity to defeat the Union forces under Major General John Schofield at Spring Hill, but most of the studies of the battle greatly exaggerate the importance of the episode due to two distinct factors. First, Southerners have woven Spring Hill into the fabric of the Lost Cause mythology of the Civil War as a point, late in the war, where the Confederacy still had a chance to win, and as a symbol of all opportunities missed by the South during the war. Second, Spring Hill is seen as a prelude to the Confederate disasters at the Battle of Franklin the next day and then the Battle of Nashville on December 15–16. This rationale states that the Confederates could have avoided those disasters by winning at Spring Hill. In reality Spring Hill did not force John

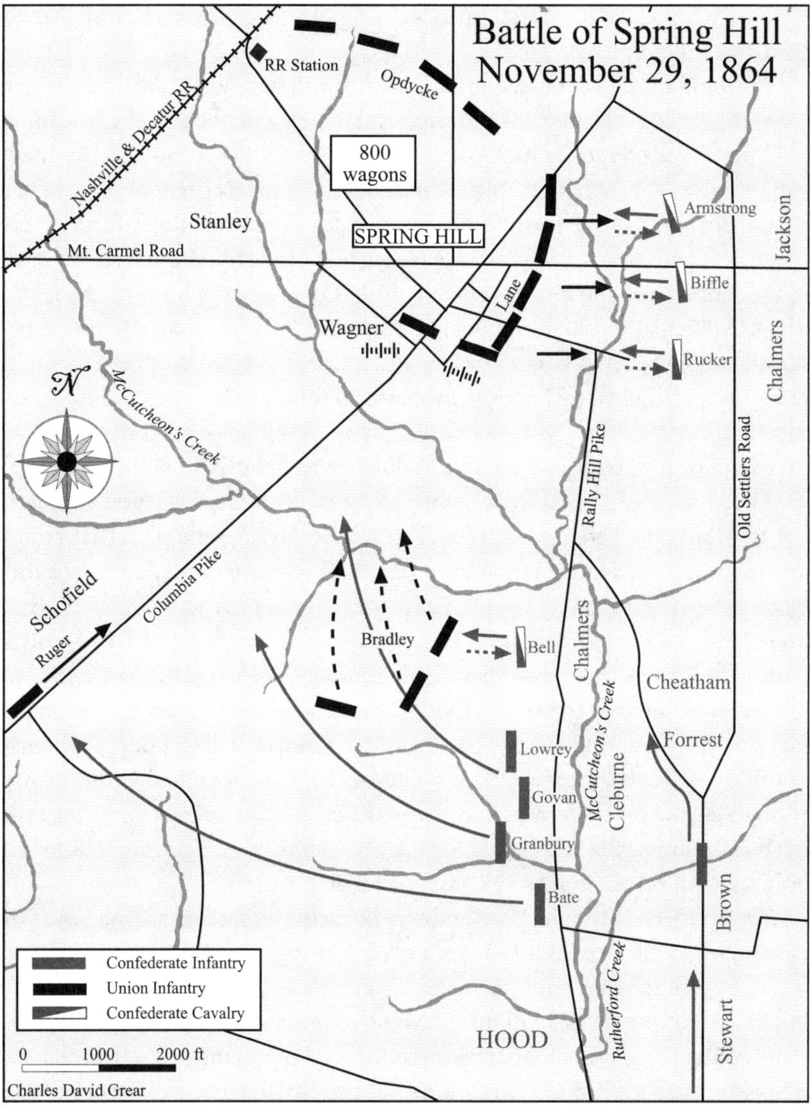

Bell Hood to pursue his disastrous decisions at either Franklin or Nashville, and should be seen as an entirely distinct episode. By November 29, 1864, nothing could have changed the course of the American Civil War. Lincoln had won reelection; scarcely five months after Spring Hill, Confederate forces would begin surrendering. While the Battle of Spring Hill had no chance to change the course of the war, it did give the Confederates an opportunity, within the limited context of the Tennessee Campaign, to deal a deadly blow to Schofield's forces and possibly compel Union forces in Nashville to confront them in battle on more even terms.[2]

Marching into Tennessee in late 1864, Hood had no specific plan other than getting to Nashville; his movements largely depended on the reactions of Union forces opposite him. On November 26, when Hood and his army approached Columbia they discovered that Union forces had already taken strong positions in the town on the north side of the Duck River. This development did not necessarily surprise Hood, but it gave him his first indication of the strength of the forces opposing him. On the north bank of the Duck River, Union major general Schofield commanded roughly twenty-eight thousand men in the Fourth and Twenty-Third Corps along with a cavalry force under Brigadier General James Wilson. Hood commanded roughly forty-four thousand infantry in the three corps of the Army of Tennessee as well as three thousand cavalrymen under Major General Nathan Bedford Forrest.[3]

On November 27, as the two armies sat opposite each other, Hood decided not to attack the Federals in front, but rather developed a plan that could destroy Schofield. Hood planned to cross the Duck River under cover of darkness on November 28, three miles east of Columbia with his Second Corps under Major General Benjamin F. "Frank" Cheatham and his Third Corps under Lieutenant General Alexander P. Stewart. With Forrest screening his movements north of the river, Hood planned to leave his First Corps under Lieutenant General Stephen D. Lee and part of his artillery in place south of the Duck River to stage a feint, hopefully keeping Schofield in place long enough for the Confederates to capture the crossroads village of Spring Hill in the Union rear. By capturing Spring Hill, Hood could cut off Schofield's only route of retreat toward Nashville and destroy him.[4]

As Hood departed the Warfield residence in the early morning hours of November 29, he faced the very real problem of logistics. John Bell Hood was clearly a general who could conceive of great plans, but he often fell short in the execution of those plans, because of poor logistics and insufficient attention to detail. The logistical difficulties of supplying the Army of Tennessee on such a circuitous march, as the one Hood made into Tennessee in late 1864, seem to have completely befuddled him. These difficulties resulted in a delay of several weeks when first marching into Tennessee, time that Schofield used well to shore up his position.

The problem of logistics once again reared its head in the early morning hours of November 29. Hood selected his best troops—Major General Patrick Cleburne's division—to lead the advance across the Duck River, but when Cleburne approached the crossing site, he discovered that the bridge remained incomplete. Cleburne hurriedly sought out the officer in charge of the bridge detail, First Lieutenant William Reddick of the 1st Florida Infantry. The lieutenant informed Cleburne that although he and his men had worked through the night, they could not finish the bridge due to a lack of men. After dressing down Reddick, Cleburne dispatched some of his own men who hurriedly finished the bridge. At 5:30 A.M. Cleburne and his division, accompanied by Hood, began crossing the river. It had taken them two and a half hours from the time Hood departed the Glenn residence until the time his first infantry crossed the Duck River, and the logistical problems were just beginning.[5]

The Confederate infantry column under Hood remained unfamiliar with the roads between their crossing and Spring Hill, largely because Hood had detached Forrest and his cavalry. On the night of November 28, Hood ordered Forrest to cross the Duck River and occupy the Union cavalry under Brigadier General James H. Wilson. Forrest crossed the river at about 11 P.M. Wilson, gathering intelligence for Schofield, almost immediately discovered Forrest's crossing, and after some skirmishing, captured a Confederate cavalryman who provided him with information. At 1 A.M. Wilson hurriedly dashed off a note to Schofield from Hurt's Crossroads, northeast of Columbia. Wilson informed his commander of Forrest's crossing and that his Confederate prisoner indicated to him that Hood and his infantry would be coming right behind the cavalry, possibly crossing the Duck River as early as 11 P.M., heading for Franklin. Wilson advised Schofield that he should be at Spring Hill with his army "by 10 A.M."[6]

At 2 A.M. Schofield received Wilson's intelligence, and although he remained unsure of exactly what the Confederates intended, he gave orders to begin a general retreat toward Spring Hill. To safeguard the wagon train, Schofield ordered Major General David S. Stanley, commander of the Fourth Corps, to accompany the train with his First and Second Divisions under Brigadier Generals Nathan Kimball and George Wagner, respectively. Schofield also ordered Colonel Sidney Post and his Third Brigade of the Fourth Division, Fourth Corps, to reconnoiter in the direction of the Confederate crossing on the Duck River. At about 7:30 A.M. Post and his men mounted a small hill along the river and from there they could plainly see Confederate infantry crossing the river, but Post could not ascertain their numbers or intentions. At 8:45 A.M., with Schofield still trying to determine Hood's objective, Stanley had his men on the road north toward Spring Hill. The race for the crossroads had begun.[7]

Even though Schofield had clear intelligence in front of him regarding Hood's intentions, he hesitated. On the evening of November 28, Schofield received a communication from Major General George H. Thomas at Nashville, asking him to hold his position as long as possible. Schofield came to believe that the bulk of Hood's army could not be crossing the river as indicated by Wilson, and the ambivalent intelligence he received from Post reinforced this impression. At 10 A.M. Schofield issued orders to stop the full-scale retreat and instructed the remainder of his forces merely to prepare for a possible withdrawal. At the same time Schofield ordered Stanley and his two divisions, along with the wagon train and the bulk of the artillery, already on the road, to continue north. Increasingly worried about a flank attack, Schofield sent orders for Kimball's division to stop and occupy a position on Rutherford Creek, some four miles north of Columbia, to protect the road and the column. That left only Stanley's corps and Wagner's division to continue on in the dusty wake of the wagon train toward Spring Hill. Although Hood's inept logistical failures continued to haunt him, it appeared that Schofield might offset that handicap with his own hesitance.[8]

As Hood marched along with Cleburne and Brigadier General Hiram Granbury, commander of the Texas Brigade, bringing up the rear of Cleburne's column, he began to fear a flank attack from the direction of Columbia. Shortly after crossing the Duck River, lacking cavalry to screen his movements, he ordered Major General John Brown to take his infantry division parallel to and west of the main road to guard against a flank attack. This spread out Brown's division for several miles, adding to their fatigue.[9]

Nathan Bedford Forrest, rather than screening the Confederate infantry, remained engaged with Wilson's Union cavalry northeast of Columbia. A skirmish developed at Mount Carmel, six miles east of Spring Hill as Wilson tried to stem Forrest's advance. Forrest initially sent Brigadier General James Chalmers's Rebel cavalry brigade against Wilson's defensive position, only to have them bloodily repulsed by Wilson's men, many of whom were armed with repeating rifles. Forrest then called off the attack and waited. Thinking that Forrest would slip around his flank, Wilson began retreating north toward Franklin just after 10 A.M. Forrest, understanding Spring Hill as Hood's objective, sent Brigadier General Lawrence Sullivan "Sul" Ross and his Texas cavalry brigade to pursue Wilson and keep him busy. Then Forrest, with all of his remaining cavalry, turned west toward Spring Hill with no one to stop him. Just before 11 A.M. the Confederate cavalry began closing in on the crossroads. It appeared as if Forrest might score a huge victory in spite of his commander's mistakes.[10]

At 11:15 A.M., just as Forrest's cavalrymen came thundering toward Spring Hill from the east, the head of Schofield's wagon train also neared the town from the south. Only a sparse Federal garrison occupied the town. The 12th Tennessee Cavalry remained the only Union force in town until two regiments from Colonel Robert Stewart's brigade arrived from Columbia. Learning of Forrest's impending arrival, all three regiments rode east out of Spring Hill to try to block the Confederate advance along the Mount Carmel Road, and Company M, 2nd Michigan Cavalry soon joined them. Just after 11:15 Forrest ordered an attack against the Union cavalrymen, who positioned themselves atop a ridge that bisected the road. The dismounted Union cavalry repulsed Forrest's first attack, and he ordered another.[11]

Between 11:20 and 11:45 A.M. additional reinforcements began to arrive in Spring Hill. Four companies of the 73rd Illinois Infantry, assigned to precede the wagon train, arrived, as did Schofield's headquarters escort, the 103rd Ohio Infantry. Soon the 120th Indiana Infantry, assigned to guard the body of the wagon train, also arrived. Battery A, 1st Ohio Light Artillery and Battery G, 1st Ohio Light Artillery also made their appearance at Spring Hill and unlimbered on a hill east of town. These reinforcements arrived just in time, because around 11:30 A.M., the Federal cavalry east of the town began to fall back toward Spring Hill. At 11:30 a courier rode up to General Stanley at the head of Wagner's division, Colonel Emerson Opdycke's brigade, still several miles south of Spring Hill. The courier informed Stanley that Confederate cavalry were bearing down on the crossroads from the east, and Stanley ordered Opdycke's men, followed by Wagner and his other two brigades, to march on the double-quick into town. At 12:30 Opdycke's men arrived in Spring Hill, huffing and puffing, only to have their commanders order them into line of battle north and east of the town. Opdycke deployed his brigade on the left of Wagner's line, with Colonel John Q. Lane's brigade in the center and Brigadier General Luther Bradley's brigade on the right. Bradley's brigade, the last to arrive, was in position by 2 P.M. Heavy skirmishing immediately broke out between Forrest's cavalrymen and the Union infantry as they arrived, and Lane and Bradley began throwing up rudimentary breastworks. Before the arrival of the Confederate infantry, Forrest tried at least twice to break the Federal line east of the village, but to no avail. Stanley, Wagner and their men had arrived just in the nick of time; if they had arrived twenty minutes later, they probably would have found Forrest in possession of Spring Hill.[12]

As the initial fighting for Spring Hill raged, Hood's lack of attention to detail hampered the Confederate infantry. Hood believed from his maps that Spring Hill lay twelve miles northwest of Davis's Ford, but the actual distance ran closer to seventeen. Instead of having his cavalry scout the road ahead of time, Hood assumed the shorter distance remained correct and hired a local man, John Gregory, as a guide. As Gregory escorted Hood and his men toward Spring Hill, the Confederate commander grew impatient.

At about noon the column halted briefly for lunch and Hood engaged in a verbal altercation with Granbury. According to Gregory, Granbury had been a "little slow" in bringing up the rear of Cleburne's column, and Hood doubtless berated Granbury for his perceived tardiness. In reality Hood should have blamed himself for not adequately scouting the routes to Spring Hill and failing to use cavalry to screen his movements, both of which slowed the progress of the Confederate infantry substantially, especially with Brown's division spread out west of the road. Finally, at 2:30 P.M. Hood, riding ahead of the column, crossed Rutherford Creek just south of Spring Hill where he could hear the sound of skirmishing coming from the direction of the town. It took the Confederates nine hours to march the seventeen miles between the Duck River and Spring Hill. Moving at a mediocre pace of less than two miles an hour, Hood wasted most of the day getting his infantry into position, leaving him only a brief window of opportunity to achieve his goal.[13]

Despite this small chance, the Confederates had no idea how quickly their window of opportunity was closing. Back in Columbia by 3 P.M., Schofield realized that Hood intended to capture Spring Hill. He could hear the sound of artillery from that quarter, and desperately sought a way to save his small army. At 3:30 he issued orders to Brigadier General Thomas Ruger and two brigades of his division to start toward Spring Hill. Schofield accompanied Ruger and issued orders to the rest of his command to wait until nightfall and then withdraw northward.[14]

At about 3 P.M. Cheatham arrived at the head of his column and Hood issued orders for him to seize Spring Hill. Known as a hard drinker and hard fighter, Cheatham had a good reputation as a field commander, but he had commanded his corps for only about a month before Spring Hill, and never in a major battle. As a relatively new corps commander, Cheatham relied heavily on the direct orders of his commanding general. Hood recalled in his memoirs that after crossing Rutherford Creek he commanded Cheatham to take the Columbia Pike south of Spring Hill and that he could clearly see the pike, as well as the wagons and men of Schofield's army moving north. However, from his vantage point at Oaklawn, it would have been impossible for Hood to see the turnpike, as a ridge, forty feet in elevation, blocked his sight. Cheatham offered a more plausible account when he recalled that Hood issued him verbal orders to "get Cleburne across the creek and send him forward toward Spring Hill, with instructions to communicate with General Forrest, who was near the village, ascertain from him the position of the enemy and attack immediately; that I should remain at the creek, assist [Major] General [William B.] Bate in crossing his division, and then go forward and put Bate's command in to support Cleburne; and that he would push Brown forward to join me." Cheatham moved to carry out these orders, helping to shepherd Cleburne's men across the creek. In accordance with his orders, Cleburne formed his line of battle with Brigadier General Mark Lowrey's Brigade on the right, Hiram Granbury's Texans on the left, staggered about one hundred yards behind Lowrey, and Brigadier General Daniel Govan's Arkansas brigade in the center, behind the other two. Hood ordered Cleburne to occupy the Columbia Pike south of Spring Hill and wheel left, facing south, to block Schofield's troops coming from the direction of Columbia.[15]

At close to 4 P.M. Cleburne began his advance, moving toward the Columbia Pike only to face danger from his right flank. Forrest rode over to accompany Cleburne in his advance, but apparently Forrest did not understand the full disposition of the Union infantry south of Spring Hill, and neither Cheatham nor Hood had bothered to reconnoiter before ordering Cleburne toward the town. As the Rebels swept forward, Bradley's Union brigade, facing southeast, opened fire on the right flank of Mark Lowrey's Alabamans and Mississippians. Under orders from Cleburne, Lowrey swung his regiments around, but because of the *echelon* formation of the division, the Irishman had difficulty getting any support into place to bolster Lowrey. By the time he got Govan's Arkansans into position, Lowrey's men had already begun to rout Bradley's troops, and Luther Bradley himself fell from his horse, badly wounded.[16]

It looked for a few moments as if Cleburne's rebels would overrun Bradley's position, threatening David Stanley's right flank. At that moment the Confederates reached the top of a slight ridge and Battery A, 1st Ohio Light Artillery opened a fierce fire that sent them scurrying for cover. Incredibly, the Ohioans managed to fire 166 rounds, sending the rebels running for their original position beyond the ridge. Company G, 1st Ohio Light Artillery added its guns to the barrage. Meanwhile, Granbury's brigade, advancing straight west, drove away the 36th Illinois Infantry and a two-gun section of artillery deployed along the Columbia Pike. At that point Cleburne halted his division, re-forming Lowrey and Govan out of range of the artillery, facing northwest, while Granbury's Texans halted facing almost due west within a hundred yards of the pike.[17]

When Bradley's men opened fire on Lowrey, Cleburne dashed off a note to Cheatham, informing him of the encounter. In response Cheatham ordered Cleburne to re-form his division and wait for Brown and Bate to come up. When Cleburne received the orders he became extremely agitated and expressed to those around him that he should press his advantage with the Federals in disarray. Cleburne immediately rode off to find his corps commander. Cheatham intended for Brown to take position on Cleburne's right and Bate on Cleburne's left for a concerted attack on Spring Hill itself. Despite this relatively sound plan of action, nightfall continued its rapid approach as time slipped away. At 4:35 P.M., roughly the time Cheatham halted Cleburne, sunset occurred, and by 5:45 P.M. complete darkness would blanket the land, making any meaningful maneuvers or attacks almost impossible.[18]

Back near Rutherford Creek, Hood established his headquarters at the Absolom Thompson plantation house, Oaklawn, and continued to press reinforcements forward, although a lack of communication between him and Cheatham created a great deal of confusion. After Cleburne's division moved beyond the creek, Cheatham trailed them and established his headquarters in a forward position. Hood met Bate, the division behind Cleburne, at Rutherford Creek and instructed him to conform to Cleburne's left. Bate crossed the creek, forming his brigades *en echelon*, but could not see Cleburne's line of advance from the Thompson house, and felt his way forward as best he could. He remembered, "As soon as ascertained, I conformed to the movement as well as I could, and pushed forward in the direction of the enemy, who held the turnpike. It was now getting dark and I had moved more than a mile in line of battle. . . . Procuring a guide, learning the exact location of the enemy, and the general direction of the turnpike, I 'changed direction to the right,' again and was moving so as to strike the turnpike to the right of Major Nathaniel Cheirs residence, which I believed would bring me near Cleburne's left."[19]

After Bate's division crossed the creek, John Brown's Confederate division also began to cross. Hood directed Brown to move directly north—toward the Caldwell residence, at that time serving as Forrest's headquarters. This line of advance would take Brown and his men beyond Cleburne's right flank. When Cheatham spotted them moving in that direction, he hurriedly sent a courier to Brown to correct his "axis of advance," so as to reach Cleburne's right flank. After issuing these orders to Brown, Cheatham rode off to find Bate, but could not find him. Instead, Cheatham sent couriers to find Bate and doubled back personally to direct Brown. Under his commander's direction Brown formed a line of battle with Brigadier General Otho Strahl's command on the right, and by 4:45 P.M. had his men in position on Cleburne's right.[20]

At about 4:45 P.M. Cleburne rode up and found Brown and Cheatham discussing the pending attack. Cleburne, having just come from his own command, expressed insistence that Cheatham allow him to advance immediately against Spring Hill. Cheatham wanted Brown to attack first, followed by Cleburne. Major Joseph Vaulx, Cheatham's assistant adjutant general, remembered that Cheatham insisted that Cleburne should attack only upon hearing the sound of Brown's guns. By the time Cheatham issued these instructions, twilight had already enveloped the combatants.[21]

As Cheatham rode south, he still could not locate Bate. More troubling to Cheatham was the fact that he could not hear the sound of Brown's attack. Impatiently, Cheatham asked his staff, "Why don't we hear Brown's guns?" Deciding that he needed to supervise the attack in person, Cheatham sent a member of his staff to find Bate. At 5:30 P.M. Bate reached the pike just north of the Cheirs residence, Rippavilla, and he was preparing to attack the Federal wagon train and troops visibly moving north to his front when Cheatham's courier reached him. The courier found Bate within two hundred yards of the Columbia Pike, and ordered him, in the rapidly gathering darkness, to halt his command and move north, parallel to the pike, and link up with Cleburne. At that time Bate already had his skirmishers busy peppering the Union column to the front, a column that included Schofield, Ruger, and the head of Ruger's division. Bate protested these orders, but even though he could clearly see the skirmishing and the retreating Union army moving north up the pike, he reluctantly obeyed.[22]

Meanwhile Cheatham soon discovered why Brown had not carried out his orders. As soon as Cheatham left Brown in search of Bate, trouble developed on Brown's flank. Otho Strahl, commander of Brown's rightmost brigade, galloped breathlessly up to his commander and reported Union troops silhouetted against the gathering darkness on his right flank. Brown rode over with him to see about the threat, and the two men observed the same line, but in the near darkness they could not ascertain the strength of the enemy. Brown also expressed dismay that Forrest, who had promised he would protect his right, had withdrawn his cavalry for the night to rest his men and horses. Afraid that the unknown Union force might outflank him, Brown halted his advance. Shortly afterward Brigadier General States Rights Gist arrived with the last of Brown's brigades, and the Tennessean placed them on the right, so that the Union line appeared to be no more than a half mile from the Confederate flank. What Brown and Strahl observed turned out to be the leftmost regiments of Colonel John Q. Lane's Union brigade, the 100th Illinois Infantry and one company of the 40th Indiana. A single regiment of Union infantry had halted an entire Rebel division. At this juncture Brown's lack of experience as a division commander came into stark relief. Brown had only commanded his division, Cheatham's old division, for about forty days and never before in a major battle. A more experienced division commander might have taken more decisive action, but Brown hesitated, in the dark, dispatched a courier to advise Cheatham of the situation, and waited for orders.[23]

In front of Absolom Thompson's palatial plantation home John Bell Hood, after ushering Brown's division across Rutherford Creek, sat down to wait for the news that Cheatham and his command had captured Spring Hill. Sitting on a log next to a pond, Hood became anxious about not hearing the sounds of an attack, and sent a courier to Cheatham to inquire about the situation. He apparently received a reply from Cheatham, informing him that the attack would begin soon. Finally, after still hearing no sound from the front, Hood dispatched Tennessee governor Isham Harris to find Cheatham. Harris first found Brown, who showed him the Union troops beyond his line. Harris dispatched a courier to Hood, suggesting that he use Alexander Stewart's corps, at that time just crossing Rutherford Creek, to bolster Brown's right flank. Harris then left Brown and found Cheatham in the rear of Cleburne's division, and the two of them set off to see Hood. Cheatham claimed after the war that before departing to see Hood he issued a second order to Brown to "throw back his right" and advance, but Brown denied that he ever received this directive and Major Vaulx also never mentioned this second order. In all likelihood Cheatham never sent the order, but instead sought clarification from Hood before doing anything more.[24]

Alexander P. Stewart's Rebel corps reached Rutherford Creek at 4 P.M. on November 29, but Hood halted Stewart on the south side of the creek and ordered him to form his men in line of battle. Finally at dark, Hood allowed them to cross the creek and proceed toward Brown's right flank. When Stewart encountered Hood near the Thompson house, Hood "complained bitterly that his orders to attack had not been obeyed," but the Confederate corps commander noted that Hood "*was there himself*." When Stewart asked Hood why he had halted his command at Rutherford Creek, Hood replied that he expected Cheatham's command to attack and scatter the enemy, and that he wanted Stewart to keep his men fresh and move to the front to cut off the Union escape route toward Franklin. Hood never addressed the point in his memoirs, but if true this represented a bizarre decision on Hood's part. Stewart pointed out that if Hood had informed Cheatham that substantial reinforcements would soon reach his flank, the information might have emboldened Cheatham and Brown to make the assault.[25]

Shortly after Stewart's conversation with Hood, Cheatham and Harris reached Hood in front of the Thompson home. What happened next remains the subject of debate. Both Cheatham and Hood claimed that Stewart was present at this meeting, but Stewart steadfastly denied that the three were ever together at Spring Hill. In any event, Hood claimed that he asked Cheatham why he had not already made his advance, and rode with him into "full view" of the enemy, instructing him to make his attack at once. On the contrary,

Cheatham claimed that when he met Hood, the commanding general ordered him, under the circumstances, not to advance, but to wait until morning to resume to attack. "I was never more astonished," wrote Cheatham, "when General Hood informed me that he had concluded to postpone the attack till daylight." Major Vaulx and General Brown also stated that Hood decided to wait until morning to renew the assault. Given that all of the principle players agree with each other and contradict Hood, it is probably safe to assume that some version of the story where Hood decided not to attack in the dark occurred. There remains no good or plausible explanation for Hood's behavior, other than fatigue. At the point where Hood, Cheatham and Harris conversed, the commanding general had been up and in the saddle or active for almost sixteen hours. It appears that with his mind clouded by fatigue, Hood decided to sleep on the matter and not pursue it again until daylight.[26]

Whether or not Hood decided to postpone the attack during his last conversation with Cheatham remains of little consequence because by that time complete darkness had fallen. Night attacks in the Civil War rarely succeeded, and in fact more often than not caused more harm than good. Cleburne understood this fact all too well, and this probably answers the question of why Cleburne did not engage in the discussions between Hood, Cheatham, Brown, and Stewart. After Cheatham halted Cleburne's initial assault and ordered him to wait for Brown, the Irishman probably gave up on the idea of the attack altogether. Cleburne and his division participated in one of the largest and best-known night attacks of the war at Chickamauga on September 19, 1863. Cleburne did not want to make the attack, and after the advance came to an end, he had accomplished nothing of substance and his division remained in such disarray that he lost an opportunity to take the ridge held by George Thomas's Union troops to his front in the early morning of September 20. The Irishman learned his lesson well, and he probably did not intend to sacrifice his division on the night of November 29, charging into the darkness without the faintest idea of the position or strength of the enemy, especially without orders or the support of either Bate or Brown on his flanks. If Hood had resumed the attack and Brown, Cleburne, Cheatham, and Stewart had all moved forward with alacrity, it probably would have accomplished nothing more than the scattering of Schofield's army and probably equally devastating results for the Confederates. The next morning the Confederate army would have been scattered in every possible direction, probably having done more harm to themselves than to Schofield through confusion and friendly fire. The brief window where the rebels had a chance to destroy Schofield came between 3 P.M. and 5:45 P.M. on November 29, and the window had passed.[27]

On the Federal side, Schofield, after arriving in Spring Hill, decided to push on to Franklin. At 8 P.M. Schofield issued orders for his men to withdraw, with Ruger's division leading the way north and Wagner's division bringing up the rear.[28]

After the last conversation with Cheatham, Hood settled down for the night at Oaklawn. On Cleburne's line, Granbury positioned his Texans along an old farm fence about one hundred yards from the Columbia Pike. The Texans heard an occasional rustling; some believed that it was merely Bate's men moving up the pike, others thought it was the enemy. Finally Captain Richard English of Granbury's staff lost his patience and said "I'll be damned if I don't find out." As he crept toward the pike on his mule, flankers from the 23rd Michigan captured him as they hastened north up the pike. At about 10 P.M. Granbury pulled his men back another one hundred yards, where they lighted campfires and made camp for the night. They still remained so close to the pike that occasionally a Federal soldier would venture up to one of the campfires to light his pipe, only to have the Texans capture him.[29]

Around 9 P.M. Bate and his command arrived on Cleburne's flank. Thinking that Union troops might turn his right flank, Bate received permission to throw back the left flank of his leftmost brigade to guard against that possibility. With no other orders, Bate and his men went into camp between 9 and 10 P.M. With his division in place, Bate, enraged by his lost opportunity to block the pike, rode off to find Hood.[30]

Even as Cleburne pulled back Granbury's brigade, Alexander Stewart's Confederate corps continued to trudge into position on Brown's right. Major General Edward Walthall's division led the way, followed by that of Major General W. W. Loring and finally Samuel French. After moving past Brown's flank about 9 P.M., Stewart halted the head of Walthall's division less than two hundred yards from the Columbia Pike. Without realizing their position, Stewart rode back to Hood's headquarters to ask for orders.[31]

In the meantime, Schofield and the head of Ruger's division reached Thompson's Station, the next stop on the road to Franklin, by 9 P.M. Forrest's cavalrymen posted along the route to Franklin informed their commander of the development, and Forrest hurried to find Hood and report the situation. When Forrest roused Hood to inform him of the situation, Hood told Forrest that Cleburne already held possession of the turnpike. After learning from Forrest that this assumption was incorrect, Hood asked him if he could obstruct the pike. Forrest informed him that Abraham Buford's and Chalmers's divisions lacked the ammunition to make an attack, but that Brigadier General William H. "Red" Jackson's division would try to block the thoroughfare. Hood's instructions in this instance are extremely strange.

His apparent knowledge of the position of his troops and anxiety about taking the Columbia Pike seem to have varied widely, depending on whom he was speaking to at the moment. Again, fatigue remains the only completely plausible explanation for Hood's behavior.[32]

After Forrest departed, Hood admitted his next visitor, William Bate. Bate expressed his dismay about not taking the pike, and he remembered that Hood assured him that Forrest would block the pike, and that Bate could "sleep easy." With no other options Bate returned to his command, pulled in most of his skirmishers, and went into camp for the night.[33]

After Bate left, at 11 P.M., Stewart finally found Hood. He reported his situation, and asked Hood for orders. Hood inquired as to whether he had found Brown's right. After Stewart replied in the affirmative, Hood told him that occupying the pike "was not material, to let the men rest; and directed me to move before daylight in the morning taking the advance toward Franklin."[34]

After most of the other Confederate infantry units had bedded down for the night, Major General Edward Johnson's division of Lieutenant General Stephen D. Lee's Confederate corps came straggling into line, having accompanied Stewart's corps for most of the day. Cheatham ordered Johnson into position on his left, south of Bate's division, and left the task of getting Johnson into position to one of his staff members, Captain Joseph Bostick, his acting assistant inspector general. Bostick placed Johnson into position and then returned to Cheatham, reporting that he could clearly hear Union troops moving along Johnson's front up the turnpike. At about the same time a private soldier reported to Hood that the Union army continued to escape north, and this alarmed Hood to the point that he sent Major Richard Mason with orders for Cheatham to have Johnson's division block the thoroughfare. Cheatham received Major Mason just as Bostick reached him with the intelligence from the pike. Cheatham ordered Bostick to return and order Johnson to block the pike. When Bostick arrived, just after 1 A.M., Johnson vehemently refused to move, protesting that darkness and unfamiliarity with the terrain made an advance impossible. Johnson then rode off to find Cheatham and object in person. After reaching Cheatham, Johnson reiterated his complaints and Cheatham, accompanied by Bostick, rode out to the turnpike. They arrived at 2 A.M. in front of Johnson's division and found nothing—all of the Union troops had already passed.[35]

At 2 A.M. Red Jackson's division finally received its orders from Forrest to advance. Sul Ross commanded the brigade nearest the pike, and the Texans readied themselves for combat. They rushed forward at 3 A.M., burning some Federal wagons in the vicinity of Thompson's Station and skirmishing with the Federal infantry there. However, without Rebel infantry support, the

Texans had to fall back in the face of the large numbers of Union infantry. At that point Forrest refused to renew the offensive. Shortly after the failed attack, the last of Schofield's infantry withdrew from Spring Hill toward Franklin. At 3:30 A.M., after twenty-four hours of maneuvering and fighting, the Battle of Spring Hill came to an end.[36]

The finger pointing for the massive Confederate debacle began within hours of the escape of Schofield's army and continued long into the postwar era. Hood blamed Cheatham, Cleburne, and Brown, and some have darkly hinted that Hood placed these divisions in the most dangerous part of the Battle of Franklin the next day because of this blame. Regardless, who was to blame for the Confederate reversal at Spring Hill? The responsibility primarily lay with Hood and his failure to grasp the importance of details, the logistics of his army. Hood came up with what, on paper, appeared to be a brilliant plan but failed to execute the plan in large part because he did not pay attention to detail. He had no idea of the distance between Davis's Ford and Spring Hill because of his failure to reconnoiter the terrain and the misallocation of his cavalry. In addition, once Hood arrived on the field, he failed to supervise the attack until his window of opportunity passed. The only possible explanation for Hood's sometimes erratic behavior at Spring Hill remains fatigue. It is not difficult to understand how a physically crippled Hood failed to take a more active role rather than remaining at Oaklawn.

Despite Hood's culpability, his subordinates also failed in many ways. Nathan Bedford Forrest experienced one of his worst days in Rebel uniform at Spring Hill. He failed to provide Hood with the intelligence he needed for the infantry to make its way to Spring Hill. Although Forrest did actively pursue the capture of Spring Hill, he also neglected to inform either Cheatham or Cleburne of the disposition of the Union forces around the town. Forrest also withdrew his divisions just as John Brown looked for them on his right flank, leading to the anxiety and apprehension that stalled the latter's attack. Finally, Forrest belatedly sought out Hood late at night, but only managed to muster token resistance to the Federal infantry at Thompson's Station.

Frank Cheatham and John Brown also bear a great deal of the responsibility for the failure on November 29. Cheatham's inexperience at corps command led directly to several of his most disastrous decisions, including his order that halted Cleburne just as the Irishman prepared to overrun Stanley's flank, and his insistence that Bate withdraw from the turnpike just as the latter began to engage the retreating Federal column. Cheatham failed to trust his two more experienced division commanders, Cleburne and Bate, instead leaving the responsibility of beginning the final assault to his least experienced commander, John Brown. Brown also cost the Confederates dearly at Spring Hill with his vacillation and lack of initiative.

Despite the fact that Spring Hill had no chance to change the larger course of the war, the battle became symbolic of the Lost Cause mythology that infected Southern thinking after the war. Spring Hill became a popular scapegoat, a point where the South could have changed the course of the war, only to have that opportunity wasted by incompetent generals. Hood, Cheatham, and most of the other Confederate generals at Spring Hill (those who did not die at Franklin the next day) engaged in a vitriolic war of words immediately following the publication of Hood's memoirs in 1880. Although these exchanges mostly produced useless self-aggrandizement and myth-making, the myriad accounts have at least given historians an opportunity to understand exactly what happened in middle Tennessee that November day. The accounts also underscore the desperate attempt of Southerners to justify their cause and come to coherent explanations about why they failed and more importantly in this case, who was most to blame.[37]

At most, Spring Hill held the promise of slightly changing the course of the war in the West, but only temporarily. If Hood had crushed Schofield, it might have altered George Thomas's plan to defeat the Confederates in Tennessee, but probably not by much. Thomas still held Nashville with far superior numbers and could easily have overcome the loss of Schofield. Despite this lack of larger significance, Spring Hill did play a pivotal part within the Tennessee Campaign itself, destroying any advantage the Rebels might have enjoyed and leading directly to Hood's disastrous decisions at Franklin the next day. The lost opportunity at Spring Hill certainly did not force Hood to order the charge at Franklin, but it put him in the ugly frame of mind that led to the disaster. Lieutenant Robert Collins of Granbury's brigade perhaps summed it up best when he wrote after the war ". . . the easiest and most charitable way to dispose of the whole matter is to say that the gods of battle were against us and injected confusion into the heads and tongues of our leaders."[38]

Notes

1. John Bell Hood, *Advance and Retreat: Personal Experiences in the United States and Confederate States Armies* (New Orleans: Fort Hood Memorial Fund by G. T. Beauregard, 1880; repr. Cambridge, MA: DeCapo Press, 1993), 283; Arthur Howard Noll, ed., *Doctor Quintard Chaplain C.S.A. and Second Bishop of Tennessee: Being His Story of the War (1861–1865)* (Sewanee, TN: The University Press, 1905), 109.

2. Hood himself and his immediate subordinates are probably most responsible for first fostering the idea that Spring Hill could have changed the course of the war. See Hood, *Advance and Retreat*, as well as the accounts of Cheatham, Stewart,

Brigadier General Mark Lowrey, Major General William Bate, and Major General John Brown in *The Southern Historical Society Papers* (December 1881), 9:518–41. Other Confederates also added to this view; see J. P. Young, "Hood's Failure at Spring Hill," *Confederate Veteran* 16, no. 1 (January 1908): 25–41, and Henry M. Field, *Bright Skies and Dark Shadows* (New York: Charles Scribner's Sons, 1890), 209–35. For the view that Spring Hill could have changed the war in the West, see Wiley Sword, *Embrace an Angry Wind: The Confederacy's Last Hurrah, Spring Hill, Franklin, and Nashville* (New York: HarperCollins Publishers Inc., 1994), 154–55; Eric A. Jacobson and Richard A. Rupp, *For Cause and for Country: A Study of the Affair at Spring Hill and the Battle of Franklin* (Franklin, TN: O'More Publishing, 2007), 169–83; Stanley F. Horn, *The Army of Tennessee* (Norman: University of Oklahoma Press, 1954), 393; Aletha D. Sayers, *The Sound of Brown's Guns: The Battle of Spring Hill November 29, 1864* (Spring Hill, TN: Rose Hill Publishing, 1995); James Lee McDonough and Thomas L. Connelly, *Five Tragic Hours: The Battle of Franklin* (Knoxville: University of Tennessee Press, 1983); Jamie Gillum, *The Battle of Spring Hill: Twenty-five Hours to Tragedy* (self-published, 2004); and David E. Roth, "The Mysteries of Spring Hill," *Blue and Gray Magazine* 2, no. 2 (October, 1984). Only Thomas Connelly in his *Autumn of Glory: The Army of Tennessee 1862–1865* (Baton Rouge: Louisiana State University Press, 1971) hints that Spring Hill may have been less important than previously thought, and only Richard M. McMurry in his *John Bell Hood and the War for Southern Independence* (Lincoln: University of Nebraska Press, 1982), states unequivocally that Spring Hill did not matter to the larger course of the war.

3. The author could not find any specific plan of action from Hood; he seems to have been largely reactionary after crossing into Tennessee, which would fit with his larger pattern of ignoring important details. For the Confederate strength, see U.S. War Department, *The War of the Rebellion: A Compilation of the Official Records of the Union and Confederate Armies*, 128 vols. (Washington, DC: Government Printing Office, 1881–1901), ser. 1, vol. 45, pt. 1: 663 (hereinafter cited as *OR*; all references are to series 1 unless otherwise indicated); for the Federal strength, see *OR*, vol. 45, pt. 1: 52.

4. Hood evidently concocted this plan on the night of November 27. Hood, *Advance and Retreat*, 282–83.

5. For a larger discussion of Hood's logistical failures in the Tennessee Campaign, see Frank E. Vandiver, "General Hood as Logistician," *Journal of Military Affairs* 16 (Spring 1952): 1–11; reprinted in Lawrence Lee Hewitt and Arthur W. Bergeron Jr., *Confederate Generals in the Western Theater: Classic Essays on America's Civil War* (Knoxville: University of Tennessee Press, 2010), 1:176–91; William W. Reddick, *Seventy-Seven Years in Dixie: The Boys in Gray from 61–65* (Santa Rosa Beach, FL: Coastal Heritage Preservation Foundation, 1999), 56.

6. *OR*, vol. 45, pt. 1: 1143.

7. John M. Schofield, *Forty-Six Years in the Army* (New York: The Century Company, 1897), 210–11; Ambrose Bierce, *Ambrose Bierce, A Sole Survivor, Bits of Autobiography*, ed. S. T. Joshi and David E. Schultz (Knoxville: University of Tennessee Press, 1998), 55; *OR*, vol. 45, pt. 1: 113–15.

8. Thomas sent this message to Schofield at 8 P.M. on November 28. *OR*, vol. 45, pt. 1: 1108; ibid., 1141–42.

9. *Southern Historical Society Papers* (1881), 9:537.

10. *OR*, vol. 45, pt. 1: 752–54, 550–54.

11. Ibid., 1152, 752–54; Letter of Mortimer Hempstead, Company M, 2nd Michigan Cavalry, to "Dear M.," December 1, 1864, Carter House Archives, Franklin, Tennessee.

12. W. H. Newlin, *A History of The Seventy-Third Regiment of Illinois Volunteer Infantry: Its Services and Experiences in Camp, on the March, on the Pickett and Skirmish Lines, and in Many Battles of the War, 1861–1865* (Decatur: Regimental Reunion Association of the Survivors of the 73rd Illinois Volunteer Infantry, 1890), 438, 446; Levi T. Scofield, *The Retreat from Pulaski to Nashville, Tenn., Battle of Franklin, Nov. 30th, 1864* (Cleveland: Caxton, 1909), 18; Jacob D. Cox, *The Battle of Franklin, Tennessee, November 30, 1864: A Monograph* (Dayton, OH: Morningside, 1983), 31.

13. The account of John Gregory, Hood's guide, can be found in Frank H. Smith, *A History of Maury County Tennessee* (Columbia, TN: Maury County Historical Society, 1969), 238.

14. *OR*, vol. 45, pt. 1: 342.

15. Hood, *Advance and Retreat*, 284; *Southern Historical Society Papers* (1881), 9:524–25, 536; Irving A. Buck, *Cleburne and His Command* (Jackson, TN: McCowat-Mercer Press, 1959), 272.

16. *Southern Historical Society Papers* (1881), 9:536; *OR*, vol. 45, pt. 1: 268–69. There has been some debate as to whether or not Cleburne disobeyed his orders by swinging around to attack Bradley instead of continuing directly toward the Columbia Pike, but this argument is ridiculous. Once Bradley opened fire, Cleburne had no choice but to swing around and face the threat. For the position that Cleburne disobeyed his orders, see Thomas L. Connelly, *Autumn of Glory: The Army of Tennessee 1862–1865* (Baton Rouge: Louisiana State University Press, 1971), 495. Connelly also states that Cleburne failed to make personal contact with Forrest, but Govan clearly stated that he was with Forrest and Cleburne as his brigade advanced. The more likely scenario is that somehow Forrest missed Bradley's Brigade in his reconnaissance. Bradley had positioned his line almost three-quarters of a mile south of Lane's right flank, in a wooded area. Forrest concentrated on dislodging Lane's men and so probably remained unaware of Bradley's presence altogether. Stephen D. Lee, in a letter written in 1878, claims that Cleburne lamented to him on the morning of November 30 that he disobeyed the spirit of his orders. Regardless of what Cleburne might have felt, Bradley's presence gave him no choice; he could not swing south, leaving an entire Union brigade in his rear. S. D. Lee to J. F. H. Claiborne June 12, 1878, Claiborne Papers, Southern Historical Collection, University of North Carolina at Chapel Hill.

17. *OR*, vol. 45, pt. 1: 330–32; Buck, *Cleburne and His Command*, 266–67.

18. Leonard H. Mangum, "General P. R. Cleburne: A Sketch of His Early Life and His Last Battle," *Kennesaw State Gazette* June 15, 1887. This is another instance in which a miscommunication between Hood and Cheatham cost the Confederates. Hood believed he had ordered Cheatham to block the Columbia Pike; Cheatham always believed that his immediate objective should have been the village of Spring Hill itself. The time of sunset and the different stages of twilight are borrowed from Jacobson and Rupp, *For Cause and for Country*, 113. The authors obtained from the U.S. Naval Observatory the exact times of these events specific to Spring Hill on November 29, 1864.

19. *Southern Historical Society Papers* (1881), 9:540.

20. Ibid., 538.

21. Henry M. Field, *Bright Skies and Dark Shadows* (New York: Charles Scribner's Sons, 1900), 215. Major Vaulx (pronounced *Voss*) related the events of Spring Hill to Dr. Field.

22. Ibid.; *Southern Historical Society Papers* (1881), 9:540–41.

23. *Southern Historical Society Papers* (1881), 9:538; *OR*, vol. 45, pt. 1: 255.

24. Hood, *Advance and Retreat*, 285; Campbell Brown and Isham Harris conversations, Brown-Ewell Papers, Tennessee State Library and Archives, Nashville, Tennessee; *Southern Historical Society Papers* (1881), 9:538; Field, *Bright Skies and Dark Shadows*, 215.

25. Hood insisted in his memoirs that he did tell Cheatham, Cleburne, and Brown that Stewart would be coming up soon, but the account of every other participant contradicts Hood. *Southern Historical Society Papers* (1881), 9:535; Hood, *Advance and Retreat*, 285.

26. There are two persistent rumors about Hood and Cheatham that have been passed down since Spring Hill. The first and most famous is that Hood was taking laudanum for the pain of his wounds, and this clouded his judgment. There is absolutely no proof that Hood was using this drug or any other, and his erratic behavior can be entirely explained by fatigue. In any event, if Cheatham had even so much as suspected Hood of using opiates, he would have shouted it from the rooftops, but he never even mentions the possibility. The other rumor is that Cheatham, known to be a hard drinker, was drunk at Spring Hill, but again there is no evidence to substantiate this claim, and Major Vaulx emphatically denied the idea. John Gregory, Hood's guide, also claimed that Hood and several other general officers were all drunk on the night of November 29, but his account is not corroborated by any others. Hood, *Advance and Retreat*, 286; *Southern Historical Society Papers* (1881), 9:526, 537; Field, *Bright Skies and Dark Shadows*, 216; Smith, *A History of Maury County Tennessee*, 238. For a compelling case against Hood's use of opiates at Spring Hill, see Stephen Davis, "John Bell Hood's Historiographical Journey; or, How did a Confederate General Become a Laudanum Addict?" in *Confederate Generals in the Western Theater: Essays on America's Civil War*, ed. Lawrence L. Hewitt and Arthur W. Bergeron (Knoxville: University of Tennessee Press, 2010), 2:217–36.

27. For Cleburne's experience with night attacks, see John R. Lundberg, "A Minute Now Is Worth an Hour Tomorrow: Cleburne's Night Attack," in *The Chickamauga Campaign*, ed. Steven E. Woodworth (Carbondale: Southern Illinois University Press, 2010), 102–15.

28. *OR*, vol. 45, pt. 1: 342.

29. Robert M. Collins, *Chapters from the Unwritten History of the War between the States* (Dayton, OH: Morningside Press, 1988), 244; John R. Lundberg, *Granbury's Texas Brigade: Diehard Western Confederates* (Baton Rouge: Louisiana State University Press, 2012), 213.

30. *Southern Historical Society Papers* (1881), 9:540.

31. Ibid., 535; *OR*, vol. 45, pt. 1: 720.

32. James Dinkins, *1861–1865, By an Old Johnnie: Personal Recollections and Experiences in the Confederate Army* (Cincinnati: The Robert Clarke Company, 1897), 232.

33. *Southern Historical Society Papers* (1881), 9:541.

34. *OR*, vol. 45, pt. 1: 713.

35. Field, *Bright Skies and Dark Shadows*, 218; Broomfield L. Ridley, *Battles and Sketches of the Army of Tennessee* (Dayton, OH: Morningside Press, 1995), 436; *Southern Historical Society Papers* (1881), 9:526–27. Oddly Major Mason "confessed" to Governor Harris on November 30 that he never delivered these orders to Cheatham, but Cheatham confirmed that Mason did reach him with the orders. The plausible explanation is that Mason was trying to redirect some of Hood's anger away from Cheatham.

36. *OR*, vol. 45, pt. 1: 769–70.

37. Hood passed away in 1879, but his memoirs, financed by P. G. T. Beauregard, appeared posthumously, in 1880. When Cheatham read the book, he became alarmed that Hood had blamed him for the Confederate failure at Spring Hill, and Cheatham immediately set out to refute the claims. Cheatham solicited accounts from most of the other generals present at Spring Hill and all of these accounts were either presented in person or read into the record of the Southern Historical Society meeting at Louisville, Kentucky, on December 1, 1881.

38. Collins, *Chapters from the Unwritten History of the War*, 244.

4

THE DESTRUCTION OF THE ARMY OF TENNESSEE'S OFFICER CORPS AT THE BATTLE OF FRANKLIN

Andrew S. Bledsoe

As the sun rose over Franklin, Tennessee, on the morning of December 1, 1864, the bodies of at least six Confederate officers lay cold and still on the back porch of Carnton, a stately plantation house owned by the McGavock family. Confederates had hastily converted it into a field hospital, and now it overflowed with casualties. Four of the dead had been generals—Major General Patrick R. Cleburne, and Brigadier Generals John Adams, Hiram B. Granbury, and Otho F. Strahl. For many years it was thought that the other two bodies on the porch at Carnton were also generals, but recent scholarship has determined that they were more likely Lieutenant Colonel Robert B. Young of the 10th Texas and Lieutenant John Marsh of Strahl's staff. It is possible that a seventh body, that of Captain James Johnston, was also at Carnton that morning.[1]

Scattered in the fields and hospitals beyond Carnton were thousands more dead and wounded Confederates of all ranks; these were the six thousand casualties of the Army of Tennessee's failed assault on the Federal works around Franklin the previous evening. A strikingly large proportion of the killed and wounded were commissioned officers. Not counting the dead at Carnton, the list of officer casualties included Major General John C. Brown and a staggering array of brigade commanders—Brigadier Generals John C. Carter, Francis M. Cockrell, Zachariah C. Deas, States Rights Gist, George W. Gordon, Arthur M. Manigault, William A. Quarles, Thomas M. Scott, and Jacob H. Sharp. In addition, an appalling number of field- and company-grade officers were killed or wounded in the attack.[2]

Years later, the enduring narrative of the Battle of Franklin is one of senseless slaughter. Sixty-eight field officers were killed, wounded, or captured. In Cleburne's division alone, one brigade and twelve regimental commanders became casualties, and losses in other divisions were almost as severe. By

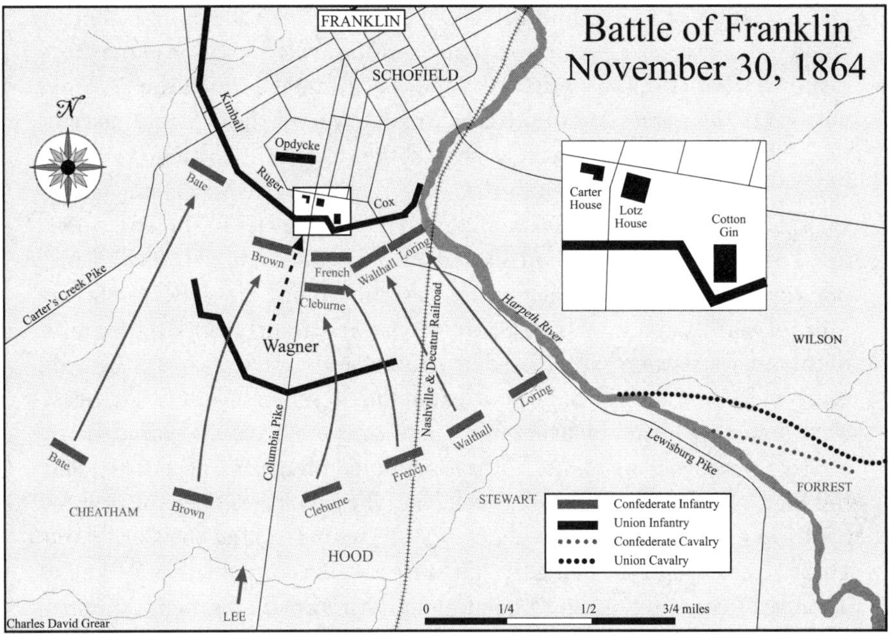

the Battle of Nashville two weeks later, the Army of Tennessee's officer corps was a shell of its former self. Lieutenant General John Bell Hood has taken his share of criticism for this bloodshed, and much of his postwar life was devoted to defending the decision to attack at Franklin. Even before the assault, some of Hood's corps and division commanders harbored doubt about the wisdom of his decision. After the battle, the wastage among the Army of Tennessee's officer corps irreparably harmed the army's morale, disrupted its command structure, and deprived it of talented and experienced commanders in what would prove to be its final campaign. The loss of so many officers in a single assault was unprecedented, even by the bloody standards of the Civil War, and such a loss of leadership proved unsustainable for the Army of Tennessee.

The explanation for this disaster lies, in part, in the timing of the attack. With the first elements of his army arriving on the field at about 1 P.M. on the afternoon of November 30, Hood decided to strike the Federal positions at Franklin immediately. Perhaps stung by his army's failure to destroy the enemy at Spring Hill the previous night, Hood was determined not to let the Federals slip away again. "I hereupon decided, before the enemy would be able to reach his stronghold at Nashville," Hood recalled in his self-serving memoir, "to make that same afternoon another and final effort to overtake and rout him, and drive him in the Big Harpeth River at Franklin, since I could no longer hope to get between him and Nashville, by reason of the short distance from Franklin to that city, and the advantage which the Federals enjoyed in the possession of the direct road."[3] Very little artillery and only two of Hood's three corps were present at the start of the battle; Stephen D. Lee's corps, along with most of the army's artillery, was still strung along the road from Columbia and would not arrive until late in the afternoon. The Federal defensive position around Franklin was extremely formidable, practically guaranteeing that any direct assault would be bloody. Nearly two miles of gently sloping fields lay before the enemy entrenchments; the hazards of this approach were exacerbated by an almost total lack of cover. The Federal line formed a rough half-moon extending from northwest to southeast around the town, and incorporated earthworks previously prepared for an earlier 1863 engagement. The left was anchored on the Harpeth River, and the right extended past Carter's Creek Pike. The center straddled the Columbia Pike, with the apex of the semicircle stretching around the Carter and Lotz Houses. Deployed along the line were the divisions of James W. Reilly, Thomas Ruger, and Nathan Kimball, along with six batteries; two additional batteries were placed in Fort Granger, an old artillery position north of the line. Jacob D. Cox, temporarily in command of the Twenty-Third Corps, made his headquarters in the Carter House, while John Schofield, the overall Federal commander on the field, would spend most of the battle directing the action from Fort Granger. As Stephen D. Lee would later report, the enemy's position "was for infantry defence one of the best I had ever seen."[4]

Moreover, the circumstances of Hood's 4 P.M. assault conspired to make such an attack especially deadly for officers. Sunset on November 30, 1864, occurred at 4:34 P.M., and civil twilight ended at 5:02 P.M., after which darkness enveloped the battlefield.[5] (Civil twilight is the limit at which light is sufficient for objects on the ground to be clearly distinguished. Once visibility surpasses the threshold for civil twilight, it becomes increasingly difficult to make out distant landmarks, people, or objects.) From sunset to the end of civil twilight, Hood's officers would have an increasingly difficult task coordinating their troops. In combat, an officer's command radius was limited to the range of his voice or line of sight. This demanded not only a great deal of personal courage, but also required that officers calmly and deliberately expose themselves to close-range fire and remain highly visible to both their soldiers and to the enemy. To preserve their ability to maintain command and control in these circumstances, many of Hood's officers went into the battle at Franklin on horseback rather than on foot, and thus made themselves obvious targets for Federal sharpshooters. Reckless as this may seem, the decision to remain mounted was the result of logical, and terrible, deliberation. The overriding imperative of Civil War leadership was that soldiers expected officers to inspire by fearless example rather than compel obedience through force, intimidation, or coercion. Likewise, the Army of Tennessee's officers had long realized that failure to present a conspicuous battlefield presence would complicate their command efforts, erode their soldiers' morale, and could ultimately hasten the assault's failure. Simply put, the men of the Army of Tennessee required that their commanders lead from the front.[6] These factors all resulted in an exceptionally challenging battlefield environment for the Army of Tennessee's combat leaders.

As Hood's arriving columns were sorting themselves out south of Franklin, Cleburne and his staff paused on Privet Knob to get a closer look at the enemy position. Having left his field glasses behind, the Irish general surveyed the Federal lines through the telescopic sight of a Whitworth rifle borrowed from a sharpshooter. The earthworks around Franklin consisted of a wall of dirt, logs, and fence rails about four feet high, backed by a trench and studded with firing positions; defenders also dug a three- to four-foot-deep trench immediately in front of the wall, and in some places had embedded abatis of sharpened wooden stakes to ward against attackers. Along the Federal left, a thick hedge of Osage orange bushes presented an almost impenetrable barrier; on the center-right, a locust grove formed another forbidding natural obstacle.[7] Sharpshooter Isaac N. Shannon was nearby when he heard Cleburne say, "They have three lines of works. . . . And they are all completed." Cleburne then remounted and "with a kindling eye and rapid movement" cantered back to Hood's headquarters at the nearby Harrison House.[8]

Between 3 and 3:30 P.M., Hood summoned the rest of his senior officers for a final council in the parlor of the Harrison House. Hood, Benjamin F. Cheatham, Cleburne, and Forrest were all present at this conference; A. P. Stewart had yet to arrive and Stephen D. Lee was still shepherding his corps toward Franklin from Columbia. After consultation, Hood's generals were all strongly against a frontal assault on the Federal works. Forrest favored crossing the Harpeth River with a mixed force of infantry and cavalry and flanking the enemy out of his entrenchments. Hood rebuffed this suggestion as impractical, deciding it would take too much time to accomplish before nightfall. This decision infuriated the hot-tempered Forrest, who may have parted from Hood with angry words.[9] Cleburne and Cheatham expressed their own concerns about the strength of the Federal position, the timing of the attack, and the lengthy exposed distance they would have to cross without adequate artillery support. Hood brushed aside their objections as well, reiterating his intention to storm the works and drive the enemy into the

Harpeth River as quickly as possible. Though the army was still assembling, sunset was swiftly approaching, and most of his artillery was not yet up, Hood had resolved that a swift and decisive blow would dislodge Schofield before he could fully entrench or escape to Nashville's defenses. There would be no flanking maneuvers, no artillery bombardment, and no delays.[10]

As the Harrison House conference concluded, Hood told Cleburne to instruct his brigades "not to fire until you run the Yankee skirmish line from behind the first line of works in your front, then [to] press them in their backs as they run to their main line; then charge the enemy's works."[11] The generals rode out to prepare their men, and in the afternoon's fading light the Army of Tennessee's commanders said their goodbyes. John M. Copley of the 49th Tennessee recalled the scene of these final exchanges. "As soon as the lines of battle were formed, a number of our field officers rode out a little in front of the lines," Copley remembered. "They were Walthall, Loring, Cheatham, Quarles, Cleburne, Granberry [*sic*], and perhaps others; these officers appeared to hold a brief consultation. . . . These officers separated, each taking his respective place with his command. A profound silence pervaded the entire army; it was simply awful, reminding one of those sickening lulls which preceded a tremendous thunderstorm."[12] From his vantage point atop Breezy Hill, Brigadier General Daniel C. Govan recalled, "General Cleburne seemed to be more despondent than I ever saw him. I was the last one to receive any instructions from him, and as I saluted and bade him good-bye I remarked, 'Well, General, there will not be many of us that will get back to Arkansas,' and he replied, 'Well, Govan, if we are to die, let us die like men.'"[13]

The Army of Tennessee had good reason to be apprehensive. Its veterans had seen similar assaults fail repeatedly in the recent past. The army's prior commander Braxton Bragg had repeatedly ground down his army in assaults at Perryville, Stones River, and Chickamauga, and Hood had continued this practice around Atlanta and at Jonesboro. The Army of Tennessee had also been on the receiving end of such assaults; most notably, William T. Sherman's disastrous attacks at Kennesaw Mountain earlier in the year. The odds were not with the attackers in such cases, and the Confederates knew it. Nevertheless, with the die cast, they were determined to succeed or die trying. Division commanders carefully instructed their men to deploy in columns of brigades. As soon as the lead elements came under fire from the first line of fortifications, brigades were to fix bayonets, charge, and carry the forward line of Federal works. This was to be accomplished, Cleburne told his men, "at all hazards."[14] Thereafter, the columns would deploy into lines of battle and break the main Federal line with a combination of speed and firepower.

It was not a particularly imaginative approach, but with daylight fading fast and few other options available, it was perhaps the only choice left.

At approximately 4 P.M., the signal to begin the assault was given. Eighteen brigades, nearly twenty thousand men, stepped out across the two-mile field with banners snapping and bayonets gleaming in the fading golden light of the autumn afternoon.[15] Field officers, most of them mounted, rode at the heads of their columns; regimental and company officers, along with noncommissioned officers, barked orders to maintain alignment and keep up the pace. Startled by the advance, rabbits and quail scurried ahead of the attackers. The Confederate right began to compress itself toward the center due to a combination of terrain and the curve of the Harpeth River, throwing off the alignment of the assaulting formations. Nevertheless, the Confederate columns of brigades managed to shake themselves out into lines of battle just before contact with Brigadier General George D. Wagner's line.[16] The 103rd Ohio's captain Levi T. Scofield crouched anxiously in the earthworks and watched the solid mass of attacking Confederates; they came on in heavy columns under fluttering banners, "with conspicuous mounted groups of general and staff officers in their midst" and driving the Federal pickets before them.[17] Shortly after 4:30 P.M., Granbury's Texans were among the first to make contact with the main enemy line just to the east of Columbia Pike. Lieutenant L. H. Mangum of Cleburne's staff was beside Granbury when "a ball struck him in the cheek and passed through his brain. Throwing his hands to his face he sank down on his knees and remained in that position until his body was taken off the field after the battle."[18] Granbury was the first Confederate general to die at Franklin, but he would not be the last.

At around the same moment that Granbury fell, Cockrell's crack Missouri brigade struck the Federal positions near the cotton gin and came under a withering crossfire of musketry and canister. The Missourians were ground to bits. Great holes were blown in their ranks while, as one Federal witness observed, "[Confederate] officers on horseback and afoot were at every gap, trying to close them up" as they fell.[19] Cockrell's men hugged the enemy works while Federal artillery blasted them at point-blank range. Cockrell was hit in the arm, the leg, and the ankle, and two horses were killed beneath him, but he managed to crawl to safety as the Missouri brigade began to disintegrate. After Cockrell fell, Colonel Elijah Gates assumed command; Gates, too, was gravely wounded with two broken arms and had to be led from the field.[20] The tenacious Missourians held fast, but deadly fire soon shredded their ranks. Years later, J. K. Merrifield of the 88th Illinois remembered the death of one of the Missouri officers. "As [Cockrell's brigade] were coming up, I noticed a flag and a large, fine-looking man, an officer, by its side. They melted away as the other line did." Seeking to capture the 1st Missouri's flag, recalled Merrifield, "I jumped over the works and ran about one hundred feet ahead and got the flag, and this fine-looking officer was wounded, and lay there with the dead and wounded in heaps upon him. He asked me to pull a dead man off his leg, as he was shot in the knee." The officer that so impressed Merrifield was Colonel Hugh Garland, commander of the 1st Missouri. Merrifield gave Garland a drink from his canteen, removed the colonel's sword, relieved him of the flag, and then dashed back to the Federal works just before the firing resumed. According to Captain John M. Hickey of the 6th Missouri, Garland "was killed by a second shot while prostrated on the ground," and expired while "weltering in their own blood" before the enemy parapet.[21] The next morning, survivors discovered the colonel's body surrounded by dead comrades.[22] Some 60 percent of the Missouri brigade fell at Franklin, along with most of its officers. According to Major General Samuel G. French, by the end of the battle Cockrell's brigade had "nearly all disappeared" from existence.[23]

Elsewhere the Confederate attack fared little better. A few minutes after the Missourians went in, Gist's brigade launched an assault on the Federal line west of the Carter House. Colonel Ellison Capers, commanding the 24th South Carolina, reported that "Gen. Gist ordered the charge in concert with Gen. Gordon. In passing from left to the right of the regiment, the general waved his hat to us . . . and rode away in the smoke of battle."[24] Gist's body servant, "Uncle Wiley" Howard, last saw the general on foot near a maple tree, leading his men in the attack. Gist's horse Joe had been shot through the neck, and the wound maddened the animal into uncontrollable rearing.[25] "Some of the [Confederate] officers waved their swords and sprang forward," reported a nearby Federal officer. "The fire then slackened as they started in close pursuit to go to the breastworks with us. . . . The cry of some of our wounded who went down in that wild race, knowing they would have to lie there exposed to all the fire of our line, had a pathetic note of despair in it that I had never heard before."[26] The locust grove in front of the enemy works impeded Gist's attack, and "[t]he smoke was so dense that one could not distinguish an object twenty feet distant."[27] Moments later, a bullet pierced his chest near the heart. Gist was eventually removed to a field hospital where Uncle Wiley Howard later discovered him. The general died later that night.[28]

At approximately 4:45 P.M., Cleburne rode up along the Columbia Pike, straight into the hottest part of the attack. "I noticed General Cleburne on a little gray horse that belonged to one of his couriers," remembered Lieutenant W. D. Mintz of the 5th Arkansas. "Cleburne's horse [had been] shot from under him. . . . [W]ith hat in hand and waving it above his head, [Cleburne] scaled the works. . . . I could not hear what he was saying, but knew he meant to go forward. Again we raised the Rebel Yell and renewed the charge to storm the enemy's last line."[29] Cleburne's headlong charge came at an opportune time, as confusion was spreading through the brigades of Granbury and Brigadier General George W. Gordon. "Gen. Cleburne came charging from our left, through his men and mine, diagonally toward the enemy's works," recalled Gordon. "His horse, running with great speed, would have plunged over and trampled [me] if [I] . . . had not checked [my] pace as [I] ran on foot."[30] "General Cleburne's object seemed to be to run into the rear line with the fleeing Federals from Wagner's division," remembered Govan. "About that time General Cleburne's horse was killed. . . . I was very near him. . . . The impetus at which he was moving carried the horse forward after his death wound, and he fell almost in the ditch on the outside of the entrenchments. One of the couriers dismounted and gave him his horse, and while in the act of mounting, this second horse was killed by a cannon ball fired . . . from the gin-house." With no other mount readily available, Cleburne went forward on foot until Govan lost sight of him in the smoke and haze. He believed Cleburne "must have met his death in a few seconds afterwards. All of this occurred near the intersection of the pike, and his body was found within 20 yards of where I saw him last waving his cap and urging his command forward."[31]

As Cleburne disappeared into the smoky shadows, Brigadier General John C. Carter was struggling to keep his own brigade from bogging down in front of the Federal works west of the Columbia Pike. Carter's Tennesseans forced their way through the locust grove and charged toward the enemy works in support of the now-dead Granbury's beleaguered Texans. It was a fool's errand. Carter's men, like Granbury's, were "mowed down like grain before the sickle" under the fire of Federal muskets and a battery of three-inch rifled artillery.[32] Carter, like many of the Army of Tennessee's brigade commanders, directed his unit from horseback. In a nearly unbelievable demonstration of bravery, Carter spurred his mount forward, placed himself directly between the Federal line and his own brigade, and urged his men on. About 150 yards from the enemy position, Carter was shot through the abdomen and fell from the saddle. His shattered brigade made it to the edge of the Federal parapet before losing momentum. Desperately wounded, Carter was carried by his staff from the field to the Harrison House, where he would linger until dying on December 10. Just to the west, William B. Bate's division was also floundering against the Federal position in a disjointed assault. Captain John William McCord of the 30th Georgia was appalled by the slaughter he saw there. "Hall & Jonathan Gillespie were both killed dead on the field," McCord wrote to his brother days after the battle. "[A]nd nearly every one of the company faced the [same] fate." He seethed that "the larger part of Genl Bates Div. acted very cowardly in the first of the fight." According to McCord, who was wounded in the attack, "Tylers & Finleys and Jacksons left would not charge the works. I was skirmishing in front of Tyler and Finley and they ran three times and left me on the hill begging them to come back." McCord added, "I am proud to say that there was no one between me and the Yankees when I was wounded."[33]

By 5 P.M., as twilight fell, the Confederate attack began to falter all along the army's front. On the right, east of the Carter family's cotton gin, Loring's division battered itself vainly against the thick natural abatis in front of the Federal works, and Brigadier General John Adams watched with mounting frustration at the lethal delays caused by the Osage orange hedges. "Maj. Garrett, who was commanding the Twenty-third Mississippi," remembered Private J. L. Boswell, "had halted his men at a rock fence about two hundred yards from the enemy's works. There were two Osage orange hedges in front of us through which Gen. Adams could not ride, making it necessary for him to ride around the ends."[34] Some enterprising officers attempted to hack their way through the barrier with their swords. Joseph Nicholas Thompson of the 35th Alabama saw a company officer die while slashing his way through the Osage orange abatis. "Poor Capt. Stewart, the last I saw of him was trying to cut a path through the hedge with his sword," Thompson remembered. "He fell with four bullets in him. I soon saw that nearly all of our company was killed or wounded and when Dick Bernard [got] by me I told him that we had better fall back on the reserve and reform."[35] Adams rode up and, according to Boswell, "passed directly in front of us, and as he did so he called out the order, 'Move forward, Maj. Garrett,' and it was not more than three minutes after this that he was shot."[36] The mounted officer presented a tantalizing target for the troops of John S. Casement's brigade defending the Federal line, and Colonel Tillman H. Stevens of the 65th Indiana was amazed at Adams's display of sheer nerve. "He rode along his line and became conspicuous while he was quite a little distance out. We could plainly see that he was very intent on doing something, and he was the one of all others that we were to do business with." Stevens could not take his eyes off the daring Confederate brigadier. "As he came closer and closer he seemed to be more and more intent. He was riding forward through such a rain of bullets that no one had any reason to believe he would escape them all, but he seemed to be in the hands of the Unseen."[37]

Desperate, Adams spurred his horse, Old Charley, toward what he thought was a thin section of the abatis and called on his men to follow him. Stunned by Adams's reckless courage, one Federal officer apparently called on his men to hold their fire. Adams had no intention of turning back, however, and urged Old Charley across the barrier and toward the 65th Illinois' colors. "Gen. Adams rode his horse over the ditch to the top of the parapet," remembered a dumbfounded Illinoisan, "[and] undertook to grasp the 'old flag' from the hands of our color sergeant, when he fell, horse and all, shot by the color guard."[38] Riddled by enemy fire, Adams's horse fell dead across the embankment and the general crumpled from the saddle. "As soon as the charge was repulsed our men sprang upon the works and lifted the horse," recalled Lieutenant Colonel Edward Adams Baker of the 65th Illinois, "while others dragged the General from under him. He was perfectly conscious, and knew his fate. He asked for water, as all dying men do in battle as the lifeblood drips from the body." Baker and the Illinoisans did what they could to ease the dying man's suffering. "One of my men gave him a canteen of water, while another brought an armload of cotton from an old gin near by and made him a pillow. The General gallantly thanked them, and, in answer to our expressions of sorrow at his sad fate, he said, 'It is the fate of a soldier to die for his country,' and expired."[39] After Adams's dramatic death at around 5:30 P.M., a well-timed Federal counterattack by Colonel Emerson Opdycke's brigade stabilized the defensive line near the cotton gin. A confused and deadly situation in Hood's army turned to chaos as officer after officer fell. "Most of our commanding officers had been killed or wounded," remembered Private William J. Rochelle of the 24th South Carolina, "and we did not know who was in command."[40] The fighting in and around the Federal works was often hand-to-hand as officers led their battered commands in repeated attacks. After so much slaughter, Confederate officers eventually had great difficulty convincing some of their demoralized troops to comply. "In vain did the officers urge their men to cross the breastworks," recalled the 5th Tennessee's Lieutenant Edwin H. Rennolds, "[but] they were too nearly exhausted and the fire was too deadly."[41]

These twilight assaults were exceptionally destructive to the Confederate regimental and company officers who led them. "A rebel colonel mounted our breastworks," Captain James A. Sexton of the 72nd Illinois remembered, "and . . . profanely . . . demanded our immediate surrender. . . . Private [John] Arbridge, of Company D, thrust his musket against the abdomen of the rash colonel, and with the exclamation, 'I guess not' instantly discharged his weapon." What happened next horrified Sexton. "The effect of the shot was horrible and actually let daylight through the victim. The doomed warrior doubled up, his head gradually sinking forward and downward until he finally plunged head foremost into the pit below, at the very feet of his slayer."[42]

Confederates who were able to breach the works faced almost certain death or capture. "Lieut. Frank H. Hale, of Co. H," remembered the 19th Tennessee's W. J. Worsham, "succeeded in scaling the works and crawled about twenty feet inside the Federal lines to the frame house . . . that stood in the yard of the Carter house, where he was killed, filled with bullets from the guns of his own regiment." Another Confederate officer, Lieutenant W. W. Etter, somehow managed to climb over the works and jump down among the enemy. According to Worsham, the Yankees "took off their hats to him, but did not take him prisoner, when he, too, reached the brick smoke house, and [he] remained unhurt until the Federals retreated, and he rejoined the regiment."[43] In the growing gloom, the Confederate attacks took on more than a hint of suicidal desperation. Shortly after 5:30 P.M., Captain Theodrick "Tod" Carter fell only yards from his boyhood home; he and his horse were pierced with multiple bullets as they charged the Federal line. The young officer lay unconscious through most of the night. Eventually Carter's father and sisters found him and carried him back to their house, where he died of his wounds.[44]

The killing only intensified as daylight failed. "Night was on now," remembered Sergeant Major S. A. Cunningham of Strahl's brigade, "so that every soldier's gun by the flash of powder made him a target" as the Confederates crouched among their own dead.[45] By around 6 P.M., Strahl's troops found themselves mired in a deteriorating firefight west of the Columbia Pike, not far from Tod Carter. Strahl, who had gone into the battle on foot, marched near the sergeant major. "Over that open area of nearly two miles he rarely spoke," recalled Cunningham, "and then directly upon the alignment of his command. A sadder face I have never seen."[46] With their comrades' bodies piling up around them, Cunningham asked Strahl what he proposed to do next. The general's reply was simple: "Keep firing."[47] The fight dragged on while Strahl and several other officers loaded muskets and passed them down the firing line.[48] Eventually a ball struck the general in the neck, though he remained conscious long enough to surrender command of his brigade to Lieutenant Colonel Fountain E. P. Stafford of the 33rd Tennessee. Staff officers tried to carry Strahl to the rear, but a second and third shot killed him before they could get him to safety. Stafford would not survive the fight at the Columbia Pike, either. His men found his body the next morning in a pile of corpses; Stafford's feet were "wedged in at the bottom, with other dead across and under him after he fell leaving his body half standing" in a gruesome imitation of life.[49]

By 7:15 P.M., a last-gasp effort failed to break the enemy line. Darkness settled and confusion reigned in the depleted Confederate ranks. Some units had lost nearly all of their senior officers in the carnage, and leaderless regiments wandered blindly in the night. "As we were moving into position the orders were changed so frequently that no one but Genl. M.[anigault] knew where to go, and he was wounded," wrote Confederate staff officer Colonel C. Irvine Walker. "Col. Shaw, next in command was wounded, Col. Davis, next was wounded, and the only staff officer who knew the instructions, Capt. Dean was wounded. Meanwhile we were advancing under a tremendous fire (all this was at night) and had gone 3 or 400 yds, through a level open field, when I found I could get no orders, nor did I know what to do[.]" With his brigade almost completely degraded, Walker decided to march his men to safety on his own initiative. "[S]o on consultation with the two Regimental Comdrs. nearest me, we withdrew to the nearest cover to await some orders. This I did as I did not see the necessity of having my brave men slaughtered for no purpose." Walker was not the only officer to see the futility of further assaults in the darkness. "On retiring I found that the remainder of the Brigade had done the same." By morning, Walker was astonished at how near they had come to the Federal position. "So we lost the credit of taking the works in our front, which we could easily have done, for we only had 75 yards to reach the enemy's line (as we discovered next day) and that distance was nothing, after having gone 300 or 400 yds. under the same fire. . . ." Walker believed the army had performed well under awful circumstances, "for we had a great deal of manoeuvring to do under fire, previous to becoming actually engaged. I never was so completely lost in my life. I could not tell where the enemy were, where any of our other troops were, whether any were in my front or not, and whether I would strike the enemy in his front or flank with my front or flank." Concerned about his brigade's reputation, Walker was emphatic about the correctness of his decision to discontinue the assault. "Everyone thinks we were right in withdrawing," he concluded, "though we all regret the unfortunate congregation of misfortune which induced it."[50]

The combination of damage and darkness precluded any further Confederate attempts to assault the works during the night, and the exhausted armies simply halted in place. Under cover of night, the Federals quietly withdrew from Franklin, leaving the wrecked Army of Tennessee in possession of the town. By dawn, it had become clear that this was no victory. "Of all the battles I have witnessed," mused the 20th Tennessee's James Litton Cooper, "this was the most bloody. Our army fought with a desperation I have never seen equaled. The ground about the Yankees was literally piled with dead. Some of them were [shot] to pieces. One man I saw had forty seven bullet holes through him."[51] Word spread quickly among the men, confirming what they already knew—the army's leadership had been utterly decimated. In at least half of the regiments and battalions in the Army of Tennessee, units that should have been commanded by colonels and majors were instead led by captains, lieutenants, or even sergeants. Sixty-eight field officers fell; fifty-five regiments lost their commanders, and twelve of these were in Cleburne's division alone. The toll among brigade commanders was also fearful. Johnson's division lost three of four, Loring's division lost two of three, and Brown's division lost all four. In short, the Battle of Franklin made a shambles of the Army of Tennessee's command structure, eliminating many of its finest combat leaders at a time when they were most urgently needed and leaving pitifully weakened for the remainder of the Tennessee Campaign.[52] If any lesson can be drawn from the loss of so many essential commanders in such a brief moment in the life of the Army of Tennessee, it is that the destructiveness of the Civil War was no respecter of persons, virtue, or raw physical courage. Hood squandered whatever thin chance the Confederacy had to salvage the war in the West by destroying the cream of his officer corps at Franklin. With their deaths went the last possibility that the South could snatch victory from the jaws of defeat and resuscitate its fading hopes for independence.

Notes

1. Eric A. Jacobson and Richard A. Rupp, *For Cause and for Country: A Study of the Affair at Spring Hill and the Battle of Franklin* (Franklin, TN: O'More Publishing, 2007), 411–12.

2. U.S. War Department, *The War of the Rebellion: A Compilation of the Official Records of the Union and Confederate Armies*, 128 vols. (Washington, DC: Government Printing Office, 1881–1901), ser. 1, vol. 45, pt. 1: 684–86 (hereafter referred to as *OR*; all references are to ser. 1, vol. 45, pt. 1 unless otherwise noted).

3. John Bell Hood, *Advance and Retreat: Personal Experiences in the United States and Confederate States Armies* (New Orleans: Beauregard, 1880), 291. Though Hood was certainly irritated by the Spring Hill affair, it is extremely unlikely that he ordered the attack at Franklin simply to punish the army for its failure. Jacobson and Rupp, *For Cause and for Country*, 237–40.

4. Jacob D. Cox, *The Battle of Franklin, Tennessee, November 30, 1864: A Monograph* (New York: C. Scribner's Sons, 1897), 280–81; John M. Schofield, *Forty-Six Years in the Army* (New York: The Century Co., 1897), 177; *OR*, ser. 1, vol. 47, pt. 1: 688.

5. Sunset and civil twilight data for Franklin, Williamson County, Tennessee (35.917044, -86.873483), November 30, 1864, U.S. Naval Observatory Astronomical Applications Department, http://aa.usno.navy.mil/data/docs/RS_OneDay.php (accessed November 30, 2014).

6. Richard Holmes, *Acts of War: The Behavior of Men in Battle* (New York: The Free Press, 1985), 341–42; Gerald F. Linderman, *Embattled Courage: The Experience of Combat in the American Civil War* (New York: The Free Press, 1987), 156–58.

7. James R. Knight, *The Battle of Franklin: When the Devil Had Full Possession of the Earth* (Charleston, SC: The History Press, 2009), 60–61; *OR*, 708.

8. Isaac N. Shannon, "Sharpshooters with Hood's Army," *Confederate Veteran* 15 (March 1907): 125–26 (hereafter referred to as *CV*).

9. Thomas Jordan and J. P. Pryor, *The Campaigns of Lieut.-Gen. N. B. Forrest, and of Forrest's Cavalry* (New Orleans: Blelock and Company, 1868), 626.

10. Contrast Wiley Sword, *Embrace an Angry Wind: The Confederacy's Last Hurrah, Spring Hill, Franklin, and Nashville* (Lawrence: University Press of Kansas, 1993), 179, with Jacobson and Rupp, *For Cause and for Country*, 237–40.

11. Statement of Judge L. H. Mangum of Arkansas regarding the death and burial of General Patrick R. Cleburne, John R. Peacock Papers, Southern Historical Collection, The Wilson Library, University of North Carolina at Chapel Hill (hereafter referred to SHC).

12. John M. Copley, *A Sketch of the Battle of Franklin, Tenn.; with Reminiscences of Camp Douglas* (Austin, TX: Eugene von Boeckmann, 1893), 48.

13. Irving A. Buck, *Cleburne and His Command* (Jackson, TN: McCowat-Mercer Press, 1908; repr. 1958), 291.

14. Ibid.

15. Cox, *Battle of Franklin*, 92.

16. Jacobson and Rupp, *For Cause and for Country*, 248.

17. Levi T. Scofield, *The Retreat from Pulaski to Nashville, Tenn., Battle of Franklin, Nov. 30th, 1864* (Cleveland: Press of the Caxton Co., 1909), 35–36.

18. L. H. Mangum, *A Memorial and Biographical History of Johnson and Hill Counties, Texas* (Chicago: The Lewis Publishing Company, 1892), 139–42.

19. Scofield, *Retreat from Pulaski*, 35.

20. Jacobson and Rupp, *For Cause and for Country*, 290.

21. John M. Hickey, "Battle of Franklin," *CV* 17 (January 1909): 14.

22. J. K. Merrifield, "Opdycke's Brigade at Franklin," *CV* 13 (December 1905): 563.

23. *OR*, 716.

24. *OR*, 734–35.

25. Statement of "Uncle Wiley" Howard, body-servant of Brigadier General States Rights Gist, Peacock Papers, SHC.

26. John K. Shellenberger, *The Battle of Franklin, A Paper Read Before Minnesota Commandery of the Loyal Legion U.S. December 9th, 1902* (Minneapolis, MN: n.p., 1897–1902), 1–29, 9.

27. David R. Logsdon, ed., *Eyewitnesses at the Battle of Franklin* (Nashville, TN: Kettle Mills Press, 2005), 26.

28. "Uncle Wiley" Howard statement, Peacock Papers, SHC, 3.

29. Logsdon, ed., *Eyewitnesses at the Battle of Franklin*, 23.

30. George W. Gordon, "Address of Gen. Gordon," *CV* 8 (January 1900): 7–9.

31. Buck, *Cleburne and His Command*, 289–91.

32. Spencer Talley Memoir, Tennessee State Library and Archives, Nashville, Tennessee (hereafter referred to as TSLA).

33. John William McCord to Dear Brother, December 5, 1864, John William McCord Letters, TSLA.

34. J. L. Boswell, "The Battle of Franklin," *CV* 12 (September 1904): 454.

35. Statement of Joseph Nicholas Thompson, *Williamson County Historical Journal* 15 (Spring 1984), 57–59.

36. Boswell, "Battle of Franklin," 454.

37. Tillman H. Stevens, "The Battle of Franklin," *CV* 11 (April 1903): 166–67.

38. James Barr, "Gens. Cleburne and Adams at Franklin," *CV* 10 (April 1902): 155.

39. Edward Adams Baker, "Gen. John Adams at Franklin," *CV* 5 (June 1897): 300–301.

40. Mamie Yeary, *Reminiscences of the Boys in Gray, 1861–1865* (Dallas, TX: Smith and Lamar, 1912), 650.

41. Edwin H. Rennolds, *A History of the Henry County Commands Which Served in the Confederate States Army* (Jacksonville, FL: Sun Publishing Company, 1904), 106.

42. James A. Sexton, "The Observations and Experiences of a Captain of Infantry at the Battle of Franklin, November 30, 1864," *A Paper Read Before the Illinois Commandery of the Military Order of the Loyal Legion of the United States, Read November 8, 1904* (Chicago: n.p., 1907), 4:466–84, 483.

43. W. J. Worsham, *The Old Nineteenth Tennessee Regiment, C.S.A.* (Knoxville, TN: Press of Paragon Printing Co., 1902), 145.

44. Rosalie Carter, *Captain Tod Carter of the Confederate States Army: A Biographical Word Portrait* (Franklin, TN: R. Carter, 1978), 43–45.

45. S. A. Cunningham, "Personal Experiences in the Battle," *CV* 18 (January 1910): 19–20.

46. S. A. Cunningham, "Death of Gen. Strahl," *CV* 1 (January 1893): 31.

47. Cunningham, "Personal Experiences in the Battle," 19–20.

48. Rennolds, *Henry County Commands*, 106.

49. Cunningham, "Death of Gen. Strahl," 31.

50. C. Irvine Walker to Orie Walker, December 6, 1864, in *Great Things Are Expected of Us: The Letters of Colonel C. Irvine Walker, 10th South Carolina Infantry, C.S.A.*, ed. William Lee White and Charles Denny Runion (Knoxville: University of Tennessee Press, 2009), 147.

51. James Litton Cooper Memoir, TSLA, 47.

52. *OR*, 684–86; Jacobson and Rupp, *For Cause and for Country*, 419–20. Researcher Tim Burgess estimates that at least 288 Confederate officers died at Franklin. Tim Burgess, correspondence with the author, April 1, 2011.

5

KILLING AT FRANKLIN

ANATOMY OF SLAUGHTER

Jonathan M. Steplyk

The Battle of Franklin holds a grim notoriety within Civil War lore. Some remember it as the "Pickett's Charge of the West," and indeed it is tempting to compare the bloody Rebel assault across the fields of central Tennessee on November 30, 1864, to Robert E. Lee's doomed third-day attack at Gettysburg. That dubious distinction, however, actually masks the ways the 1864 battle surpassed the Gettysburg climax in size and scope. Pickett's Charge consisted of about twelve thousand men attacking across three-quarters of a mile, compared to twenty thousand veterans of the Army of Tennessee crossing two miles of ground. The assault by the divisions of George Pickett, J. Johnson Pettigrew, and Isaac Trimble was preceded by a massive artillery bombardment, while the Army of Tennessee attacked with minimal artillery support. Moreover, Confederate forces in Pickett's Charge—attacking Union troops protected by only minimal field works—secured only a limited lodgment in the enemy position before their repulse, whereas the Army of Tennessee, through audacity and serendipity, created a dangerous breach in the heavily fortified Union line at Franklin, one which was fiercely contested for several hours and into the night before it was ultimately closed. In short, the Confederate charge at the Battle of Franklin was "larger, longer, and deadlier" than the final attack at Gettysburg.[1]

Blame for the Confederate bloodletting at Franklin has rested chiefly on the commanding general who on that November day threw his men at the Yankee defenders, John Bell Hood. "They charge me with having made Franklin a slaughter-pen," Hood bristled in an 1879 reunion for veterans of the Army of Tennessee, "but, as I understand it, WAR means FIGHT, and FIGHT means KILL." Regardless of Hood's culpability, his statement contained two truths: the Battle of Franklin was a case of great slaughter, and the soldiers blue and gray that fought there were faced with the task of killing in war. The chapter does not offer a simple retelling of the battle, nor does it seek to evaluate the senior generalship of the opposing sides. Instead, it offers answers to compelling questions regarding the deeply personal side of the face of battle in the Civil War. It examines the emotional and psychological factors relating to the prospect and reality of killing on the battlefield. What were the soldiers' experiences of killing at Franklin like? What details did they leave us about the nature of combat, and what do they tell us about the soldiers themselves?

The question of what it meant to a soldier to kill in combat is particularly compelling in regards to the American Civil War, which as a civil war was by its very nature fratricidal. The conflict was fueled by intense political and sectional animosities, even as it pitted against one another countrymen who shared much in terms of history and culture. The Civil War was truly a brothers' war, waged between brothers in spirit and sometimes even dividing brothers in blood. Scholars of Civil War soldiers and combat have addressed killing in some detail but not necessarily systematically. James McPherson, who to his credit considers the subject in his influential *For Cause and Comrades*, has noted elsewhere that "the ways in which ordinary northerners and southerners, inside and outside the army, managed to rationalize the killing is a subject in search of a historian." The essay represents a foray into examining the nature of killing in the Civil War.[2]

The subject of killing in combat has garnered increasing interest in military history, particularly thanks to Dave Grossman's *On Killing: The Psychological Cost of Learning to Kill in War and Society*. In what he terms a study of "killology," Grossman argues that the task of having to kill, just like the fear of being killed, acts as a potential stressor on men in battle. To kill in combat requires the soldier to overcome natural and cultural inhibitions against taking the life of one's fellow man, especially for the citizen-soldier only recently removed from the norms of civilian life. Grossman offers a sophisticated matrix of factors which alternately facilitate or inhabit killing in battle and also affect how much or how little strain it places on the soldiers' psyche.[3]

Although space does not permit exhaustively considering the factors acting on Civil War soldiers in general, we can identify some factors that would have prepared those who fought at Franklin for the ordeal of battle. Most of the combatants were veterans of at least two years' service who had already "seen the elephant." Also, the nature of Civil War combat would have partially shielded them from knowing and seeing that they personally were killing in battle, one of the key factors Grossman presents as mitigating the strain of combat. In a modern nineteenth-century army, the type of fighting most of these soldiers participated in would have been firefights, conducted at progressively longer ranges as the war progressed, and using black-powder weapons that produced clouds of acrid white smoke, which often left soldiers firing blindly at one another through a literal fog of war. For these veterans, Franklin would be one of their most harrowing experiences with battle at close quarters.

One fascinating generalization that can be made about Civil War soldiers comes from numerous observations of how Rebs and Yanks remarkably could go from trying to kill each other in battle to conducting formal and informal truces amongst themselves, then returning to fighting once again. This was particularly true of the protracted campaigning and siege warfare around Atlanta. Orson Young of the 96th Illinois wrote his parents that summer of how the opposing sides traded shots with one another "for amusement" at 200 yards' distance from their respective rifle pits. "When we would be tired of shooting at one another," he explained, "we would stop and talk to each other a while to vary the amusement." It was as if Civil War soldiers had a veritable on/off switch when it came to alternately fighting or fraternizing with one another.[4]

War came to Franklin as Union forces under John M. Schofield retreated through Tennessee on their way to link up with George Thomas's command in Nashville, pursued by Hood's Army of Tennessee. Remembered by one Confederate veteran as "a beautiful little county town," Franklin nestled within a bend in the Harpeth River. Because it would take time for the engineers to improve the local bridges and ford to allow his artillery and wagons to cross, Schofield elected to make a stand with his back to the Harpeth. He sent most of the Fourth Corps under David S. Stanley across to the north bank and arrayed Jacob D. Cox's Twenty-Third Corps for battle south and west of town. His battle line took the shape of a rough semicircle, somewhat mirroring the bend in the river, with both flanks anchored on the Harpeth.

Tired by long marches and sleepless nights, Union soldiers nevertheless set about with a will fortifying their position, particularly the veterans who fully appreciated the life-saving value of earthworks. Among those who had dug their way through Atlanta's siege, an Ohio lieutenant boasted, "Every man was an engineer." According to a teenage resident of Franklin, "they worked like beavers, using houses, fences, timber, and dirt." The town had witnessed a small skirmish the previous year, and since then Union soldiers had already begun some defenses south of town, so now many of Schofield's men found they had a head start digging in. Soldiers such as Adam Weaver of the 104th Ohio found that he and his comrades had only to deepen the ditches on each side of their earthen wall and make other improvements, so that "by 10:30 this morning our regiment had the strongest defensive mainline I can recall."[5]

By midday this line would have proved formidable indeed, amounting to the most sophisticated field fortifications possible to arrange in the time available. Union soldiers enjoyed the cover of shoulder-high earthworks, surmounted by head logs several inches above the top to provide a gap wide enough to fire through while providing maximum protection from enemy fire. A three-foot ditch in front of the wall not only provided additional earth but also effectively made the five-foot-high works an eight-foot obstacle for attackers. Embrasures were cut into the wall at points for artillery emplacements to bolster Union firepower still further. The southern portion of the line, astride the Franklin and Columbia Turnpike—from which Hood's army would approach the town directly—received the most protection, but would also contain an Achilles' heel. Here the line bulged outward to take advantage of the slopes of Carter Hill and to encompass the buildings of Fountain Branch Carter's farm, including a large cotton-gin house just east of the pike and on the opposite side from Carter's handsome brick home and several outbuildings. The line in front of the gin house faced almost due south—perpendicular to the pike—angled inward toward the road, turned back to cross the pike parallel to the wall fronting the gin house, and angled back as the Union line wrapped around to face more southwesterly. South of the Carter House grew a locust grove from which Union soldiers harvested trees, arranging them in front of their lines with their branches toward the enemy to make effective abatis. East of the road on the Union left, the defenders found a thorny hedge of Osage orange trees. These they cut and repositioned in front of their own works to form a similar obstacle. The ground in front of the wall astride the Franklin and Columbia Turnpike was clear, however, and a gap was left in the earthworks for the road itself to allow Union traffic through. To protect this potential weak spot, Union soldiers began on their own initiative a second, parallel line of earthworks about seventy yards to the rear. This retrenched line actually crossed the turnpike, stretching west in front of Carter's farm office and smokehouse until it finally intersected with the angling main Union line on the right.[6]

Schofield hoped the Twenty-Third Corps' defenses would avert a battle at Franklin by dissuading Hood from attacking and thus buy time to fall back to Nashville. Many of his men, however, looked forward to putting the earthworks to good use with a grim anticipation. By this stage of the war it was almost reflexive for veteran troops in the presence of the enemy to begin entrenching immediately during any substantial halt. Understandably, after putting in much back-breaking labor they experienced some disappointment if they were called on to march away without having been able to reap the benefits of their work. Moreover, these veterans knew well both the perils of assaulting such positions and the comparative ease with which they could be defended. Many of these veterans were reconciled enough to killing their enemies that they could relish the opportunity to turn the tables on foes who had bloodied them from behind the security of earthworks. "[W]hat a comfort to know that we, who in the Georgia campaign had to do most of the bucking against fortifications, were on the right side of the works, and in such a splendid position, with a gentle slope away from us, and not even a mullein-stalk to obstruct our fire for a good third of a mile," wrote staff officer Levi Scofield. "Our men felt that now was their time for wiping out many an old score." Grossman theorizes that soldiers experience progressively less resistance to killing the greater their physical distance from the enemy and the easier the actual means of killing. For troops behind stout defenses, attackers would have greater difficulty closing the distance between them, while their own protection would reduce their fears of being killed. A Texan at Chattanooga the year before had enthusiastically described picking off Union attackers struggling up the slopes of Missionary Ridge. "Now the fun of all this is that we are behind these logs and are not getting hurt one particle," he explained. "Oh this is fun to lie here and shoot them down and we not get hurt. . . ." The Twenty-Third Corps soldiers anticipating giving a similar reception to the Army of Tennessee would soon find themselves in pitched battle at closer quarters than many had ever experienced before.[7]

While most of the Twenty-Third Corps had by noon produced an impressive fortified line ringing the outskirts of Franklin, down the pike several thousand of their comrades had yet to start their own digging. The next few hours set in motion a series of events that would jeopardize the security of those defenses and of Schofield's entire army. From the south had arrived the rearguard, Brigadier General George D. Wagner's division from the Fourth Corps, which had been fending off the pursuit by Forrest's cavalry. Around 11 A.M. Wagner had rested two of his three brigades, those of Joseph Conrad and John Q. Lane, on Winstead Hill, about two miles south of the main line, leaving the third under Emerson Opdycke on watch on nearby Breezy Hill. An hour later, when another brigade from the Fourth Corps was ordered off Winstead Hill and back to Franklin, Wagner began marching his division north to town as well. These orders did not apply to his division, however, and Wagner soon received a dispatch from Fourth Corps commander David Stanley instructing him to "hold the heights you now occupy until dark, unless severely pressed," and to relieve Opdycke. Wagner reoccupied the hills, but by 1:30 he elected once more to fall back as Hood's leading columns came into view. During the withdrawal, he deployed Conrad's brigade on a small rise of ground about half a mile south of the main line, perhaps trying to fulfill the spirit of Stanley's orders and delay the Rebel advance. If this was the case, it was "reckless discretion" on Wagner's part, according to historian Eric Jacobson, considering that his orders applied only to the heights further south and to no other terrain.[8]

As Opdycke's brigade came marching up the pike, Wagner rode up and directed Opdycke to deploy his men west of the road on Conrad's right. Opdycke refused. Not only had the division commander failed to relieve his weary brigade, but, as Opdycke pointed out, putting the men so far forward would leave them terribly exposed "in a good position to aid the enemy and nobody else." Both Wagner and Opdycke were known to be bad tempered when crossed, both were now sleep deprived, and to boot Wagner was nursing an injured leg from his horse falling. A shouting match between superior and subordinate now ensued, a scene made all the more ludicrous because Opdycke kept his brigade on the march to Franklin even as Wagner demanded he turn it around. As the brigade filed through the gap in the Federal line, Wagner gave up the fight. "Well, Opdycke, fight when and where you damn please," he snapped. "We all know you'll fight." Opdycke chose to rest his men in a reserve position two hundred yards north of the Carter House. Wagner put John Lane's brigade in the position he had intended for Opdycke. Both men's decisions would dramatically shape the battle soon to erupt.[9]

The men of Conrad's and Lane's brigades started digging in as best they could, forming a salient resembling a flattened "V," while newly arrived Confederate soldiers occupied Winstead and Breezy Hill. The Federals were at distinct disadvantages compared to their comrades a half mile to the rear. There were no previously begun works here and fewer fences or buildings to provide extra material. Like most Civil War soldiers, they carried few entrenching tools, so most men set to work digging with bayonets, plates, cups, and bare hands. The brigades were a mix of veterans and green recruits, but both perceived how precarious their forward position was. "The opinion was . . . universal that a big blunder was being committed," recalled Captain John K. Shellenberger, commanding a company in the 64th Ohio. "The indignation of the men grew almost into a mutiny." One of his men complained, "What can our generals be thinking about in keeping us out here? We are only in the way. Why don't they take us back to the breastworks?" Levi T. Scofield, General Cox's staff engineer, was with Wagner back at the main line and heard several staff officers make similar remonstrances to the division commander. Hood's whole army was massing to the front, they warned, and Wagner's orders were to stand only "against cavalry and skirmishers." His men, Wagner repeated, would stand and fight. David Stanley, Wagner's corps commander, insisted after the war that Wagner had been "'full' of whiskey, if not drunk," and "in a vainglorious condition." Just about every Civil War general who blundered on the battlefield was accused of drunkenness, and at the time Stanley was on the opposite side of the Harpeth River, so Wagner's true condition cannot be known with certainty. What is certain is that George Day Wagner had decided to fight.[10]

Across the valley on Winstead Hill, Hood had resolved with equal surety to "make the fight." He had on hand the corps of Alexander P. Stewart and Benjamin F. Cheatham, plus two batteries of artillery; Stephen D. Lee's corps and the remaining artillery were still en route. Hood had seen the Yankees abandon Columbia and Spring Hill and likely believed Schofield would give way if aggressively pressed at Franklin. Indeed, Schofield hoped to avoid a fight, but a frontal assault would still have to contend with the Federals' formidable defenses. Hood also seethed at the missed opportunity to bag Schofield's army at Spring Hill, and he was described by General John C. Brown as having been "wrathy as a rattlesnake . . . striking at everything" that morning. He overruled the protests of his subordinates, declining to wait for Lee or to ford the Harpeth River downstream and turn Schofield's position. Instead, he arrayed his available troops in a two-mile-long battle line astride the Franklin and Columbia Turnpike, Stewart taking the right wing and Cheatham the left. The Army of Tennessee was to attack straight ahead, aimed at the Yankees atop and in front of Carter's Hill.[11]

At about 4:00 P.M., a signal flag on Winstead Hill sent the Confederates forward. The disciplined line of butternut and gray "was the grandest sight I ever beheld," remembered the 5th Tennessee's Lt. Edwin H. Rennolds. Across the valley the Yankees, many of whom had not expected an attack, also marveled. The spectacle "was a military pageant such as is rarely seen in actual war, such as I never beheld before or since," wrote a Union surgeon. The Confederates "were so long in plain view, that our men almost forgot the deadly errand of the foe." For Wagner's two forward brigades, the deadly pageant meant it was time to stop digging and to ready their rifles. The two Confederate corps came on at the double quick, in such strength that the two brigades' firepower could do little to stop them. The 64th Ohio triggered "a wall of blazing guns all along our front," wrote Private William A. Keesy. "We are working like demons ourselves, loading and firing till the gun-barrels burn our hands with every touch. But our fire only maddens the foe and they come charging down upon our line and we are all mixed up in hand to hand conflict." With the Rebels upon them, the Yankees in the salient had only three options available to them: fight it out hand to hand, surrender, or run for the rear. Numbers of Federals—mostly the raw recruits—actually ran *toward* the oncoming Confederates, empty hands raised in surrender, and were hustled off to the rear. A company officer in the 79th Illinois saw the Rebel tide come within 35 or 40 paces of his regiment, and, hearing no command to retreat, "I assumed the responsibility and gave the order. About half of the command got up and retreated while the rest remained and continued to fire; so I gave the order the second time." Captain Shellenberger ordered his company to retreat, then immediately "gave an example of how to do it by turning and running to the breastworks."[12]

Stewart's and Cheatham's men plowed into the salient. They had charged with loaded muskets but under orders not to fire until they reached the first line. Now they loosed deadly volleys into the backs of stampeding Federals. Tennessean J. B. Wynn coolly described how "I discharged my gun and the man in front of it fell." Behind the slain Yankee another one leveled his musket at Wynn, but "at one leap I sprang past the muzzle of his gun, grasping it with the left hand." With his now empty musket raised like a club in his right hand Wynn demanded—and received—the second Yankee's surrender. Wynn's prisoner was fortunate indeed, assuming he survived the rest of the battle. One of the most dangerous moments for a soldier in battle is going from active combatant to accepted prisoner of war, considering that his captors, nerved to battle and with adrenaline pumping, must have the presence of mind to recognize him not as a threat to be eliminated but as a prisoner to be taken. Another Tennessean spotted a Union soldier who was perhaps even luckier to be taken alive. W. M. Crook was reloading his musket when he saw ten feet from him a Yankee captain shoot down one of his comrades, then throw up his hands when another Rebel pointed a musket at him. Crook recalled, "A Southern lieutenant, not seeing the captain shoot our man, and thinking his man ought not to shoot an enemy with his hands up, knocked the gun down, and pointed the Federal captain to the rear." Crook's account implies that he felt the captain deserved to be killed at that moment and that perhaps he also believed the Confederate lieutenant would have agreed had he seen the entire episode. Military history is replete with accounts of so-called "surrender-executions," usually carried out according to an unspoken rule among men in battle that an enemy who resists too long deserves no quarter, especially in cases where they have just seen the enemy kill one of their comrades. Under the laws of war, the Federal captain was fully entitled to quarter once he surrendered, but nonetheless under the circumstances he was fortunate indeed to survive the encounter.[13]

Flush with victory, the Confederate attackers were not about to stop at the first line of works. Numerous accounts from Franklin tell how at this point shouts of "Go into the works with them!" erupted from the ranks. With two shattered Union brigades stampeding up the turnpike for the safety of the main line, their foes charged after them in hot pursuit. The pursuit reflected not only the boldness and élan of the Army of Tennessee's veterans but their tactical savvy as well. Following at the heels of Conrad's and Lane's men, they would be able to close on the Union entrenchments behind a human shield of refugees, men who were at this moment blocking their comrades' aim and who would also disrupt the defenders' cohesion as they fled through their ranks. Also acting on Hood's men at this moment were the flush of victory and the released tension of men nerved to battle. Joseph Boyce, a captain in Cockrell's brigade of Missourians, described how "we crossed the enemy's advance line of rifle pits, raised the glorious old yell, and rushed upon the main works a frantic, maddened body with overpowering impulse to reach the enemy and kill, murder, destroy." Kill the enemy they did, recorded an officer from Granbury's Texas Brigade in his diary, "yelling like fury and shooting at them at the same time."[14]

Studies of the nature of combat and killing help us better understand the zeal and slaughter that characterized the Confederate pursuit during this phase of the battle. Grossman speaks directly to this kind of combat scenario, noting, "It is when the bayonet charge has forced one side's soldiers to turn their backs and flee that the killing truly begins, and at some visceral level the soldier intuitively understands this and is very, very frightened when he has to turn his back to the enemy." Nor is this a recent insight, he assures us. Carl von Clausewitz and Ardant du Picq "both expound on length" how in battles throughout history the greatest casualties tended to be inflicted during the victors' pursuit of a broken enemy. Grossman identifies two probable factors that contribute to this proclivity to kill a fleeing enemy. The first he identifies as the "chase instinct," evidenced among all predatory animals that literally close in for the kill in pursuit of fleeing prey. Second, since both physical and emotional distance from the target make killing easier, Grossman explains that a human target whose back is turned is dehumanized in the eyes of a human assailant: "The eyes are the window of the soul, and if one does not have to look into the eyes when killing, it is much easier to deny the humanity of the victim." Furthermore, a point that Grossman does not directly address is that a retreating enemy is far less able to fight back, making for a combat scenario in which the aggressor's own fear of being killed is greatly diminished.[15]

Running their half-mile gauntlet back to the Union main line, the fugitives of Conrad's and Lane's brigades had more than just their pursuers to fear. The retreating mob largely blocked the defenders in the main line from firing into the Rebels. Survivors of the retreat remembered the terror of running toward the muzzles of comrades desperately waiting for a clear field of fire. William Keesy wrote:

> A more frightful danger . . . confronted me as the works were almost reached. Our men behind those works rose up and leveled their guns to fire into us. Oh, my God! The fire from the enemy is bad enough; by a miracle we have escaped that, now to be mown down by our own comrades! Their officers plead with them nobly to hold their fire until we should get in. I could hear the men respond by saying, "Why, they are all coming in together! The Rebels are right with them!" But the flash and the roar of those leveled guns do not come until nearly all our men are in, although many of them find shelter in the outside ditch.[16]

As Keesy's harrowing account attests, the wait to fire for the defenders in the main line was almost as agonizing as the fugitives' flight to the rear. For the awaiting Federals, belonging to Thomas Ruger's and James Reilly's divisions of the Twenty-Third Corps, the situation must have seemed desperate indeed if the enlisted men were so willing to fire into their own comrades in order to stop the Rebel onslaught. The episode also reveals much about the combat motivation of the soldiers in the Battle of Franklin. In one of the first modern studies of soldiers' behavior in combat, U.S. Army historian S. L. A. Marshall famously (and controversially) claimed that during World War II only 15 to 20 percent of GIs in combat fired their weapons. Granted, infantry tactics differed greatly between the Civil War and Second World War. Still, this episode at Franklin seems to point to the Twenty-Third Corps soldiers' exceptional readiness to fire with deadly effect. Perhaps no part of the battle more clearly illustrates that most basic of rationalizations for killing in combat—kill or be killed.[17]

Although Wagner's fugitives significantly shielded the Confederate attack, the Rebels were not spared entirely from the Twenty-Third Corps' firepower. As Private Keesy's and other accounts suggest, most of the runners put enough distance between themselves and their Confederate pursuers to leave time for the main line to fire. Furthermore, most of the Yankees who retreated for the salient headed for the point of least resistance, the stretch of works intersected by the turnpike that was not protected by any kind of abatis. This gave Union defenders behind the more formidable works on the left and right clearer fields of fire, and they opened up with deadly enfilade fire into the Confederate attack. Once they came within one hundred paces of the defenses, recalled General George W. Gordon, "hell exploded in our faces." The Battle of Franklin infamously claimed the lives of six Confederate generals, and it was this Union fusillade that slew two of them. Hiram Granbury fell at the head of his brigade, and Irish-born Patrick Cleburne, perhaps the ablest and most talented general in the Army of Tennessee, was shot not long after.[18]

Deadly though it was, Yankee firepower could not stop the Rebel juggernaut, and Confederate attackers crashed into the unobstructed section of the earthworks. Men from the 50th, 100th, and 104th Ohio regiments reeled from the breach, along with the artillerymen of the 1st Battery, Kentucky Light Artillery. Confederates wheeled the deserted cannons around to fire into the Union defenders but were unable to load or fire the guns. Had they succeeded, canister blasts from their own guns would have wrecked still more havoc on the Twenty-Third Corps and may have decisively comprised their defense. West of the Ohioans' position, the breach widened as the left of the 72nd Illinois, grappling hand to hand with the Rebels, buckled. Captain James A. Sexton of the 72nd saw a wounded comrade wade into the attackers, swinging a pickaxe "with the strength and desperation of a madman." Sexton also vividly recalled the moment when "a rebel colonel mounted our breastworks, and in language not choice, but profanely expressive, demanded our immediate surrender." An Illinois soldier answered by jabbing his loaded musket in the colonel's belly and grimly uttering "I guess not" as he pulled the trigger. The blast "actually let daylight through the victim" and toppled him into the ditch.[19]

Having forced a widening gap in the Union defenses, Cleburne's and Brown's divisions had given Hood's army its best chance of winning the day, but now Federals to the rear surged forward to deny them that chance. In disobeying Wagner's order, Colonel Opdycke had fortuitously placed his brigade in ideal position to support the main line. The veterans of his six regiments had stacked arms and were enjoying a much-needed rest and repast when fugitives from the center came stampeding toward them. Opdycke ordered his men into ranks, intending to shift his brigade east of the pike so as to clear them out of the path of the fugitives and to avoid the obstacle of the Carter farm on the road's west side. Seeing the Rebel breakthrough and the security of the retrenched line to their front, however, many of Opdycke's officers and men interpreted the order as a straightforward advance. "Go for them, Boys," yelled Major Thomas W. Motherspaw to his 73rd Illinois; then, mounting his horse, he ordered, "Forward, 73rd, to the works!" The 73rd's sister regiments surged forward to join in the impulsive charge. Opdycke at first tried to call back Motherspaw, but then, accepting the inevitable, called out, "First Brigade, forward to the works" as he spurred into action.[20]

The brigade's mad dash and the Carter farm buildings and fences prevented Opdycke's men from approaching the enemy with any kind of cohesion or order. Instead the two sides "met on the run," according to a Michigan soldier, colliding in a furious melee. From the east of the pike, the 12th and 16th Kentucky also sprang forward to seal the gap. J. K. Merrifield of the 88th Illinois remembered seeing a Confederate knock a 16th Kentucky soldier to the ground with his musket butt, only to be clubbed to the ground by another Kentuckian. The first Federal, regaining his feet, then bayonetted his fallen assailant. Men on both sides used whatever weapons were handiest—"bayonets, butts of guns, axes, picks, shovels"—even their bare hands. Merrifield saw an officer from his own regiment take on the Rebels with "a little old four-barrel pistol" and a camp hatchet. An officer from Conrad's brigade, having survived Wagner's blunder, now witnessed the gruesomeness of hand-to-hand fighting. "I saw a Confederate soldier, close to me, thrust one of our men through with the bayonet," he reported, "and before he could draw his weapon from the ghastly wound his brains were scattered on all of us that stood near, by the butt of a musket swung with terrific force by some big fellow whom I could not recognize in the grim dirt and smoke that enveloped us all."[21]

A testament to the desperate nature of the frenzied brawl around the Carter farm was that officers were drawn into melee right alongside their men. Generally, the role of regimental officers was to direct and inspire their men in battle, not to take part as combatants themselves. More often than not, their swords served as symbols of their authority and flashy pointers than as weapons. Not so at Franklin. Major Arthur MacArthur spurred his mount at a Confederate color bearer, only to have his horse shot out from under him. Struggling forward on foot, he took a bullet to the shoulder; then a nearby Rebel major put a pistol ball in his chest. MacArthur ran the officer through with his sword, receiving another pistol ball in the knee as the two collapsed on the ground. MacArthur survived his grievous wounds, going on to father a son, Douglas, who would add further laurels to the family name during both World Wars.

Meanwhile, Emerson Opdycke emptied his revolver into the butternut ranks, and then, alighting from the saddle, reversed the weapon and began clubbing away. Writing home to his wife, he told only of having used the clubbed revolver to chivvy Union soldiers back into the fight. Other Union sources—including a postwar letter by Opdycke—claim that he bashed away at the Confederates with the revolver, breaking it in the process, and then picked up a fallen musket to club with that. At the west side of the breakthrough among the 72nd Illinois, "every officer was busy with his revolver," wrote Captain Sexton. "I discharged my own weapon nine times and the most distant man I shot at was not more than twenty feet away."[22]

So hellish was the close-quarter fighting, it is no wonder survivors turned to infernal imagery to describe it. Combatants characterized men of both sides as fighting like "demons." One Confederate veteran wrote that it was "as if the devil had full possession of the earth." The devil's domain could not even compare with the horror of Franklin, insisted an Illinois officer: "The contending elements of hell turned loose would seem almost as a Methodist love-feast compared to the pandemonium that reigned there for the space of ten or twenty minutes." The memory of Franklin stood out for veterans in large part because such combat was so exceptional in their wartime experiences. "You read about hand-to-hand fighting, which does not come very often," explained J. K. Merrifield. "[I]t was the only time I ever saw the bayonet and musket butts used," wrote a soldier in the 73rd Illinois, "and, let me tell you, both were used freely there." W. M. Crook of the 13th Tennessee fought in all of the Army of Tennessee's battles "from Shiloh to Bentonville, but Franklin was by far the closest quarters that I was ever in."[23]

To close with the enemy with fixed bayonet or clubbed musket was a fearsome prospect, and it is a wonder that so many men on each side managed to throw themselves into such combat so boldly. Certainly it was not a condition devoutly to be wished among most Civil War soldiers. "I surely do not want to ever witness the like again," wrote Wayne E. Morris, the Michigander who described the collision of blue and gray in the Carter farmyard. There were a host of reasons for Civil War soldiers to shun the fury of close combat. Dave Grossman observes, "At hand-to-hand range the instinctive resistance to killing becomes strongest." Doing so is killing at its most personal. The soldier can look directly into his opponent's face, hear him, smell him, and see firsthand the results of the damage and pain he inflicts. Hand-to-hand killing constitutes a kind of "intimate brutality." Pulling a trigger allows powder and ball to do the physical work of killing, whereas stabbing, slashing, or clubbing requires the combatant to interact bodily with the foe. Soldiers throughout history have innately preferred to club or slash with their weapons rather than stab, a reluctance that training tries to overcome. To stab is more likely to prove fatal, but simply bashing an enemy out of the way seems more psychologically tolerable than piercing human flesh.[24]

Furthermore, killing at hand-to-hand range is simply more dangerous to the soldier attempting it than killing at longer ranges. "We can understand then that the average soldier has an intense resistance toward bayonetting his fellow man," explains Grossman, "and that this act is surpassed only by the resistance to *being* bayonetted."[25] In contrast to the relative ease and effectiveness of killing by shooting (and accounts from Franklin reveal that many soldiers were shooting amidst the melee), physically battling an enemy requires hazarding one's own life in a contest of strength, reaction time, skill—even chance. We should consider that the average Civil War solider was not trained for hand-to-hand combat. Union and Confederate infantry fought primarily through musketry. The manual of arms in American drill books of the day contained a few basic combat stances for the soldier with a fixed bayonet, but it was far more important that he be drilled to load his musket in the proper sequence so that he could load and fire reliably, reflexively, and quickly. Some soldiers did train using an elaborate bayonet drill based on a French manual translated by George B. McClellan, but its use was rare, especially in the western armies. Much has been made of the fact that many Civil War soldiers had never fired their weapons before being thrust into combat, but wartime accounts suggest many officers were much more likely to arrange live-fire and even target practice for their men than they were to try to school them in bayonet drill.

After perhaps twenty minutes of melee, the disorganized crowds of Yankees and Rebels in the Carter farmyard parted from one another like bloodied boxers going to their respective corners, the Federals forming behind their retrenched line and the Confederates taking cover behind the reverse slope of the earthworks they had initially overrun. This, however, was no pause between rounds. Instead, the two lines exchanged a brisk fire between their respective dirt ramparts, returning to the Civil War infantryman's basic function of loading and shooting. Union soldiers crowded together in masses six to eight men deep behind the retrenched line, those in the rear loading and passing forward ready muskets to those up front. Confederates, sheltered up against the forward slope of their captured portion of the main Union line, replied in kind, though they could not bring as many guns to bear as their opponents. Brigadier General Otho F. Strahl joined his men in the work of loading and passing muskets before a neck wound took him out of the fight. Near the general was Sergeant Major Sumner A. Cunningham of the 41st Tennessee, who handed his own rifle to one of the shooters on the embankment. "The man who had been firing had cocked it and was taking deliberate aim, when he was shot and tumbled down into the ditch upon those killed before him," Cunningham remembered. "As the men so exposed were shot down, their places were supplied by volunteers until these were exhausted, and it was necessary for Gen. Strahl to call upon others."[26]

This musketry duel continued even as darkness came to the field of Franklin. Union and Confederate soldiers had stalemated one another. Circumstances had allowed the Rebels to breach the Union line, but they lacked the numbers to exploit the breakthrough. The Federals had the numbers for the successful counterattack that contained the breakthrough, but circumstances prevented them from driving the Rebels back and recapturing their own fortifications, so the ground south of the retrenched line remained a no-man's-land for the remainder of the fighting. Union attempts to retake their works faced more than just the spirited fire from the Confederates clinging to the embankment. James Sexton led one such sortie and successfully reached the Federal side of the works, "but to our dismay we were soon compelled to return because our own troops on our right and left, mistaking us for the enemy . . . opened fire on us." Sexton took part in a second attempt, met the same results, and with that he and his men gave up the effort. Many of the soldiers responsible for the friendly fire were those in new regiments like the 44th Missouri. Darkness, close proximity to the enemy, and the desperate nature of the fight made many of the men trigger-happy, and it was this overeagerness to fire that bedeviled their comrades.[27]

East and west of the breakthrough, Hood's attacks stalled in front of the well-defended Union works. The stampede of Wagner's men had not disrupted these portions of the line, and the Confederates faced the formidable obstacle of the abatis. East of the Columbia Pike, the attackers of A. P. Stewart's corps became entangled in the refashioned Osage orange hedge, which lived up to its reputation of being "pig tight, horse high, and bull strong." One Alabama officer slashed vainly with his sword at the tough but springy wood, only to be felled by four Yankee bullets. Particularly deadly was the fire from the 65th Indiana and 65th Illinois. Fighting alongside one another, both regiments included a number of men armed with 16-shot Henry repeating rifles. Levi Scofield surmised that "their execution must have been terrible." Indeed it was, confirmed one of the Indianans, for "there was nothing but death for anybody that came in front of them."[28]

Despite the withering fire, some Confederates managed to force paths through the abatis and seek shelter in the ditch along the forward slope of the earthworks. Now the two sides tried to shoot or stab one another with only a dirt wall separating them, fighting "over the works almost hand to hand for two mortal hours," according to an officer in the 16th Kentucky (U.S.). "[W]e fought them across their breastworks," remembered General Gordon, "both sides lying low and putting their guns under the head logs . . . firing nervously, rapidly, and at random, and not exposing any part of the body except the hand that fired the gun." In the ditch, Tennessean John Copley found a dead Yankee with two loaded revolvers in his belt: "I quickly removed them . . . and with one in each hand emptied them under the head-logs at the mass of men across the works in my front."[29]

The Union salient in front of Carter's cotton gin stood fast against the Confederate onslaught, rendered especially strong by two 12-pounder Napoleons from the 6th Battery, Ohio Light Artillery. Although their position sat perilously close to the Confederate breakthrough to their right and rear, the Ohio gunners stubbornly stuck to their guns and fired blast after blast of deadly canister into their attackers. After each discharge, Confederates tried to crawl through the embrasures in desperate attempts to silence the cannons, but the artillerymen fought back with "sponge staves, axes, and picks." Lieutenant Aaron P. Baldwin, commanding the two-gun section, reported how Private Jacob Steinbaugh threw an ax to kill a "daring rebel" coming through the embrasure, then "disabled another with a pick." John Copley, exchanging his captured revolvers for his own rifle, tried to get a shot at the Ohioans but each time had to drop back to escape the muzzle blast as the cannon fired. "After getting my face blistered and eyebrows burned off," he explained, "I abandoned that dangerous place by getting back away from the blaze of these guns." In another attempt to silence the artillery, a young Confederate drummer climbed up to the embrasure and shoved a fence rail into one of the cannons' muzzles. Just as he did so, the gun fired, "and nothing was ever found of the drummer boy." The Ohio gunners could have no doubt as to the deadly effect of their canister blasts. With each discharge Lieutenant Baldwin could hear "two sounds—first the explosion, and then the bones."[30]

West of the turnpike, the Confederate attacks fared little better. General States Rights Gist led his brigade of South Carolinians and Georgians toward the locust abatis, only to die much like Patrick Cleburne, with a bullet in his chest. Further west along the line, two companies of the untested 183rd Ohio had been ordered up to the works. Unexpectedly, the green troops suddenly bolted for the rear in the face of the Rebel attack. Tennesseans and Georgians from William B. Bate's division poured over the vacated wall and fought hand to hand with the defenders on either side of the breakthrough. Mervin Clark, the 183rd Ohio's twenty-one-year-old lieutenant colonel, seized the colors and led his men back into the fight. Clark fell mortally wounded, however, and his men once more fled. Veteran infantrymen from Illinois, Indiana, and Michigan and a Pennsylvania battery rushed to the scene, and a combination of Union musketry and artillery closed the breach.[31]

Fighting at Franklin ultimately came down to killing. The desperate nature of the battle meant many men on both sides consciously fought with lethal intent, and some soldiers could even tell amongst the fury that they personally had successfully killed. Amidst the night fighting, Mississippian George W. Leavell could make out the silhouette of a Union soldier ramming down a cartridge. "I leveled my rifle till the outline darkened the sight and fired," Leavell wrote, wryly adding, "I feel sure the ball he pushed never whistled by a Rebel's ear to make him dodge." Still other men fired almost blindly at the enemy, shooting through the powder smoke at the muzzle flashes. As in many other Civil War firefights, close range and low visibility meant sheer volume of fire could matter more than well-aimed shots. Firing under such conditions was not far removed from what modern fighting men call "spray and pray." From soldiers' accounts, one gets the sense that as the fighting dragged on, the weary soldiers on both sides began to wish that the enemy would just simply *go away*, yet circumstances and both sides' conduct conspired to keep the battle raging. Schofield's men, with their backs to the river but protected by strong field works, had neither the inclination nor the need to abandon the fight. Hood's men, pinned down on the forward side of the fortifications, "held the works in pure desperation," explained a Confederate officer in Strahl's brigade. "It was certain death to retreat across that plain, and equally as bad to remain." With the two armies locked together in close combat, seemingly unable to break off the fight, both Union and Confederate soldiers heeded the advice of General Strahl: "Keep firing."[32]

Once again, Dave Grossman's work provides valuable insight into the nature of the fighting at Franklin, this time regarding the intent of the men who desperately traded volleys at one another well into the night of November 30. Grossman suggests we look beyond the assumption that the soldier in combat follows the alternate instinctive responses of "fight or flight." To this model he adds the options of posturing and submitting. Thus far in the Battle of Franklin we can find evidence of flight (the stampede of Wagner's forward brigades), submission (the surrender of Union soldiers in Wagner's salient), and aggressive fighting (the melee around the Carter farm). Posturing seems to characterize partially the musketry duels between the two sides once the Confederates gained a limited foothold along the Union line. In Grossman's usage, "posturing" refers to aggressive behavior that seeks to intimidate the enemy but falls short of possible life-and-death combat, behavior which we see extensively among both humans and the animal kingdom. The use of gunpowder weapons, he suggests, granted soldiers "superior *posturing* ability," and in this sense the act of firing could reflect soldiers' desire simply to drive away the enemy rather than kill the enemy. Grossman approvingly cites British historian Paddy Griffith's observation that many Civil War regiments would "blaz[e] away uncontrollably . . . until all ammunition was gone or all enthusiasm spent." Griffith explains from this that firing was "a positive act" for Civil War soldiers that provided "a physical release for their emotions." Sure enough, we find many accounts in soldiers' writings in which they described feeling tremendous anxiety just before a battle which suddenly passed away once they were able to blaze away at the enemy.[33]

Firing certainly provided a certain posturing function at Franklin; soldiers on both sides of the works appreciated the fact that keeping up a steady rate of fire could effectively deter an enemy at such precariously close quarters. However, such firing often provided limited lethality. Hence we read of Civil War musketry shredding trees well above the heads of troops and of officers constantly admonishing their men to "aim low." The men at Franklin who raised their muskets over the works with one hand to fire because the bullets flew so thickly might also be described as posturing. Lieutenant William Mohrman reported a drastically more ineffective example of posturing. As the officers of the 72nd Illinois distributed much needed cartridges to their men, he "saw a fellow squatting on the ground who fired his piece in the direction of Jupiter, and the times were too busy to call him to order." Posturing, however, only partially accounts for the behavior of the combatants at this stage in the battle. While some men fired blindly through clouds of powder smoke, as the night wore on men on both sides fired at the enemy's muzzle flashes. Enough bullets flew low enough to suggest many men still fired with lethal intent. The shooters who dropped around Sergeant Major Cunningham proved such firing was decidedly lethal. Confederate soldiers also had good reason to fear going back across the open plain. General Otho Strahl died not from the wound he received in the ditch but from two Yankee bullets that struck him through the dark as he was being carried to the rear by his staff. On the other side of the works, the friendly fire that plagued Captain Sexton and his men attests to the trigger-happiness of their fellow defenders.[34]

Throughout the battle both sides displayed contrasting extremes of brutality and mercy. During the rout of Wagner's forward brigades, some Rebel attackers paused to collect prisoners while others gunned down fleeing Yankees with a will. As the battle turned in the Federals' favor, it increasingly fell to the defenders whether to offer or deny mercy. On the Union left, Brigadier General John Adams led his Mississippians forward to the works on horseback, prompting Lieutenant Colonel W. Scott Stewart to call on his 65th Illinois to spare such a brave man. At first the Illinoisans held their fire, but when the color guard perceived that Adams was riding straight for their banners, they loosed a volley that dropped the gallant general out of the saddle. Other defenders were still less inclined to spare the foe. In front of the 175th Ohio, Confederate attackers became trapped in the abatis and so "hollered to the boys to cease firing—they would surrender." However, the 175th, a new regiment in their first battle, refused and continued to fire away into the helpless Rebels. "So much the better," Private Isaac Miller of the 93rd Ohio wrote approvingly. "All they kill we won't have to fight or feed anymore." Miller specifically attributed the Ohioans' refusal to spare the Rebels to their being a new regiment, seemingly implying that a veteran unit would have been more likely to show the willingness or wherewithal to spare fellow fighting men under such circumstances.[35]

As the firing wore on, weary and desperate Confederates sought to end their ordeal in the death-filled ditches and so began calling on Union soldiers to let them surrender, some lifting their hats over the parapets as a sign of truce. "Drop your guns and climb over," came the defenders' reply. As George W. Gordon came over the works as a prisoner, a nervous Yankee drove his musket butt at the general's head, but a more alert comrade intervened. "Don't strike him. He is surrendering," the second soldier called out as he deflected the blow, which instead glanced off Gordon's shoulder. For the Federals, taking the pinned-down Rebels' surrenders was not only merciful but a wise move for their own safety, since it took out of the fight armed opponents who could otherwise still prove dangerous. During these informal truces, as some Confederates clambered over the works into the safety of Union lines, others used the lulls as chances to escape the ditches and slip through the darkness back to their own lines. Remaining on the field were the wounded and dying who moaned and cried out piteously throughout the night. Such sounds prompted one of the battle's most eloquent expressions of mercy. Hearing one of his lieutenants opine that the Union army "ought to remain here and wipe hell out of" the Rebels, Colonel I. N. Stiles replied, "There is no hell left in them. Don't you hear them praying?"[36]

On the battlefield, the firing eventually faded away like a dying fire, with occasional bouts of flame but eventually burning itself out. "[A]fter 10:30 P.M. there was very little firing anywhere," reported Lieutenant Gus Smith of the 111th Ohio, and shortly afterward Schofield, his engineering along the river complete, began withdrawing his army from Franklin. By 2 A.M., the entire Union army was across the Harpeth and marching north to Nashville. Just over two weeks after the battle, the combatants once more marched through the town of Franklin, only this time the armies' roles were reversed.[37]

In the wake of Hood's crushing defeat at Nashville, now the Confederates were the pursued and the Federals the pursuers. How the veterans of Franklin spoke of the battlefield in the immediate aftermath and years later provides further clues as to how they perceived the nature of killing in combat. While men on both sides were appalled by the human carnage in the battle's wake, many of them primarily mourned their own dead but spoke ambivalently of their slain enemies. "The battlefield of Franklin was truely [*sic*] a sad and at the same time a glorious sight," wrote Alexander Thain of the 96th Illinois in January 1865. "It was sad to see so many graves for although they were rebels still they were men," he explained, adding, "But it was glorious to see the evidences of so great a victory." James Sexton declared the deaths of "hosts of brave souls" to be "a bitter wrong, a monstrous injustice," but he spoke specifically of those given "a scanty burial by rebel hands." The "butchery" at Franklin haunted Confederate Sam Watkins, who wished "to God I could tear the page from these memoirs and from my own memory." As with Sexton, however, when Watkins mourned the "brave and gallant heroes" who fell, he spoke of those from his own side.[38]

If the survivors of Franklin voiced few regrets over loss of life among the enemy, many nevertheless warmed to feelings of fraternity and comradeship with their former foes in the postwar years. Many Franklin veterans embraced the spirit of sectional reconciliation that swept the nation in the 1880s and later decades. Southern subscribers to S. A. Cunningham's *Confederate Veteran* magazine read with interest Northern submissions that offered accounts from the "other side" at Franklin. A number of Union veterans' contributions paid tribute to the "immutable valor" of fallen Confederate heroes such as General John Adams. Addressing fellow Union officers, Levi Scofield spoke of meeting former Confederate general Benjamin F. Cheatham, who told him, "Any man who was in the battle of Franklin, no matter which side, is my friend." Former Yankees and Rebels shared the bond of having survived what many agreed was the most terrible encounter of the war they could remember. "The battle of Franklin . . . was the worst slaughter pen and the most bitterly contested of all of our battles," wrote an ex-Confederate from Cockrell's Missouri brigade. An Illinois veteran from Opdycke's brigade similarly judged Franklin "the hardest, bloodiest, and most wicked fight I was ever in."[39]

What conclusions then can be drawn from the Battle of Franklin about Civil War soldiers and the nature of killing in combat? Surely experiencing the prospect and reality of killing was as different as the thousands of unique individuals who made up the contending armies, yet some general observations can be made. Significantly, close study of the battle corroborates many of the arguments and paradigms Dave Grossman presents in *On Killing*, which in turn bodes well for further applying his ideas to the study of Civil War soldiers. Accounts from Franklin corroborate his matrix of factors which alternately encourage or inhibit killing in battle, not all of which could be addressed in the space of this essay. Physical distance and a fleeing or otherwise vulnerable enemy encouraged aggressiveness, while the unusual prospect of fighting and killing hand to hand proved a fearsome reality, one most of the veterans could never forget and never wished to repeat.

After a furious melee, Union and Confederate forces drew apart only short distances from one another, but settled into their default fighting mode of loading and firing rather than closing again with the enemy. The battle bears out Grossman's fourfold model of soldiers' responses in combat, offering numerous examples of men fleeing, submitting, killing, and even posturing. Franklin offers evidence of other phenomena identified by Grossman and other students of combat, such as the chase instinct, surrender-executions, the emotional benefit of being able to fire away at the enemy, and even some soldiers' preference to clubbing over stabbing the enemy.

At the same time, soldiers at Franklin behaved in ways not necessarily accounted for by Grossman. Notably, few accounts from the battle present killing the enemy as psychologically daunting or burdensome. In some cases men hesitated or declined to kill—often in favor of taking prisoners instead—but the survivors offered little evidence of trauma or guilt related to killing. Of course, we must consider the possibility that some veterans hid such feelings, perhaps fearing what their peers or society at large might say about such sentiments. Historians have found Civil War soldiers who expressed misgivings along these lines, but the study of Franklin does not offer them readily. Moreover, a number of accounts from the battle forthrightly described having killed in laconic or even sardonic tones, even those written decades after the war. Perhaps the fact that Franklin pitted primarily seasoned veterans against one another played a role. In addition, Grossman addresses the role of self-defense in facilitating killing somewhat sparingly. Self-defense factors into his matrix primarily as a function of the "value" or "payoff" the target's death represents to the soldier. "Even if he kills in self-defense," Grossman argues, "there is enormous resistance associated with killing an individual who is not normally associated with relevance or payoff." In comparison, James McPherson suggests the sense of "kill or be killed" must have been a key factor in "overcom[ing] the sanctions against killing." In fact, at Franklin the principle of self-defense might account not only for individual behavior but also group behavior. A number of times during the battle we find soldiers aggressively throwing themselves into the fray, risking their personal safety because the fate of the army seemed to hang in the balance. This helps to account for the boldness and tactical awareness displayed both by the Confederates who seized on the chance to follow retreating defenders into the works and the Federals who charged headlong into the breach that resulted. Many in the ranks seem to have appreciated that closing with the enemy and killing could mean in the course of a battle the difference between their own lives or deaths. Future study of Civil War soldiers and killing must further consider this question.[40]

The armies of both John M. Schofield and John Bell Hood played for high stakes at the Battle of Franklin. Union soldiers faced the challenge of holding back the veterans of the Army of Tennessee, or being driven into the Harpeth River and captured. Confederate soldiers faced the prospects of trapping and eliminating an enemy that had narrowly escaped them time and again, or being slaughtered and repulsed in attacks on a well-protected foe. The foolish placement of two Federal brigades in a highly vulnerable salient jeopardized the security of a seemingly impregnable line, a blunder that gave a fighting chance of success to what might otherwise have proved a hopeless and equally foolish frontal assault. The ensuing clash found the two armies locked in deadly embrace in the dying light and dark chill of November 30, making the hills and fields south of Franklin, Tennessee, into slaughter yards where Union and Confederate soldiers had to choose between dying, fleeing, surrendering, or fighting—and killing.

Notes

1. Civil War Trust, "Ten Facts about the Battle of Franklin," *Civil War Trust*, http://www.civilwar.org/battlefields/franklin/ten-facts/ten-facts-about-the-battle-of.html (accessed April 22, 2013).

2. James M. McPherson, "Afterword," *Religion and the American Civil War*, ed. Randall M. Miller, Harry S. Stout, and Charles Reagan Wilson (New York: Oxford University Press, 1998), 411.

3. Dave Grossman, *On Killing: The Psychological Cost of Learning to Kill in War and Society*, rev. ed. (1995; New York: Back Bay Books, 2009), 53–58, 186–94.

4. Orson Young to "Dear Parents," June 6, 1864, Orson Young letters, 92.33.67, Lake County History Archives, Wauconda, Illinois.

5. John M. Copley, *A Sketch of the Battle of Franklin, Tenn.; with Reminiscences of Camp Douglas* (Austin, TX: E. Von Boeckmann, 1893), 36; Wiley Sword, *Embrace an Angry Wind: The Confederacy's Last Hurrah, Spring Hill, Franklin, and Nashville* (New York: HarperCollins, 1992), 159–60; Gus F. Smith, "Battle of Franklin," *Papers of the Military Order of the Loyal Legion of the United States*, 66 vols. (various publishers and dates; repr., Wilmington, NC: Broadfoot Publishing Company, 1991–96), 51:255 (hereinafter cited as *MOLLUS*); Hardin Figuers, Adam J. Weaver, quoted in David R. Logsdon, ed., *Eyewitnesses at the Battle of Franklin*, 3rd ed. (Nashville: Kettle Mills Press, 1991), 3.

6. Sword, *Embrace an Angry Wind*, 164–65.

7. Levi T. Scofield, "The Retreat from Pulaski to Nashville," *MOLLUS*, 2:131; Grossman, *On Killing*, 97–98; Samuel T. Foster, *One of Cleburne's Command: The Civil War Reminiscences and Diary of Capt. Samuel T. Foster, Granbury's Texas Brigade, CSA*, ed. Norman D. Brown (Austin: University of Texas Press, 1980), 62.

8. Eric A. Jacobson and Richard A. Rupp, *For Cause and for Country: A Study of the Affair at Spring Hill and the Battle of Franklin* (Franklin, TN: O'More Publishing, 2007), 230–33, 240–41.

9. Ibid., 243–44; Sword, *Embrace an Angry Wind*, 173–75.

10. John K. Shellenberger, quoted in Logsdon, *Eyewitnesses at the Battle of Franklin*, 13–14; Scofield, "The Retreat from Pulaski to Nashville," *MOLLUS*, 2:131–32; David S. Stanley, quoted in Logsdon, *Eyewitnesses at the Battle of Franklin*, 16.

11. James R. Knight, *The Battle of Franklin: When the Devil Had Full Possession of the Earth* (Charleston, SC: History Press, 2009), 55–56, 51; Jacobson and Rupp, *For Cause and for Country*, 256–60; Sword, *Embrace an Angry Wind*, 183.

12. Jacobson and Rupp, *For Cause and for Country*, 270–73; Edwin H. Rennolds, quoted in Logsdon, *Eyewitnesses at the Battle of Franklin*, 15, 18; Fred. W. Byers, "Battle of Franklin," *MOLLUS*, 46:233–34; W. A. Keesy, *War as Viewed from the Ranks: Personal Recollections of the War of the Rebellion by a Private Soldier* (Norwalk, OH: Experiment and News Co., 1898), 107.

13. Logsdon, *Eyewitnesses at the Battle of Franklin*, 17; W. M. Crook, "W. M. Crook's Heroism at Franklin," *Confederate Veteran* 11 (1903): 303 (hereinafter cited as *CV*); John Keegan, *The Face of Battle* (1976; New York: Penguin Books, 1978), 47–49; Grossman, *On Killing*, 201–3.

14. Joseph Boyce, "Missourians in the Battle of Franklin," *CV* 24 (1916): 102–3; Foster, *One of Cleburne's Command*, 92.

15. Grossman, *On Killing*, 127–29.

16. Keesy, *War as Viewed from the Ranks*, 108.

17. Grossman, *On Killing*, 3–4; James M. McPherson, *For Cause and Comrades: Why Men Fought in the Civil War* (New York: Oxford University Press, 1997), 72–73.

18. George W. Gordon, speech, in "Confederate Monument at Franklin," *CV* 8 (1900): 7; Jacobson and Rupp, *For Cause and for Country*, 308; Wiley Sword, *Courage under Fire: Profiles in Bravery from the Battlefields of the Civil War* (New York: St. Martin's Griffin, 2007), 62.

19. Jacobson and Rupp, *For Cause and for Country*, 312–17; James A. Sexton, "The Observations and Experiences of a Captain of Infantry at the Battle of Franklin, November 30, 1864," *MOLLUS*, 13: 478–79.

20. Sword, *Embrace an Angry Wind*, 199–201.

21. "Opdycke's Brigade at Franklin," *CV* 13 (1905): 563; Logsdon, *Eyewitnesses at the Battle of Franklin*, 28.

22. Logsdon, *Eyewitnesses at the Battle of Franklin*, 30; William J. K. Beaudot, *The 24th Wisconsin Infantry in the Civil War: The Biography of a Regiment* (Mechanicsburg, PA: Stackpole Books, 2003), 337–38; Emerson Opdycke to Lucy Opdycke, December 2, 1864, in *To Battle for God and the Right: The Civil War Letterbooks of Emerson Opdycke*, ed. Glenn V. Longacre and John E. Haas (Urbana: University of Illinois Press, 2003), 248, 250; "Opdycke's Brigade at Franklin," 563; Sexton, "Observations and Experiences," *MOLLUS*, 13:478.

23. James Dinkins, quoted in Jacobson and Rupp, *For Cause and for Country*, 323; George W. Patten, statement, in *History of the Seventy-Third Illinois* (Springfield, IL: n.p., 1890), 462; "Opdycke's Brigade at Franklin," *CV* 13: 564; J. D. Remington, statement, in *History of the Seventy-Third Illinois*, 450; Crook, "W. M. Crook's Heroism at Franklin," *CV* 11: 303.

24. Sword, *Embrace an Angry Wind*, 202; Grossman, *On Killing*, 120–25, 131.

25. Grossman, *On Killing*, 125.

26. Sexton, "Observations and Experiences," *MOLLUS*, 13:479–80; S. A. Cunningham, "Disastrous Campaign in Tennessee," *CV* 12 (1904): 340.

27. Sexton, "Observations and Experiences," *MOLLUS*, 13:480–81.

28. Stephen Lyn Bales, *Natural Histories: Stories from the Tennessee Valley*, Outdoor Tennessee Series (Knoxville: The University of Tennessee Press, 2007), 194–95; Logsdon, *Eyewitnesses at the Battle of Franklin*, 46; Scofield, "The Retreat from Pulaski to Nashville," *MOLLUS*, 2:139; Tillman H. Stevens, quoted in Logsdon, *Eyewitnesses at the Battle of Franklin*, 40.

29. Morris C. Hutchins, "The Battle of Franklin, Tennessee," *MOLLUS*, 5:281; Gordon, speech, in "Confederate Monument at Franklin," *CV* 8 (1900): 8; John M. Copley, quoted in Logsdon, *Eyewitnesses at the Battle of Franklin*, 42.

30. U.S. War Department, *The War of the Rebellion: A Compilation of the Official Records of the Union and Confederate Armies*, ed. Robert N. Scott, 128 vols. (Washington, DC: Government Printing Office, 1884), ser. 1, vol. 45, pt. 1: 334; Logsdon, *Eyewitnesses at the Battle of Franklin*, 42; Scofield, "The Retreat from Pulaski to Nashville," *MOLLUS*, 2:143, 139.

31. Sword, *Embrace an Angry Wind*, 237–40; Jacobson and Rupp, *For Cause and for Country*, 363–67.

32. George W. Leavell, "Battle of Franklin Remembrances," *CV* 10 (1902): 501; W. E. Cunningham, quoted in Smith, "Battle of Franklin," *MOLLUS*, 15:262–63.

33. Grossman, *On Killing*, 5–9; Paddy Griffith, *Battle Tactics of the Civil War* (New Haven, CT: Yale University Press, 1989), 112.

34. Ibid., 9–11; Logsdon, *Eyewitnesses at the Battle of Franklin*, 34; Cunningham, "Disastrous Campaign in Tennessee," *CV* 12, 340.

35. Logsdon, *Eyewitnesses at the Battle of Franklin*, 49; Jacobson and Rupp, *For Cause and for Country*, 342–43; Sword, *Courage under Fire*, 164.

36. W. W. Gist, "The Other Side at Franklin," *CV* 17 (1909): 14; Gordon, speech, in *CV* 8: 8; Logsdon, *Eyewitnesses at the Battle of Franklin*, 56–57; Thomas E. Milchrist, "Reflections of a Subaltern on the Hood-Thomas Campaign in Tennessee," *MOLLUS*, 13:461.

37. Smith, "Battle of Franklin," *MOLLUS*, 51:257; Sword, *Embrace an Angry Wind*, 254–55.

38. Alexander R. Thain to Sue Smith, January 9, 1865, Minto Family papers, 95.45.415, Lake County History Archives, Wauconda, Illinois; Sexton, "Observations and Experiences," *MOLLUS*, 13:483; Sam R. Watkins, *"Co. Aytch," Maury Grays, First Tennessee Regiment; or, A Side Show of the Big Show* (1881; Wilmington, NC: Broadfoot Publishing Company, 1990), 220–22.

39. Union contributions to *Confederate Veteran* include: "Opdycke's Brigade at Franklin," *CV* 13: 563–64; Gist, "The Other Side at Franklin," *CV* 17: 13–16; "Gen. John Adams at Franklin," *CV* 5 (1897): 299–302; Thomas Gibson, "Particulars of Gen. John Adams's Death," *CV* 12 (1904): 482–83; S. C. Walford, "From 'the Other Side' at Franklin," *CV* 17 (1909): 15–16; Scofield, "The Retreat from Pulaski to Nashville," *MOLLUS*, 2:137; J. M. Hickey, "Battle of Franklin," *CV* 17 (1909): 14; Remington, statement, in *History of the Seventy-Third Illinois*, 449–50.

40. Grossman, *On Killing*, 173–174; McPherson, *For Cause and Comrades*, 73.

6

A FAILURE TO COMMUNICATE
GRANT, THOMAS, AND THE NASHVILLE CAMPAIGN

Brooks D. Simpson

One of the problems with history is that we usually know how the story turns out. We tend to view events looking backward, with a fairly good idea of the result, even if we are less than sure how that result came about. Thus it is a challenge to write about an event or to make assessments about what happened in light of that knowledge—knowledge that was not available to the very people we choose to write about and seek to understand.

Nowhere is that more evident in studying the military history of the American Civil War than when it comes to the relationship between Ulysses S. Grant and George H. Thomas in the weeks leading to the battle of Nashville. In the end, so we are told, Thomas delivered a decisive blow, nearly destroying John Bell Hood's Army of Tennessee. In retrospect, we today look askance on the concerns expressed by Grant as to why Thomas did not move with more dispatch and count as a fortunate near miss that the Union general in chief did not replace Thomas before the Rock of Chickamauga commenced his devastating attack. Since nothing succeeds like success, we wonder why Grant criticized Thomas for being slow when we know that in any case he was sure.

There have been some rather passionate denunciations of Grant's behavior. Stephen Z. Starr delivered a particularly scorching one to the Cincinnati Civil War Round Table in 1961.[1] Claiming that Abraham Lincoln had backed Thomas against an "unreasonably angry" Grant, T. Harry Williams declared that the result demonstrated that "again, the President had been more right than Grant."[2] More than a few studies point out that Thomas was in a far better position to judge circumstances than was Grant; here and there one comes across mention of the fact that Grant was not nearly so active in his continuing operations against Robert E. Lee's Army of Northern Virginia as he wanted Thomas to be against Hood. Authors speculate that Grant resented Thomas or was jealous of his subordinate; they portray Grant as impatient and unreasonable.

What these evaluations cannot quite escape, however, is that we know what happened next. Of course Grant seems petty and churlish, while Thomas comes off as patient and long-suffering, a victim of verbal abuse and threats. We know more than the major characters knew, although we do not always apply that knowledge. For example, Thomas clearly outnumbered Hood, but he did not think so; in portraying his force as inferior he served to foster fears that something might go wrong. Emphasizing just how out of touch Grant was with the situation at Nashville begs the question as to why he did not know better. Perhaps the interaction of Grant and Thomas is rendered more understandable by assessing how each man communicated with the other; perhaps Grant's reactions were grounded in the information he did and did not have.

What happened between Grant and Thomas in the weeks leading up to the Battle of Nashville? What explains the growing rift between the two men? To what can we attribute Grant's impatience and uneasiness? Why did Thomas seem so unwilling to communicate freely with Grant?

Both Grant and Thomas faced serious challenges in mid-November 1864. Although the reelection of Abraham Lincoln removed all doubt about the United States' commitment to a war for reunion, Grant still wrestled with the problem of bringing the Confederacy to its knees. In Georgia William T. Sherman embarked on his march through the interior of the state, a move that seemed as risky as it was daring. Grant had to contend with opposition to the operation from Lincoln and Secretary of War Edwin M. Stanton, and they would hold him responsible if his most trusted subordinate failed to come through. In the Shenandoah Valley Philip H. Sheridan preferred to rest on the laurels he had earned at Winchester, Fisher's Hill, and Cedar Creek, and showed no sign of a willingness to comply with Grant's wishes for him to cut off the James River canal, sever the Virginia Central Railroad, and threaten Richmond from the west. At the same time Grant began to formulate a plan to take Fort Fisher by amphibious assault before advancing upon Wilmington, North Carolina, the Confederacy's last significant port. He hoped to use men drawn from the Army of the James without having to put its commander, Benjamin F. Butler, in charge of the army's part in that operation. Finally, he was well aware of Thomas's assignment to keep John Bell Hood's Army of Tennessee in check, telling Thomas, "Do not let Hoods forces get off without punishment."[3]

As Thomas well knew, this was easier said than done. In preparing for his excursion through Georgia, Sherman had picked the best units under his command, leaving Thomas to scrape together what he could to defend Tennessee and defeat Hood. As Sherman himself had failed for several months to pin Hood down in the aftermath of the capture of Atlanta, it would be no mean feat for Thomas to do the same with inferior forces and reinforcements scattered all over the place. As he told Grant in late November, Hood's army "so greatly outnumbers mine at this time that I am compelled to act on the defensive."[4]

Grant was not pleased with this reply. He fed Thomas reports from southern newspapers about Confederate troop movements, several of which Thomas rightly discounted; however, Grant remained eager for Thomas to take the offensive if he could.[5] News of John Schofield's triumph over Hood at Franklin on November 30 simply spurred calls for action. Grant learned of the result at Franklin on December 1, with news of between six and seven thousand Confederate casualties (including a thousand prisoners) against small Federal losses. However, those totals by themselves failed to convey the degree to which Hood's army had been damaged by Franklin, and so Grant concluded that it remained a potent offensive force that was perfectly capable of more mischief. "If Hood is permitted to remain quietly around Nashville you will lose all the road back to Chattanooga and possibly have to abandon the line of the Tenn.," he telegraphed Thomas. "Should he attack you it is all well but if he does not you should attack him before he fortifies."[6]

As tough as it was for Thomas to gather together enough men to strike at Hood, he found it especially difficult to obtain sufficient mounts for his cavalry. He was reluctant to take the offensive until he had enough horsemen to keep Nathan Bedford Forrest's cavalry in check. Back in Washington, however, the authorities could not believe that horses were in short supply. Some twenty-two thousand mounts had been sent westward, according to Henry W. Halleck. Where had they gone? Stanton told Grant that Thomas was already empowered to impress into military service horses owned by civilians.[7] Nor did Thomas's comments about lacking manpower please his superiors. Halleck informed Grant that Thomas had been authorized to call upon governors for militia, and that other commands had drained their reserves to bolster Thomas's ranks. "I believe that every possible effort has been made to supply Genl Thomas' demands and wants so far as the means at the disposition of the government permitted."[8]

The authorities in Washington shared their displeasure about Thomas with the general in chief. On December 2, Stanton informed Grant, "The President feels solicitous about the disposition of Thomas to lay in fortifications for an indefinite period 'until [James] Wilson gets equipments.' This looks like the [George B.] McClellan & [William S.] Rosecranz [*sic*] strategy of do nothing and let the rebels raid the country. The President wishes you to consider the matter."[9] Thus nudged, Grant wired Thomas: "With your citizen employees all armed you can move out of Nashville with all of your army and force the enemy to retire or fight upon ground of your own choosing." He added that while he believed the troops "should have taken the offensive against the enemy" after Franklin "instead of falling back to Nashville," it might well be that "at this distance . . . I may err as to the best method of dealing with the enemy."[10]

This last comment was on the mark. Grant did not understand the situation at Nashville. He did not fully grasp the damaged condition of Hood's army in the wake of Franklin, nor did he have a good sense of how Thomas was hurrying to construct a force from disparate elements that would be able to take the offensive. Pressed by Washington, he betrayed his anxiety about what Hood might do as well as his suspicion, honed the previous fall at Chattanooga, that Thomas required constant prodding to act. The usually imperturbable general seemed a bit rattled and nervous about what might happen with Hood on the loose. After all, he reasoned that if he was in the Confederate commander's place, he would leave Thomas and Nashville behind and head for the Ohio River, where he could do some real damage. He urged that Thomas be reinforced, only to hear that every available man had already been funneled to Nashville.[11]

On December 2 Thomas explained the situation to his superior. At the time of the Battle of Franklin he had just five thousand infantry to send forward to reinforce Schofield. His cavalry force under James H. Wilson was badly outnumbered, so much so that while Thomas had now gathered enough infantry to feel comfortable with taking the offensive, he wanted to await the arrival of even more horsemen before he struck. He reminded Grant that Sherman had left him with his two weakest corps and dismounted cavalry, all of which took time to organize, supply, and prepare. Several delays had frustrated that process, which "enabled Hood to take advantage [of] my crippled condition"; nevertheless, Thomas hoped to take the offensive in a few days.[12]

Grant was not reassured. How could he be, given Thomas's characterization of his "crippled condition"? Might not Hood do what Grant had feared all along—break north to the Ohio, spreading chaos as he advanced? After all, Grant's major objection to Sherman's plan to march through Georgia was that Hood would be left to his own devices; better, he believed, to deal first with Hood. Sherman had persuaded him otherwise, in the process singing Thomas's praises. Sherman trusted Thomas, and Grant trusted Sherman. Now that trust was to be put to the test, under the scrutiny of those in Washington who had questioned the wisdom of Sherman's march for months.

To Sherman Grant wrote that while some of Thomas's "falling back was undoubtedly necessary and all of it may have been," he did not truly think so. "I hope yet Hood will be badly crippled if not destroyed."[13] Nevertheless, so long as Thomas attacked in a few days, the crisis might well pass.

Besides, Grant was engaged in planning other offensive operations. On December 3 he directed George G. Meade to prepare to send several divisions southward to destroy the Weldon Railroad; the next day he urged Butler that it was time to launch the expedition against Fort Fisher and Wilmington. Once more he pressed Sheridan to strike at the Virginia Central Railroad.[14] Such directives challenge claims that Grant was doing nothing at Richmond and Petersburg at the same time he was ordering Thomas to do something. Rather, he wanted to pin Lee in place while he continued to shred his logistical network. Elsewhere he wanted the armies set in motion—including Thomas's command.

Thomas had told Grant on December 2 that he hoped to attack Hood in a few days; on December 5 Grant inquired as to what had happened. He had heard that Forrest's cavalry was on the move along the Cumberland River. Would the Confederate horsemen cross the river and push northward? It seemed to him that it was time to attack Hood: "Time strengthens him in all probability as much as it does you."[15] Thomas responded the next evening. He still lacked sufficient cavalry to contend with Forrest, although he believed that within three days that shortcoming would be remedied. He conceded that the Confederates were looking to cross the Cumberland River, but trusted that gunboats patrolling the river would prove an adequate defense.[16] In any case, Grant would have to wait a few days more for Thomas to attack.

By the time Thomas composed his explanation, Grant was running out of patience. On the afternoon of December 6, he wired Thomas: "Attack Hood at once and wait no longer for a remount of your cavalry. There is great danger of delay resulting in a campaign back to the Ohio River." To Sherman he declared that he had refrained from ordering Thomas to attack, but that had changed: "I could stand it no longer and gave the order without any reserve."[17] The next morning Stanton added to the pressure, telling Grant, "Thomas seems unwilling to attack because it is hazardous as if all war was anything but hazardous. If he waits for Wilson to get ready, Gabriel will be blowing his last horn." Having by this time received Thomas's explanation of why he had not attacked already, Grant was inclined to agree. If Thomas did not attack "promptly," Grant recommended replacing him with Schofield.[18]

Upon receiving Grant's rather blunt directive, Thomas replied on December 6 that he would comply, "though I believe it will be hazardous with the small force of cavalry now at my service."[19] It was thus understandable that Grant expected to hear that on December 7 Thomas had taken the offensive. However, the wires remained silent, and no news was not good news.

By December 8, Grant, having considered Thomas's explanations for his delay, moved closer toward relieving him. He instructed Halleck to dispatch reinforcements to Thomas, then remarked that if Thomas still had not attacked, "he ought to be ordered to hand over his command to Schofield." Grant believed that "there is no better man to repel an attack than Thomas—but I fear he is too cautious to ever take the initiative."[20]

Given what Stanton and Halleck had already said about Thomas, Grant was simply following their cues as well as his own preferences in suggesting Thomas's replacement. But he should have known better when it came to Halleck. The chief of staff had been critical of Grant for some time in private conversation, and he had meddled in several of Grant's command decisions earlier that year. Moreover, Halleck and Thomas had already established an open line of communication, with Thomas's explanations of delays perhaps falling on somewhat sympathetic ears (as Steven E. Woodworth once put it, "Halleck was inclined to be patient with a slow-moving general, as well he might, given his own record in field command"[21]). Thomas had shared with Halleck his concern about his shortage of mounted cavalry and about the Confederates crossing the Cumberland River below Nashville.[22] On December 5 he had assured Halleck that if all went well, he would advance against Hood in two days.[23] It would have been a good idea had Thomas explained without prodding what the situation was.

Learning that Grant was contemplating whether to displace Thomas, Halleck saw a chance to interject himself. "If you wish Genl Thomas relieved from command, give the order," he told Grant on December 8. "No one here will, I think, interfere. The responsibility, however, will be yours, as no one here, so far as I am informed, wishes Genl Thomas's removal."[24] That news brought Grant up short. Either Halleck was out of touch with Stanton, or Grant had read too much into Stanton's harsh comments, including those referring to Lincoln's own discomfort. "I want Gen. Thomas reminded of the importance of immediate action," he quickly replied. "I sent him a dispatch this evening which will probably urge him on. I would not say relieve him until I hear further from him."[25]

Looking to prod Thomas into action, Grant's dispatch warned him that it looked as if the Confederates were scattered south of the Cumberland River as they sought a place to cross it. "Why not attack at once? By all means avoid the contingency of a footrace to see which, you or Hood, can beat to the Ohio." Grant told Thomas to mobilize state militia to defend Kentucky and then move out to meet the enemy. "Now is one of the farest opertunities ever presented of destroying one of the three Armies of the enemy. If destroyed he can never replace it. Use the means at your command and you can do this and cause a rejoicing that will resound from one end of the land to the other."[26]

By the time Thomas received this telegram, circumstances had changed yet again. Freezing rain made it impossible to do anything. It was just as Grant had feared: waiting too long led to another reason for delay. Moreover, having expressed the hope that he would attack first on the December 5, then the seventh, and now the ninth, Thomas had failed to advance, and in each case Grant had to contact him to find out what had happened. It would have been far wiser for Thomas to have informed Grant of what was going on—best to deliver the bad news without prodding. After all, he had no trouble keeping Halleck up to date. In turn, Halleck did nothing to improve communications between Grant and Thomas. If anything, he made things worse in his next missive to Nashville. "General Grant expresses much dissatisfaction with your delay in attacking the enemy," he informed Thomas. "If you wait until General Wilson mounts all his cavalry, you will wait till doomsday, for the waste equals the supply."[27]

Thomas replied, reporting that he had to postpone his attack once more due to weather conditions. "I regret that General Grant should feel dissatisfaction at my delay in attacking the enemy," he told Halleck. "I feel conscious that I have done everything in my power to prepare, and that the troops could not have been gotten ready before this, and if he should order me to be relieved I will submit without a murmur."[28] Had Thomas known that an order was framed to do exactly that, he might have been even more offended.[29] Instead, he contacted Grant directly on December 9, explaining that the poor weather prevented undertaking offensive operations, and indicated that Halleck had told him of Grant's dissatisfaction. At the same time, he confirmed one of Grant's suspicions: "There is no doubt but that Hood's forces are considerably scattered along the river with the view of attempting a crossing, but it has been impossible for me to organize and equip the troops for an attack at an earlier time." Thomas remained sure that Union gunboats would thwart a crossing.[30]

By the time Grant heard from Thomas, he had also learned of the storm from Halleck, who forwarded Thomas's dispatch describing the weather conditions.[31] Although Grant decided to suspend the order removing Thomas, he remained frustrated at that general's inactivity. "Gen. Thomas has been urged in every way possible to attack the enemy even to the giving the positive order," he explained. "He did say he thought he would be able to attack on the 7th but did not do so nor has he given a reason for not doing it." Still Grant was "very unwilling to do injustice to an officer who has done as much good service as Gen. Thomas," so for the moment he would wait and see what happened.[32] "I have as much confidence in your conducting a battle as I have in any other officer," he told Thomas. "But it has seemed to me that you have been slow and I have had no explanation of affairs to convince me otherwise." Only Thomas's message to Halleck had stayed Grant's hand: "I hope most sincerely that there will be no necessity of repeating the order and that the facts will show that you have been right all the time." Thomas replied late that night, reporting that difficulties in concentrating his men and addressing transportation needs had consumed more time than he had anticipated . . . and then there was the storm, which continued throughout the day and into the night.[33]

This set of exchanges highlights two important problems. First, telegraphic communication was far from instantaneous. It took a while for word from Nashville to reach Washington and City Point, and vice versa. In the meantime conditions could change radically; moreover, one might assume that no one was saying anything when in fact a reply was already on its way across the wires. Thus decisions were made and orders framed in ignorance of the current situation. What in retrospect might look like foolish or ill-tempered conclusions were in fact products of the delays inherent in the available technology. Those conditions added to Grant's frustration and impatience; so did Thomas's reluctance to communicate with Grant directly except as a response to a message from his superior. Having Halleck in the middle was not a guarantee of improved understanding.

Had the situation in Nashville been the only issue on Grant's mind, one might well wonder what was going on. But it was not. Indeed, once he had learned that bad weather had forestalled Thomas's attack, Grant could turn his attention elsewhere, and he had plenty on his plate. On December 10 Grant endeavored to learn the location of [G. W.] Warren's expedition. Afraid that Warren might be in trouble, he mobilized reinforcements to launch a rescue mission.[34] It was not until the next afternoon that he returned his focus to Thomas. Having again heard nothing from Nashville, he wired Thomas that if Hood crossed the Cumberland, "you will be forced to act, accepting such weather as you can find. Let there be no further delay." Hood's army could not survive an attack intact. "I am in hopes of receiving a dispatch from you to-day announcing that you have moved. Delay no longer for weather or reinforcements."[35]

Thomas's reply proved disappointing. There had been no attack on the tenth or the eleventh: the freezing rain had turned the ground to a sheet of ice, making it impossible to move men into position or to conduct combat operations. Thomas cancelled his planned attack for December 10 and suggested that any advance would be made "under every disadvantage," although he pledged to move "as promptly as possible."[36]

Much has been made of Grant asking Thomas to do the impossible. To attack under such conditions would have been difficult if not a disaster. What Grant's critics miss is that Thomas did not keep Grant informed of the situation. Instead, Grant waited for news that never came—it was up to Grant to initiate these exchanges, leading one to wonder whether Thomas might have been somewhat passive-aggressive in his dealings with Grant. After all, this was yet another case of Thomas indicating that he planned to attack, leaving it to Grant to find out that nothing had happened when he asked for an update. It looked as if Thomas was pushing Grant's buttons. While he said nothing to Grant on December 10 about weather conditions, he shared that information with Halleck; apparently Halleck did not relay that news to Grant.[37]

Indeed, one might well wonder what Henry W. Halleck's role was in this growing rift. It was reasonable for Thomas to conclude that Halleck would be consulting with Grant concerning Thomas's situation, but Halleck was at best erratic in conveying information. It is not clear that all of Thomas's messages to Halleck were forwarded to City Point in timely fashion (and Thomas would have no way of knowing whether this was the case). In considering Grant's reactions, one must not only set aside the outcome of the battle at Nashville, but also reflect on exactly what he knew and when he knew it. From Grant's letters to Thomas one divines that in many cases Grant lacked good information needed to make good decisions, express reasonable expectations, and offer helpful advice. After all, Halleck had possession of information about the bad weather in Nashville before Grant, who directed Thomas's replacement without having that information in hand (which explains why he suspended the order). To cite Thomas's correspondence with Halleck overlooks the key question of exactly how much did Halleck share with Grant—and why Grant, who was well aware of Halleck's tendency to meddle, did not insist that Halleck forward all correspondence to him so he would have a better understanding of the situation at Nashville. In any case, the so-called modern command system celebrated by T. Harry Williams in *Lincoln and His Generals* was not working very well in December 1864.

Thomas made clear to his cavalry commander, James H. Wilson, his irritation with the "Washington authorities," as he put it (recall that Grant was not at Washington), declaring that they treated him "as if I were a boy." In response, Thomas tended to sulk. Perhaps he thought that sharing information with Halleck was sufficient notification of what was going on. It is evident that just as Grant lacked complete confidence in him, he would not take Grant into his own confidence. It is also reasonable to suggest that

Thomas may have believed that keeping Halleck up to date was sufficient, although several of Grant's other commanders, including Sherman and Sheridan, maintained direct contact with the general in chief. If such was the case with Thomas, perhaps he might have heeded the lessons of previous exchanges and kept Grant apprised of what was going on directly, and to do so without waiting for an impatient inquiry.[38]

Meanwhile, there were other matters on Grant's mind. Meade suggested on December 11 that he might attack Lee's lines; later Grant and Meade agreed that such a move probably would not succeed.[39] At the same time Grant tried once more to push Sheridan into action against the Virginia Central Railroad and the James River canal.[40] Two days later he prodded Butler to commence his operation against Fort Fisher and Wilmington.[41] In each case the subordinate general kept in touch with the general in chief, explaining delays (including poor weather) or offering his views, so that Grant remained informed of what was going on. Such was not the case with Thomas, who still seemed reluctant to say anything to Grant until Grant said something to him. That did not prevent him from informing Halleck on the evening of December 12 that the weather conditions precluded making an attack, for it "would only result in a useless sacrifice of life."[42] The following evening he shared with Halleck the news that the weather was finally improving, allowing him to attack in the near future.[43]

On December 13 Grant snapped. He had waited, and waited, and waited. There was no need to ask again what was going on. It so happened that John A. Logan, one of Grant's old division commanders with the Army of the Tennessee, was at City Point visiting Grant. Logan received orders to proceed to Nashville via Louisville.[44] If he arrived at Nashville to find that Thomas had not attacked, he was to present an order from Grant relieving Thomas and putting Logan in charge. Perhaps Grant did not know that it had been Thomas who advised Sherman to name Oliver O. Howard and not Logan to the command of the Army of the Tennessee to replace the fallen James B. McPherson in July 1864, but Grant had confidence that Logan was a fighting general who would not hesitate to go after Hood.

Grant's impatience increased on December 14. Deciding to go to Nashville to see things for himself, he left City Point for Washington late in the day.[45] Meanwhile Halleck informed Thomas of the consequences of the delay in moving against Hood. "It has been seriously apprehended that while Hood, with a part of his forces, held you in check near Nashville, he would have time to operate against other important points left only partially protected. Hence, General Grant was anxious that you should attack the rebel force in your front, and expressed great dissatisfaction that his orders had not been carried out," he explained. "Moreover, so long as Hood occupies a threatening position in Tennessee, General [Edward] Canby is obliged to keep large force upon the Mississippi River, to protect its navigation and to hold Memphis, Vicksburg, &c., although General Grant had directed a part of these forces to co-operate with General Sherman. Every day's delay on your part, therefore, seriously interferes with General Grant's plans." Thomas replied that evening that he would attack the following morning, adding, "Much as I regret the apparent delay in attacking the enemy, it could not have been done before with any reasonable hope of success."[46] Once more he said nothing directly to Grant.

Compounding problems at this point was a collapse in the telegraph line linking Nashville to Washington.[47] Thus, as Grant made his way north, there was no way to find out what was going on in Nashville. Thomas's message to Halleck of December 14 promising to attack the next day had not yet arrived because of the break. Thus no one knew what Thomas might (or might not) do. Arriving in Washington on December 15, Grant, having heard nothing new from Thomas, prepared to continue his trip west to Nashville. Although David Homer Bates claims that Grant directed by telegram for Thomas to be relieved (with John M. Schofield taking command pending Grant's arrival), no such text survives. Bates also recalled a meeting between Lincoln, Stanton, Grant, and Halleck where he claims that both the president and the secretary of war opposed Thomas's removal. Whether such a meeting took place is unknown; that anyone else (namely War Department staffer Major Thomas T. Eckert, who manned the military telegraph) would know what was said is unlikely; that Bates's claim (via Eckert) that Stanton protested loudly against Thomas's removal is questionable given the harsh comments he had previously made about Thomas.[48]

That evening telegraphic service between Nashville and Washington was restored. If Bates is to believed, Eckert took it upon himself to wait for news from Nashville before transmitting Grant's order relieving Thomas. Late that evening Thomas's December 14 promise to attack the next day came through, followed shortly after by news of Thomas's military success on the fifteenth, as first reported by John C. Van Duzer, a captain who operated the military telegraph in Nashville (and who had been carrying on a correspondence with Eckert). Reading the dispatch, Grant returned to the hotel and informed telegraph operator Samuel Beckwith, "I guess we will not go to Nashville after all. Thomas has licked Hood." Immediately he wired Thomas to congratulate him on his "splendid success," adding, "Push the enemy now and give him no rest until he is entirely destroyed.... Much is now expected." Moments later he sent a second telegram upon receiving

Thomas's own report of the operations of that day . . . a report Thomas had sent to Halleck, not Grant.[49]

By the next day all was well in Washington. Of note was Lincoln's own message to Thomas late that morning. After congratulating Thomas on the triumph of the fifteenth, he added, "You made a magnificent beginning. A grand consummation is within your easy reach. Do not let it slip." Such a message suggested that Lincoln shared Grant's concerns about Thomas. Otherwise he would not have felt the need to exhort him to an even greater achievement. A relieved Grant decided to visit his family in Burlington, New Jersey; on December 17, Logan, having reached Louisville, learned of Thomas's victory, and Grant told him to report to Sherman.[50]

The crisis, in short, was over. However, the friction between Grant and Thomas continued. Responding to a suggestion from Stanton that Thomas should be awarded a major generalship in the regular army for his victory, Grant thought it would be better to wait a few days to see how complete the victory was. It was not until December 23 that he approved of the idea. (For his part, Thomas groused that he had earned that promotion as a result of Chickamauga.) At the same time, Grant and Sherman continued to exchange opinions about Thomas, with Sherman offering conditional praise of his West Point classmate while conceding that he was deliberate if not slow. Before long, Grant began to strip away forces from Thomas, notably Schofield's Army of the Ohio—the Hero of Nashville would not direct another major operation during the remainder of the war.[51]

Thomas's victory at Nashville overshadowed all that came before it, and in retrospect Grant's concerns seem unrealistic. As James H. Wilson, who served under both Grant and Thomas, later put it, in contemplating the possibility of Hood crossing the Cumberland River and striking northward, Grant entertained fears about a movement Wilson deemed "the wildest and the most desperate and hopeless military undertaking possible to imagine." Indeed, according to Wilson, "Grant lost his head and failed to act with his usual sound sense."[52] But these claims were made in light of learning what was on Hood's mind after Franklin; unfortunately for all concerned, no one had bothered to understand that no one on the Union side had divined his intentions at the time.

Reviewing Grant's messages, Wilson claimed they showed that Grant "had a good memory for injuries, real or fancied, with an utter lack of sympathy or active friendship for Thomas"; such sentiments were rooted in previous slights. The telegrams "disclose a willingness, if not a settled purpose, on Grant's part to cause Thomas's removal and downfall, provided the authorities at Washington could be induced to take the responsibility for such radical action."[53]

Several biographers and historians hostile to Grant have echoed these descriptions, and indeed, if Grant's telegrams are taken out of context and compared to the situation as we understand it in hindsight, it makes sense to draw these conclusions, although in several cases the actual evidence for them is scant. Much fairer is telegraph operator Samuel Beckwith's observation that it was hard to explain Grant's "extreme impatience," but that his "persistent demands" for action "impressed me at the time as being rather strange."[54]

Still, one cannot deny that there was friction between Grant and Thomas. Simply put, Grant did not trust Thomas as he trusted Sherman, Sheridan, or even Meade. Whatever the origins of this friction, it was evident during the Chattanooga Campaign and the winter of 1863–64. While one may safely dismiss claims that Grant was jealous of Thomas, felt inferior around him, or was afraid of his abilities—claims sometimes made but not persuasively argued by people who tend to believe that to think highly of Thomas one must degrade Grant and Sherman—one cannot evade the conclusion that Grant was reluctant to give Thomas the same slack he extended to Sherman, Sheridan, and, to a lesser, extent, Meade. Simply put, Grant was more willing to listen to the advice these generals gave; he did not hold them to account the same way he did Thomas when these subordinates did not immediately comply with his orders or offered different perspectives. As Wilson later observed, Grant refused to extend to Thomas "that freedom of judgment and action which he so generously extended to Meade, Sherman, Sheridan, and Schofield." He even displayed more patience with Ben Butler than he did with Thomas, although in the end Butler would try that patience too much. Still, Grant did hold back on acting on his desire to remove Thomas, and that willingness to second guess himself paid off.

Moreover, a review of Grant's headquarters correspondence reveals that during this period the commanding general had other matters on his mind, and the resulting stress may have contributed to his curtness toward Thomas. For days he was not sure of the whereabouts of either Sherman or Warren; he also found it hard to spur either Phillip H. Sheridan or Benjamin F. Butler into action. Within a month Butler's fumbling generalship at Fort Fisher cost him his command. Nor can it be denied that Grant was receiving mixed messages from Washington. Lincoln, Stanton, and Halleck all placed pressure on him to do something about Thomas, with each expressing doubts about Thomas's generalship; however, when Grant wanted to act, these same three people advised inaction. Nevertheless, it is clear they were concerned; Lincoln himself restricted his commentary on the war in his fourth annual message, delivered on December 6, to two short paragraphs buried deep within his text, as if not to call attention to the situation.

Less has been made of Thomas's own contributions to the miscommunication. The general promised several times to attack within a short period of time, only to fall silent when those attacks did not come off. Had he volunteered to Grant his reasoning for delay in breaking the news to his superiors instead of waiting for another lecture to which he would offer a response, he might well have avoided much of the ensuing confusion and ill feeling. As even Thomas B. Buell, an avowed admirer of Thomas, admits, Thomas's messages "worked against him," for they argued that Hood's army posed a threat (thus justifying Grant's concern) and that the Confederate commander was seeking a way across the Cumberland (although such a move would have been difficult to support with a significant force). Nor did they highlight Thomas's desire to form a powerful strike force with his cavalry designed to cut off Hood's retreat. As Buell suggests, "To Grant and those in Washington, [Thomas's] telegrams confirmed their notion of Thomas as a conservative, slow-moving plodder."[55]

Thomas did, though, inform Halleck of circumstances and notified him of delays promptly. In examining the communication breakdown between Thomas and Grant, one needs to consider that Halleck was not as cooperative as he could have been. Even as he reminded Thomas of the importance of doing something, he did not always keep Grant informed of what Thomas was telling him, thus adding to the friction between a worried superior and a recalcitrant subordinate. Although Halleck may have played an important role in holding back Grant's order to relieve Thomas until he had informed Grant of the weather conditions that prevented Thomas from taking the offensive, one wonders whether in the end it would have been better to dispense altogether with Halleck and force Grant and Thomas to deal directly with each other.

There were also structural issues in the process of communication that go beyond explanations based on personal conflicts or real and imagined slights but which may help explain why communication between Grant and Thomas was so flawed. Reconstructing the lines of communication between Nashville, Washington, and City Point as well as the actual sequence of telegrams (paying as much attention to when they were received as when they were sent) suggests that there were several dysfunctional patterns at play. One was simply the delay in transmitting messages between the three points: it took longer for Thomas to communicate with Grant than it took him to communicate with Halleck, and so in several cases messages were being composed at the very moment when other information was on its way that would change the circumstances as understood by all parties. Moreover, there is no evidence that Halleck forwarded all of Thomas's communications to Grant. Grant specifically cited the telegrams to which he was replying, and he did not mention a majority of the messages that Thomas sent Halleck. Delays are bad enough in the best of circumstances, but they are worse when the parties are impatient and prone to act hastily or snap back in reply . . . or rely upon incomplete information because someone fails to foster the flow of complete information.

As if understanding the dynamics involved in the Grant-Halleck-Thomas triangle was not enough, in later years some participants and scholars added another player to the mix: John M. Schofield. The story was that Schofield telegraphed Grant that Thomas was "certainly too slow in his movements."[56] So testified James M. Steedman. According to this rumor, Schofield was eager to supplant Thomas, in part to pay off an ancient grievance dating back to Schofield's time at West Point as a cadet. However, nothing supported this tale: Grant specifically denied it in a letter to Schofield in 1881.[57]

Nor did the parties involved make full use of alternative avenues of communication. Another source of information between Nashville and Washington was the wires between Major Thomas Eckert at the War Department and John C. Van Duzer, a military telegraph operator stationed at Nashville. Both men thought they needed to do more than simply transmit messages: Eckert had withheld military telegrams from the president, while Van Duzer had already come under fire for exercising prerogatives over military communications. However, Van Duzer kept Eckert informed of the situation at Nashville, including the storm of December 9. Some of the messages they exchanged contained information useful to their superiors. And James H. Wilson, who had served under Grant, did nothing to clear the air, although Wilson had often thought of himself as an important go-between in Grant's relations with other generals.

In short, the frayed relationship between Ulysses S. Grant and George H. Thomas in the weeks prior to Thomas's decisive victory over John Bell Hood's Army of Tennessee can be understood partly as a clash of personalities for which both men are responsible, partly as a result of the awkward command structure in which Henry W. Halleck operated, and partly due to problems inherent in long-range telegraphic communication during the Civil War. Grant's biographers have been more willing than Thomas's more defensive biographers to accept the notion that both of the principals bore some responsibility for the near-complete collapse of trust between the two men, suggesting that a more dispassionate approach offers a more fruitful understanding of what happened. That in the end Thomas smashed Hood outside Nashville meant that such friction fortunately did not alter the conduct of the war, regardless of whether it continues to irritate some people to this day.

Notes

1. See Stephen Z. Starr, "Grant and Thomas: December, 1864," http://www.cincinnaticwrt.org/data/ccwrt_history/talks_text/starr_grant_thomas.html (accessed June 14, 2014).

2. T. Harry Williams, *Lincoln and His Generals* (New York: Knopf, 1952), 344–45.

3. Grant to Thomas, November 24, 1864, John Y. Simon et al., eds., *The Papers of Ulysses S. Grant*, 32 vols. (Carbondale: Southern Illinois University Press, 1967–2012), 13:21 (hereafter *PUSG*).

4. Thomas to Grant, November 25, 1864, *PUSG*, 13:24.

5. Grant to Thomas, November 27, 1864, *PUSG*, 13:27–28; Thomas to Grant, November 28, 1864, *PUSG*, 13:28; Grant to Thomas and Halleck, November 30, 1864, *PUSG*, 13:33; Thomas to Grant, November 30, December 1, 1864, *PUSG*, 13:34.

6. Grant to Meade, December 1, 1864, *PUSG*, 13:54; Grant to Thomas, December 2, 1864, *PUSG*, 13:52–53.

7. Halleck to Grant, December 5, 1864, *PUSG*, 13:50; Stanton to Grant, December 2, 1864, *PUSG*, 13:50.

8. Halleck to Grant, December 3, 1864, *PUSG*, 13:51.

9. Stanton to Grant, December 2, 1864, *PUSG*, 13:50.

10. Grant to Thomas, December 2, 1864, *PUSG*, 13:53. See Adam Badeau, *Military History of Ulysses S. Grant*, 3 vols. (New York: D. Appleton and Co., 1881), 3:215–16, for showing that Grant's first telegram of December 2 was sent prior to Stanton's telegram of December 2; also see Grant to Stanton, December 2, 1864, *PUSG*, 13:49.

11. Grant to Halleck, December 2, 1864, *PUSG*, 13:51; Halleck to Grant, December 3, 1864, *PUSG*, 13:51.

12. Thomas to Grant, December 2, 1864, *PUSG*, 13:53–54.

13. Grant to Sherman, December 3, 1864, *PUSG*, 13:56–57.

14. Grant to Meade, December 3, 1864, *PUSG*, 13:55; Grant to Butler, December 4, 1864, *PUSG*, 13:61; Grant to Sheridan, December 4, 1864, *PUSG*, 13:62.

15. Grant to Thomas, December 5, 1864, *PUSG*, 13:67.

16. Thomas to Grant, December 6, 1864, *PUSG*, 13:67–68.

17. Grant to Thomas, December 6, 1864, *PUSG*, 13:77; Grant to Sherman, December 6, 1864, *PUSG*, 13:73.

18. Stanton to Grant, December 7, 1864, *PUSG*, 13:79; Grant to Stanton, December 7, 1864, *PUSG*, 13:78–79.

19. Thomas to Grant, December 6, 1864, *PUSG*, 13:77.

20. Grant to Halleck, December 8, 1864, *PUSG*, 13:83.

21. Steven E. Woodworth, "George H. Thomas," in *Grant's Lieutenants: From Chattanooga to Appomattox*, ed. Steven E. Woodworth (Lincoln: University of Nebraska Press, 2008), 41.

22. U.S. War Department, *The War of the Rebellion: A Compilation of the Official Records of the Union and Confederate Armies*, 128 vols. (Washington, DC: Government Printing Office, 1881–1901), ser. 1, vol. 45, pt. 2: 18, 29, 43 (hereinafter cited as *OR*; all references are to series 1 unless otherwise indicated).

23. *OR*, vol. 45, pt. 2: 55.

24. Halleck to Grant, December 8, 1864, *PUSG*, 13:84.

25. Grant to Halleck, December 8, 1864, *PUSG*, 13:84.

26. Grant to Thomas, December 8, 1864, *PUSG*, 13:87–88.

27. *OR*, vol. 45, pt. 2: 114.

28. Ibid.

29. Grant to Halleck, December 9, 1864, *PUSG*, 13:90. See the draft order in *OR*, vol. 45, pt. 2: 114.

30. Thomas to Grant, December 9, 1864, *PUSG*, 13:88.

31. Halleck to Grant, December 9, 1864, *PUSG*, 13:90.

32. Grant to Halleck, December 9, 1864, *PUSG*, 13:90–91. In *Lincoln in the Telegraph Office* (New York: Century, 1907), 312–13, David Homer Bates claimed that Lincoln held up the order to remove Thomas, but it is clear from the correspondence that Grant decided to suspend it upon receiving information about the weather from Halleck.

33. Grant to Thomas, December 9, 1864, and Thomas to Grant, December 9, 1864, *PUSG*, 13:96.

34. Grant to George F. Shepley, December 10, 1864, *PUSG*, 13:101; Grant to Meade, December 10, 1864, *PUSG*, 13:96–97.

35. Grant to Thomas, December 11, 1864, *PUSG*, 13:107.

36. Thomas to Grant, December 11, 1864, *PUSG*, 13:107.

37. *OR*, vol. 45, pt. 2: 130. See also Thomas to Halleck, December 11, 1864, *OR*, vol. 45, pt. 2: 143, for an update provided to Halleck before he received Grant's telegram, including information about Confederate efforts to cross the Cumberland River—just what Grant feared.

38. James H. Wilson, *Under the Old Flag*, 2 vols. (New York: D. Appleton, 1912), 2:102.

39. Meade to Grant, December 12, 1864, and Grant to Meade, December 12, 1864, *PUSG*, 13:108.

40. Grant to Sheridan, December 12, 1864, *PUSG*, 13:110.

41. Grant to Butler, December 14, 1864, *PUSG*, 13:119.

42. *OR*, vol. 45, pt. 2: 155.

43. Ibid., 168.

44. Special Orders No. 149, December 13, 1864, *PUSG*, 13:128.

45. Grant to Meade and Edward O. C. Ord. December 14, 1864, *PUSG*, 13:120.

46. *OR*, vol. 45, pt. 2: 180.

47. Bates, *Lincoln in the Telegraph Office*, 314.

48. Ibid., 315. In *Recollections of President Lincoln and His Administration* (New York: Harper and Brothers, 1891), 363, Lucius E. Chittenden recalled a conversation between Lincoln and Grant where Lincoln reminded Grant that the man on the scene might be the best judge of what was in front of him—a piece of advice Lincoln himself did not always follow with his generals. According to Horace Porter, *Campaigning with Grant* (New York: Century, 1897), 348, Grant arrived in Washington in the early evening, and immediately learned of Thomas's intentions to attack upon debarking from his steamer, precluding a visit to the War Department or the White House; however, Samuel Beckwith, who accompanied Grant, said that Grant arrived on the afternoon of the fifteenth, went to the Willard, then to the War Department, where he met with Lincoln, Stanton, and Halleck prior to penning an order for dismissal. John Y. Simon and David L. Wilson, "Samuel H. Beckwith: 'Grant's Shadow,'" in *Ulysses S. Grant: Essays and Documents*, ed. John Y. Simon and David L. Wilson (Carbondale: Southern Illinois University Press, 1981), 117–18.

49. Simon and Wilson, "Beckwith," 118; Bates, *Lincoln in the Telegraph Office*, 317–18; Grant to Thomas, December 15, 1864, *PUSG*, 13:124 (two telegrams); Thomas to Halleck, December 15, 1864, *OR*, vol. 45, pt. 2: 194. If Beckwith's account is to be believed, the claim that Eckert did not transmit Grant's order on his own initiative loses force, for Beckwith has Grant at the War Department when the news came of Thomas's victory.

50. Logan to Grant, December 17, 1864, and Grant to Logan, December 17, 1864, *PUSG*, 13:127–28.

51. Brian Steele Wills offers a summary of these events in *George Henry Thomas: As True as Steel* (Lawrence: University Press of Kansas, 2012), 331–33, 338–44. This volume is the most detailed and deeply researched biography of Thomas.

52. Wilson, *Under the Old Flag*, 2:65.

53. Ibid., 2:66–67.

54. Simon and Wilson, "Beckwith," 116.

55. Thomas B. Buell, *The Warrior Generals: Combat Leadership in the Civil War* (New York: Crown, 1997), 398, 399–400.

56. Freeman Cleaves, *Rock of Chickamauga: The Life of General George H. Thomas* (Norman: University of Oklahoma Press, 1948), 259–60.

57. Grant to Schofield, August 1, 1881, *PUSG*, 30:252–53.

Union brigadier general John M. Corse held the fort at Allatoona Pass against vastly superior Confederate numbers. Library of Congress

Confederate major general Patrick R. Cleburne kept a diary during the campaign and later fell at Franklin. Library of Congress

Confederate lieutenant general Benjamin Franklin Cheatham was one of several officers involved in the confused affair at Spring Hill. Library of Congress

Confederate general John B. Hood hurled his army in a mass frontal assault at an entrenched Union force at Franklin. Library of Congress

Union major general George H. Thomas commanded the army that met Hood's Confederates at Nashville. Library of Congress

Ulysses S. Grant, general in chief of all Union armies, worried that Thomas was not moving quickly and aggressively enough to remove the threat of Hood's invasion. Library of Congress

Union major general Andrew Jackson Smith commanded a three-division detachment of the Army of the Tennessee that made important breakthroughs on both days of the Battle of Nashville. Library of Congress

7

WHERE GENIUS CANNOT EXIST

THE GENERALSHIP OF GEORGE H. THOMAS

Paul L. Schmelzer

> The student may be tempted to look for genius in places where it does not and cannot exist.
> —Carl von Clausewitz

Major General George H. Thomas enjoys an undeserved reputation for greatness among many Civil War historians. Thomas's advocates mistakenly find in his victory at Nashville evidence of military genius. Some go so far as to find Thomas the outstanding general of the war on either side. They find him superior to both Major General William T. Sherman and General Ulysses S. Grant, and attribute much of those soldiers' successes to him. They credit Thomas with "winning" the war in the West (and by implication to some the war as a whole), and speculate on the course of the war if Thomas rather than Grant had been raised to high command. Grant, in his memoirs, detailed problems with Thomas that nearly resulted in Thomas's dismissal on the very eve of his near total destruction of Hood's army. Thomas's reputation, according to the critics, unjustly suffered due to Grant's and Sherman's widely circulated accounts after the war. Writing no memoir left Thomas open to the unfair criticisms by Sherman and Grant. "Rehabilitating" Thomas requires a devaluing of Grant. Thomas's advocates contrast his systematic and careful planning with the more "improvisational" nature of Grant, who is "uninterested" in staff work. Such historians describe Grant as "less intelligent" than Thomas. They also credit Thomas with "coming nearer than any other general in the Civil War to the complete destruction of an opposing army," or achieving "what no other army commander achieved in the Civil War—the battle of annihilation."[1]

Advocates for Thomas are consistent in their critique of Grant's attempt to relieve Thomas and "freeze" him out of any major role in closing out the war, as well as of Grant's dispersing of most of Thomas's troops after the Battle of Nashville. Examining Grant's critics, both in their positive views of Thomas and negative assessments of Grant, it is possible to come to some conclusions about the relative merits of each man and his achievements.

A Question of Genius

Those effusive enough in their praise of Thomas to label him a military "genius" neglect to define the term. Genius is perhaps an overused expression, but any comparison/evaluation of a commander's performance requires a common standard. The German military writer Carl von Clausewitz is unique in his ability to provide such a standard. Clausewitz identified special conditions for using the term "genius" in the context of war and suggested a method and logic behind its application. Using Clausewitz's formulation, Thomas's advocates are "looking for genius where it cannot and will not exist." In general terms, Clausewitz reserves use of the word for those whose successes contribute politically to ending the war. "The effects of genius show not so much in novel forms of action as in the ultimate success of the whole." In short, Clausewitz suggests that those who look for genius in matters military should avoid looking to the battlefield itself, as genius cannot be found in tactics.[2]

Those critics who rate Thomas superior in intelligence to Grant may be correct. Those who comment on his attention to detail, the comprehensiveness of his plans and systematic methods (in contrast to Grant) may be correct as well. The question remains open if these qualities illustrate military genius, or if they describe something else entirely. Clausewitz prefers "a special type of mind . . . a strong, rather than a brilliant one," and suggests "rather than try to outbid the enemy with complicated schemes, one should on the contrary, try to outdo him in simplicity."[3] Genius in a military sense defines something other than mastery of some esoteric skill set of great complexity one might attribute to "genius" in a general sense. Whatever the merits of Thomas's comprehensive planning, systematic staff work, and preparedness for battle, he cannot be accused of outbidding his enemy with simplicity.

There are several reasons for Clausewitz's view. Historians tend to admire effective battlefield commanders and descriptions of decisive battles while neglecting the effects of such men and their battles on the "organic whole" as Clausewitz suggests. Clausewitz could be describing some of Thomas's advocates in his description below, some which seem particularly applicable to the Battle of Nashville. "Thus, such a commonplace maneuver as turning an opponent's flank may be hailed by critics as a stroke of genius, of deepest insight, or all-inclusive knowledge. Can one imagine anything so absurd? Where execution is dominant, as it is in the individual events of a war whether great or small, then intellectual factors are reduced to a minimum."[4]

If strategy is difficult, tactics seem less so. A. L. Conger also commented on the relative simplicity of tactical choices available to a commander: "roughly speaking, on the offensive one has the choice of attacking on the right flank, the left flank, or the center, or maneuvering against the rear."[5] The permutations of these simple choices are all easily countered and subject to chance and probability. Thomas at Nashville chose to attack his enemy's left flank. Thomas included feints that successfully distracted his enemy, and his cavalry maneuvered against Hood's rear. Hood did fail to counter Thomas's choices. His army proved unable to maintain its cohesion in the two-day battle, revealing perhaps as much about Hood's leadership and the state of his army as it does about Thomas's "genius." To apply Clausewitz's argument and take it to its logical conclusion, it is just as likely that Hood could have outguessed Thomas. He could have supported his flank, and not have been fooled by feints. Had Nathan Bedford Forrest been present, he might have stalemated Major General James H. Wilson's painstakingly remounted cavalry. In short a myriad of options were open to Hood, which could have made Thomas's assault on a fortified position miscarry, as so many assaults had in the past. Also Hood could have retreated, effectively negating all of Thomas's plans and meticulous preparations.

Clausewitz finds little of value in those critics who examine only the material factors of such battlefield combinations, excluding the moral and political factors driving strategy: "They reduce everything to a few mathematical formulas of equilibrium and superiority, of time and space, limited by a few angles and lines. If that were really all, it would hardly provide a scientific problem for a schoolboy."[6]

In contrast to almost all other theorists, Clausewitz fails to find that "*falling on an enemy's rear* is an accomplishment in itself." Like any other tactical formulation, "it has no value in isolation." In both strategy and tactics "forces sent to operate against the enemy's rear and flank are not available for use against his front." A flank attack in battle clearly comprises a tactical device, possibly advantageous, but typically precautions are taken against such attacks. A particular commander may excel in cunning, in the "game" element of tactics, outguessing or surprising his opponent during the execution of a flank attack (or through some other expedient), but the decisive confrontation might just as easily occur elsewhere (the front, for example).[7]

Clausewitz places battle in its proper place, not as an end in itself but as a means for attainment of some other goal. "War should be conceived as an organic whole whose parts cannot be separated, so that each individual act contributes to the whole and itself originates in the central concept."[8]

Clausewitz is also unique in attributing no special skill or advantage to another concept dear to the heart of many historians. B. H. Liddell-Hart, Herman Hattaway, and Archer Jones, along with many other military historians, find targeting weakness a laudable objective in and of itself. Such a view displays a serious disconnect in their analysis, failing to identify the links between the political goals of the war and the actual movements on the battlefield. Hattaway and Jones also suggest a method for strategy's application (similar to Liddell-Hart), finding the goal in strategy the same as in tactics: that of "producing tactical contact with the enemy at his weak spot."[9]

Clausewitz also found this line of thought wrongheaded. Targeting weakness often leaves enemy strength intact. Instead "the victor . . . must strike with all his strength and not just against a fraction of the enemy's. Not by taking the easy way but by constantly seeking out the enemy's power." Grant's directness, often mistaken for simplemindedness or a lack of imagination, always targeted his enemy's power.[10]

Armchair generals, like Monday-morning quarterbacks, often obsess over trivialities. Orders of battle, tactics, surprise, and matching strength to weakness do not comprise the heart of war. The "cunning" of a commander, like the false admiration critics reserve for an attack on the flank or rear, has "so little strategic value that they are used only if a ready-made opportunity presents itself."[11] While historical examples exist of success achieved through targeting weakness, through "brilliant" tactical combinations, through the "game" element on the battlefield, generally this is not the case.

Clausewitz continues, "Yet however much one longs to see opposing generals vie with one another in craft, cleverness, and cunning, the fact remains that these qualities do not figure prominently in the history of war. Rarely do they stand out amid the welter of events and circumstances."[12]

The sagacious critic looks to strategy, political results, and the success of the whole, a complexity that "Newton himself would quail before." Few would find George H. Thomas's tactics deficient, "where execution is dominant" and "intellectual forces are reduced to a minimum," on the battlefield itself. A more important question regards his understanding of the use of battle to further the aims of the war and his role in that process.[13]

A Question of Strategy, Tactics, and Victory

> Strategy is the use of the engagement for the object of war.
> —Carl von Clausewitz

Thomas's reputation must rise or fall on his performance in the Nashville Campaign, where he enjoyed the greatest measure of independence. As a theater commander Thomas's responsibilities grew tremendously as oversight by superiors diminished. At Chickamauga, Thomas's stand earned him the nickname "Rock of Chickamauga." There his tactical prowess and battlefield courage salvaged to some extent his superior's mistakes. At Chattanooga, his army again saved a failed tactical situation as his attack on the Confederate center succeeded when Sherman's flanking movement was effectively countered. But Thomas's principle independent achievement, the Battle of Nashville, and the moves leading to it, remained tactical. Thomas sought the perfect plan, sought the perfect instrument of war, and viewed the engagement itself as the overriding perfection of his craft.

Colonel Henry Stone of Thomas's staff admiringly said of his commander, "He realized too keenly the importance of victory to allow anything that might secure it to be neglected." Stone betrays his own and Thomas's lack of understanding of the true purpose of battle, stating, "compared with the destruction of Hood's army nothing else was of any account." However desirable "victory" in battle and the "destruction" of Hood's army, destruction in and of itself guarantees nothing. Just as Thomas's army operated in one of the multiple theaters under Grant's command, winning battles provided just one of the many components of his strategy to end the war. Grant's strategy required that Thomas negate Hood and unleash his army in the interior of the Confederacy *à la* Sherman, as rapidly as possible, regardless of the *degree* of Hood's defeat.[14]

Robert E. Lee, perhaps the foremost tactician of the Civil War, "won" most of his battles but arguably failed to turn tactical ability into a lasting strategic advantage. The link between tactical triumph in Northern Virginia and winning the war remained as elusive for the generally "successful" Lee as it did for generally unsuccessful other commanders. In contrast, Grant's Overland Campaign closing out the war included many tactical reversals, draws, and victories of only marginal tactical value. Thomas's tactical successes at Chickamauga and Chattanooga (as a subordinate commander) and at Nashville are only relevant, as Clausewitz suggests, in their contribution to winning the war as a whole.

Clausewitz distinguishes between actions whose effects reach into the political dimension (strategy), and the nuts and bolts of individual battles or even theater-size engagements, that may or may not have larger strategic implications. Above all, strategy in a Clausewitzian sense defines something essentially separate from and superior to tactics and the winning of battles.

There are situations when fighting a battle, even a successful one, may in itself be counterproductive. Clausewitz described this irony: "Strategy decides the time when, the place where, and the forces with which the engagement is to be fought. Once the tactical encounter has taken place and the result—be it victory or defeat—is assured, strategy will use it to serve the object of the war."[15]

After interminable delays to reequip (especially his cavalry), Thomas delivered a crushing blow at Nashville, wrecking Hood's army. This carefully orchestrated and technically well-organized demolition of Hood reaped no commensurate strategic (read, political) advantage. Sherman outmaneuvered Hood; or rather Hood had outmaneuvered himself strategically, months before his actual destruction. The construct designed by Grant and Sherman rendered both Thomas and Hood almost moot to the final results of the war before their battle even took place. Hood accomplished his own irrelevance by moving north rather than continuing to confront Sherman. Hood then mistakenly waited at Nashville for his own demolition while Thomas reequipped. Certainly his self-destructive assault at Franklin achieved results far beyond those Thomas could have inflicted offensively in the same time period. Thomas's continued delays allowed Hood time to fortify, requiring yet more delays to ensure the success of the set-piece battle he desired. Secretary of War Edwin M. Stanton remarked to Grant of his and Lincoln's concerns: "This looks like the [Major General George B.] McClellan and [Major General William S.] Rosecrans strategy of do nothing and let the rebels raid the country."[16]

The political climate of the period, the pressures from Washington and Grant, seem to have had little or no effect on Thomas. Convinced of the rightness of his plan and his perception of the situation, Thomas entered his fortifications, built his army, and allowed Hood to fortify. Thomas seemed unconcerned about the political implications of his actions, or lack thereof. Every military move makes policy. Much as Lee repeatedly "terrified Washington" by sending a Stonewall Jackson or a Jubal Early into the Shenandoah Valley, Hood's move also "terrified Washington." Whatever the true potential of Jackson or Early to seriously threaten Washington, or Hood's ability to actually cross the Cumberland, the political effects were real and Thomas should have dealt with them on their own terms. Political pressures to attack, justified or not from a purely military standpoint, nearly resulted in Thomas's dismissal. Regardless of one's views of the political climate driving exhortations from Washington, or Grant's supposed "micromanagement" in advocating immediate action, Thomas's dismissal would have rendered his "correct" strategy, correct tactics, "perfect" plan, and supposed military genius immaterial.[17]

Thomas's supporters laud his resistance to political pressure and question the appropriateness of "Washington's shackles," as if battles take place in a political vacuum. Clausewitz's most famous thesis describes war as merely an extension of politics. Clausewitz replied to critics of this view: "When people talk, as they often do, about the harmful political influence on the management of war, they are not really saying what they mean. Their quarrel should be with the policy itself, not its influence."[18]

A Question of Time

> Our belief then is that any kind of interruption, pause, or suspension of activity is inconsistent with the nature of offensive war.
> —Carl von Clausewitz

> I determined to retire to the fortifications around Nashville, until General Wilson can get his cavalry equipped.
> —George H. Thomas

> Why not attack at once?
> —Ulysses S. Grant

Time accrues to the advantage of the defender. Clausewitz explained some of the reasons for this phenomenon. While halting "could make offensive war easier," it does not make its results more certain. The reasons given for halting "usually camouflage misgivings on the part of the general or vacillation on the part of the government." In addition, anything time allows an attacker to accomplish generally will equally benefit a defender (such as the bringing up of supplies and reinforcements or refitting and reorganizing). Time also generally benefits the weaker psychologically. It allows a defender time to recover his moral balance and exploit other options, look for additional allies or methods to weaken or divide his enemies.[19]

Clausewitz typically qualifies his views; none of these observations is absolute. In this case supplies and reinforcements probably worked to Thomas's advantage more than Hood's. Time did allow Hood to "refit and reorganize," and most significantly fortify. Clausewitz's other observations seem to apply fairly to Thomas before Nashville. Thomas had "misgivings" about facing an enemy with "deficient" cavalry. In this case "government" had no reservations but rather advocated an attack. The time Thomas took did allow Hood at least to some extent to "recover his moral balance." Fortunately for the Union, Hood largely wasted his reprieve and failed to exploit other options.

Grant's views on offensive war mirrored those of Clausewitz. Grant suggested to Thomas, "time strengthens him in all possibility as much as you." Clausewitz offered, "offensive war requires above all a quick, irresistible decision." Grant suggested to Thomas that after the repulse of Hood at Franklin, instead of falling back to Nashville and entering its fortifications, "we should have taken the offensive against the enemy where he was." Clausewitz disdained the use of fortifications in offensive war, as "fortifying towns and positions is no business for the army and therefore no excuse for suspending operations."[20]

Grant also advised, "you should attack him before he fortifies," before Hood's troops regained their moral balance. Grant's experience at Vicksburg led him to similar conclusions as Clausewitz. At Vicksburg a beaten enemy quickly recovered its moral balance once behind its fortifications, bloodily repulsing Grant's assaults.[21]

Some of the options available to Hood given Thomas's delays were laid out by Grant: "It looks to me evident the enemy are trying to cross the Cumberland River. . . . There is great danger of delay resulting in a campaign back to the Ohio River." Grant also expressed concern (similar to that of Lincoln and Stanton) about Confederate raiders: "Is there not danger of Forrest moving down the Cumberland to where he can cross it?" Grant also offered, "You will now suffer incalculable injury upon your railroads if Hood is not speedily disposed of."[22]

Grant intuitively knew of the condition of Hood's army despite being hundreds of miles away in Washington. At the time, not subject to hindsight, he wrote Thomas: "Hood cannot even stand a drawn battle so far from his supplies of ordnance stores. If he retreats and you follow, he must lose his material and much of his army." In his memoirs Grant was more explicit: "He [Thomas] had troops enough even to annihilate him in the open field." When the battle actually took place Hood's army disintegrated.[23]

A Question of Victory

> One may marvel just as much at the remarkable results of some victories as at the lack of results of others.
>
> —Carl von Clausewitz

Sherman commented on some remarkable results of his own "victories." "I regard my two moves from Atlanta to Savannah and Savannah to Goldsborough as great blows as if we had fought a dozen successful battles." Sherman was commenting in purely moral or political terms, as in material terms he had fought no great battles and few general engagements at all.[24]

Clausewitz asks a simple question: "what exactly does 'defeat' signify?" He could also have phrased the question differently and reached the same conclusion: what exactly does "victory" signify? In multiple examples from the Napoleonic and French Revolutionary wars, he illustrates the impossibility of an answer to these simple questions. Instead, keeping the dominant characteristics of both belligerents in mind, "a certain center of gravity develops, the hub of all power and movement on which everything depends." Defining the center of gravity defines the proper target of military operations, "the point against which all our energies should be directed." Clausewitz suggests three rather obvious possibilities, derived from general experiences, and typically qualifies each: destruction of an enemy's army, "*if it is at all significant*"; seizure of his capital, "*if it is not only the center of administration, but also that of social, professional and political activity*"; defeat of a principle ally, "*if that ally is more powerful than he.*"[25]

By the time of Sherman's march to Savannah, Hood's army had lost much of its significance. Hood's move into Tennessee guaranteed it would play no part in closing out the war. The center of gravity by this time existed in the East, with Lee's army (rather than with Hood's in the West) and that "center of administration, social, professional and political activity," Richmond. If not for Union misperceptions of Hood's potential for further offensive action, his army at Nashville could have been left in place to wither while Sherman's men "were absolutely annihilating the Southern Confederacy."[26]

Clausewitz observed: "Yet both these things may be done (destruction of the enemy's forces and the country occupied) and the war . . . cannot be considered to have ended so long as the enemy's will has not been broken." One could argue that Hood's army's will was broken as much by Hood's ill-advised attacks at Franklin as by Thomas's actions as Nashville. In the Confederacy as a whole Sherman's depredations proved decisive in breaking the enemy's will. Sherman predicted before his famous march, "Even without battle the results, operating upon the minds of sensible men, would produce fruits more than compensating for the expense, trouble, and risk." Union troops marching through Georgia confirmed: "war and individual ruin are synonymous terms" in a way a victory in Virginia or a defeat in Tennessee are not. Predictably, individual soldiers from the areas transited by Sherman deserted in large numbers and Southern governors retained or recalled troops from national service. Grant's use of Sherman demolished the faith, hopes, and wishful thinking propping up the Confederate war effort. If we include Nashville along with Sherman's "dozen" victories, plus those by Grant targeting Lee's army and Richmond, we get a clearer understanding of the use of the engagement to achieve the ends of war and also the relative significance of the Battle of Nashville in that process.[27]

A Question of Annihilation

Thomas pulled off what no other army commander achieved
in the Civil War—the battle of annihilation.
—Geoffrey Perret

He came nearer than any other general in the Civil War
to the complete destruction of an opposing army.
—Peter Parish

A headcount revealed barely half the 40,000 who had
marched northward seven weeks earlier.
—James McPherson

Whatever the merits of Thomas's demolition of Hood it probably does not properly qualify as a "battle of annihilation." Annihilation implies total destruction, a situation demonstratively untrue materially. Thomas's advocates have a better case for moral annihilation—annihilation of the enemy's will. Hood's army never operated as a coherent unit after Nashville, though many of its "annihilated" component units served with Joe Johnston confronting Sherman in the Carolinas. Of some forty thousand present at the beginning of the Tennessee Campaign, Thomas at Nashville inflicted somewhere around eight thousand casualties and Hood suffered some twenty thousand casualties in the entire campaign.[28]

Although definitions of a "battle of annihilation" can properly differ, the term implies near if not total destruction. Alfred von Schlieffen looked to Hannibal's triumph at Cannae as a model and meticulously evaluated great battles throughout history in relation to that model. In von Schlieffen's view, battles of annihilation require envelopment; double is better than single; a flank attack (turning movement too) is better than head on. By von Schlieffen's criteria Nashville would represent at best a "marginal" battle of annihilation. Von Schlieffen also suggested other criteria necessary for pulling off battles of annihilation: "a Hannibal is needed on one side, and a Terentius Varro on the other."[29]

At Nashville Hood provided the Terentius Varro. After failure to trap or damage Major General John M. Schofield at Springhill, Hood "was now inspired by a berserker frenzy akin to madness." It is difficult to take issue with evaluations such as David Eicher's: "If Hood mortally wounded his army at Franklin, he would kill it two weeks later at Nashville." Von Schlieffen of course, had chosen the wrong model. In common with many of the greatest battles of annihilation in history, whether brought about by flank attack, maneuver toward the rear, or double envelopment, Cannae proved politically indecisive. Rome won the war. Cannae, as Clausewitz suggests, provides just another example of clever constructs that "do not stand out amid the welter of events and circumstances" in the history of war. Historically, even true battles of annihilation provide surprisingly mixed results in winning wars. The near-absolute destruction at Cannae, like the "marginal" annihilation at Nashville, produced no war-winning results. The greatest such battle in material terms, fought by the Germans at Kiev in 1941, in a similar manner produced no decisive results.[30]

Grant captured three armies during the Civil War, in contrast to all other Civil War generals who, taken together, captured none. Grant's triumphs, all of which included the use of maneuver and fortifications, comprise the only "battles of annihilation" in the Civil War. The last of these, coupled with the fall of Richmond, provided the final significant act of the war.

Grant bests all other Civil War generals in using engagements, be they "victories" or "defeats," for the object of war. Defining policy at the point of bloodshed (the engagement) and coupling the engagement further to a campaign, and multiple campaigns to the achievement of the object of war, defines a great complexity. The difficulty lies in determining how killing, occupying territory, or even destroying armies creates "war-winning" political change. Then as now, most soldiers and scholars fail to distinguish between two essentially distinct military acts: killing and victory. Military success, in and of itself, often generates great political change, but even a brief examination of the historical record reveals many exceptions to the "rule" that theory cannot ignore. The killing at Nashville generated political change only tangential to ending the war.[31]

Grant versus Thomas

> I have carefully searched the military records of both ancient and modern history, and have never found Grant's superior as a general.
>
> —Robert E. Lee

Francis F. McKinney, author of *Education in Violence*, considered Thomas the man most responsible for Grant's success. Grant himself probably deserves that credit. However much one admires Thomas's building of folding pontoons, innovative use of railroads, and organization of a cavalry corps, "like had never been seen on the American continent," however great his tactical contribution to Grant's victories at Chattanooga and Nashville, and however great his administrative abilities, one ultimately finds little commonality to make a truly valid comparison possible.[32]

As interesting as these discussions may be for some historians, as much as we long "to see opposing generals vie with one another in craft, cleverness, and cunning," a historian making such a comparison is comparing apples and oranges, or in this case tacticians and strategists. Thomas's great battlefield success at Nashville represents something far less than and apart from Grant's function as commander of all the Union armies. This is more than a problem of semantics. Whatever choices the historian makes (for example, one could label Grant a *grand* strategist, Thomas a *battlefield* strategist), Thomas exhibits no equivalency with Grant in level of responsibility or political accomplishment no matter how one defines the term "strategy," or whatever parameters one chooses in making such a comparison.[33]

One would speculate that Clausewitz would find such comparisons and controversies trivial, given his disdain for any discussion of war divorced from its political context. The question of a couple of weeks delay, whether the advantages Thomas derived from attacking later balances out other advantages gained from attacking before Hood's entrenchment, whether the "completeness" of Thomas's victory would have been diminished by prompter action all represent the minutia of war, not its substance.

In a larger sense we can never know if Thomas could have handled Lincoln, Stanton, and a Benjamin Butler on the road to a final victory, or if he could have brought a Robert E. Lee to defeat. Any direct comparison with Grant as general in chief is purely speculative. Battlefield success generally makes politics easier. If Thomas's advocates have correctly evaluated his martial abilities, he may have done well, especially in comparison to McClellan, Halleck, and the many other Union generals who proved unable to win battles.

Grant always claimed his risky moves at Vicksburg were determined by political circumstance: "The elections of 1862 had gone against the prosecution of the war. Voluntary enlistments had nearly ceased and the draft had been resorted to; this was resisted, and a defeat or backward movement would have made its execution impossible." As even some of Thomas's supporters would concede, it is difficult to imagine him improvising operations or launching a campaign to satisfy purely political conditions.[34]

A great deal of the controversy regarding Thomas's being "slow" revolves around his remount of Wilson's cavalry. Organizationally and administratively Thomas did organize a highly effective unit, "like had never been seen on the American continent." Grant weighed in on Wilson's operations and others after Nashville, typically looking to the political effects generated rather than their military effectiveness. Grant found Wilson's and Stone's clear tactical successes failed to serve the object of war: "they were all eminently successful, but without any good result." Coming too late in the war to contribute to the final destruction of the Confederacy they proved potentially damaging to the war aim of reunion and reconciliation. Grant lamented the unnecessary loss of lives and property destroyed when he wished to spare them, for their wastefulness and also for their negative effects, both moral and material, on opponents soon expected to return to the Union.[35]

Clausewitz perceptively conceded that though it remains the first consideration, "the political aim is not a tyrant." The political aim "must adapt itself to its chosen means, a process which can radically change it." The question remains whether Grant, in his dealings with Thomas, was turning the political aim into a tyrant. Politics required that Thomas act. Grant deferred to him, as the man on the spot, repeatedly. As the process unfolded the weather intervened, again preventing action. The weather, of course, would not have been a factor had Thomas not retired to his fortifications and taken time to remount his cavalry, as Grant advised.[36]

Though he did begin the process to accomplish Thomas's removal, the steps he took were systematic and ultimately involved removing himself from his own command and traveling west to deal with Thomas personally. At this point Thomas acted, fulfilling the requirements of policy and those of Grant. Clausewitz observed that freedom of choice, often available in tactics, is not necessarily available in strategy. While Thomas enjoyed the luxury of tactical choice, to fortify, to remount cavalry, to plan and reorganize his army, fewer options were available to Grant. Hood's advance appeared to the north as a great menace and a defeat as cities such as Nashville had not been threatened for years. Sherman had not yet emerged from his great march. Northerners feared that if Sherman were destroyed, as Jefferson Davis had predicted, and if Hood reached the Ohio, as Lincoln feared, that the course of the war could turn. All of these concerns made up the political context in which Thomas operated and seemingly ignored.

Clausewitz stated in one of the last writings before his death, "War cannot be divorced from its political life." Any thinking about war removed from its political whole leaves us "with something pointless and devoid of sense." Thomas's reluctance to act and think politically was pointless and devoid of sense. Though an excellent tactician and courageous fighter, he failed to tailor those excellent qualities to Grant's overall strategy to win the war. Thomas, in J. F. C. Fuller's correct estimation, remains strategically "a man of parochial vision."[37]

Notes

1. Francis F. McKinney, *Education in Violence: The Life of George H. Thomas and the Army of the Cumberland* (Detroit: Wayne State University Press, 1961), 300, for a description of Thomas as a military genius; viii, identifies Thomas as the man "who, above all others, made Grant's career a success." See 301, 302, for Grant's deficiencies as a staff officer with a penchant for improvisation. See Thomas B. Buell, *The Warrior Generals: Combat Leadership in the Civil War* (New York: Crown, 1997) and Albert Castel, *Decision in the West: The Atlanta Campaign of 1864* (Lawrence: University of Kansas Press, 1992) for Thomas's superiority to all other Civil War generals. Donn Piatt, *General George H. Thomas: A Critical Biography* (Cincinnati: Robert Clarke and Co., 1893) offers a "what-if" approach to historical analysis. See Peter Parish, *The American Civil War* (New York: Holmes and Meier, 1975), 483, and Geoffrey Perret, *A Country Made by War* (New York: Random House, 1989), 248, 251, for battle of annihilation quotes.

2. Carl von Clausewitz, *On War* (Princeton: Princeton University Press, 1984), 178.

3. Ibid., 108, 229, 103.

4. Ibid., 178.

5. A. L. Conger, *Rise of U. S. Grant* (New York: Century, 1931), 298.

6. Clausewitz, *On War*, 460.

7. Emphasis in original; ibid., 585–86.

8. Ibid., 607.

9. Herman Hattaway and Archer Jones, *How the North Won* (Chicago: University of Illinois Press, 1983), 711, 420–21.

10. Clausewitz and Grant of course understood that you could target power indirectly, and achieve positive results, even if no fighting actually occurs. Clausewitz, *On War*, 596.

11. Ibid., 198–203; Conger, *Rise*, 221, 243.

12. Ibid., 202.

13. Ibid., 586.

14. J. F. C. Fuller, *The Generalship of Ulysses S. Grant* (London: Da Capo Press, 1929), 327.

15. Clausewitz, *On War*, 88, 194, 256.

16. Hattaway and Jones, *How the North Won*, 649.

17. J. F. C. Fuller, *Grant and Lee: A Study in Personality and Generalship* (Bloomington: Indiana University Press, 1957), 253, finds "terrifying Washington," Lee's grand strategic principle.

18. McKinney, *Education in Violence*, 300; Clausewitz, *On War*, 112.

19. Clausewitz, *On War*, 599, 598.

20. Ibid.; Ulysses S. Grant, *Personal Memoirs of Ulysses S. Grant* (New York: Charles L. Webster and Company, 1885–86), 1:566, 567.

21. Grant, *Memoirs*, 2:277.

22. John A. Wyeth, *Life of Nathan Bedford Forrest* (Baton Rouge: Louisiana State University Press, 1989), 546–51, details Forrest's "raiding the countryside" as Lincoln and Stanton feared.

23. Grant, *Memoirs*, 2:379–80.

24. William T. Sherman, *Home Letters of General Sherman*, ed. M. A. deWolf Howe (New York: Scribners, 1909), 337.

25. Emphasis in original; Clausewitz, *On War*, 595–96.

26. Ibid., 90. *Battles and Leaders of the Civil War*, 4 vols. (New York: Thomas Yoseloff, repr. 1956), 4:249.

27. Clausewitz, *On War*, 90; U.S. War Department, *The War of the Rebellion: A Compilation of the Official Records of the Union and Confederate Armies*, 128 vols. (Washington, DC: Government Printing Office, 1881–1901), ser. 1, vol. 38, pt. 3: 162 (hereafter referred to as *OR*; all references are to ser. 1 unless otherwise noted); Walter Millis, *American Military Thought* (New York: Bobbs-Merrill, 1966), 159; Joseph T. Glatthar, *Partners in Command: The Relationships Between Leaders in the Civil War* (New York: Free Press, 1994), 158; *OR*, vol. 39, pt. 3: 378.

28. James McPherson, *Battle Cry of Freedom: The Civil War Era* (New York: Oxford University Press, 1988), 815. Hattaway and Jones, *How the North Won*, 652, cite substantially lower figures (six thousand total losses) for Hood.

29. Alfred von Schlieffen, *Cannae* (Leavenworth, KS: U.S. Army Command and General Staff College Press, 1931), quoted in Hattaway and Jones, *How the North Won*, 683.

30. See Albert Seaton, *The Russo-German War 1941–45* (New York: Praeger, 1971), 141–52, for a description of the Kiev double envelopment and its indecisiveness. Henry Coppee, *General Thomas* (New York: D. Appleton, 1893) 254; David Eicher, *The Longest Night: A Military History of the Civil War* (New York: Simon and Schuster, 2001), 771.

31. William S. McFeely, *Grant: A Biography* (New York: W. W. Norton, 1981), 78, credits Grant with a superior understanding of the simple notion that "to make war is to kill." While "true," Grant's superiority stems from his ability to make something out of a battle beyond mere killing.

32. McKinney, *Education in Violence*, viii, ix.

33. Fuller, *Generalship*, 7, finds the term "grand strategy" would be more comprehensible if labeled "political strategy," while the more commonly used term "strategy" (like that of Thomas at Nashville) should be called "field strategy."

34. McKinney, *Education in Violence*, 302; Grant, *Memoirs*, 301.

35. Grant, *Memoirs*, 571.

36. Clausewitz, *On War*, 87.

37. Fuller, *Generalship*, 337, 168; John Y. Simon, *Papers of Ulysses S. Grant*, vol. 13, *November 16, 1864–February 20, 1865* (Carbondale: Southern Illinois University Press, 1985), 273.

8

"NO MORE AUCTION BLOCK FOR ME"
THE FIGHT FOR FREEDOM BY THE U.S. COLORED TROOPS AT THE BATTLE OF NASHVILLE

D. L. Turner and Scott L. Stabler

On October 16, 1905, a letter to the editor of New York City's *Sun* newspaper appeared expressing the belief that black soldiers had *not* actively participated in preserving the Union during the Civil War. The writer also questioned, "Can it be proved that any of our colored soldiers killed any rebels? If so, where?"[1] Within days, a rebuttal appeared from an eyewitness to the Battle of Nashville—a decisive engagement during which two provisional brigades of U.S. Colored Troops (USCT) played significant roles. Referencing the conflict the respondent stated, "On the occasion of the charge at Nashville, the negroes fought like savages. . . ."[2] Aside from winning acclaim for their valor in combat, for the first time black soldiers played a prominent role in the initial combat of a major battle during the Civil War. With their assistance, Union forces broke the back of the Confederate army in the West. The USCT were significant protagonists at the Battle of Nashville. Because of this role, they fulfilled the first line of a slave liberation song that proclaimed, "No more auction block for me, No more, no more!"[3] They also helped to preserve the Union, won respect, opened new doors of opportunity, and earned an important place for themselves in history.[4]

Despite these accomplishments, the perception that African Americans served as the only people in the history of the world that made no effort of their own to win their freedom existed well into the twentieth century. Historians too often focused predominantly on white generals.[5] Fortunately, efforts to recognize and understand the military contributions of the USCT during the Civil War prevail today. Preeminent historian James McPherson writes in his 1965 *Negro's Civil War*, "Blacks were active in the movements to bring education, suffrage, and land to Southern freedmen. And perhaps most importantly of all, the contribution of Negro soldiers helped the North

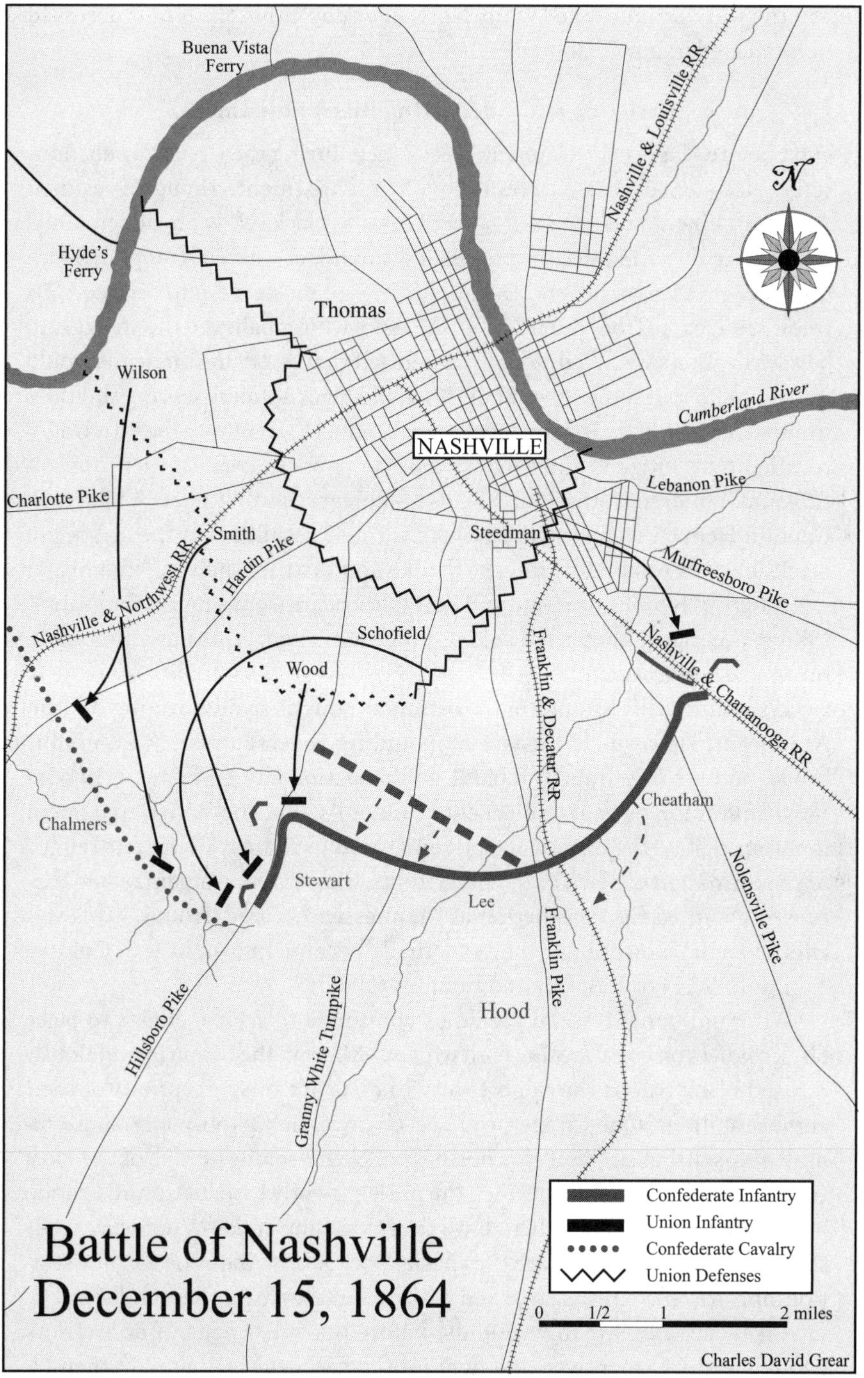
Buena Vista Ferry
Hyde's Ferry
Thomas
Wilson
Nashville & Louisville RR
N
Cumberland River
NASHVILLE
Lebanon Pike
Charlotte Pike
Smith
Steedman
Hardin Pike
Murfreesboro Pike
Nashville & Northwest RR
Schofield
Nashville & Chattanooga RR
Wood
Franklin & Decatur RR
Cheatham
Chalmers
Stewart
Lee
Nolensville Pike
Franklin Pike
Hood
Hillsboro Pike
Granny White Turnpike
Confederate Infantry
Union Infantry
Confederate Cavalry
Union Defenses
Battle of Nashville
December 15, 1864
0
1/2
1
2 miles
Charles David Grear

win the war and convinced many Northern people that the Negro deserved to be treated as a man and an equal."[6]

Resisting and Advocating Black Enlistment

Even before "facing the elephant," black men during the Civil War encountered many encumbrances on the path to enlistment. Though President Abraham Lincoln realized the value of arming blacks early on, he remained reluctant to do so. In 1862, the president dismantled "colored" troops in South Carolina that Union general David Hunter had mustered into service.[7] His trepidation came from public opinion. Many whites believed the struggle to be a white man's war. Additionally, others felt that African Americans would not fight and found the thought of white and black soldiers serving shoulder to shoulder repulsive. Former Lieutenant Colonel E. H. Low of the 55th USCT recalled that "citizens and soldiers took no pains to conceal their opposition and contempt for; saying 'the d——d negroes won't fight.'"[8] Likewise, Captain Henry Romeyn of the 14th USCT also recalled that the arming of blacks elicited remarks of intense dislike and distrust such as, "The nigger won't fight"; "No white private will ever take orders from a nigger Sergeant!"; "When the nigger becomes a soldier I'll resign!"; and, "Don't ask me ever to recognize a nigger officer!"[9]

Lincoln initially listened to the dissonant sounds against arming African Americans. However, in the face of mounting Federal losses, he eventually broadened his war aims to include emancipation and enlistment. In May 1863, Union forces began to accept black enlistees. The War Department then established the Bureau of Colored Troops to address all matters related to the formation of black or "colored" units. Those troops organized in Tennessee obtained the designation as "Tennessee Colored Troops." This was later changed, however, as they eventually became known as U.S. Colored Troops (USCT) or U.S. Colored Infantry (USCI).[10]

After enlistment, racial prejudice continued to stymie efforts to place black soldiers on equal footing with whites.[11] Many in the Union incredulously refused black troops the opportunity to disprove misperceptions of their combat abilities. One Copperhead speech given on October 1, 1864, exemplified this disbelief: "Now this business of Negro soldiers is one of the most contemptible and foolish in which the pre-eminently foolish Administration has ever been engaged. Where have they done any good? Where have they stood under fire? Yet they are the special pets of this Abolition Administration, and are receiving its favor and praises. But they are useless and worse."[12]

Likewise, an Ohioan wrote just before his enlistment, "I don't think enough of the Nigger to go and fight for them. I would rather fight them."[13]

Sergeant Enoch Baker also wrote his wife about the controversy, stating, "It Will raise a rebellion in the army that all abolitionists this Side of hell could not Stop."[14] Laboring under this general attitude, General William T. Sherman refused to have blacks serve as soldiers in his command. Instead, he used them predominantly as common laborers. The commander even banned their recruitment, writing, "I believe that negroes better serve the Army as teamsters, pioneers, and servants, and have no objection to the surplus, if any, being enlisted as soldiers, but I must have labor and a large quantity of it."[15]

Attitudes such as these frequently contributed to the "Sambo" effect, or the perception that African Americans by nature were docile, weak-minded human beings who needed guidance from whites in order to survive. Anecdotes illustrating this notion appeared frequently in local newspapers. These items featured blacks named "Sambo" or "Cuffee" as comic foils. Editorials and commentaries also stated that black men did not comprehend the meaning of freedom and were therefore incapable of self-support or full citizenship.[16] One editor expressed this sentiment as follows: "So far, the Government has thought for him, acted for him, fed and clothed him and lionized him. Thus cared for and freed from labor, Sambo's most exalted conception of freedom has been fully realized. But alas! For him, the dream will soon be dissipated. True, Uncle Sam will still think for him, through the Bureau [Freedmen's Bureau] but then, Sambo will have to go to work again—'to lay down the fiddle and the bow,' and take up 'the shovel and the hoe.'"[17]

Time and expediency eventually worked to overcome such inhibitions, but not without their own peculiar set of circumstances. Many newly freed men exhibited signs of abuse, both physical and emotional. Some bore scars from whips and lashes on their bodies or were unaccustomed to full rations—habitually consuming several days' worth in a single sitting. Many men also required instruction and encouragement in acquiring desirable military attributes related to comportment and personal hygiene due to a lifetime of forced groveling as slaves. Despite these initial hurdles, many recruits proved quick studies and within a short time overcame most of the unhealthy habits.[18]

Transformation in attitudes toward blacks in the army also came as some white soldiers reached the conclusion that a black body could stop a bullet as well as a white one. This attitude was reflected in an irreverent but popular poem that circulated for several years entitled "Miles O'Reilly on the 'Naygurs.'" Sung to the tune of "The Low-Backed Car," the lyrics of this tune appeared on the front page of one Kansas newspaper on the first day of the Battle of Nashville. It read in part:

Some tell us 'tis a burnin' shame
To make the naygurs fight,
An' that the thrade of being kilt
Belongs but to the white;
But as for me, upon my sowl!
So liberal are we here,
I'll let Sambo be murthered in place of myself,
On ivery day in the year!
On ivery day in the year, boys,
An' ivery hour of the day,
The right to be kilt I'll divide wid him,
An' divil a word I'll say . . . [19]

In a more respectful tone, changes in the demeanor of black enlistees often convinced whites that this new approach could provide a foundation for these men to begin their transformation from former slave into that of citizen. One outside source gave an example of this after inspecting the camp of the 14th USCT, a force made up of 950 enlisted men, all but eight of which were former slaves:

> Their camp was the cleanest we had ever seen, and their appearance and drill unsurpassed. The colonel has full confidence in their fighting qualities, and one of the captains remarked that they could not fail in action with such stuff as their men are made of. The chaplain teaches them three hours a day, and many can read and write. The sight of that regiment on dress parade, with every head bare to heaven as the chaplain lifted up his voice and prayed that they might be strong and quit themselves like men in the day of battle, was one never to be forgotten. Adjoining their camp was that of the 42nd U.S.C.T., a regiment now forming and containing about 150 men. The contrast between the slouching gait and slovenly appearance of the raw recruits, some of who still had on their plantation clothes, and the soldierly bearing of the disciplined men, was very marked.[20]

The best example of transformation came from a private. In letters to his wife in March 1863, Charles Willis, of the 8th Illinois, initially compared USCT troops to eight-year-olds. Only one month later, he made an "honest confession." At that time, he wished to "put muskets in the hands of the latter." By June, he had come full circle writing home that he was considering "applying for a position in a [black] regiment myself." Changes in Union soldiers' attitudes continued to take place throughout the war.[21]

The experiment proved successful nearly everywhere the USCT fought. Two particular brigades of black infantry fought bravely at Nashville, most of whom hailed from Tennessee. Comprising Colonel Thomas J. Morgan's First Brigade were the 14th, 17th, 18th, and 44th USCT. Colonel Charles R. Thompson commanded the Second Brigade, a unit that included the 12th, 13th, and 100th USCT.[22] These troops eventually rewarded Lincoln and General George H. Thomas, commander of the Army of the Cumberland, through their heroics on the field during the Battle of Nashville.[23] The president later wrote in response to critics of his decision to enlist black troops, "More than a year of trial now shows . . . no loss by it any how or any where."[24]

While black troops were novel, so too were their white officers. Early on, officials of the Bureau of Colored Troops determined that only white officers of high caliber could lead black troops. In a civil service–style policy shift, the U.S. Army made a conscious effort—perhaps for the first time ever on a large scale—to match skill and leadership ability to job demands.[25] Advocating a greater degree of professionalism, examination boards felt duty bound to produce the best white leaders possible to command black troops.[26]

White officers of black troops faced additional challenges not presented to their counterparts. Service amongst the USCT proved life threatening off the field as well as on. Members of USCT units suffered greater animosity from their Confederate enemies than their white Union counterparts. For black soldiers, capture often meant reenslavement or execution.[27] White officers likewise were threatened with death upon capture. One example of this took place on February 2, 1865. At that time Colonel L. Johnson reported from Chattanooga that on December 20, 1864, soon after the Battle of Nashville, that Captain Charles G. Penfield of the 44th USCT, Lieutenant George W. Fitch of the 12th USCT, and Lieutenant Cooke of the 17th USCT were apprehended by Confederate scouts under General Nathan Bedford Forrest. As captives, southerners marched these men to a spot near Columbia, Tennessee, and shot them all. Left for dead, Lieutenant Fitch survived and escaped to tell the tale.[28]

Undeterred and despite their inexperience in combat, USCT leadership in Tennessee worked tirelessly to gain recognition of the combat ability of black troops and a front-line position in the fight. Though his men habitually performed guard and picket duty, hard manual labor, or foraged for supplies, Colonel Morgan argued tirelessly for opportunities that allowed his men to prove themselves in battle. His petitions acquired strength when the USCT evidenced their worth in actions fought at Decatur, Alabama, Pulaski, Tennessee, and Dalton, Georgia.[29] At Dalton, an engagement that occurred on August 15, 1864, the 14th and the 44th USCT served admirably.[30] Encounters such as these not only impressed whites, but also gave black soldiers confidence. The USCT did so well during the engagement at Dalton that the white regiment serving with them, according to Morgan, "swung their hats and gave three rousing cheers" when the black troops passed.[31] These experiences militated white concerns.

The Battle of Nashville

Black troops figured prominently into Union goals of retaining possession of western lands. Approximately fifty thousand black men mustered into service, with thirteen thousand of them stationed at Nashville under General George Thomas.[32] Though General Thomas supported emancipation as a means to stop the Confederates ability to "bear against us all the strength of their so-called Confederate States," he, and others were not yet convinced of the black soldier's ability to fight—an attitude that would soon change.[33]

Four major Union commands took part in the Battle of Nashville. These included troops under the command of Major General James Blair Steedman, then commander of the provisional detachment in the district of the Etowah. Included as part of Steedman's command were two black regiments, the 14th and 44th.[34]

Like Thomas, Steedman initially held reservations regarding black soldiers.[35] By the time of the Battle of Nashville, however, his doubts had already evaporated. This occurred during the battle at Dalton when the black regiments under his command performed so worthily.[36] Following this, he also witnessed the 14th USCT in action when they turned back Forrest's cavalry at Pulaski and then fought bravely again at Decatur, Alabama. Despite this, the crowning achievement of the USCT came during the Battle of Nashville.

By the time of the Battle of Nashville, Hood had already suffered terrible losses at the Battles of Atlanta and Franklin. Nevertheless, he remained undaunted despite facing increasingly concentrated Union forces at Nashville. Hood arrived in Nashville with approximately twenty-two thousand men. Though greatly outnumbered, his seasoned and dedicated veterans hoped that a successful strike would distract Sherman's march southward and prevent Union forces from further entrenching themselves in Nashville, thus making the North susceptible to invasion.[37] Holding high hopes and an iron-willed determination, Hood promised his troops that they would eat their Christmas dinner in Nashville.[38] The Confederate general immediately commenced to entrench his army two and a half miles south of the city along some heights that ran nearly parallel to the ground occupied by Union forces. By December 3, Hood had capitalized on this strong geographical position and fortified his ground by mounting siege guns and constructing earthworks.[39]

As part of Union preparations at Nashville, all USCT in the Department of the Cumberland concentrated at the Tennessee capital under General Steedman. Arriving from Chattanooga in a destitute condition, the black troops helped to provide the Union with a numerical advantage, boosting troop numbers to around fifty-five thousand.[40] Still, save the 14th, this mighty force lacked experience and the full confidence of its leaders. Thomas, a Virginian from a slave-owning family, reiterated to Morgan that he did not believe black soldiers would fight unless behind breastworks. Realizing the imminent commencement of a great battle, Morgan remained undeterred in his cries for an opportunity for his black troops to fight.[41]

Weather played a part in the Battle of Nashville. On December 8, the weather in the city turned bitterly cold as a severe storm blew in and temperatures dipped to eight degrees. This inclement climate lasted a week, during which time freezing rain and sleet coated the landscape with a sheet of ice two to three inches thick.[42] Lacking food and proper clothing, the ragged Confederates suffered greatly. Likewise, though General Thomas's army as a whole was well equipped—black troops suffered along with their Confederate foe due to exposure to the elements.[43] Morgan stated, "For a few days our sufferings were quite severe. We had only shelter tents for the troops, with very little fuel, and many of our men who had lost their blankets keenly felt their need."[44] Likewise, Captain Romeyn recalled that men slept fully clothed and packed by threes, like sardines, in dog tents designed for two.[45]

The cold lifted as temperatures began to warm on the eve of December 14. As the ice melted, battle plans revealed that the USCT would open the fight. Thomas ordered General Steedman to address the enemy right flank with a two-fold purpose: (1) To attract attention as part of a feint attack and (2) to hold Confederate forces as long as possible in order to prevent reinforcements from moving to the flank, the place of the principle attack. Steedman chose Morgan to lead the entire division to begin the struggle.[46]

The USCT's attack on the Confederate right would not go well, but would serve its purpose. USCT camps stirred at 4 A.M. on the morning of December 15. As the day dawned, the troops stood ready to move out by 6:30 A.M. Carrying two days rations and one hundred rounds of ammunition, men left their tents standing as they fell into formation to bow their heads and listen while their commander gave last-minute instructions and their chaplain "invoked the blessing of the God of battles."[47]

A dense fog enveloped the region, limiting visibility to about a hundred yards. Despite this, Federal troops moved out with the 14th leading the advance. As the sun rose, the fog burned off revealing to Confederates a host of Federal forces menacing their front and flank. Among their aggressors were the two brigades of former slaves, specifically, the 12th, 13th, and 100th USCT under Colonel Thompson (Second Colored Brigade), and the 14th, 17th, 44th, and a detachment of 18th USCT as part of Colonel Morgan's command (First Colored Brigade).[48]

Hostilities commenced at about 8 A.M. Steedman's First Colored Brigade and a rear echelon of "green" white troops under the command of Lieutenant Colonel Charles H. Grosvenor moved out from the Union left.[49] Though the frozen earth had now turned into a great, sticky sea of mud, Steedman's men continued to move southwest in order to attack Hood's right flank. Following the Murfreesboro Pike toward what is known today as Granbury Lunette (near present day Polk Avenue), the Union infantry advanced hoping to deceive the Confederate commander into believing that this formed the true attack. From their elevated position, Confederates, comprised of Granbury's Texas Brigade, patiently watched the approaching men in blue.[50] At the appropriate moment, the Confederates opened fire on the Yankees, reigning down a heavy barrage. Despite the fusillade, Union troops continued to move forward in a great rush led by Morgan's men. Pushing skirmish lines and Confederate pickets back in their thrust, Federal forces succeeded in clearing rebel rifle pits. In steady resolve, Morgan's men moved southeast along the Nashville and Chattanooga Railroad tracks. Before the rebels could react, the black troops had captured a portion of their works.[51]

Despite this momentary gain, Union troops unwittingly walked into a trap set by Confederate troops as they proceeded up the railroad line. Confederates had camouflaged their lunette behind some vegetation on one side of the tracks and now waited behind it patiently for an opportune moment to strike at their foe. Official sources describe the lunette as strong, ". . . with ditch in front and heavy head-logs on top of parapet, forming a very safe cover. . . ."[52] Additional rebels were entrenched above the "Rains cut," or deep railroad cut, on the other side. Once the Union troops passed near the lunette, Confederates released an enfilade from both sides down into the "Rains cut" that created confusion and forced a briefly disorganized Union retreat, leaving a large number of dead and wounded on the field. Withdrawing to the abandoned Confederate rifle pits did not help. The slant of the hill proffered little protection to Union troops. As a result, the exposed USCT troops faced concentrated fire from the mainline of the enemy while trying to retreat further. Steedman's men retreated, but kept within range of the Confederates the rest of the day, but in well-protected entrenchments.[53]

Moving across Brown's Creek between the Nolensville and Murfreesboro turnpikes, Thompson's USCT command experienced greater success. Stationed to the east of Morgan and on the extreme Union left, Thompson had moved up near the Murfreesboro Pike. Once they heard the initial engagement, Thompson received orders to assault the Confederate works as well.[54] Overly excited to participate in their first combat experience, Thompson and his men turned the diversionary attack "into an actual assault." The 12th USCT captured the front works at Nolensville Pike surprising the Confederates who had to re-aim their artillery. Well protected, Thompson's men suffered few casualties from the barrage of Confederate cannon fire. Thompson received no more orders for further action that day.[55]

Early in the engagement, Hood recognized Steedman's attack as a feint and withdrew troops to strengthen his right.[56] Steedman, while he followed orders, failed to advance against the now-weakened Confederate line. Although unsuccessful in overrunning the Confederates, the initial attack briefly delayed reinforcements to the Confederate left, but at a huge cost of lives.[57] The 17th Michigan USCT under Colonel Rufus Shafter suffered particularly heavy casualties as canister from the guns in the redoubt and shells from a battery shredded their ranks. In all, the 17th lost 119 of their comrades, a portion of which comprised nearly its entire color.[58]

Steedman's report did not speak frankly of the day's results.[59] The battle's first day ended in a Union victory when Thomas crushed the Confederate left flank. In fact, Thomas praised Steedman in his report: "He accomplished with great success and some loss, succeeding, however, in attracting the enemy's attention to that part of his lines, and inducing him to draw re-enforcements from toward his center and left."[60]

Nevertheless, at the cost of 350 men and amid congratulations from General Steedman, the USCT had done their duty.[61] Black military historian George Washington Williams later wrote of the battle: "All day these troops behaved with great courage. They executed every movement, obeyed every order."[62] The skirmish proved "severe but glorious," particularly for the USCT troops. For their efforts, Morgan received glowing praise from General Steedman:

> We had done all he [Steedman] desired, and more. Colored soldiers had fought side by side with white troops. They had mingled together in the charge. They had supported each other. They had assisted each other from the field when wounded, and they lay side by side in death. The survivors rejoiced together over a hard-fought field, won by a common valor. All who witnessed their conduct gave them equal praise. The day that we had longed to see had come and gone, and the sun went down upon a record of coolness, bravery, manliness, never to be unmade. A new chapter in the history of liberty had been written. It had been shown that marching under a flag of freedom, animated by a love of liberty, even the slave becomes a man and a hero.[63]

Despite this praise and the fact that black soldiers proved they would fight bravely when they "saw the elephant," full recognition and respect were not so easily won from the American public and the popular press. A chance encounter between one USCT soldier and a New York newspaper correspondent as the troops fell back illustrates the racist stereotypes and general disregard held toward black soldiers: "I met one of those sable warriors—a regular mud pie—returning from the front. 'Are you hurt?' I exclaimed. 'Oh, lor, massa, yes. Cannon ball struck this 'ere nigger right on de brest, and rolled me over, killing Jim at de oder side.' He looked very well for a man whom a cannon ball had made a shuttle cock of."[64] Later, Thomas had USCT troops transport prisoners back to Nashville. Confederates objected, stating that they would rather die than have "nigger soldiers" escort them to Nashville. Thomas replied caustically, "Well, you may say your prayers and get ready to die, for these are the only soldiers I can spare."[65]

The Second Day

The events of the second day brought new challenges and opportunities for the USCT when it was discovered that Hood's army had withdrawn roughly two miles from its original position. The new Confederate line stretched thinly from Shy's Hill to Peach Orchard or Overton's Hill. Morgan's command remained on the far left flank of Union lines in order to guard against surprise attack. The Second Colored Brigade under Colonel Thompson formed on the right of Morgan. Action began at 6 A.M. when Steedman's forces first found the Confederate works empty.[66]

Steedman's men next continued to move up the Nolensville Pike to the left of Brigadier General T. J. Wood's command to face the entrenched enemy. There they faced Hood's strongest and most aggressive corps. Stephen D. Lee's fresh troops, who had seen no action on the first day, were already deeply entrenched on Overton's Hill.[67] At 1 P.M., combined Union forces under Steedman and Brigadier General Wood took initial measures for an all-out frontal assault. Thompson and the Second Colored Brigade would undertake the assault on Overton's Hill. Slogging one hundred yards through a muddy plowed cornfield, Union troops struggled over rocks, through thick underbrush, and between fallen treetops, all while facing heavy Confederate artillery. This fusillade rained down a "murderous fire of cannon and musketry," so fierce that though Union forces often reached the enemy's works, they were quickly driven back.[68] Reports termed the encounter as a great slaughter. Local sources later substantiated this remarking that it would have been possible to "walk across the slope of the hill stepping from one dead Yankee to another."[69]

The assault proved lethal. Though enthusiastic, the men of the 18th USCT lost five color bearers during their repulse. Trailing them, the 13th USCT attacked the rebels, virtually alone. Cheering wildly, they carried the parapet and held on until Hood sent two brigades of reinforcements from his left. The 13th failed to obtain support from either its left or its right. On the right, Colonel Philip S. Post of the white First Brigade was grievously wounded in the hip. Without leadership, his men floundered and failed to charge when the 13th needed support most. On the left, Morgan wrongheadedly ordered his men to spread out instead of charge at the time the 13th took the works. Without support and devastated by heavy casualties, those few men of the 13th still able to retreat did so.[70]

The next assault proved the most successful of the USCT's campaign at Nashville. Following the first failed attempt at taking the hill, the Second Colored Brigade retired behind the First Colored Brigade in order to reform. At 3 P.M. they mounted a second and final assault. During this effort, six thousand soldiers under the cover of a barrage of Union artillery fire, charged Confederate forces. Swarming over the top of the hill, Union soldiers overwhelmed their foe, giving them little opportunity to retreat. Morgan later wrote of the engagement and the colored troops: "The army climbed the hill with steady resolve which nothing but death could check. The assaulting column reached the earthworks; the enemy gave way and began a precipitous retreat. We pushed forward and joined in the pursuit until the darkness and the rain forced a halt." The assault weakened the Confederate right, fitting perfectly into Thomas's plan.

The potency of the USCT's attack on Hood's right flank caused Hood to bring three brigades of A. J. Smith's command to support Stephen D. Lee's men, thus weakening the Confederate left. By the time Smith's men arrived, Lee's force had stymied Steedman's initial attempt at advance, but it proved too late to send them back to the Confederate left. Hood had made a major mistake as Thomas planned another sweeping motion from his right on the Confederate left. As in day one of the battle, Thomas again cleared the Confederate left forcing an all-out retreat. The battle was a complete triumph.[71]

While the USCT suffered enormous casualties, they also enjoyed effuse praise for their actions in battle. The 13th alone recorded 220 casualties or 40 percent of its force. Most of these casualties occurred within their brave 30-minute assault on day two. One Confederate commander who praised USCT actions said he "never saw dead men thicker than in front of my two regiments."[72] Following the engagement, an officer of the 100th USCT surveyed the battlefield and stated, "The blood of the white and black men has flown freely together for the great cause which is to give freedom, unity, manhood and peace to all men, whatever birth or complexion."[73] C. B. Leitner of

Geneva, Georgia, a soldier in Hood's army, at one point attempted to persuade President Jefferson Davis to consider recruiting black troops as well. Believing that the presence of black Confederate troops might have helped the Southern army push Union forces back to the Ohio River, he wrote, "[If you] could have reinforced the Army of Tennessee with 40,000 Negro troops today it would have been upon the banks of the Ohio [River]."[74] "Falling like wheat before a mowing machine," southerner James Holtzclaw later wrote, "they gallantly dashed up to the abates [*sic*], forty feet in front, and were killed by hundreds."[75] Lastly, one Ohioan wrote, "I never saw more heroic conduct shown on the field of battle than was exhibited by this body of men so recently slaves."[76]

Superiors also commended USCT troops. Their actions had converted General Thomas from slaveholder to a leader who supported black troops as equal combatants on the battlefield. Seeing the many bodies of black soldiers at the "foremost on the very works of the enemy," Thomas turned to his fellow officers and said simply: "Gentlemen, Negroes will fight."[77] Thomas later stated, "This [Nashville] proves the manhood of the Negro."[78] Colonel Thompson wrote of the 13th's efforts: "These troops were here for the first time under such a fire as veterans dread, and yet, side by side with the veterans of Stone's River, Missionary Ridge, and Atlanta, they assaulted probably the strongest works on the entire line, and though not successful, they vied with the old warriors in bravery, tenacity, and deeds of noble daring."[79] Steedman, once reluctant to use black troops, now praised them and decried segregation, stating, "The larger portion of these losses [casualties at Nashville], amounting in the aggregate to fully 25 percent of the men under my command who were taken into action, it will be observed fell upon the colored troops. I was unable to discover that color made any difference in the fighting of my troops. All, white and black, nobly did their duty as soldiers, and evinced cheerfulness and resolution such as I have never seen excelled in any campaign of the war in which I have borne a part."[80]

Despite this, complete acceptance of black troops would come slowly. Just a few months following the remarkable performance by the USCT, one newspaper correspondent observed new white Federal recruits in Nashville harassing a passing black soldier, "jeering at Sambo's expense." The writer observed the incident and then concluded, "The colored soldier took it all in good part, convinced that a year or so of wholesome active service would completely change their tune. No soldier in a veteran white regiment would, under the circumstances, have offered the slightest disrespect to a colored compatriot."[81]

By the end of the Civil War, roughly 15 percent of the U.S. Army was comprised of black soldiers serving in one of 138 USCT infantry regiments. Over two hundred thousand black men enlisted in the Union army or navy, with a little over half coming from the eleven seceded states. Of these, thirty-eight thousand died. In addition, the USCT suffered a casualty rate of 23.8 percent.[82] Historian James McPherson states that, "Without their help [black soldiers], the North could not have won the war as soon as it did, and perhaps could not have won at all."[83]

Following their demise in Nashville, the dispirited Confederate survivors fled toward Franklin and Spring Hill. The USCT assisted in the pursuit of the fleeing foe.[84] Hood's Tennessee campaign proved disastrous to the Confederacy as his forces were eviscerated.[85] Without the ability to gain reinforcements, the Army of Northern Virginia could not sustain itself and in four months, the war ended without another large-scale engagement. For this reason, the Battle of Nashville deserves greater attention. As an important part of this, that attention must also focus on the USCT troops who served there so valiantly. While black soldiers actively participated in a number of encounters, the Battle of Nashville serves as the last major engagement in which the USCT partook during the war. The battle also bolstered the USCT's contemporary reputation—as regimental losses and recollections attest.[86]

Notes

1. "A Union Veteran's Questions," *Sun* (New York City), Oct. 16, 1905, 4.

2. "Negro Soldiers," *Sun* (New York City), Oct. 18, 1905, 6.

3. This song is dated circa 1863, around the time of the Emancipation Proclamation. Words and music may be found in Edith Fowke and Joe Glazer, *Songs of Work and Protest: 100 Favorite Songs of American Workers Complete with Music and Historical Notes* (1960; repr. Mineola, NY: Dover Song Collections, 2012), 173.

4. Budge Weidman, "Preserving the Legacy of the United States Colored Troops," *The National Archives.Gov*, accessed May 31, 2012, http://www.archives.gov/education/lessons/blacks-civil-war/article.html.

5. W. E. Woodward, *Meet General Grant* (New York: Literary Guild of America, 1928), 372.

6. James M. McPherson, *The Negro's Civil War: How American Negroes Felt and Acted during the War for the Union*, 3rd ed. (1965; repr. New York: Vintage Books, 2003), xi.

7. Jennifer Edwards-Ring, *Chattel, Soldier, Citizens: The United States Colored Troops in the Battle of Nashville 15–16 December 1864* (master's thesis, Western Illinois University, 2005), 9.

8. E. H. Low, "At Guntown: What the Colored Troops Did There," *National Tribune* (Washington, D.C.), December 29, 1887, 3.

9. Henry Romeyn, "The Colored Troops," *National Tribune* (Washington, DC), July 14, 1887, 1. Reader's note: Due to a spelling error, Henry Romeyn's last name is sometimes spelled "Romyen" in early military records.

10. Romeyn, "The Colored Troops," 1; Weidman, "Preserving the Legacy of the United States Colored Troops."

11. Henry Romeyn, "With Colored Troops in the Army of the Cumberland," *War Papers, Being Papers Read Before the Commandery of the District of Columbia* (Wilmington, NC: Broadfoot Publishing Company, 1993), 49.

12. "Extracts from the Copperheads Speeches," *Big Blue Union* (Marysville, KS), October 1, 1864, 1.

13. Randall M. Miller and Jon W. Zophy, "Unwelcome Allies: Billy Yank and the Black Soldier," *Phylon* 39, no. 3 (1978): 234.

14. Ibid., 234–35.

15. Anne J. Bailey, "The USCT in the Confederate Heartland, 1864," in *Black Soldiers in Blue: African American Troops in the Civil War Era*, ed. John David Smith (Chapel Hill: University of North Carolina Press, 2002), 229–30.

16. For an example of Sambo as a comic character see "Iced Champagne," *Jeffersonian* (Stroudsburg, PA), September 28, 1865, 1.

17. "To Be or Not to Be," *Anderson Intelligencer* (Anderson Court House, SC), September 13, 1866, 3.

18. Romeyn, "The Colored Troops," *National Tribune*, 14 July 1887 and 21 July 1887; Thomas J. Morgan, *Reminiscences of Service with Colored Troops in the Army of the Cumberland, 1863–65* (Providence: Rhode Island Soldiers and Sailors Historical Society, 1885), 20 (hereafter referred to as *Reminiscences*).

19. "Miles O'Reilly on the 'Naygurs,'" *White Cloud Kansas Chief* (White Cloud, KS), December 15, 1864, 1.

20. Pennsylvania Relief Association for East Tennessee, *Report to the Contributors to the Pennsylvania Relief Association for East Tennessee* (Philadelphia: 1864), 23.

21. Miller and Zophy, "Unwelcome Allies," 236–38.

22. Hondon B. Hargrove, *Black Union Soldiers in the Civil War* (Jefferson, NC: McFarland and Company, Inc., Publishers, 1988), 192.

23. John David Smith, "Let Us All Be Grateful," in *Black Soldiers in Blue*, 63.

24. Lincoln to Albert G. Hodges, April 4, 1864, accessed June 27, 2015, http://showcase.netins.net/web/creative/lincoln/speeches/hodges.htm.

25. John H. Taggart, *Free Military School, for Applicants for Commands of Colored Troops* (Philadelphia: King and Baird, Printers, 1863), 4.

26. Bobby L. Lovett, "The Negro's Civil War in Tennessee, 1861–1865," *Journal of Negro History* 61:1 (January 1976): 39; Taggart, *Free Military School*, 3–4.

27. James Lee McDonough, *Nashville: The Western Confederacy's Final Gamble* (Knoxville: University of Tennessee Press, 2004), 36–37.

28. Colonel L. Johnson to Brigadier General L. Thomas, Headquarters, 44th U.S. Colored Infantry, Chattanooga, Tennessee, February 2, 1865, U.S. War Department, *The War of the Rebellion: A Compilation of the Official Records of the Union and Confederate Armies*, 128 vols. (Washington, DC: Government Printing Office, 1881–1901), ser. 2, vol. 8: 171 (hereinafter cited as *OR*; all references are to series 1 unless otherwise indicated).

29. Joseph T. Wilson, *The Black Phalanx: African American Soldiers in the War of Independence, The War of 1812, and the Civil War* (New York: Da Capo Press, 1994), 297; Anne J. Bailey, "The USCT in the Confederate Heartland, 1864," in *Black Soldiers in Blue*, 233.

30. Jim Burran, "Civil War Anniversary: The Emancipation Proclamation," *Daily Citizen* (Dalton, GA), accessed September 23, 2012, http://daltondailycitizen.com/local/x403278048/Civil-War-anniversary-The-Emancipation-Proclamation.

31. Morgan, *Reminiscences*, 30.

32. Hargrove, *Black Union Soldiers in the Civil War*, 176–77; Smith, *Black Soldiers in Blue*, xviii.

33. George Washington Williams, *A History of the Negro Troops in the War of the Rebellion, 1861–65* (New York: Harper and Brothers, Franklin Square, 1888), 109.

34. General Jacob D. Cox, *Sherman's March to the Sea: Hood's Tennessee Campaign and the Carolina Campaigns of 1865* (1882; repr. New York: Da Capo Press, 1994), 100.

35. McDonough, *Nashville*, 159–60.

36. Benson Bobrick, *Master of War: The Life of George H. Thomas* (New York: Simon and Schuster, 2006), 276.

37. Patrick Brennan, "Last Stand in the Heartland: The Fight for Nashville, December 1864," *North and South* 8:3 (May 2005): 26; Williams, *A History of the Negro Troops*, 283.

38. Leverett M. Kelley, "Battle of Nashville," *War Papers. Being Papers Read Before The Commandery of the District of Columbia* (Wilmington, NC: Broadfoot Publishing Company, 1993), 31.

39. Henry Stone, *The Battle of Nashville, Tennessee, December 15 and 16, 1864* (Boston: Military Historical Society of Massachusetts, 1908), 490.

40. Kelley, "Battle of Nashville," 32.

41. Bobrick, *Master of War*, 4; Ezra J. Warner, *Generals in Blue: Lives of the Union Commanders* (Baton Rouge: Louisiana State University Press, 1964), 500–502; McDonough, *Nashville*, 159.

42. Kelley, "Battle of Nashville," 34.

43. Romeyn, "With Colored Troops," 69.

44. Morgan, *Reminiscences*, 40.

45. Romeyn, "With Colored Troops," 69.

46. Wilson, *The Black Phalanx*; John Walker, "Blood on the Snow," *Military Heritage* 8:5 (2007), 39–40.

47. Romeyn, "The Colored Troops," *The National Tribune*, 4 August 1887, 1.

48. Stanley F. Horn, *The Decisive Battle of Nashville* (Baton Rouge: Louisiana State University Press, 1991), 74–75; Wiley Sword, *The Confederacy's Last Hurrah: Spring Hill, Franklin, and Nashville* (Lawrence: University Press of Kansas, 1993), 324–25.

49. Report of Major General James B. Steedman. U.S. Army, Commanding Provisional Detachment (District of the Etowah), The Battle of Nashville, January 27, 1865, accessed June 27, 2015, http://www.civilwarhome.com/steedmannash.htm.

50. Walker, "Blood on the Snow," 39; McDonough, *Nashville*, 163–64.

51. Report of Colonel Thomas J. Morgan, 14th U.S. Colored Troops, commanding First Colored Brigade, of operations November 29, 1864–January 12, 1865, *OR*, vol. 45, pt. 1: 534–38; Sword, *The Confederacy's Last Hurrah*, 324–25.

52. Morgan Report, *OR*, vol. 45, pt. 1: 536.

53. Henry V. Freeman, "A Colored Brigade in the Campaign and Battle of Nashville," *Military Essays and Recollections: Papers Read Before the Commandery of the State of Illinois, Military Order of the Loyal Legion of the United States* (1891), 412–413; Brennan, "Last Stand in the Heartland," 33–34.

54. Steedman Report; McDonough, *Nashville*, 163–64.

55. Report of Colonel Charles R. Thompson, 12th U.S. Colored Troops, commanding Second Colored Brigade, of operations December 7, 1864–January 15, 1865, *OR*, vol. 45, pt. 1: 542; Steedman Report.

56. Horn, *The Decisive Battle of Nashville*, 76–77.

57. Steedman Report; Christopher J. Einolf, *George Thomas: Virginian for the Union* (Norman: University of Oklahoma Press, 2007), 272.

58. Colonel Reuben D. Mussey to Captain C. P. Brown, December 21, 1864, in *Freedom: A Documentary History of Emancipation, 1861–1867, Series II, The Black Military Experience*, ed. Ira Berlin, Joseph P. Reidy, and Leslie S. Rowland (Cambridge, UK: Cambridge University Press, 1982), 560–62.

59. Einolf, *George Thomas*, 272.

60. Report of Major General George H. Thomas, U.S. Army, Commanding Department of the Cumberland, Battle of Nashville, January 20, 1965, accessed June 27, 2015, http://www.civilwarhome.com/thomasnash.htm.

61. Berlin et al., *Freedom*, 560–62.

62. Williams, *A History of the Negro Troops*, 287.

63. Morgan, *Reminiscences*, 41.

64. D. P. Conygham, "Thomas. The Battles before Nashville," *New York Herald*, December 22, 1864, 1.

65. Bobrick, *Master of War*, 294.

66. Cox, *Sherman's March to the Sea*, 117.

67. Horn, *The Decisive Battle of Nashville*, 118–19.

68. Morgan, *Reminiscences*, 46.

69. Ross Massey, "The Battle of Nashville," Battle of Nashville Preservation Society, Inc., accessed September 10, 2012, http://www.bonps.org/the-battle/.

70. Report of Lieutenant General Stephen D. Lee, C. S. army, commanding Army Corps, of operations November 2–December 17, 1861, *OR*, vol. 45, pt. 1: 689; Report of Major General Henry D. Clayton, C. S. army, commanding division, of operations November 20–December 27, 1864, *OR*, vol. 45, pt. 1: 698; Report of Brigadier General James T. Holtzclaw, C. S. army, commanding brigade, of operations November 20–December 27, 1861, *OR*, vol. 45, pt. 1: 705; Berlin, *Freedom*, 560–62; Einolf, *Thomas*, 5, 277–78; Freeman, "A Colored Brigade in the Campaign and Battle of Nashville," 416–18.

71. Report of Colonel John A. Hottenstein, 13th U.S. Colored Troops, of operations November 30, 1864–January 15, 1865, *OR*, vol. 45, pt. 1: 548–49; Report of Major General George H. Thomas, U.S. Army, Commanding Department of the Cumberland, Battle of Nashville, January 20, 1965, accessed June 27, 2015, http://www.civilwarhome.com/thomasnash.htm; Walker, "Blood on the Snow," 44.

72. Hottenstein Report, *OR*, vol. 45, pt. 1: 548–49; Lee Report 689, 698; Holtzclaw Report, 705; Steedman Report.

73. Joseph T. Glatthaar, *Forged in Battle: The Civil War Alliance of Black Soldiers and White Officers* (New York: The Free Press, 1990), 160.

74. Quoted in Bobby Lovett, "Blacks in the Battle of Nashville," December 15–16, 1864, *Tennessee State University Faculty Journal* (1976): 44.

75. Brennan, "Last Stand in the Heartland," 40.

76. Ibid., 40.

77. Morgan, *Reminiscences*, 48.

78. Quoted in Einolf, *George Thomas*, 5.

79. Thompson Report, *OR*, vol. 45, pt. 1: 542–46.

80. Steedman Report.

81. "The Coming Campaign in Tennessee," *Daily Dispatch*, March 6, 1865, 2.

82. Paul D. Renard, "Reuben Delavan Mussey: Unheralded Architect of the Civil War's U.S. Colored Troops," *Military Collector and Historian* (2006): 181; Walker, "Blood on the Snow," 41.

83. Quoted in Howard Zinn, *A People's History of the United States* (New York: Harper Collins, 2003 [1980]), 194.

84. Steedman Report; Thompson Report, *OR*, vol. 45, pt. 1: 543–44; Horn, *The Decisive Battle of Nashville*, 159.

85. Horn, *The Decisive Battle of Nashville*, 166.

86. Hargrove, *Black Union Soldiers in the Civil War*, 193.

9

A. J. SMITH'S DETACHMENT IN THE BATTLE OF NASHVILLE

Steven E. Woodworth

The army with which George H. Thomas fought the Battle of Nashville was composed of detachments from several previous commands. There was the Fourth Corps, which had been part of the Army of the Cumberland; the Twenty-Third Corps, which had comprised the Army of the Ohio; a cavalry corps; and a division of U.S. Colored Troops. Each contingent played an important role in the battle: the cavalry did well, and the USCT division was conspicuously courageous. None, however, was as successful as the highly aggressive contingent of three divisions from the Army of the Tennessee under the command of Major General Andrew Jackson (A. J.) Smith.

Smith was an 1838 West Point graduate, a veteran of the Mexican-American War and the prewar regular army. He commanded a division in Grant's army during the Vicksburg Campaign, as well as in the late-winter 1864 raid on Meridian, Mississippi.[1] His next assignment was to a three-division—thus corps-sized—detachment of the Army of the Tennessee that took part in the Red River Campaign.[2] Arriving back on the east bank of the Mississippi too late to join Sherman's campaign in Georgia as intended, Smith's command became the North's strategic reserve, a sort of rapid-reaction force, marching hundreds of miles to respond to crises in northern Mississippi and Missouri before embarking at St. Louis for the steamboat ride to Nashville to join Thomas.[3]

Smith's command numbered about nine thousand men in three divisions, totaling eight brigades, containing some twenty-nine infantry regiments, nearly all from the Ohio and Mississippi Valleys. Legend has it that Smith's men were veterans of Vicksburg, but just over half (sixteen) of his regiments had taken part in that campaign. Overall the records of Smith's regiments were a mixture of combat experience and long stints of garrison duty punctuated by efforts to suppress Confederate guerrillas. One regiment

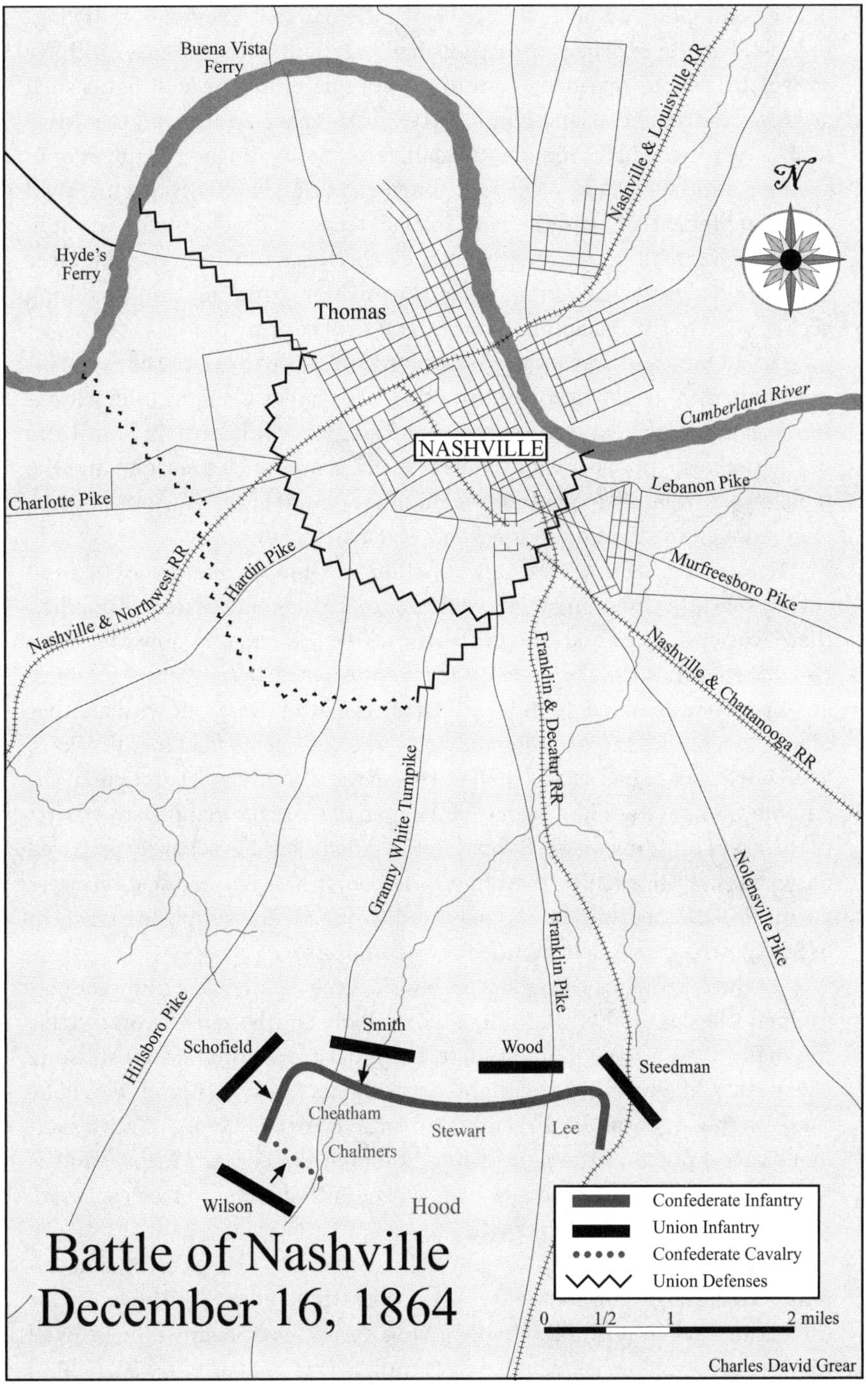

Buena Vista Ferry
Hyde's Ferry
Thomas
Nashville & Louisville RR
N
Cumberland River
NASHVILLE
Lebanon Pike
Charlotte Pike
Murfreesboro Pike
Hardin Pike
Nashville & Northwest RR
Nashville & Chattanooga RR
Franklin & Decatur RR
Granny White Turnpike
Nolensville Pike
Franklin Pike
Hillsboro Pike
Schofield
Smith
Wood
Steedman
Cheatham
Stewart
Lee
Chalmers
Wilson
Hood
Confederate Infantry
Union Infantry
Confederate Cavalry
Union Defenses
Battle of Nashville
December 16, 1864
0
1/2
1
2 miles
Charles David Grear

of the command had been at Fort Henry the day that Confederate stronghold fell back in February 1862. Four had fought at Fort Donelson and five at Shiloh. Various regiments within the command had been at fights such as New Madrid and Island Number Ten, Iuka and Corinth, and two Minnesota regiments had even fought against the Sioux during the uprising in their state in 1862. After Vicksburg, fourteen of the regiments had marched with the Meridian Expedition and then sixteen had fought under Smith in the Red River Campaign. Their wartime experience consisted of a few large battles and a great deal of marching, skirmishing, camping, and becoming accustomed to the discipline, routine, and drill of army life.[4]

Two of Smith's three divisions debarked in Nashville in the early morning hours of November 30, and the third, Brigadier General John McArthur's, landed the next day. Smith's men had great confidence in Smith and in themselves. Thomas assigned them a sector on the Union right, and the men immediately got to work entrenching the new line, building breastworks stout enough to stand up to musketry and artillery fire.[5]

As was the case whenever units of different Union armies were deployed side by side after spending their war hitherto in different theaters of conflict, there was curiosity about the unknown fellow soldiers and how they went about their duties. On December 2 one of McArthur's regimental commanders, Lieutenant Colonel John H. Stibbs of the 12th Iowa, went with another officer to visit the neighboring Fourth Corps and see its field fortifications. The Fourth Corps had served in the Army of the Cumberland throughout the Atlanta Campaign. "I had been told the men of that command were experts in the art of building forts," Stibbs later recalled, "but I was hardly prepared for what I saw on reaching their line." The Fourth Corps's fortifications were far more elaborate than he had expected and made the simple breastworks of Smith's troops seem insignificant by comparison.[6]

On the evening of December 14 Smith received an order from Thomas to open the attack next morning at six o'clock. Smith's corps would strike the main blow, aimed at Hood's left. Brigadier General James H. Wilson's cavalry would advance on his right, covering his flank. To his left would be the Fourth Corps, under Brigadier General Thomas J. Wood. Smith's left flank would pivot on the point where it joined the Fourth Corps, and the whole detachment would make a left wheel until it came to face eastward, ready to fall on Hood's flank.[7]

Morning came with thick fog. An officer in Smith's corps estimated visibility at about fifteen to twenty feet. Delay occurred as Smith waited for the cavalry get in position. Finally giving up on the horsemen, he ordered McArthur's division, which led the column, to move out at 7:00 A.M. Behind

McArthur's three-brigade division marched the three brigades of Brigadier General Kenner Garrard's division. Behind them, followed the two-brigade division of Colonel J. B. Moore in reserve. McArthur advanced with his two lead brigades in line of battle, his skirmishers trading fire with Confederate cavalry vedettes.[8]

Meanwhile, at the far end of the battlefield, on Thomas's left, Steedman launched a "demonstration" against the Confederate right, which turned out to be an ill-starred assault by two brigades of U.S. Colored Troops and two regiments of white troops against a strongly entrenched stretch of Rebel lines, held by some of Hood's toughest troops. The attackers met fierce resistance and suffered heavy casualties. By noon the assault had ended in complete failure without much disturbing the defenders.[9]

By that hour, another stage of Thomas's attack had ended in embarrassment. In the center, Thomas J. Wood's Fourth Corps had advanced under cover of a very intense and prolonged bombardment from the heavy guns of the Nashville defenses. Despite all the sound and fury, however, Wood's advance captured merely an outer line of Confederate works that turned out to be manned only by the Rebel skirmishers. The main Confederate defenses were some distance farther on, but by 2:00 P.M. Wood had ordered his troops to stop and entrench. So far the day was not progressing very well for General Thomas.[10]

Hood knew his left flank was vulnerable to attack. With about twenty-five thousand men, his army was not large enough to stretch its line to the Cumberland River downstream from Nashville. So he refused that flank. When his line reached the Hillsboro Pike, which angled south-southwest from Nashville, the Confederate front bent back, away from the city and the enemy, at roughly a ninety-degree angle, generally following the course of the pike. This was the line McArthur's men were advancing to attack.

In fact Hood did not have enough men to hold that line either—at least not with a continuous line of breastworks. So he and his engineer officers devised a plan for holding a mile of westward-facing front with minimum manpower. It called for building five small earth-and-log redoubts, numbered one through five, each sheltering two to four field guns and manned by one hundred to two hundred men. They were sited at high points, with Redoubt Five on the southern end of the line, about a mile and three-quarters from Redoubt One, at the bend of the line. Each redoubt was within range of the cannon and small arms of its neighboring forts. These posts would be independent but mutually supporting. The plan called for backing up the redoubts with what infantry Hood might be able to deploy along the Hillsboro Pike if an attack on this line seemed imminent. Hood was betting the redoubts would stop any Union attack against his left flank, and to see that they were built right, he ordered the corps commander in that sector, Lieutenant General A. P. Stewart, to supervise their construction in person. That line of redoubts was Smith's target.[11]

Throughout the late morning, Smith's command continued its enormous left wheel on a two-division front, pivoting on its left flank, where it made contact with the right flank of the Fourth Corps, as Thomas had ordered the night before. By this movement the detachment's line swung in a counterclockwise direction so that instead of facing southwest it came to face almost due east. This brought Smith's line to face head on Hood's refused left flank along the Hillsboro Pike. By now, the Union cavalry, dismounted for the fight, had caught up and was keeping pace on Smith's right.[12]

Shortly after 1 P.M., Smith's troops came to grips with the Confederate left flank. The first of the little forts they encountered was Redoubt Five, the southwesternmost of the strongpoints guarding Hood's flank. It was thus the flank of the flank, the last outpost on Hood's left, located on "a prominent knob," as a Union officer described the hill. The redoubt contained about 150 men and mounted four twelve-pounder brass cannon, all well protected by stout earthen embankments. A brisk southerly wind sprang up about this time, driving away the remains of the fog banks on this part of the battlefield and revealing Federals and Confederates to each other at a distance of between nine hundred and thirteen hundred yards. The garrison of Redoubt Five immediately opened fire on Smith's approaching lines with its four cannon. McArthur pressed on, advancing his lines several hundred yards closer to the redoubt and brought up the two batteries of artillery attached to his two lead brigades, Cogswell's battery and the 2nd Iowa, to shell the redoubt from the very close range of 400 yards—actually somewhat ahead of the lines of the Union infantry. By 2:15 P.M., the Union gunners were beginning to run low on ammunition, but the Confederate guns in the fort had fallen silent. This was partially the result of the shelling by McArthur's two batteries and partially the work of Union skirmishers picking off gunners through the embrasures of the redoubt and driving the other artillerymen from their pieces. Captain William F. Notestine led his Company E, 11th Missouri, deployed as skirmishers, to within a dozen yards of the redoubt, and Captain Benjamin S. Williams had his Company D, 8th Wisconsin, almost in the ditch that skirted the redoubt's parapet.[13]

Ordered by Smith to take two brigades and storm the redoubt, McArthur sent in William L. McMillen's brigade, followed closely by Colonel Lucius F. Hubbard's. Simultaneously Colonel Edward Hatch, commanding a division of Wilson's cavalry, launched one of his brigades in a dismounted charge against the opposite face of the redoubt.[14] Though it was supported by Redoubt Four, located about 400 yards to the north, well within range of its two twelve-pounder cannon, Redoubt Five lacked infantry support. Major General Edward C. Walthall's division was in position along the stone wall bordering the Hillsboro Pike, several hundred yards in rear of the line of redoubts, but Walthall lacked sufficient numbers to stretch his line all the way south to Redoubt Five. So by order of his corps commander, Stewart, Walthall's left flank lay approximately in rear of Redoubt Four. Redoubt Five was on its own. Informed of the situation, Hood ordered reinforcements from Lieutenant General Stephen D. Lee's corps, but they were still far from the scene of action when Hatch and McMillen began their assault.[15]

The fight for Redoubt Five developed very quickly. McMillen had his brigade in textbook formation with the 72nd Ohio out in front as skirmishers, the 95th Ohio and 10th Minnesota in line of battle behind that, and the 114th Indiana and 93rd Indiana as the second line of battle farther to the rear. At McArthur's order they plunged up the slope. "The brigade struck the works like a cyclone," wrote a sergeant of the 10th Minnesota. The defenders' fire was heavy but high, and McMillen's men did not stop to return it. Almost simultaneously Hatch's dismounted troopers leapt over the parapet on one side while McMillen's men surged over the breastwork on the other and Notestine's skirmishers clambered over their section of the redoubt. Most of the Confederates went over the back wall with equal speed. A few seemed inclined to linger and dispute possession, but Federal bayonets hurried them on their way. Within minutes the fight was over. The victorious Federals raised "a mighty cheer" and then wheeled the captured cannon to fire on those of the Confederates who had fled the redoubt rather than surrender.[16]

The celebration of Hatch's and McMillen's men inside Redoubt Five proved short lived. Four hundred yards away—within prime artillery range—Redoubt Four stood on higher ground, and its commander, Captain Charles L. Lumsden, had pulled his two twelve-pounders out of their embrasures and turned them to fire into the neighboring earthwork that had until moments before been occupied by his comrades in gray. Redoubt Four's two-hundred-man infantry detachment deployed on the hillside in front of their fort, facing toward Redoubt Five, and added the fire of their rifles.[17]

After a brief pause beyond Redoubt Five during which the troops went to ground to shelter from the Rebel fire, McMillen and Hatch set out to take Redoubt Four as well, and McArthur ordered Hubbard, whose brigade has passed mostly to the left of Redoubt Five, to join the attack. Hubbard's brigade was one of the most experienced units in Smith's corps. Three of its four regiments were veterans of Iuka, Corinth, and some of the heaviest fighting around Vicksburg. Especially famous was the 8th Wisconsin, whose bald eagle mascot, Abe, had earned the whole brigade the moniker "Eagle Brigade." Abe, however, had not reenlisted and was back in Wisconsin, so the brigade fought without its mascot at Nashville.[18]

Over in the ranks of McMillen's brigade, Lieutenant Colonel Samuel P. Jennison of the 10th Minnesota was distressed that Hatch's cavalrymen might have gotten their flags into Redoubt Five before his own regiment's flag went in. He was determined not to be outdone this time, so he decided to seize the colors and race ahead with them himself. What he did not figure on was his red-headed Irish color sergeant, a tall, powerfully built man named Connor O'Keefe, who was determined not to let the flag pass from his hands on any account. As one of the Minnesotans described it, "Up the hill they both went amidst the leaden hail, the colors swaying to and fro as they tugged away."[19]

The regiment was right behind them, though, and this attack turned out much like the previous one. The two brigades of infantry and one of dismounted cavalry raced toward the redoubt, disregarding the Rebel fire, and then surged up and over the parapets and into the fort. Hand-to-hand fighting was brief, and then those Confederates who still could do so fled toward Redoubt Three. Some 200 of the graycoats—both infantrymen and artillerists—remained behind as prisoners of war. Meanwhile, Lieutenant Colonel Jennison seemed satisfied with the outcome of his race. With the regiment's flag, still wielded by the formidable O'Keefe, waving exultantly over the redoubt's parapet, the colonel grabbed one his captains shouting, "Glory! Hallelujah!"[20]

McMillen's brigade was ready to go for Redoubt Three. The infantry marched down into the swale between the hill on which Redoubt Two stood and that on which Redoubt Three was situated, and Cogswell's battery fired a short preparatory bombardment. Then McMillen gave the order to advance, and the brigade was just starting up the slope when several staff officers arrived with orders to halt. Smith wanted McMillen's brigade to catch its breath and also guard his right flank. "Tired as the soldiers were," wrote one of them later, "they would most assuredly have carried that hill."[21]

The job instead went to Hubbard's brigade, which now set out toward Redoubt Three while also angling toward the Hillsboro Pike. The brigade had not gone far, though, before Hubbard noticed the Confederate infantry lining the stone wall along the pike and realized that he might be moving into a dangerous situation with his right flank exposed to enemy troops. Halting and deploying flank guards, he sent back word to McArthur and Smith that he would need reinforcements.[22]

These were already on the way. Smith had been holding McArthur's third brigade in reserve. Its men had watched from a ridgetop several hundred yards to the rear as McMillen's and Hubbard's men had charged the first two redoubts and had cheered as their comrades had captured the strongpoints. They were growing increasingly impatient, however, to get into the action themselves. As the fight for Redoubt Four was playing out, Smith had ridden past the brigade's position. Its soldiers, who were already, in the words of one of their officers, "wild with excitement," began to shout, "Bring us a fort! Bring us a fort!"

"Never mind," Smith replied. "I'll get a fort for you. You won't have to wait long for it either."[23]

After studying the ground and the formidable appearance of the redoubt, Smith rode over to the brigade's commander, Colonel Sylvester G. Hill, and commented, as a bystander recalled, that "it seemed a rather hazardous undertaking to charge there."

"Oh, no," Hill replied, "our men will go right up there. Nothing can stop them. They will go up without a bit of trouble."

Apparently still not quite convinced, Smith replied, "Well, just hold them where they are until you hear my bugle. I will go over and have the second brigade pushed forward to the pike, and they will then be in a position to enfilade the enemy's line." With that Smith turned his horse and galloped off toward Hubbard's position.[24]

Hill may not have understood Smith's order, or he may have simply decided to disregard it. Smith had been gone hardly sixty seconds when Hill ordered his own bugler to sound the charge, and the brigade eagerly surged down the intervening valley and up the slope toward Redoubt Three. They were halfway up when Smith's own bugle sounded the charge on their right, sending Hubbard's brigade into the attack. Once again the Confederate defensive fire was heavy but high. In fact, the four cannon in Redoubt Three could not be depressed sufficiently to hit the charging Federals. Hill's men held their fire as they advanced, following Hill's order that they should not discharge their rifles until they were inside the redoubt.[25]

The Rebels in Redoubt Three may well have been discouraged both at their inability to deliver effective cannon fire against the rapidly advancing Federals and by the sudden fall of redoubts four and five a few minutes before. As Hill's brigade approached the earthwork, the Confederates pulled their cannon out of the embrasures and tried to limber up and head for the rear. At this point a number of Hill's men disregarded their orders and loosed a volley at the escaping artillerists, some of whom scampered away, leaving behind two of their guns. The rest of the defenders of Redoubt Three scrambled over the rear parapet and made off before Hill's men came pouring over the front of the breastworks. Moments later, the skirmishers of Garrard's division came over the parapet on the other side. One of the Rebels may have turned back to fire, or shots may have already been striking the redoubt from the next Confederate stronghold in line, for just as the brigade passed over the breastworks, a bullet struck Colonel Hill in the forehead. He died a few minutes later, without having spoken another word. Nevertheless, a third Rebel strongpoint had now fallen to Smith's troops.[26]

Hood's decision to place the redoubts several hundred yards in front of a scant line of infantry was not paying off for him so far. One thing could be said, however, and that was that the redoubts were indeed positioned in such a way as to be mutually supporting, at least to some degree. Thus, as had been the case in each of the other redoubts, as soon as the Federals had overrun Redoubt Three they found themselves under fire from the next redoubt up the line, in this case, Redoubt Two. "A terrible fire was poured into us," wrote a Union officer after the battle.[27]

As before, the Union commander reacted by ordering an immediate attack toward the new source of firing. This time it was Colonel William R. Marshall of the 7th Minnesota, who had taken command of the brigade when Hill went down. In the confusion resulting from overrunning Redoubt Three and from the sudden change of command, only about a quarter of the brigade's troops—some two hundred men—heard Marshall's order and followed him toward Redoubt Two. By this time, however, the effects of the overall attack's momentum were such that the weakness of the attacking force hardly mattered. Whereas the defenders of Redoubt Five had stayed at their post to thrust bayonets and swing rammer staffs against the fifteen hundred attackers of McMillen's and Hatch's brigades, the Rebels in Redoubt Two, who were scarcely outnumbered by the two hundred attackers, fled before Marshall's brigade reached the earthwork. The successful attackers found a cannon the Confederates left behind and turned it to fire on the retreating graybacks.[28]

It was about this time that the reinforcements Hood had ordered Stephen D. Lee to send from his corps to support Stewart's refused line along the ridge west of the Hillsboro Pike began to arrive. Lee, perhaps reluctant to part with any more combat power than absolutely necessary, had chosen to send Edward Johnson's division, the only part of his corps that had suffered heavy casualties at Franklin and thus its weakest formation. The division was composed of two brigades, one under Arthur M. Manigault and the other under Zachariah C. Deas.[29]

By the time Manigault and Deas approached the rear of Stewart's line along the Hillsboro Pike behind redoubts four and five, McArthur's Federals had already overrun those positions. Manigault's and Deas's men halted and took position behind the low stone wall on the east side of the Hillsboro Pike, but there they made a poor showing. No sooner had they taken up their position along the pike than Hubbard's brigade, now supported on its right by Major General Darius Couch's division of the Twenty-Third Corps, began advancing toward them. Near Redoubt Five, on the Rebels' left flank, the 2nd Iowa Battery opened on them as well. Johnson's Confederates bolted for the rear, dashing across a field east of the pike, but as the Iowans' shells burst thickly over the field, the Rebels turned and scrambled back to the wall. Staying there seemed safer than retreat, at least for the moment. They soon changed their minds again. Several of McArthur's regiments moved up to the stone wall on the west side of the pike and began firing at the Rebels across the roadway at point-blank range. Then two companies of Hubbard's skirmishers, Williams's Company D of the 8th Wisconsin along with Company D of the 11th Missouri, got astride the Hillsboro Pike beyond (south of) Johnson's left and came charging down the road with bayonets fixed. At that the two Confederate brigades collapsed and fled eastward again, while the two skirmish companies rounded up some 450 prisoners. The rest of the Confederate division streamed eastward.[30]

The rout of Johnson's division created a critical situation for Walthall's division, which was holding the northern half of Stewart's refused line, in rear of redoubts one, two, and three. If Walthall's line gave way, Stewart's other division, that of Major General William W. Loring, which still faced north, would be doomed. Stewart decided the situation was hopeless and ordered both divisions to pull back, but events on the battlefield quickly outran the Confederate corps commander's ability to react. Walthall had already ordered his division to retreat, even as his troops were beginning to fall back from the Hillsboro Pike without orders. Several of Hubbard's regiments as well as elements of Schofield's corps, which had by that time arrived on Smith's right, advanced east across the Hillsboro Pike, capturing scores of Rebels and driving the rest before them about a mile, all the way to the Granny White Pike. There Hubbard's men bagged two more abandoned pieces of artillery, which the fleeing Rebels had abandoned in the road.[31]

The sun set about that time, just after 4:30. Smith's corps and other Union troops on the western side of the battlefield spent the remaining minutes of daylight rounding up prisoners while the remnants of A. P. Stewart's routed corps retired eastward to regroup. Smith ordered his men to hold the positions they had taken, and after entrenching, the command rested on its arms that night. It was not a pleasant night. The rain showers that had swept through intermittently throughout the day returned occasionally during the night, and as a sergeant of the 93rd Indiana later recalled, "Every comrade was wet to the skin." But the men built scanty fires to boil their coffee and got through the night as best they could. It had been a successful day for McArthur's division, Smith's corps, and Thomas's army. The total haul for the army on December 15 was sixteen captured cannon and between eight hundred and one thousand prisoners taken.[32]

During the night Hood pulled his army back about a mile to a new and more compact position a little more than two miles from flank to flank. Its right flank, just east of the Franklin Pike, was anchored on Overton's Hill, while its left, just west of the Granny White Pike, was similarly fastened to Shy's Hill, another commanding eminence.[33] The Confederate line bulged forward at each hill, so that its center section was recessed between the hills. On the outer end of each hill the line was refused, once again bending backward at about a ninety-degree angle. Thus the line wrapped around the north and west sides of Shy's Hill and the north and east sides of Overton's. The center was naturally the strongest part of the Confederate position, and there Hood placed Stewart's battered corps. On his flanks, holding the key hills, he placed his more battle-worthy formations, Lieutenant General Stephen D. Lee's corps holding Overton's Hill on the right and Lieutenant General Benjamin F. Cheatham's corps holding Shy's Hill on the left.

In arranging his army to renew the attack the next day, Thomas placed A. J. Smith's corps on his right-center, between Wood's Fourth Corps on the left and John M. Schofield's Twenty-Third on the right. Smith's right lay just west of the Granny White Pike, facing the northeast slope of Shy's Hill, while most of Smith's line extended to the east of the Granny White Pike along the Confederate left-center, facing its foes of the day before, Stewart's corps. During the night Schofield asked Smith to lend him a division as reinforcements for the Union right. In response Smith dispatched Moore's division, retaining Garrard's and McArthur's.[34]

December 16 dawned foggy but less so than the day before. Smith got his two divisions in motion before the fog burned off, marching at about 8:00 A.M. The detachment had finished the previous day's fight facing eastward, the direction in which they had pursued Walthall's fugitives the evening before, and in that formation they had rested throughout the night. With the new day it became apparent that the Confederates had withdrawn some distance to the south. So the full detachment performed a right wheel, the reverse of the previous morning's maneuver, so as to face the foe in his new position. "To watch a single company execute a perfect wheel, is at all times a matter of interest to a military men," wrote Lieutenant Colonel Stibbs many years later. "The wheel of a regiment is of still greater interest, but to watch an army corps wheeling in line as we did that morning, with banners waving and bayonets glistening in the early morning sunlight, was a sight which once seen could never be forgotten."[35]

Smith's corps advanced with Garrard's division once again on the left and McArthur's on the right. They found the Confederates, in the words of Smith's report, "at the base of a chain of hills called the Brentwood Hills." The Rebels had dug in, throwing up breastworks and planting batteries.[36]

The Confederate entrenchments looked remarkably formidable, especially considering the Rebels had built them overnight. Smith advanced to within 600 yards of the Rebel works and halted about 9:00 A.M. Confederate sharpshooters and artillery opened fire, and Smith brought up all six of his batteries to reply. The Union gunners again proved effective. The 2nd Iowa had the satisfaction of seeing one of its shots detonate the ammunition chest on a Confederate limber. A column of white smoke suddenly shot up from within the Confederate lines, and the Federals could see a man, arms and legs splayed wide, cartwheeling through the air twenty feet above the ground. Only then did the tremendous sound of the explosion reach Union lines. For two hours the guns roared steadily, until the Confederate batteries fell silent for the most part. Smith then had his guns keep up a slower harassing fire. During the artillery duel, Smith's infantry dug in, and his skirmishers worked their way forward to scarcely 100 yards from the Rebel breastworks.[37]

Throughout the morning and early afternoon, Smith's troops waited for Thomas to order an advance. The army's lack of aggressive action "seemed inexplicable to us," wrote a Hoosier soldier in McMillen's brigade. On the Union left, Wood persuaded Thomas to let his Fourth Corps attempt to storm the Confederate right on Overton's Hill, the easterly of the two hills the anchored opposite ends of Hood's line. Along with Steedman's detachment Wood made the attack, but the Federals were slaughtered, despite the thinness of the Confederate lines—scarcely one defender to every five feet of the breastworks. The position was simply too strong to be carried by assault.[38]

While Wood's attack failed, Smith's troops had grown increasingly impatient. McArthur was chief among those dissatisfied with the situation. He eyed Shy's Hill as Wood had done Overton's at the other end of the line and, like Wood, judged the high point to be a key that would unhinge the entire Confederate line. Overton's Hill had proven a death trap for attacking Federals, and Shy's Hill looked equally formidable. It was very steep. One of McArthur's regimental commanders noted that it was "so precipitous that it seemed foolhardy to attempt its capture by direct assault." Still, as McArthur studied it further, he decided it was too steep to allow the cannon on its crest to be depressed sufficiently to hit infantry charging up the slope.

Confederate foot soldiers on the crest would also have difficulty covering the slope with their fire. The Confederate works were set back too far, so that the bulge of the slope partially blocked the defenders' field of fire. It was a mistake the Confederate Army of Tennessee had made at Missionary Ridge a year and three weeks before and from which it had apparently not taken the appropriate lesson.[39]

McArthur and his troops had not been at Missionary Ridge, but his conclusion was that Shy's Hill could be taken. Since it lay directly in front of the sector of Major General Darius Couch's division of the Twenty-Third Corps, just to the right of McArthur's division, he went over to talk to Couch about coordinating an assault. Couch was not interested. What he heard from his corps headquarters was that the Rebels were likely to do the attacking, and the Federals might just have enough strength to hold them off. Attacking was not on the agenda of any element of the Twenty-Third Corps. Disappointed, McArthur returned to his division and continued to wait discontentedly. Sometime later, he tried Couch again, and again met with no encouragement.[40]

By 2:00 McArthur worried that if the attack were postponed much longer there would be insufficient time to carry it out before nightfall, and the Confederates could be expected to use another night to make their field fortifications even stronger. Going over to see Couch again, McArthur this time did not ask him anything but instead told him that his, McArthur's, division was going to assault the hill. Couch said he could not participate but would send a brigade over to watch the trenches McArthur's men would be vacating, so that they would have someplace to regroup after their repulse.[41]

At 2:30 P.M. McArthur ordered McMillen to lead off the advance and "take that hill." The colonel was startled but ordered the men of his brigade to put down the shovels with which they had up to that moment been strengthening their trenches and form up for the assault. Moving out of the trenches, McMillen's brigade marched 500 yards to its right, taking up a position directly in front of Couch's division. Then McMillen saw to it that his men's cartridge boxes were full and oversaw the placement of Cogswell's battery so that it could provide the best possible bombardment in support of the charge. In McArthur's plan, McMillen's men would spearhead the charge, neither cheering nor firing but advancing silently with loaded rifles. They would be covered by a heavy artillery barrage overhead and a heavy skirmish line out front, both intended to keep the Rebels' heads down as much as possible. McArthur's other two brigades would support McMillen by advancing in echelon on the left of his brigade.[42]

In preparation for the assault, McMillen recalled the skirmish details that had been out for most of the day and replaced them with a special detail of sharpshooters for the assault. When Sergeant Amos E. Glanville of Company F, 10th Minnesota, got back to the regiment along with the rest of its skirmish detail, he found the men lying on the ground with bayonets fixed. A number of men in his company were singing George F. Root's popular sentimental song "Just before the Battle, Mother," which Glanville found depressing. Down at the far end of the regiment he could see Lieutenant Colonel Jennison giving a pre-battle speech to the men on that flank. Then Jennison came down to Company F's end of the line, and repeated his pep talk. "Boys," he said, "you can see the job set before us." He gave some instructions for how he wanted the attack carried out. Then he pulled a letter from his pocket and told the men it was from his father. It said that a number of people in the neighborhood had been asking about the regiment. "They had not heard from it lately." He put the letter back in his pocket, paused, and then said, "Boys, I propose that they shall hear from [the] regiment today!"[43]

As they continued to wait, First Sergeant Hiram A. Mosher of Company F, looking over the ranks of waiting soldiers, spied Private Jesse J. Ferguson, one of the quietest members of the company, whom the regimental surgeon had that morning excused from duty because of sickness. Mosher ordered Ferguson to fall out and go to the rear. "Mosher," the private replied, "I would rather die than be out of my place today."[44]

The attack was nearly ready to step off when the commander of McMillen's attached artillery battery reported that his guns were nearly out of ammunition. Delay ensued while ammunition was sought. While more shells were being brought up, McArthur, shortly before 3:00 P.M. sent Smith a dispatch claiming that he could take the hill in his front, Shy's Hill, and stating his intention to attack unless ordered not to do so. Smith was with Thomas when he received the message, and Thomas ordered Smith to have McArthur wait while Thomas tried to set up a coordinated assault that would include the army's other commands. Smith sent a staff officer to convey the order to McArthur, and Thomas trotted off to find Schofield.[45]

It was nearly 4:00 P.M., and sunset was less than forty-five minutes away before McArthur was finally able to launch his attack. The commander of McMillen's battery had managed to borrow enough ammunition from a neighboring battery to allow each of his guns to fire ten rounds. Smith's staff officer still had not arrived with the order to wait for Schofield, so on McMillen's order the guns opened up and the infantrymen prepared to advance. All eighteen guns in McArthur's division were soon in action. Captain Joe Reed of the 2nd Iowa Battery told a fellow officer that by then he had the range so perfectly that he could burst every shell "squarely over the enemy's works." McArthur's plan was for McMillen to attack Shy's Hill from the northeast, and when his line was halfway up the hill, Hubbard's and Hill's brigades, the latter now under the command of Colonel William R. Marshall, were to advance on McMillen's left against the Confederate lines on the lower ground east of Shy's Hill.[46]

McMillen started the advance with his brigade in two lines. The regiments of the first line were, from left to right, the 10th Minnesota, 93rd Indiana, and 114th Illinois. Behind them, the 95th Ohio and 72nd Ohio formed the second line. As the brigade crossed the low ground in front of Shy's Hill, it took flanking fire from the left. In response to this, regimental commanders on the left of the brigade changed course so as to advance more directly toward this threat. This opened a gap in the center of the line, into which the 72nd and 95th Ohio advanced. Thereafter the brigade continued its advance in a single line of all five regiments.[47]

Out in front was a detachment of skirmishers from the 72nd Ohio under Captain James Fernald, assigned to function as sharpshooters and help the artillery keep the Rebels' heads down. The men of the two main battle lines were neither to fire nor to cheer but to press on rapidly toward the Confederate lines with bayonets fixed, rifles at "trail arms," depending on the fire of the skirmishers in front of them and their artillery, firing over their heads, to suppress the defenders' fire. Bullets buzzed past them as they started toward the hill, but for most of the climb they enjoyed the protection of the bulge of the hillside, which made them almost immune to Rebel fire.[48]

As they scrambled up the slope, McMillen's men could hear the "whiz and whirl" of their own artillery's shells passing uncomfortably close over their heads—and loved it. Twenty years later First Lieutenant Henry W. Phelps of the 95th Ohio wished he knew the name of the battery or batteries that had supported his attack so that he could give them due credit. "Those guns were 'sweet' shooters," he wrote, "and the gunners brave men." Simultaneously, from a vantage point several hundred yards to the rear, a sergeant of the Twenty-Third Corps was impressed at how the "continuous artillery firing prevented the enemy from firing upon the charging column." When McMillen's men reached the brow of the hill, only a few yards short of the breastworks, they paused and went to ground, no doubt partially to catch their breath, but also because a further advance would have taken them directly into the path of the shells that were continuing to batter the defenses.[49]

Presently, the guns fell silent. Some soldiers of the 93rd Indiana and 114th Illinois had begun to fire their rifles during this pause in the advance. The adjutant of the 93rd was yelling at them to cease firing and charge over the works. Near him another soldier raised his rifle, and the adjutant struck him across the shoulder with the flat of his sword, shouting, "Cease! Charge over!"[50]

McMillen's whole line sprang up and surged forward. Behind the breastwork a thin line of Rebels, men of Brigadier General Thomas B. Smith's Tennessee brigade, hastily rose up, brought their muzzles down, and fired. Most of the hurried volley went high, passing over the heads of McMillen's charging Federals. Then they were over the breastworks and among Smith's men, firing their rifles point blank and thrusting with their bayonets. An Indiana sergeant noted that some of the Rebels had been cowering behind the breastworks when McMillen's men climbed over and had offered no resistance. Others fought desperately. A Rebel shot Sergeant James Pride, color-bearer of the 95th Ohio, just as he was crossing the parapet. A few yards away, Confederate Lieutenant Colonel William M. Shy was fighting alongside his men when summoned to surrender. He refused, and moments later a rifle bullet tore through his head.[51]

Only the far left of McMillen's line suffered severely. There the breastworks curved away from the brow of the slope so that the 10th Minnesota had to cross more open ground to reach them. Just as the Minnesotans were entering the zone swept by friendly artillery fire, the point in the charge at which the other regiments of McMillen's brigade had taken shelter behind the brow of the hill, they found themselves on open sloping ground above the brow of the hill, fully exposed, front and flank, to a volley that members of the regiment years later still remember as "that . . . crash."[52]

Sergeant Amos Glanville estimated that some 70 members of the 10th Minnesota fell from the combined effects of that volley and the friendly artillery fire from rear. He especially remembered "a handsome, fair-haired Norwegian" named Hans Oleson, "a great favorite" in Company F, who fell, shot through the heart. A Rebel bullet smashed the lock of Jesse Ferguson's rifle. He dropped the now useless weapon, but as he stooped to pick up the rifle of a fallen comrade, another bullet struck him in the forehead.[53]

Still the regiment pressed forward to the breastworks. As Lieutenant Colonel Jennison climbed onto the parapet something hit him in the head and he toppled back. Someone said it had been an axe, thrown at Jennison by a Rebel inside the breastworks. Nearby Con O'Keefe leapt atop the breastworks still firmly gripping the flagstaff. A Rebel scrambled up and tried to wrest the flag away from him, but O'Keefe knocked him down and then stood on the parapet waving the colors. By this time the rest of the regiment was streaming across the breastworks. "The boys just went over those works like a tornado," recalled Glanville. Just behind the breastwork, in the bottom of the Confederate trench, was another image that remained vivid in the sergeant's memory. There sat a Confederate soldier without a head. Enough other dead Rebels lay in the trench that the little rivulets of rainwater that ran trickled down the hillside from it were red, "like a stream of blood." The living Confederates surrendered or fled. Total casualties for the 10th Minnesota came to seventy-seven, including seventeen out of its twenty-three officers. Amazingly Lieutenant Colonel Jennison recovered from his wound.[54]

The hilltop fight was over within minutes. Not only Smith's brigade but the rest of Major General William B. Bate's Confederate division disintegrated. Here and there a small knot of soldiers strove to keep up resistance. All around the hilltop and down the reverse slopes other Confederates legged it for the rear, where even then the Union cavalry, pushing past Hood's extreme left flank, was beginning to threaten their retreat. Hundreds of other Confederates on the hill threw down their weapons and raised their hands in surrender. Atop Shy's Hill McMillen's men cheered wildly and his color-bearers waved their flags vigorously above the Rebel parapet. McMillen's brigade took prisoners slightly greater than its own numbers: 1,533 enlisted men and eighty-three officers, including General Smith. Along with them, McMillen's men took four battle flags and eight cannon.[55]

As Sergeant Lacock looked around the hilltop, he was impressed at the effectiveness of the Union artillery bombardment that had prepared the way for his brigade's assault. "The ground was literally plowed up like a field ready for grain," he wrote. "The dead and mangled lay in all directions, many bodies lying scattered in fragments as the huge exploding shells had torn them."[56]

Meanwhile, the start of McMillen's attack against Shy's Hill had been the signal for what quickly became a general advance. To the left of McMillen, McArthur's other two brigades, Hubbard's and Marshall's, advanced toward the Confederate lines just east of Shy's Hill. Instead of waiting until McMillen was half-way up the hill, Hubbard led his troops forward as soon as McMillen's attack got underway. McArthur's order may well have reached Hubbard in garbled form, for he reported receiving it only at 4:00 P.M., and noted that he had obeyed it by advancing immediately. His men were impatient to attack, and when the order was announced in the 9th Minnesota, the men sent up a tremendous shout. Marshall, on the other hand, received no attack order at all. Seeing McMillen's brigade charge toward Shy's Hill and then Hubbard's set out across the cornfield, Marshall ordered his own brigade to join the assault. His regimental commanders had anticipated the order and had already directed their men to put down their entrenching tools, pick up their rifles and be ready to advance. As a result of its late start, and perhaps also because for part of the distance of its advance it had the cover of corn stalks left standing in the field, Marshall's brigade did not suffer as many casualties as Hubbard's during the charge.[57]

The task facing the men of Hubbard's and Marshall's brigades might have looked easier to an unpracticed eye, with no steep hill to climb, but their route of advance led them through muddy fields of corn stubble, over ground that was soggy from recent rains, and fields bisected occasionally by ditches and stone fences. Worse, the gentler slope in this sector in fact offered an ideal field of fire for the defending Confederates, who could sweep the field with frontal and enfilading fire and punish the attackers severely. With fixed bayonets the Federals trotted forward at the double-quick. Confederate rifle fire and blasts of canister toppled men in scores. The 5th Minnesota lost two color-bearers, and the 11th Missouri three, and had its flagstaff broken in three pieces by a Rebel shell. Hubbard had three horses shot out from under him. In all, his brigade lost 315 of the 1,421 men it took into battle. The commander of one of the two Confederate brigades holding this sector of the line was confident that his men were successfully beating off the Union attack when the Rebel line on Shy's Hill went to pieces and McMillen's victorious troops wheeled left and swarmed down toward the flank of the defenders there, driving the fugitives of Bate's shattered division in front of them.[58]

The Confederates to the east of Shy's Hill were still crouching behind their breastworks, however, when the two regiments in Hubbard's first line, the 5th and 9th Minnesota, stormed over the parapet. The 11th Missouri and 8th Wisconsin were right behind them. Many of the defenders simply surrendered where the stood, while others fled to the rear or toward what had been the seemingly impregnable stronghold of Shy's Hill, just west of their position, unaware that McMillen's men were even then bursting onto its crest. Hubbard sent his right two regiments, the 9th Minnesota and 8th Wisconsin in pursuit up the slope toward Shy's Hill, where the Rebels would soon be trapped between them and McMillen's men. In addition to prisoners, the two regiments also captured three pieces of artillery.[59]

Meanwhile, Hubbard wheeled the 5th Minnesota and 11th Missouri to the left and led them sweeping along the back side of the Confederate parapets, rolling up the Rebels as they went. The 11th Missouri captured an entire a four-gun battery of artillery that had hit them hard during their advance. First Lieutenant William T. Simmons saw the color-bearer of the 34th Alabama trying to make off with that regiment's flag and ordered him to halt and surrender. The Confederate refused, and Simmons threatened to shoot him. That persuaded the man to stop and give up his colors. Corporal James W. Parks of the 11th Missouri's color guard captured another Confederate flag. First Lieutenant John F. Bishop of the 5th Minnesota personally received the surrender of Confederate brigadier general Henry R. Jackson. With that the 5th had outdone its fellow Minnesota regiment of the brigade. The 9th's biggest capture was a colonel.[60]

Marshall's troops surged over the breastworks just to the east of Hubbard's breakthrough only moments later, even as Hubbard's two Minnesota regiments were beginning to roll up the Confederate line there. Back inside the Union lines, Smith sat on his horse watching the success of his troops. Thomas, having heard the noise of battle while on his way to see Schofield, turned and galloped back. Finding Smith and seeing the men of Marshall's brigade streaming into the Confederate works, Thomas exclaimed, "General, what is the matter? Are your men being captured there?" Not at all, Smith assured him. "My men are capturing them. Those are Rebel prisoners you see." Smith later related that this occasion was the only time he had ever heard—or heard of—Thomas laughing out loud.[61]

The entire Confederate left, from Shy's Hill eastward for the better part of a mile, had now collapsed, and the rest of Hood's line continued to unravel from west to east, the beginning of the overwhelming rout that swept the Rebels from the field and gave George Thomas one of the greatest victories of the Civil War. McArthur's division rounded up prisoners and captured guns, and Hubbard's and Marshall's brigades pressed forward as much as a mile. Indeed, Hubbard had to rein in the eager men of the 8th Wisconsin, who would have pursued further in the darkness. In addition to the haul McMillen was rounding up, Hubbard's brigade captured nine cannon, seven Confederate battle flags, and some 2,000 prisoners of war, while Marshall's took two more cannon, bringing the total take for McArthur's division that day to twenty-four cannon, thirteen flags, and more than 4,273 prisoners of war. The total for Smith's entire detachment for the two-day battle came to thirty-six cannon, sixteen flags, and 5,123 prisoners of war, including a major general and two brigadier generals.[62]

A careful consideration of the part played by Smith's detachment, and especially McArthur's division, in the Battle of Nashville reveals several reasons for the amazing success achieved. The first reason that might be suggested is the weakness and demoralization of the Confederate defenders after the severe bleeding their army had suffered at the Battle of Franklin, little more than two weeks before. This was undoubtedly a factor but does not explain the phenomenon completely. At other times and places during the war Confederate troops who had suffered severely and would have seemed to have had every reason for demoralization had nevertheless fought stubbornly, especially when they occupied strong defensive positions with stout breastworks, as was the case at Nashville. Examples of such tough defensive fighting can be seen in the defense of the Vicksburg fortifications against

Union assaults on May 19 and 22, 1863, as well as in the April 2, 1865, struggle for Forts Gregg and Whitworth, as the Confederates waged an ultimately doomed struggle to hold on to the defenses of Petersburg and Richmond. Indeed, Hood's own Confederate army handily beat off Union assaults in other sectors on both days of the Battle of Nashville. That it collapsed so suddenly and completely on the afternoons of both days was a result of particularly bold and skillful fighting by Smith's guerrillas.

Five different factors about Smith's command itself can be identified as contributing to its unusual success at Nashville. The first of these was the skillful and aggressive role played by Smith's skirmishers. Both at Redoubt Five and Shy's Hill, the skirmishers were effective in forcing the defenders to keep their heads down. Officers throughout the Army of the Tennessee had been developing the use of skirmishers into a flexible and highly effective tactic during the second half of the war. They were finding that their highly experienced troops no longer needed close-order formations in order to maneuver and maintain cohesion. The troops of Smith's detachment may well have been especially suited for the skirmishing role because of their prolonged counterguerrilla experience, emphasizing independent and small-unit action and good marksmanship.

Another factor that may have contributed even more to the success of Smith's attacks on both days of the Battle of Nashville was his command's unusually well-served artillery. McArthur credited his artillery for the capture of Redoubt Five, the first Confederate stronghold to fall on December 15. By the time the assaulting infantry and dismounted cavalry charged, he wrote, "the fort had been rendered untenable by the fire from my batteries."[63] The artillery was, if anything, even more effective the following afternoon when Smith's batteries maintained a close bombardment of Confederate lines on Shy's Hill until McMillen's attackers were within a few yards of the parapet, not only prompting some of the defenders to cower in the bottom of their trenches until they were captured but also inflicting heavy casualties.

This kind of barrage, lifting only moments before attacking infantry surged over the parapet, was the ideal for which World War I artillerists would strive but which they would not often achieve until the last year of that war. Smith's gunners had an advantage over the artillerists of the First World War in that they could use direct fire for their barrage, but they also labored under serious disadvantages relative to their twentieth-century successors in that their shells were far less lethal and were ignited by fuses that had to be appropriately cut by the gunners. Cutting the fuses too long would have rendered the bombardment ineffective, and cutting them too short would have precipitated a slaughter among the attacking troops. Great precision and confidence were necessary. Artillery was the branch of service that required both the most technical knowledge and the most teamwork. Smith's artillerists had apparently profited from their two to three years of experience.

Smith's troops also had good leadership. Experienced, aggressive, and skillful officers filled the chain of command from Smith himself and the redoubtable John McArthur down to aggressive and inspirational brigade and regimental commanders like William McMillen, Lucius Hubbard, and Samuel Jennison. These men seemed to know almost instantly in each combat situation during those two days not only exactly the right course of action, but exactly the course of action their fellow brigade and regimental commanders would adopt. Long experience again paid off for Smith's guerrillas.

Another factor that characterized both the officers and the enlisted men of Smith's detachment was the well-established habit of aggressiveness they all seemed to share. Nearly all of the regiments in Smith's detachment had had their introduction to military life and first learned the art of war as part of the Army of the Tennessee. That army, in turn, had been organized and welded into a fighting force under the command of Ulysses S. Grant. He had inculcated into his troops the assumption that they would always be on the offensive and would be victorious. This had not necessarily occurred 100 percent of the time in their experience of war, but close enough to keep the assumption alive. Officers and men tended to take it as assured that the enemy was afraid of them and that as soon as they could find a way to get a fair fight with their foes, they would whip the Rebels almost as a matter of course. This pattern was still visible in the performance of Smith's detachment at Nashville.

The same trait of aggressiveness may have been especially cultivated by the unusual service career of Smith's detachment. One officer believed that the guerrillas were more accustomed than their fellow Union troops to operate in the open and on the move. Lieutenant Colonel John H. Stibbs, commander of the 12th Iowa, one of McArthur's regiments, wrote in 1907, "I will not presume to say that we were better officered, or that we had better soldiers than those of any other division of the army, but I thought then, and so stated, and I'm still of the opinion, that it was a part of God's providence to train and fit the men of McArthur's division to meet the requirements of that important engagement." He mentioned the fact that Smith's command had spent less of its time fighting from entrenchments than had the rest of Thomas's army. "Our service and fighting had all been in the open."[64] This primed them to show "reckless daring" in the face of enemy field works and "led them to a wild rush onto and over every obstacle placed in their way."[65]

Overarching all of these factors and providing a unified explanation for them is the particular experience of Smith's troops. Most of Smith's regiments had seen at least one full-scale, pitched battle. Several had participated in a number of such encounters, yet even they had suffered through less intense, sustained combat and bloodletting than had most of the regiments that had participated in the Atlanta Campaign, to say nothing of the troops in Virginia, whose regiments were scarcely shadows of their former numbers and spirit. All of Smith's regiments had spent at least two years under arms, many three—marching, camping, drilling, and growing accustomed to army ways, to obeying orders, and to functioning as a unit. All of the regiments had extensive experience with small battles, allowing their men to become somewhat accustomed to being under fire without too many of them becoming casualties. In short, Smith's regiments were seasoned but not exhausted, toughened but not bled white. These factors helped build in them the confidence, aggressiveness, and skill that enabled them to achieve spectacular success at the Battle of Nashville and to play the key role in achieving the overwhelming Union victory there.

Notes

1. U.S. War Department, *The War of the Rebellion: A Compilation of the Official Records of the Union and Confederate Armies*, 128 vols. (Washington, DC: Government Office, 1881–1901), ser. 1, vol. 32, pt. 1, 168–69 (hereinafter cited as *OR*; except as otherwise noted, all references are to series 1).

2. *OR*, vol. 34, pt. 1, 304–12; John W. Lacock, "Battling with Hood: Smith Guerrillas at the Siege of Nashville," *National Tribune*, November 7, 1895, 1.

3. *OR*, vol. 34, pt. 1, 31, 33; vol. 39, pt. 2, 179; vol. 41, pt. 1, 307–16, 314–15, 322–23; Lacock, "Battling with Hood," 1–2.

4. *OR*, vol. 45, pt. 1, 94; Frederick H. Dyer, *A Compendium of the War of the Rebellion*, 3 parts (Des Moines: Dyer Publishing Company, 1908), pt. 3, 1068, 1072–73, 1077, 1081, 1086–87, 1094–98, 1139, 1151–52, 1170, 1176, 1178–79, 1298–1301, 1327–28, 1330–31, 1335–36, 1469, 1530, 1538–39, 1676, 1678, 1686–87.

5. *OR*, vol. 45, pt. 1, 35, 54, 433, 452; Lacock, "Battling with Hood," 2; John H. Stibbs, "McArthur's Division at Nashville as Seen by a Regimental Commander," *Military Essays and Recollections: Papers Read before the Commandery of the State of Illinois, Military Order of the Loyal Legion of the United States*, 10 vols. (Chicago: Cozzens Beaton Company, 1907; repr., Wilmington, NC: Broadfoot Publishing Company, 1992), 4:488–89 (hereinafter *MOLLUS*); Wiley Sword, *The Confederacy's Last Hurrah: Spring Hill, Franklin, and Nashville* (Lawrence: University Press of Kansas, 1993), 276.

6. Stibbs, "McArthur's Division at Nashville," *MOLLUS*, 4:489.

7. Lacock, "Battling with Hood," 2; Stibbs, "McArthur's Division at Nashville," *MOLLUS*, 4:489; *OR*, vol. 45, pt. 1, 433.

8. *OR*, vol. 45, pt. 1, 38, 433, 437, 441, 444–45, 450, 457; Lacock, "Battling with Hood," 2; Stibbs, "McArthur's Division at Nashville," *MOLLUS*, 4:489–90; A. E. Glanville, "Battle of Nashville: The Rout and Destruction of Hood's Army," *National Tribune*, July 8, 1886, 1; Sword, *The Confederacy's Last Hurrah*, 321.

9. *OR*, vol. 45, pt. 1, 38; Sword, *The Confederacy's Last Hurrah*, 322–26.

10. *OR*, vol. 45, pt. 1, 38–39; Sword, *The Confederacy's Last Hurrah*, 328–29.

11. Sword, *The Confederacy's Last Hurrah*, 315–16.

12. *OR*, vol. 45, pt. 1, 433, 437–38; Sword, *The Confederacy's Last Hurrah*, 329–34.

13. *OR*, vol. 45, pt. 1, 38, 434, 437–38, 441, 445, 450, 452, 457–58, 460; Stibbs, "McArthur's Division at Nashville," *MOLLUS*, 4:490–91; Sword gives the number of cannon as two and the garrison as one hundred. Sword, *The Confederacy's Last Hurrah*, 333–34.

14. *OR*, vol. 45, pt. 1, 38, 434, 437–38, 441; Sword, *The Confederacy's Last Hurrah*, 333–34.

15. *OR*, vol. 45, pt. 1, 433–34, 445; Sword gives the number of cannon in Redoubt Four as two. Sword, *The Confederacy's Last Hurrah*, 334–35.

16. *OR*, vol. 45, pt. 1, 39, 441, 445, 453, 455; Glanville, "Battle of Nashville," 1; Stibbs, "McArthur's Division at Nashville," *MOLLUS*, 4:491; Sword, *The Confederacy's Last Hurrah*, 335–36.

17. *OR*, vol. 45, pt. 1, 434; Sword puts the number of troops in the Redoubt Four at one hundred. Sword, *The Confederacy's Last Hurrah*, 336.

18. *OR*, vol. 45, pt. 1, 434, 438; Glanville, "Battle of Nashville," 1.

19. Glanville, "Battle of Nashville," 1.

20. *OR*, vol. 45, pt. 1, 38, 434, 438, 459; Lacock, "Battling with Hood," 2; Glanville, "Battle of Nashville," 1; Sword, *The Confederacy's Last Hurrah*, 336.

21. Glanville, "Battle of Nashville," 1.

22. Sword, *The Confederacy's Last Hurrah*, 336–37.

23. Stibbs, "McArthur's Division at Nashville," *MOLLUS*, 4:491–92.

24. Ibid., 4:492; *OR*, vol. 45, pt. 1, 438; Sword, *The Confederacy's Last Hurrah*, 337–38.

25. Stibbs, "McArthur's Division at Nashville," *MOLLUS*, 4:492–93; *OR*, vol. 45, pt. 1, 460, 465; Sword, *The Confederacy's Last Hurrah*, 338.

26. *OR*, vol. 45, pt. 1, 434, 460, 467; Lacock, "Battling with Hood," 2; Sword, *The Confederacy's Last Hurrah*, 338.

27. Sword, *The Confederacy's Last Hurrah*, 338.

28. *OR*, vol. 45, pt. 1, 434, 460, 463; Stibbs, "McArthur's Division at Nashville," *MOLLUS*, 4:493; Sword, *The Confederacy's Last Hurrah*, 338.

29. Sword, *The Confederacy's Last Hurrah*, 338.

30. *OR*, vol. 45, pt. 1, 438, 445, 457, 459; Sword, *The Confederacy's Last Hurrah*, 338–39.

31. *OR*, vol. 45, pt. 1, 433–34, 446, 451, 453, 457; Sword, *The Confederacy's Last Hurrah*, 339–41.

32. *OR*, vol. 45, pt. 1, 446, 451. 457; Stibbs, "McArthur's Division at Nashville," *MOLLUS*, 4:495; Lacock, "Battling with Hood," 2; Sword, *The Confederacy's Last Hurrah*, 343–44, Thomas places the number of prisoners taken at twelve hundred, *OR*, vol. 45, pt. 1, 39.

33. The name Shy's Hill was not attached to this eminence until after the battle. However, it is used throughout this account in order to avoid confusion.

34. *OR*, vol. 45, pt. 1, 39–40, 434; Sword, *The Confederacy's Last Hurrah*, 351.

35. *OR*, vol. 45, pt. 1, 434–35; Stibbs, "McArthur's Division at Nashville," *MOLLUS*, 4:495; Sword, *The Confederacy's Last Hurrah*, 350.

36. *OR*, vol. 45, pt. 1, 39–40, 434–35, 438, 446–47, 451; Sword, *The Confederacy's Last Hurrah*, 350–51.

37. *OR*, vol. 45, pt. 1, 39–40, 434–35, 438, 441–42, 447, 451, 455, 457, 459; Stibbs, "McArthur's Division at Nashville," *MOLLUS*, 4:497–98; Sword, *The Confederacy's Last Hurrah*, 350–51.

38. *OR*, vol. 45, pt. 1, 39–40, 457; Lacock, "Battling with Hood," 2; Sword, *The Confederacy's Last Hurrah*, 354–63.

39. Stibbs, "McArthur's Division at Nashville," *MOLLUS*, 4:497; Sword, *The Confederacy's Last Hurrah*, 365.

40. *OR*, vol. 45, pt. 1, 438; Sword, *The Confederacy's Last Hurrah*, 365–66.

41. *OR*, vol. 45, pt. 1, 438–39, 442; Sword, *The Confederacy's Last Hurrah*, 366.

42. *OR*, vol. 45, pt. 1, 435, 438, 442, 444; Sword, *The Confederacy's Last Hurrah*, 366.

43. Glanville, "Battle of Nashville," 1.

44. Ibid.

45. *OR*, vol. 45, pt. 1, 435, 438; Stibbs, "McArthur's Division at Nashville," *MOLLUS*, 4:498; Sword, *The Confederacy's Last Hurrah*, 366–67.

46. *OR*, vol. 45, pt. 1, 435, 438, 442; Stibbs, "McArthur's Division at Nashville," *MOLLUS*, 4:497; Sword, *The Confederacy's Last Hurrah*, 367.

47. Henry W. Phelps, "Up on Bald Hill: That Was a Great Charge at Nashville, and No Mistake," *National Tribune*, May 17, 1894, 3.

48. *OR*, vol. 45, pt. 1, 435, 442; "D.C.," "Famous for Charging: More about Old Town Creek and the Battle of Nashville," *National Tribune*, March 15, 1894, 3; Sword, *The Confederacy's Last Hurrah*, 373.

49. Lacock, "Battling with Hood," 2; Henry W. Phelps, "A. J. Smith's Troops: How They Fought at Nashville and Chased Rebels in Missouri," *National Tribune*, February 3, 1887, 3; Samuel C. Miles, "A Critical Moment: An Incident in which a Lieutenant Figures Heroically," *National Tribune*, August 23, 1894, 3.

50. "D.C.," "Famous for Charging," 3; Oliver W. Case, "Battling with Hood: One of Cox's Men Corroborates Comrade Lacock's Story," *National Tribune*, December 12, 1895, 3.

51. *OR*, vol. 45, pt. 1, 442; Miles, "A Critical Moment," 3; Lacock, "Battling with Hood," 2; Phelps, "Up on Bald Hill," 3; Sword, *The Confederacy's Last Hurrah*, 373.

52. *OR*, vol. 45, pt. 1, 435, 442; "D.C.," "Famous for Charging," 3; Miles, "A Critical Moment," 3; Glanville, "Battle of Nashville," 1; Sword, *The Confederacy's Last Hurrah*, 373.

53. Glanville, "Battle of Nashville," 1.

54. *OR*, vol. 45, pt. 1, 435, 442; Glanville, "Battle of Nashville," 1; Phelps, "Up on Bald Hill," 3; Sword, *The Confederacy's Last Hurrah*, 373.

55. *OR*, vol. 45, pt. 1, 40; Lacock, "Battling with Hood," 2; Sword, *The Confederacy's Last Hurrah*, 374.

56. Lacock, "Battling with Hood," 2.

57. *OR*, vol. 45, pt. 1, 435–36, 438–39, 447, 453, 460, 463–64; Stibbs, "McArthur's Division at Nashville," *MOLLUS*, 4:496, 499; Sword, *The Confederacy's Last Hurrah*, 374–75.

58. *OR*, vol. 45, pt. 1, 435–36, 438–39, 451–52, 455, 457, 467; Sword, *The Confederacy's Last Hurrah*, 374–75.

59. *OR*, vol. 45, pt. 1, 447, 451, 453.

60. *OR*, vol. 45, pt. 1, 453, 455–56.

61. Stibbs, "McArthur's Division at Nashville," *MOLLUS*, 4:500–501.

62. *OR*, vol. 45, pt. 1, 436, 439, 442, 455, 457, 461; Sword, *The Confederacy's Last Hurrah*, 375–76.

63. *OR*, vol. 45, pt. 1, 438.

64. John H. Stibbs, "McArthur's Division at Nashville as Seen by a Regimental Commander," *MOLLUS*, 4:487.

65. Stibbs, "McArthur's Division at Nashville," *MOLLUS*, 4:488.

10

CIVILIAN PARTICIPANTS AND OBSERVERS DURING THE FRANKLIN-NASHVILLE CAMPAIGN

John J. Gaines

Just as enlisted soldiers and officers bore witness to terrible combat and the aftermath of battles during the Civil War, so too did the civilian population that resided in and around those fields. As the armies quickly moved on after battles, the civilians who experienced them continued to be active participants in the narrative by caring for the dying and wounded. Furthermore, the Franklin and Nashville Campaign occurred in an urban area with many civilians unable or reluctant to leave their homes and possessions. The greater numbers of civilians at the center of these battles provided ancillary support in a variety of ways.

Following the brief encounter between Confederate lieutenant general John B. Hood's and Union major general John M. Schofield's forces at Spring Hill, both armies moved toward Franklin in a lethal race. Schofield's forces arrived well ahead of Hood's and quickly erected breastworks through the center of town. Unfortunately, those breastworks enveloped houses and other structures of the local community.

Initially, a mix of apprehension and curiosity gripped the residents of Franklin. A few civilians immediately sought shelter, while others ventured out to witness the excitement, just as some civilians cautiously prepared for the coming battle. The Franklin Female Institute even opened for classes in the morning as soldiers poured into the town. Soon enough, the teachers at the institute reconsidered and rang the school bell to dismiss the students.[1] In one of the Franklin homes, Frances McEwen recalled that her "mother, who never knew what fear meant in her life, was a little reluctant to go and leave the upper part of the house to the tender mercies of soldiers, but she finally joined us in the basement."[2] F. B. Carter asked Major General Jacob D. Cox if the family should leave the house prior to the battle. Cox replied that they should only leave if battle were imminent; otherwise he would not be able to see to the "safety of its contents."[3] Unfortunately, the decision to remain and safeguard their belongings or flee to safety was a very risky one.

Other civilians looked forward to the excitement of the coming battle. Carrie Snyder spent the morning playing backgammon while Union soldiers constructed fortifications. "I began to fear there would be no fight. I wanted to see a battle or hear one. . . . We kept playing backgammon until about three o'clock, then the firing began to get thicker and sounded . . . like a snapping roar. We got up and walked about the house and yard; bullets occasionally whistled over our heads. We did not fear them much if we had the brick house between us."[4] Likewise, teenager Hardin Figuers met the news of the pending battle with absolute joy. He stated, "No mortal can tell with what a thrill of excitement I heard this announcement, but my mother and the General were in a more serious mood." Figuers traveled along the line inspecting the growing fortifications. "I spent the entire afternoon upon the top of the barn and woodshed, in a tree top, and other high places, seeing all that could be seen."[5]

The citizens of Franklin looked on as work on the fortifications continued through the morning. In the early afternoon, the reality of the battle began to set in as Confederate forces approached the town and began to form into a skirmish line at around 3:30. Figuers was in awe of the sight. "The imagination could not picture a more magnificent panoramic view than that scene as Hood's army, with perfect line and steady step, moved through the open field, with bands playing and battle flags flying, while the Federals stood still in their breastworks in the evening sun."[6]

As the firing started, many of the people of Franklin still did not recognize the danger of the looming conflict. According to Fannie Courtney, "I was sitting at the dinner table, when I heard the roar of artillery. I ran into the yard to listen."[7] The bewilderment did not last long once the reality of the dangerous situation became apparent. Carrie Snyder, like many other younger witnesses, remained outside until an artillery round flew over the house, then she rapidly joined "the old folks into the cellar." Many residents stayed to witness the events until it was obviously too hazardous to remain exposed. According to Fannie Courtney, a nineteen-year-old Union sympathizer, "the bullets were falling so thick it was unsafe to remain longer. Men, women, and children were running in every direction, together with unmanageable teams, loose horses and mules. . . . I hastened to the cellar with the rest of my family and neighbors who sought protection with us."[8]

The Carter House basement also filled with civilians seeking shelter during the battle. Located in the center of the Union line, just feet behind the breastworks, the basement contained seventeen civilians including F. B. Carter, his four adult daughters, a daughter-in-law, several grandchildren, and two female servants. During the Confederate charges against the Union line, several Union soldiers tried to run down to the cellar but were rebuked by Grandpa Carter who "talked pretty rough to them."[9]

Finally, teenager Hardin Figuers lingered outside until, "I concluded I was as liable to be hit as a soldier and retreated to the cellar. Just before entering the cellar, while standing at the front gate, I saw a Yankee get shot just across the street." Unfortunately, the perceived safety of the basements and cellars of Franklin did not last. An artillery shell later hit the Hardin home, scaring the occupants.[10]

Interestingly, the degree of naiveté among the witnesses to the battle was not only restricted to the younger generation. Residents at the McEwen house sent one of their slaves upstairs into the kitchen to prepare a meal while a group of whites cowered in the cellar. "A few minutes later, there was a crash! And down came a deluge of dust and gravel. The usually placid face of our old black mammy, now thoroughly frightened, appeared on the scene. She said a cannon ball had torn a hole in the side of the meat house and broken her wash kettle to pieces. She left the supper on the stove and fled precipitately into the cellar."[11] A similar situation occurred in another Franklin cellar when an elderly woman began to complain about the comfort of her surroundings during the battle. According to Carrie Snyder, "the old lady, [was] bewailing the fact that we had not caught up some bedding and brought (it) down with us. She . . . wanted us to go upstairs and get them."[12] Apparently, Snyder thought better of the request and refused to endanger herself.

As the battle raged on into the evening outside, curiosity drew several residents out of their cellars and into active participation. Hardin Figuers reported that an artillery shell landed very close to the house causing several occupants of the cellar to venture upstairs. The scene of the wounded around the house along with their cries forced Figuers and the other occupants to render aid. They went to the town square to get the local doctor claiming that all of the houses just inside the Union fortifications "were full of wounded Confederate prisoners and that no doctor was with them." He refused to return to the Hardin home, stating, "If they are as bad off as you say, I could not do them any good, and it is too dangerous to risk going up there." Hardin continued, "I was ashamed of him then and am ashamed of him now, and I will not give his name."[13] Figuers continued to aid the wounded, with his mother returning in the morning to assist him. Over the next several days, the family cooked meals and tended the wounded as best they could.

Soon afterward, many residents gave a sigh of relief as the Union forces moved on to Nashville. Fannie Courtney noted that the Union troops began moving out at around ten o'clock in the evening. Fannie emerged to give aid to passing wounded soldiers as did other people of Franklin.[14] Sallie Carter noted, "There was a stampede. Many federals ran by my house. Several wounded came by. Some of them asked me for water. One was very weak from loss of blood, and I gave him some whisky [*sic*]. Another was badly shot, and I tore one of my lace curtains for a bandage."[15] Finally, at around midnight, the battle drew to a close with only very sporadic firing. In tense anticipation, both residents and soldiers awaited evidence that the battle would resume or had completely concluded.

Although it appeared that the battle had officially ended, residents remained apprehensive that the danger was not over. In fact, as the Federals retreated, they used occasional harassing cannon fire to deter the Confederate forces from pursuit. Anna Toone Sloan had gone to bed when "a shell came whizzing through the wall close to the chimney knocking the mantel down, putting out the lights, and then falling right into the bed with us. . . . It did not explode, as it fell on the feather bed . . . but it scared us to death." Sloan immediately returned to the cellar of a neighbor.[16] Rumors circulated among the residents as they ventured out that the retreating Federals were going to burn the town following the fire at the cotton gin. According to Carrie Snyder, "It seems the Federal army . . . had set fire to the government stables, in which there was nothing left but a few tons of hay and some worthless saddles, harness, etc. That was the only building destroyed, unless by accident, or if in the way." A couple of other buildings burned in town but were put out by soldiers and civilians.[17] Fannie Courtney feared, "We thought of nothing else but being burned alive in the cellar, as there was no way of getting out if the fire continued to spread."[18]

Following the battle, the emotional impact of the carnage hit the civilians of the community. In spite of hours of combat, a few of the residents of the town realized the magnitude and barbarism exhibited in the previous day's event. Making an effort to impress the soldiers after the battle, Frances McEwen's sisters donned their new dresses in order to "look their best." Several soldiers openly questioned the prudence of the young ladies wearing store-bought clothing rather than homespun items. Fairly quickly, however, the family worked to bring water and wine to the soldiers. According to McEwen, "Instead of saying lessons at school the day after the battle, I watched the wounded men being carried in. Our house was full as could be; from morning until night we made bandages and scraped linen lint with which to dress the wounds, besides making jellies and soups with which to nourish them."[19]

Down the street, Hardin Figuers emerged to explore the battlefield with a slave. "The first dead person that I found was a little Yankee boy, about my own age, lying in the middle of the street with his hands thrown back over his head, pale in death. The sight of this boy somehow impressed me more than the thousands of dead men I was to look upon."[20] Like Figuers, Alice McPhail was overwhelmed as she explored the area around the Carter House in the morning. "I remember when day came the awful sight I saw. Men dead lying in the yard." Carrie Snyder would express the most telling words concerning the impact of the battle: "God forgive me for ever wishing to see or hear a battle."[21] These images stayed with them both for the rest of their lives.

While the aftermath of the battle was a horrific experience for the civilians that were unaccustomed to seeing combat, the extraordinary slaughter of the battle traumatized the soldiers themselves. Tennessean Sam Watkins later wrote: "Would to God that I never witnessed such a scene!"[22] Confederate captain John M. Hickey of the 11th Missouri went on to describe the morning. "Nothing could be heard but the wails of the wounded and the dying, some calling for their friends, some praying to be relieved of their awful suffering, and thousands in the deep, agonizing throes of death filled the air with mournful sounds and dying groans that can never be described." Hickey experienced the attention and care of the people of Franklin firsthand. During the battle, he was wounded several times, including a wound that would claim his right leg. He spent a week awaiting medical attention in one of the churches of the community.[23]

Even General John Bell Hood, a man who had ordered thousands of men into combat and often to their deaths, was flabbergasted by the spectacle. As he moved through the village,

> his sturdy visage assumed a melancholy appearance, and for a considerable time he sat on his horse and wept like a child. . . . The most heart-rending scenes . . . were citizens of Franklin and the surrounding country. They appeared on the battlefield about sun-up. Fathers, mothers, brothers and sisters looking for fathers, husbands, sons, brothers and friends. A large part of Hood's army was from Tennessee, some from Franklin and many from the vicinity of Franklin. . . . While the General was weeping the . . . cries . . . and wailing were heard from little groups all over the field. . . . Frail women clasping their hands above the mangled bodies . . . ; and little children frantic with fear and grief.[24]

If the scene affected the soldiers in such a way, it is impossible to gauge the impact on the civilian witnesses.

The Carter family soon emerged from the basement of the home seeking their relative, Captain Tod Carter, a member of Hood's army. Brigadier General Thomas Benton Smith located the family and helped them to find young Tod. The family retrieved Tod from a point about 150 yards from his childhood home. He had been shot nine times in the arms and legs with one shot embedded above his left eye. Confederate surgeon Dr. Deering Roberts removed the ball over Tod's eye and treated the remaining wounds. Unfortunately, Tod died of his wounds two days after the battle, leaving his family heartbroken.[25]

Not all families in Franklin had such a sad reunion fortunately. About the time the Carter family set out on their quest to find Tod, Fannie Courtney and her mother opened the front door of their home. To their absolute joy, Fannie's brother and one of her cousins of Lieutenant General Nathan Bedford Forrest's command stood there. "My mother was overjoyed that she was once more permitted to clasp her boy to her heart. He remained with us one day and night, and then rejoined his unit near Murfreesboro. We saw him no more . . ."[26]

After her brother's departure, Fannie and her mother, as well as many other citizens of Franklin, became nurses and orderlies to care for the nearly four thousand wounded soldiers. Within the town, forty-four homes, schools, churches, and other buildings were pressed into service as hospitals and convalescent buildings for wounded soldiers. As the Confederate rations lacked quality and quantity, the citizens often served any food that was available in their own homes to feed the wounded. Fannie Courtney stated that many of the soldiers her mother and she attended to claimed they had not eaten in two days. As most of the soldiers had lost their blankets and overcoats, Fannie and others brought any bedding they could find to provide comfort. They endeavored to "do all in [their] power to make the wounded more comfortable until they could be brought to hospitals."[27]

Carrie McGavock ordered her own home, the Carnton House, to be converted to a hospital. She had any cloth in the house, including "old linen, then her towels and napkins, then her sheets and tablecloths, then her husband's shirts, and her own undergarments," torn apart to make bandages. Mrs. McGavock filled her home with wounded soldiers, allotting two to each bed and more in any space that was available. As the house filled, McGavock put her lawn to use as well. She and the rest of the household worked tirelessly to care for all of the patients in her home. Ultimately, "it was [thanks] to her thoughtfulness and oversight that a full list of the dead that rest there was made. She had a true record, and always kept it in her own possession. Until the close of her life no sign of neglect showed in any part of the cemetery, it being her chief pleasure to see that no stray weeds crept upon the hallowed ground, and that the grass and inclosures [*sic*] showed in their careful keeping the love she bestowed upon that spot."[28]

As so many soldiers recovered in local hospitals with surgeons, aides, and nurses attending to them, several romances bloomed in the midst of misery. A surgeon from Missouri married one of the local young women. At least one of the wounded soldiers found love during his recovery and married another local girl. Finally, "a young soldier who was an artist, met on the field one of our young ladies, who was also of an artistic turn of mind, and the year following they were married."[29]

During the closing hours of the battle, the Union Army of the Ohio began moving toward Nashville with the Confederate forces following several hours later. As the Union soldiers moved through populations of Confederate supporters, many civilians worried about pillaging by soldiers. Mary Claiborne, a guest at Travelers Rest outside of Nashville, wrote that as Union forces flowed by, two guards (known only as David and Silas) remained at the house "for the protection of the family from stragglers." Annie Maxwell retrieved her husband's rank insignia and urged one of the soldiers to accept an impromptu promotion in the hopes that his new rank would dissuade looters. The newly minted Captain David stationed himself next to the smokehouse so that he would be in full view of passing soldiers. One of the passing soldiers proclaimed, "A captain, by God, guarding these damned rebels." The family repaid the two soldiers with a fine dinner, but unfortunately their extended stay caused them to get cut off from their comrades by the marching Confederate forces. For the time being, David and Silas dressed in civilian clothing and were hidden by the family.[30]

As the columns of soldiers paraded from Franklin into Nashville, thousands of civilians came out of their homes to see the throngs of Confederate prisoners of war. In a fit of pent-up hostility, several small groups of African American civilians stationed themselves along the route of the passing Confederate prisoners. The two groups openly exchanged insults.[31] The Union soldiers themselves had lost their novelty since Nashville had been occupied by Union forces for two years at this point. However, the realization of a likely battle near the city impressed many residents. Rachel Carter Craighead noted in her diary, "they expect a battle by day light. Good Lord protect us."

As the soldiers marched into the Nashville area and began constructing fortifications for the coming battle, they confronted the same problem that occurred at Franklin and other previous battles near urban areas. Existing houses and other structures lay within the lines of fortifications and risked destruction in order to solidify the line. The chancellor of the University of Nashville, John Berrien Lindsley, later expressed his gratitude in his diary that Union forces built their breastworks in order to save as many "houses as possible. Dr. Hoyte's and mine were directly in the line, but that were made to fall immediately behind it."[32]

Margaret Lawrence Lindsley, a twenty-four-year-old Unionist, noted in her journal that the civilians in the area of East Nashville were extremely nervous and consumed with thoughts of the battle, especially concerning rumors that General Nathan Bedford Forrest would soon be arriving. Like the younger residents of Franklin, the youth of Nashville exhibited a profound sense of excitement for the coming battle. Margaret wrote, "The servants and children are utterly unmanageable—simply wild—the former stand and stare at the line of soldiers in petrified terror, the latter equally magnetized but the attraction being one of unmitigated delight at the idea of a battle 'right here!' No finer fun could be conceived of; and Lettie, Lou, Frank, John and Baby Bess, are all ready, decked in warlike paraphernalia, . . . all eager for the fray!"[33]

Margaret went on to disclose a bit of harsh fun at the expense of an African American servant or slave at the home:

> I have been laughing at, and trying to encourage old Aunt Cynthia, who persists in declaring "No! No! No! I can't do no cooking this hyar day!" "because Miss Maggie, dem dar bullets kill me sure in de kitchen!" I have offered her the front parlor if she thinks that safer—anywhere in the house if she will only prepare some fuel to sustain and keep burning all this fire and flame of valor and patriotism in the Lindsley family—but to no purpose—cook she will not, nor any of her numerous assistants—my only answer being: "How kin you—jest and laugh at sich a time as this Miss Maggie, when de rebs done dum sure, and we all be killed!"[34]

Several days of unseasonably warm weather for early December led many civilians to believe the battle would begin quite soon. The flurry of activity by soldiers erecting breastworks as well as their friends and neighbors preparing to leave the area and hiding their possessions largely legitimized the panic. Civilians living near the Belmont mansion fled with the expectation that the battle would likely rage directly through the vicinity.[35]

As the region experienced a sudden cold snap, another concern facing the residents of Nashville was the destruction of the groves of trees, fences, and smaller wooden structures used by both armies to fend off the sudden onset of freezing temperatures in the area. According to a Confederate chaplain, the hills around the city were recently overgrown with trees. Within a few days of the arrivals of both armies, much of the area had been clear cut. In her journal, Margaret Lindsley lamented, "still destruction at least goes bravely on." Fortunately, however, the cold weather postponed the battle and allowed the soldiers to have a brief respite following the conflict at Franklin.[36]

In addition to the confiscation of lumber for various projects, Union major general George Thomas, commander of Union forces at Nashville, ordered that all suitable horses within the general area, including Middle Tennessee and Southern Kentucky, to be confiscated in an attempt to replenish the army. With the appropriation of an estimated seven thousand relatively fresh horses, Thomas resupplied the entirety of his dismounted cavalry. Unfortunately, the civilian owners of these horses were left only with the promise that "the government [would] settle for them afterward."[37]

While many civilians in the region suffered due to the military confiscation of livestock, others benefited from the presence of so many soldiers, especially the Union soldiers with somewhat regular visits by federal paymasters. Abram Stafford of the 103rd Ohio enjoyed his time in Nashville, especially after witnessing the horrors of Franklin. Stafford remarked in his diary that on the days prior to the battle he had his shoes resoled for two dollars, had six pictures made for ninety-five cents, mailed several packages and letters, and saw the play *Aladin and the Wonderful Lamp.*[38] Many other soldiers took advantage of the lull in campaigning and their proximity to an urban area to embark on adventures of their own.

Despite the occasional skirmishing between pickets on the front lines, "some of the boys got passes and went into the city."[39] William Hunzinger of the 79th Indiana could not get a pass for himself initially, so he sent his watch into town with his brother Levi in order to get it cleaned. Levi returned with a bounty of goods purchased in Nashville. "Levi brought us a basket of pies, cakes, and apples, and we had a good mess. He got my watch cleaned." Several days later, William was able to get a pass for himself and likely spent a significant amount of money in town. "I got a pass and went to town and enjoyed myself fine eating apples, pies, cakes and drinking sider [*sic*]. And I hardly knew the town for it had improved so much since I last saw it and is such a buisness plase [*sic*]. I went back to camp and found Levi and James Mitchell and we went to town and eat cakes and pies together." The next day, on December 8, William returned to town for goods and services rather than eating. "Levi and I set for photographs at the Cumberland gallery and I bought Genls Wm. T. Shereman, George H. Thomas and Wm. P. [*sic*; James B.] McPhersons Photographs. I purchased a diary for 1865."[40]

So many soldiers ventured into the town to spend their pay, vendors actually had trouble meeting the needs of their new customers. A couple of soldiers from the 7th Minnesota visited several galleries in the area before they were able to find one that would schedule a sitting for the two since all of the photographers were overwhelmed with soldiers seeking sessions. John Hiestand of the 123rd Indiana documented one of the more extravagant incidents of soldiers spending money in the local economy. Following their time guarding railroad stock, Hiestand and several others "went to [the] circus, [and then] got supper at [a] saloon tonight."[41]

Although many people in the area, both soldiers and civilians, expected the Battle of Nashville to begin very soon, the firing simply did not start. Instead, the civilians of Nashville took in the spectacle of the Union soldiers constructing fortifications throughout the community. Rachel Craighead wrote in her diary on December 4: "I expected to be aroused this morning by the booming of cannon but all seems quiet. . . . I went over to see Sister Joe. We went on top of the house. Heard and saw the work on a number of cannon."[42]

While some residents opted to watch the work from afar, others endeavored to gain a more intimate look and ended up regretting their decision to do so. Several different soldiers recorded their memories of this group of civilians. According to Dr. Stephen Ayres of the Cumberland Hospital, "When our men were busily at work in the trenches, . . . they had quite an interested group of lookers-on from the city. These were clerks and bookkeepers and employees of various kinds, and with their nice clean suits and polished boots they presented quite a contrast to our veterans at work. Suddenly, and to their great surprise, they were corralled by the corporal's guard and ordered to serve their turn with the picks and shovels which they had been watching with so much interest." R. B. Stewart of the 15th Ohio followed up by remarking, "An hour's work in the trenches satisfied their curiosity and they came no more to camp." Though the soldiers undoubtedly delighted in granting the civilian spectators a bit of comeuppance for their unabashed gawking, the soldiers did have a logic to their actions. A first lieutenant from the 49th Ohio justified the temporary drafting of civilians as laborers by noting: "Did we not do this they would throng our line so much as to be in our way."[43]

Civilians also ventured to other parts of the line and found themselves in harm's way there as well. Unfortunately, many did not realize the reach of the rifled muskets and wandered into range of the opposing lines. Union chaplain Elijah Edwards of the 7th Minnesota Infantry found amusement at the reactions of a group of civilians that strolled too close to the Confederate forces. "Today I rode around our outer line, and to my astonishment found that we were in minie [ball] range of the rebs. I noticed some civilians who had come out to be spectators of the fray and being . . . reminded by the whizzing of a few bullets of the demands of home left hurriedly. One was standing near a gunner when a bullet whizzed by his ear. I shall not ever forget his scared comical expression . . . on the haste with which he decamped."[44]

As in the cases of hopeful reunions prior to the Battle of Franklin, civilians of Nashville likewise looked for relatives among Hood's forces on the outskirts of the city. As the Confederates constructed their camps, some civilians braved the occasional musket fire to locate long-missed relatives. Though rare, some of these attempted reunions were successful. Confederate captain William Gale documented one such in a letter to his wife. "When we got to John Overton's place I saw some ladies by the roadside in high excitement, and on riding up found them to be Mary Bradford, Miss Maxwell, Miss May, Misses Becky Allison, Mary Hadley and Buck Correy. Mary Hadley was married to Maj. Clare, of the Staff of Gen. Hood, and was left behind after her three days' honeymoon."[45] Mary and William honeymooned in the Confederate camp from the twelfth until their bliss was interrupted on the morning of the fifteenth by erupting musket fire of the coming battle. William quickly returned to duty and Mary took a group of children to the basement of Travelers Rest. The couple had courted for several years through correspondence and were ultimately married a few days before the Battle of Nashville in the Brentwood Methodist Church by Bishop Charles Quintard. After the end of the war, the major and Mary were reunited and remained in Nashville until he passed away in 1873.[46]

After more than a week of minor skirmishes between Confederate pickets and Union soldiers enjoying the benefits of an encampment in an urban area, the weather, rather than violence, put an end to most activity in the area. On December 8 it turned very cold. In a memoir of the war, Alexis Cope, adjutant of the 15th Ohio, remembered the extent of the chill more than fifty years later:

> The morning of December 8, was the coldest we had so far experienced during the winter and it was difficult to keep warm. . . . On Friday, December 9, early in the morning, there was a storm of sleet and snow which continued all day, and it grew so cold the men crowded together in their tents to keep warm. It was reported that an order to move against the enemy next morning had been issued, but was afterwards countermanded because of the storm. . . . December 10, the storm had practically ceased, but it was very cold and the ground was covered with sleet and snow, and it was very difficult to get about. . . . December 11, was still cold and the sleet and snow did not melt. The men kept their tents, or huddled about their fires. There was but little picket firing. At 10 A.M. there was a meeting of corps commanders at General Thomas' headquarters and it was decided that we could not attack the enemy with any show of success until the weather moderated and the snow and sleet melted. . . . December 12, it was still cold and although the sun shown in the morning it did not have the power to melt the ice and snow which covered the ground.[47]

One of the very few instances of commerce to continue during the incredible cold snap was by Dr. John Tilford, a surgeon with the 79th Indiana. The storm forced Tilford to leave camp in order to purchase a small camp stove for the considerable price of seven dollars in order to warm his tent.[48] As most privates earned only sixteen dollars a month in 1865, it is somewhat likely that the price of the stove can be taken as evidence that the civilians of Nashville engaged in slight price gouging.

Though the temperature reached six degrees below zero and many soldiers found themselves freezing in their tents, civilians in the area apparently also had some influence among the Union officers in the city concerning the fate of their trees to procure firewood. Sergeant Lyman Pierce of the 2nd Iowa Cavalry complained, "At first the boys cut the gum trees in camp, and with them made fires on the company grounds, around which they clustered to keep from freezing. This we thought severe enough to satisfy any disciplinarian, but facts showed differently, and on the morning of December 9, a bitter cold day, we were greeted by an order *to cut no more trees.* Had this order been obeyed, every soldier in the command must *inevitably have frozen to death,* except such generals as toasted their toes by warm parlor fires."[49]

Finally, on December 16, a combination of somewhat warming weather and pressure from General Ulysses S. Grant moved Thomas to begin his attack on the Confederate forces encamped on the outskirts of Nashville. Fortunately for the people of the city, the bulk of the fighting took place as a running battle with the Confederates retreating away from the city. Perhaps with the city having been garrisoned for a number of years and with both armies encamped in the area for more than a week, the novelty of masses of soldiers had worn off and most civilians did not endeavor to become spectators of the battle. Many sheltered themselves in basements and cellars during the fighting. Younger people at Travelers Rest peeked out of ground-level windows from cellars and "watched the bomb shells that were flying through the air and lighting in various parts of the grounds and garden."[50] For the most part, the Union soldiers pursuing the fleeing Confederates passed by so quickly that most civilians witnessed only a brief scene with only small-arms fire. While minié balls were certainly lethal, civilians found relief that artillery rounds flew over them only during the opening moments of the battle and the terror of the entire event lasted only a single day. Fortunately, the war would be over within a few months.

Though they became obstacles and annoyances to the passing armies at times, civilians provided a tremendously wide range of direct assistance to the armies and soldiers themselves. Civilians served as impromptu sutlers, offering a great variety of goods and services that aided and bolstered morale among the soldiers. They also, albeit often unwillingly, were sources of food stocks and livestock that allowed armies to replenish their own dwindling supplies. Furthermore, civilians became amateur medical personnel who rendered much-needed help to the surgeons left behind after engagements, aiding the recovering and comforting the dying. Finally, civilians supplemented the military participants as chroniclers of the events, passing on their memories, a sense of the gravity of the event they witnessed, the amazement at the gathering of so many soldiers, and ultimately the horror at the destruction brought by those forces.

Notes

1. David R. Logsdon, *Eyewitnesses at the Battle of Franklin* (Nashville: Kettle Mills Press, 1991), 3.
2. Ibid., 11.
3. Ibid., 2.
4. Ibid., 10.
5. Hardin Figuers, "A Boy's Impressions of the Battle of Franklin," *Confederate Veteran Magazine* (January 1915): 4.
6. Ibid.
7. Logsdon, *Eyewitnesses at the Battle of Franklin*, 10.
8. Ibid., 11
9. Frances McEwen, "Inside the Lines at Franklin," *Confederate Veteran Magazine* (January 1895): 72.
10. Figuers, "A Boy's Impressions of the Battle of Franklin," 4.
11. McEwen, "Inside the Lines at Franklin," 72.
12. Logsdon, *Eyewitnesses at the Battle of Franklin*, 12.
13. Figuers, "A Boy's Impressions of the Battle of Franklin," 4.
14. Logsdon, *Eyewitnesses at the Battle of Franklin*, 57.
15. Sallie Carter, "A Lady Who Writes of the Battle," *Confederate Veteran Magazine* (November 1909): 542.
16. Logsdon, *Eyewitnesses at the Battle of Franklin*, 63.
17. Ibid., 61.
18. Ibid., 60.
19. McEwen, "Inside the Lines at Franklin," 72–73.
20. Logsdon, *Eyewitnesses at the Battle of Franklin*, 68.
21. Ibid., 71.
22. Sam Watkins, *Company Aytch: Or, A Side Show of the Big Show* (New York: Touchstone Books, 1997), 232.
23. Captain J. M. Hickey, "Battle of Franklin," *Confederate Veteran Magazine* 17 (January 1909): 14.
24. Byron Bowers, Ferguson's Battery, Cheatham's Corps: Review Appeal, February 24, 1972, "Reminiscences of Byron Bowers," *Middle Tennessee Eyewitnesses to the Civil War*, accessed February 1, 2014, http://www.midtneyewitnesses.com/eyewitness-book-series/franklin/confederate-soldier.
25. Logsdon, *Eyewitnesses at the Battle of Franklin*, 67.

26. Frances "Fannie" Courtney, *Williamson County Historical Journal* 7, "Tinth" Anniversary Edition, 1966–1976, *Middle Tennessee Eyewitnesses to the Civil War*, accessed February 1, 2014, http://www.midtneyewitnesses.com/eyewitness-book-series/franklin/civilian.

27. Ibid.

28. Colonel William Dudley Gale, "The Good Samaritan at Franklin," *Confederate Veteran Magazine* 30, no. 1 (December 1922): 448.

29. McEwen, "Inside the Lines at Franklin," 73.

30. "Travelers Rest," *Middle Tennessee Eyewitnesses to the Civil War*, last modified 2012, accessed February 27, 2014, http://www.midtneyewitnesses.com/still-standing/nashville/travellers-rest.

31. Logsdon, *Eyewitnesses at the Battle of Nashville*, 4.

32. Ibid., 7.

33. Ibid., 13.

34. Ibid.

35. Ibid., 10.

36. Ibid., 9, 17.

37. James Fowler Rusling, *Men and Things I Saw in Civil War Days* (New York: Eaton and Mains, 1899), 91.

38. Abram Harrison Stafford, "The Civil War Diaries of Abram Harrison Stafford and Elizabeth Churchill of Chardon, Geauga County, Ohio," accessed March 12, 2014, http://www.rootsweb.ancestry.com/~ohgeauga/abram.htm.

39. George W. Morris, *History of the Eighty-First Regiment of Indiana Volunteer Infantry in the Great War of the Rebellion, 1861 to 1865* (Louisville, KY: The Franklin Printing Company, 1901), 145.

40. William H. Hunzinger, *The Camp Life and Campaigns of William H. Huntzinger and Brothers, A Day to Day Record, 1862–1865*, accessed March 14, 2014, http://www.lafavre.us/huntzinger/huntzinger.htm.

41. Logsdon, *Eyewitnesses at the Battle of Nashville*, 22, 35.

42. Ibid., 13.

43. Ibid., 14.

44. Ibid., 15.

45. Colonel William Dudley Gale, "Confederate Disaster at Nashville," *Confederate Veteran Magazine* 2 (February 1894): 46–47.

46. "Amiable and Beloved Mary Hadley Clare," *Confederate Veteran Magazine* 19 (July 1911): 347.

47. Alexis Cope, *The Fifteenth Ohio Volunteers and its Campaigns, War of 1861–5*, (Columbus, OH: Published by the author, 1916), 635–36.

48. Logsdon, *Eyewitnesses at the Battle of Nashville*, 28.

49. Lyman B. Pierce, *History of the Second Iowa Cavalry* (Burlington, IA: Hawkeye Steam Book and Job Printing Establishment, 1865), 140–41.

50. Logsdon, *Eyewitnesses at the Battle of Nashville*, 83.

11

"OUR PEOPLES ARE DEPRESSED IN SPIRIT"

TEXANS' REACTIONS TO HOOD'S TENNESSEE CAMPAIGN

Charles D. Grear

The winter of 1864–65 proved difficult for most throughout the South. While civilians experienced hardships created by the Union blockade and destruction from the numerous campaigns throughout the South, General Robert E. Lee's Army of Northern Virginia was under siege at Petersburg, Virginia, and General John Bell Hood led the disastrous Tennessee Campaign of 1864. Though not short on supplies nor suffering any significant Union presence, the people of Texas, the Confederate state farthest from the chaos of these campaigns, reacted to the events on the other side of the Mississippi River, particularly Hood's campaign through Tennessee. Distance isolated Texans from the hardships of their sister states, but they still felt the pressure of a prolonged war, particularly a disastrous campaign that dipped morale to its nadir.[1] Contemporary newspapers, letters, and diaries of the soldiers in the field and citizens back home reveal their thoughts and attitudes. How Texans reacted to the tragic Tennessee Campaign highlights a region whose home front many historians have ignored or considered too provincial to include in studies of the Civil War.

Texas was unlike other Confederate states. It was the only southern state that shared a border with a foreign country, had a frontier, or featured a population diverse enough to include significant numbers both of the foreign-born and of native northern settlers.[2] Three-fourths of the Texas population was not born in the Lone Star State. Texans, being on the western flank of the Confederacy, had more choices of locations to serve; thus, soldiers from Texas served in all theaters of the war and in more states and territories than men from any other Confederate or Union state. Essentially, Texans had many more connections to people and places outside of the state, which motivated many of them to fight east of the Mississippi River despite a major drought and the potential for Indian raids back home, as well as incursions from disgruntled Tejanos in Mexico.[3]

By the start of the Tennessee Campaign, Texas soldiers had experienced many hardships and setbacks. Previous events had already diminished Texan morale. One such was the loss of Vicksburg, which isolated Texas and the Trans-Mississippi from the rest of the Confederacy. Since mid-May 1863, when General Ulysses S. Grant led his assaults on Vicksburg, correspondence between Texas soldiers and their family members and friends had decreased significantly. The loss of Vicksburg spurred many Texans to desert, most returning home to defend against an anticipated Union invasion. Texans who remained in the Cis-Mississippi were those who had the strongest devotion to the Confederate cause and had the continued desire to protect their extended families in the more easterly part of the Confederacy. Most recently the capture of Atlanta, Georgia, was a significant loss to the Confederacy. Despite all this, many Texans wanted to continue the fight. Stationed near the Texas-Louisiana border in September 1864, H. P. Edwards of the 20th Texas Infantry met three Texans returning home before the fall of Atlanta. "I think the war is over now at lest the fighting. I dont think there will be any more hard fighting. I saw three men from Atlanta. . . . They say the yanks cant take Atlanta."[4]

False news spurred Edwards's hopes, but even those who participated in the failed defense of Atlanta shared his optimism. Captain James P. Douglas, commander of the 1st Texas Battery, appeared confident of the Confederate cause and particularly Hood in the days after Atlanta. In a letter home to his wife, Douglas reassured her that "he [Hood] may design a flank movement on the enemy yet, with a view to drawing Sherman out of Atlanta, which I think could be successfully accomplished. We are in a plentiful country and living well so far as provisions are concerned though I pay a very high price for all articles of food."[5] A few days later Douglas expressed his continued belief in the Confederate army's abilities: "I am not willing to close this campaign with Atlanta in the hands of the Yanks. We can retake it without any trouble, if reinforced, by flanking it."[6]

Even when Francis Lubbock, the former governor of Texas, encouraged Texans to return to the Trans-Mississippi to defend the Lone Star State, Douglas disagreed. "I believe his ideas are correct and would myself prefer to stay on this side if everything were arranged to suit me, but as I am now situated, I am bound to differ with him and shall not take his advice if an opportunity offers for me to get to the trans-Mississippi department."[7] Hood's marching orders on September 29 further buoyed Douglas's spirits and those of his comrades in the Army of Tennessee. Faith in their army and an opportunity to strike back at the victors of Atlanta encouraged the Texans and raised morale.[8]

Texans, both soldiers and civilians, anticipated the new campaign to redeem their loss of Atlanta and continue the fight against the Union. Writing from Florence, Alabama, Corporal William G. Young of the 15th Texas Cavalry expressed his faith in the continued campaign to stop Sherman in a diary entry on November 17. "This [Atlanta] campaign is not ended yet," Young wrote. "My opinion is we will have another fight, but where or when or if ever I can't say."[9] These sentiments were echoed back in the Lone Star State when news arrived that Hood was on the move. Houston's *Tri-Weekly Telegraph* reported to its readers that "Gen. Hood has at last struck the right chord. . . . No matter what the critics may say—no matter what the books might say—we lose more in retreat than we do in advancing." Like most Texans, the editor viewed Hood's movements as a continuation of the Atlanta Campaign. As long as the Army of Tennessee remained intact and appeared active, Texans remained confident that their chances to continue and possibly win the Civil War stayed alive.[10]

Maintaining soldier morale depended on many factors. Though men could for a time forgo good food and tolerable conditions, the dwindling of supplies and poor weather began to take its toll. When Hood started the Tennessee Campaign the men had rested nearly a month since the fall of Atlanta. Soon after the Army of Tennessee moved to threaten General William Tecumseh Sherman's line of communication and entice him to follow the Confederates to ground of their choice, the weather turned nasty. On October 26 Young recorded in his diary, "Thru the mud up to our knees, we go it all day, 18 miles."[11] The rained continued. On November 9 Young again wrote, "Rain, rain all the time." He mentioned wet weather again on the seventeenth and twentieth of the month until the conditions worsened on November 21, when Charles A. Leuscher, a German Texan in the 6th Texas Infantry, recorded in his diary, "We marched of[f] from Florence while the snow came down thick, & we were bound for Tennessee."[12] Young concurred on the twenty-third, commenting, "The ground still frozen, barefooted."[13] Misery set in early for the men in Hood's army, and the foul weather continued from December 7 through 13 in the form of sleet and freezing rain.[14]

Dwindling supplies compounded the soldiers' miseries. Almost from the start of the march to Tennessee, Young noted the lack of rations: "Lay up all day [October 2] expecting rations." Later that month, he again chronicled, "Rations short, two ears of corn to the men." The only reprieve the Texan recorded was on November 17 while camped at Florence. "As for rations and clothing," he wrote, "we have done very well since here." A week later and many miles farther on the march, the army reduced the men's rations by half.[15] As the campaign entered Union-occupied territory in Tennessee, Hood's men relied more on captured Union supply trains and railroad cars for food.[16]

Victuals were not the only topics on the minds of Texans. Throughout the fall of 1864, people across the divided nation awaited the presidential election in the Union states and the prospect of another year of war in January 1865. Texan H. P. Edwards pored over any news he could find of the election. On September 19 he received a newspaper from a blockade runner and noted his excitement that the peace candidate, "[George B.] McCelland [*sic*] was nominated for president."[17] Less than two months later news of Abraham Lincoln's reelection received mixed reactions from Texans. Young of the 15th Texas Cavalry saw Lincoln's reelection as a new opportunity to regain the honor lost at Atlanta. "Lincoln is elected. . . . We will get a chance to whip him good. . . . With this army we can tough it out four years longer."[18] Private Georg Wilhelm Schwarting, a captured German soldier in the 17th/18th/24th/25th Texas Cavalry Consolidated, exhausted with the war, noted, "Should the Union have the misfortune to re-elect the current president, meaning that peace will be postponed for another 4 years, then I'll be going to Texas in the fall or the spring, and probably from there back to Germany. I just don't feel comfortable here in Yanky-land." He never fulfilled his threat and returned to the Confederate army as a cavalryman in Louisiana.[19] Similarly, T. J. Dilliard of the 28th Texas Cavalry expressed his frustration while at Camp Gano in Arkansas:

> Reliable news has reached here that Abe Lincoln is President for the next 4 years. This is discouraging to soldiers of this department with Abe as the President of the United States is expected a continue of the war for the next 4 years. There are but few of our soldiers that are willing to fight for another 4 years without pay or any other Thing furnish by the government. I find more dissatisfaction and discontent in Camp Than I have seen before The greater part of this Brigade declare That They will not serve any longer Than Spring all have been looking forward to the year 65 as the ending of the war and if their hopes are not realized I know not what wille be the Course taken but believe that a great many of our men will go home.[20]

Lincoln's reelection and the start of the new year served as an artificial deadline for the men. If the new year came and victory did not appear closer, their morale would diminish further.

Even after the fall of Atlanta, the morale of Texans had initially been good, but as Hood advanced into Tennessee it steadily declined. The Battle of

Franklin initiated a fundamental change in even the most motivated Texans. Though the number of letters after the battle dropped significantly because of the soldiers' isolation from the Trans-Mississippi, the number of men who died in battle, and the distractions of an active campaign, there was a more subtle reason why Texans rarely mentioned the battles of Franklin and Nashville: they rarely write about defeats. When Texans rode and marched off to war, their letters and speeches contained many references to the martial past of the Lone Star State. Soldiers and leaders mentioned the Texas Revolution and Mexican-American War, but not once did they mention the failed Santa Fe and Mier expeditions of the Republic Era. Examination of hundreds of collections of letters, diaries, and memoirs turned up only three that mentioned those battles. The lack of documentation demonstrates these soldiers' true reaction to this campaign; it proved to be the final conflict that broke their morale and general belief in the Confederate cause.

The ever-optimistic James P. Douglas and Robert Franklin Bunting are the only two Texans to write directly about the Battle of Franklin. In a letter to his wife Sallie, Douglas wrote, "I have seen many battles, but this one for the short time it lasted and the small ground it was fought upon (the line of the conflict was about 500 yards in length), was the bloodiest I have ever seen."[21] Bunting concurred, lamenting the loss of Patrick Cleburne and Hiram Granbury, "But alas! how great the cost in precious, noble, heroic life . . . the blood of Arkansians and Texians flowed freely in the conflict . . . those Patriots rushed triumphing to the conflict, conscious that Heaven smiled on their efforts."[22] Another soldier, Jim Turner of the 6th Texas Infantry, remembered years after the war, "We had to charge across an open field through the most deadly fire it was ever our misfortune to face. . . . Our men were mowed down like grass. Although almost our entire division had been shot down, we pressed steadily."[23] The best description of the carnage and sentiment of the battle came from Lieutenant Linson Montgomery Keener of the 7th Texas Infantry: "As we walked over the field after the battle was over the whole earth seemed covered with the dead bodies of Southern soldiers. 'Tell your boy that if he could have walked with me over that battle ground and witnessed that sight, with the bodies of the dead so close together one could barely move without stepping on them, he would have seen enough of the sorrow and the horror of war to far outweigh all the glory and glamour. Never, never, have I seen so many Confederates sacrificed as at the Battle of Franklin.'"[24]

The gore and death at Franklin shocked the Texans, but Douglas and Bunting attempted to view the battle in a positive light by regarding it as a Confederate victory. This claim seemed plausible since Major General John Schofield surrendered the battlefield when he retreated for Nashville. Douglas commented, "Our men are in fine spirits."[25] Bunting recorded in his diary that "Tonight the spell is broken, the lightening flashes of glad tidings of our great victory at Franklin"[26] Though Texans recognized the cost in lives at Franklin, they attempted to justify it by claiming success.

Unfortunately the defeat at Nashville humbled these proud and devoted men. Again Douglas, who barely escaped capture, was the only Texan to write directly about the battle immediately after its conclusion. In another letter to his wife he mentioned only that "Our fight around Nashville was so humiliating a defeat that I will not dwell upon it."[27] Similarly in Douglas John Cater's reminisces, he found the battle a pointless exercise. "For what purpose I could not tell. Sherman could easily send troops by railroad to Nashville to repeat the Atlanta tragedy. But he was not needed. Gen. Thomas had men enough without calling on Sherman to drive us out of Tennessee."[28] These battles proved a significant and final turning point for Texan morale, though it took some time for the truth to reach the Texas public.

Initial newspaper reports throughout the Trans-Mississippi were favorable to the Confederate army. The *Tri-Weekly Telegraph* of Houston informed the public, "Great consternation prevailed in Nashville, and with good cause. The city was surrounded and the Cumberland blockaded. Hood with a victorious army appears to be in position to dictate terms to Yankees, and, has we trust ere this taken possession."[29] The *Daily True Delta* of New Orleans reported that at Franklin "the Federal army was defeated, that the Confederate army was victorious, that the enemy was saved from disaster by the advent of night, and has found safety only in the fortifications of Nashville." The rest of the article spins the truth, arguing that the Union forces did not repulse the Confederates, who instead had enjoyed the "prettiest victory of war" and "cleanest victory of the war"[30] By the end of December the press revealed the truth with the headlines "Rebel Retreat in Tennessee," "Richmond Papers Say Their Defeat in Tennessee Was Disastrous," and "The Confederacy Tumbling."[31] Despite the grim newspaper reports, Sergeant Major Nathan Gregg of the 3rd Texas Cavalry, writing a letter to his hometown newspaper, the *Marshall Republican*, tried to put a positive spin even on this disastrous campaign. "Hood's army is in a high state of discipline, and as determined as if no disasters had occurred to it. This was all we had really to fear; for its losses can be repaired, and with Gen. Joseph E. Johnston once more in command of it, as is reported, it will soon recover all that has been lost."[32] The 3rd Texas Cavalry had relatively few casualties during both battles, which could have influenced Gregg's immediate reaction to the campaign.[33] The words and actions of Gregg's fellow Texas soldiers tell a completely different story.

Texans in Hood's army and elsewhere clearly expressed their dismay in their reactions to the failed campaign in Tennessee. Ebenezer Albert Kellogg of the 27th Texas Cavalry served as part of the rearguard during the army's retreat from Nashville. His memoir provided a matter-of-fact description of the campaign and concluded with the entry, "So ends the disastrous campaign."[34] Similarly Cater, a member of the 3rd Texas Cavalry, with the help of years of reflection, reminisced, "How different now! A wrecked and shattered army with nothing but gloom before us. Comment is unnecessary."[35] Morale of Texas soldiers plummeted after the failed campaign, and the gloom of that time remained a significant memory of the men who participated in it.

Even the ever-optimistic James P. Douglas confided to his wife that "our country is in much the worse condition it has ever been. If a great deed is not done this winter, the Yanks will close the war in the spring. I fear many of the officers and men in the army are demoralized. We should be prepared for the worst, while we strive and hope for the better . . . unless something is done more than has yet been done, our great cause must fail. I loathe to write it, but the truth forces itself upon me." He even considered resigning his commission and blamed the poor result on "the refusal of our men [Trans-Mississippians] to cross the Mississippi when ordered."[36]

Other disillusioned Texas soldiers began to exhibit a disconnect with the men not serving in the army. Andrew J. Fogle of the 9th Texas Infantry was encamped at Mobile, Alabama, when he wrote his first letter home since Hood's campaign. In it he claimed that it was the people back home and cowards who had left him and his comrades in their current dire position. "[T]here is lots of men that is redy now to submit to lincon he has ishud a new order he ses if we will lay down our arms and free the negros and give up our land and com back in the union that he would stop this war and there are lots of men that is willing to do it but it isent men that is in the army hit is men that is at hom and men that is in the brush sneaking and hiding a bout to ceat out the army."[37] John Wesley Rabb, of the famed Terry's Texas Rangers serving under General Joseph E. Johnston in Georgia, mirrored the other men's despair. "I think that we got the worst of it, & I am not in the best spirits," he wrote. "We lost Atlanta & Savanah because the troops on the west side of the Miss. river refused to come over here & help ous. If they had come over here, our line would have been on the Comberland River, & Savanah & Atlanta would never have been taken. But it is hard to tell now where our line is now. . . . Things look rather dark over here at this time."[38]

The campaign influenced not only the men that fought the battles, but also the morale of Texans throughout the South. The men's state of mind was evident in their letters, both by what they wrote and, just as tellingly, by what they left unwritten. After the Battle of Franklin, Henry Orr, a member of the 12th Texas Cavalry, which was camped in Arkansas for the winter, wrote his sister, "The Northern armies are pressing on all sides and our peoples are depressed in spirits. . . . The future is dark."[39] Writing from Mobile, John Simmons noted, "Men are getting more anxious to get out of this war than ever. For my part I cannot see any stopping place but, as the saying is, the darkest part of the night is just before day." He even described in detail the cost for a Texan to hire a substitute equivalent to $700 in Confederate money. A considerable amount, when the average pay for a soldier was $18 a month after June 1864. Most interesting about the numerous letters Simmons wrote after the Battle of Franklin was that in them he gave his wife constant updates about most activities east of the Mississippi with the noted exception of Hood's Tennessee Campaign.[40] Texans could not escape the pall spreading across the South. The dreadful battles of Franklin and Nashville forced Texans to reassess their suffering and sacrifices over the past four years. They also began to reprioritize what mattered to them most, the cause of the South or the defense of their homes.

During the winter of 1865 the Confederacy began to debate seriously the arming of slaves to serve in its army. The right to maintain the institution of slavery was a significant element of the claimed justification for secession and was included in the Texas Ordnance of Secession, which outlined all the reasons Texas wanted to leave the United States. Chief among the reasons—consisting of two-thirds of the document—was slavery.[41] Lieutenant Leonidas J. Storey of the 26th Texas Cavalry expressed his change of opinion by April 1865 when he wrote home that "we would prove ourselves unworthy of our ancestors if we failed to make the sacrifice. Let the negro go—he is not worth a peuter button compared to the great cause for which we are struggling. If independence is worth the sacrifice of a million of white men, let us add to the list a million of negroes together with the very last of our resources ere we give up the struggle." Stationed in Richmond, Texas, Storey had as his main motivation the continuance of the war in the East so that the scene of combat could not reach the Lone Star State. The more southern men fighting back east, the less likely Lincoln could successfully invade Texas.[42]

Texans fighting east of the Mississippi began to lose their motivation to fight there, and soon after the retreat from Nashville they looked for ways to return home. Almost immediately after Hood's defeat at Nashville, the war's largest fight for furloughs began. Furloughs were the most honorable way for Texans to leave the East. Once back home, a Texas soldier could then usually find a way to justify joining a Trans-Mississippi unit rather than return to his previous regiment. Since the surrender of General John Pemberton's army at Vicksburg, Trans-Mississippi soldiers developed a greater sense of isolation. From the start of the war these men viewed the Mississippi River as a physical and psychological barrier between the bulk of the Union army and their homes. Once the river fell to Union control, communication with their families back home diminished significantly. This collective struggle developed a stronger sense of camaraderie between soldiers whose homes were in the Trans-Mississippi. An Arkansas soldier best conveyed this after the 4th Arkansas Infantry received orders to Meridian, Mississippi

> where we were delighted to find our old comrades, "THE CHUBS" (Gen. [Mathew] Ector's Brigade of Texians) were soon to arrive and be united in the same division with us, under Maj. Gen. [Samuel G.] French. An account of the meeting of these two brigades, after such a long separation, would make one of the most affecting episodes of the war. Both commands, a like exiled from their homes and almost entirely cut off from every communication with their families and friends by the intervention of the Mississippi river. Their long-continued service side by side in camp, on the march and on the battle-field, had stimulated a feeling of reliance upon, and confidence in each other, which I have never known to exist anywhere else in the army.[43]

Trans-Mississippi troops serving east of the river had regularly felt neglected by Confederate officials early in the conflict. Witnessing Cis-Mississippi soldiers consistently receiving furloughs to visit their homes and families while they rarely, if ever, received any began to take a toll, especially when demoralization began to set in after the campaign in Tennessee that fall. Confederate officials were reluctant to issue Trans-Mississippi soldiers furloughs because it took so long for men to get home and back, and more importantly many men would not return to their units once west of the river. The day after the defeat at Nashville, men from the famed Texas Brigade, once commanded by Hood, "wrote out a application to president Davis and all of the Brigade Signed it and Sent it to him. We Stated in it that we wanted to be on an equality withe the rest of the troops, that they were getting furloughs and our Brigade was getting non."[44] On the same day other members of the Texas Brigade noted other petitions such as James T. Hunter of the 4th Texas Infantry who wrote a friend about the unit's application for a furlough sent to General Robert E. Lee and another sent to President Jefferson Davis. Both "were conched in strong language."[45]

Even Texans closer to the Lone Star State petitioned for furloughs. John C. Dunn of the 17th/18th/24th/25th Texas Cavalry Consolidated, then in Mississippi, complained to a friend that officers promised the Texans furloughs but had yet to give any to the men. Brigadier General Lawrence Sullivan "Sul" Ross wrote to former Texas governor Francis Lubbock that the men in his brigade "have despaired of receiving furloughs."[46] The most vocal of the Texans' call for furloughs was a member of Ross's Brigade. Using the pen name "Alamo," the most notable symbol of Texas defiance, he wrote a "Letter on Wrongs of Ross's Brigade, January 1865" to the *Daily Clarion* in Meridian, Mississippi. This letter to the newspaper editor listed the brigade's grievances, most notably the lack of furloughs. After three and a half years of service "only about five men and two officers to the company have been permitted to visit their homes." He argued that according to Confederate law they deserved time to visit their homes. "Yet the troops from the Trans-Mississippi Department, have received the benefits of just such an abused interpretation, while those from East Mississippi Department, whose uninterrupted communications with their homes ensured them to obtain the common necessities of a soldier, or the means for their purchase, have all received their furloughs, some as many as five or six times." Also "it is contended that Trans-Mississippians, without having great merit probably, have had greater need of them," since "Texans have been as effectually isolated from their homes as they would be if the Atlantic ocean rolled in the place of the Mississippi." Alamo further argued that Texans left behind families on the frontier exposed to Indians, and he continued to list many other promises given to them that the government never fulfilled. Further demoralization would follow if not treated correctly, "And lastly shall she [Texas] be made to regret that she did not listen to the wisdom of her most aged statesman, [Sam Houston] and, plant the 'lone star' in her own territory, free and independent of all powers, save that of heaven? There is danger. Let Ross's Brigade be furloughed, and others, where it can be done without immediate injury to the service."[47]

Furloughs even became an issue for soldiers guarding the home front. L. D. Bradley of Waul's Texas Legion wrote his wife about an incident in Galveston that he tried to prevent. "About 150 to 200 men, with arms assembled, at about 8 o'clock on the night of the [February] 26th, and proceeded to Genl [James Morrison] Hawes H. D. Qrts with the armed intention of making him grant furloughs, or to hang him."[48] Fortunately Hawes was not there, and as his popularity diminished further he "left Galveston on Wednesday's train, to provide, as we learn, for the removal of his family to another locality. He leaves many friends, but many of the soldiers and their families rejoice at his departure."[49]

Though Texans and Civil War soldiers expressed their thoughts and feelings in letters, diaries, and memoirs, their actions and grievances speak louder. Distraught with their situation, Lone Star soldiers began to take their own "furloughs." Desertions by Texans increased in the months following the Battle of Nashville. Camped in Shreveport, Louisiana, John Simmons of the 22nd Texas Infantry commented on stories that soldiers passing through the town conveyed to him. "One evidence of the fact is that they are a-furloughing every seventh man on the other side of the river that belongs on this side, and disbanding all them that live in one hundred miles of the army. This is only the case with Hood's old army [Army of Tennessee], as there have been a great many from there passed through our camps and tell the same tale."[50] A month later Simmons realized that, "Most of the soldiers from the other side of the river that come home professing to have furloughs, the furloughs were of their own making." Serving alongside men far from their homes, Simmons believed "some of these days I better think our boys will do the same if they aren't treated better."[51]

Denial of furloughs was not the only reason Texans began to desert. General discontent and demoralization influenced men even during the retreat from Tennessee. The men of the 9th Texas Cavalry, who served in Hood's rearguard, noticed that the Army of Tennessee "became a disheartened and disorganized rabble of half-armed and barefooted men, who sought every opportunity to fall out by the wayside and desert their cause to put an end to their suffering." When the issue of furloughs plagued the Trans-Mississippians, 180 men deserted the army on the "owl train," a term generally used to describe a train that runs at night but used this instance to describe their unauthorized departure. Soldiers of the 9th Texas Cavalry that stayed behind commented, "Not a harsh word was said to them, nor was any effort made to stop them." Unfortunately the "owl train" did not make it past Alexandria, Louisiana, where authorities captured the men. Since there were too many men to arrest and court-martial, they received a sixty-day furlough to visit family back in Texas.[52]

Regardless of the specific issue, many Texans deserted their units in the months after the Franklin-Nashville Campaign. After Hood's retreat ended at Tupelo, Mississippi, more men left the ranks. Cater of the 3rd Texas Cavalry noted while at West Point, Mississippi, "Here I lost sight of the army, except for a brigade which was very small now."[53] So many issues demoralized Texas soldiers in the months following the campaign and influenced them to desert the army. Samuel S. Watson of the 1st Texas Infantry in Richmond, Virginia, summed it up best: "I will say to you that Evry thing looks Sad and gloomy at this time in and a round Richmond, great many people has become dispondant and Sum disertion Sum dissatisfaction in difrant ways Sum for putting the Negros—to fight I do—they will stop all there foolishness and let the men go home."[54] As the war dragged on and Texas appeared more threatened by Union advances and attempted invasion, this motivation to defend the people they left behind waned. They were motivated instead to return home and defend what they still had: their immediate homes and families not yet threatened by an invading army.

Even before the campaign, Texans in the Trans-Mississippi, with the exception of young unmarried men, refused to serve east of the Mississippi River. Confederate president Jefferson Davis continually asked Edmund Kirby Smith, commander of the Trans-Mississippi Department, for more men to fight in the Cis-Mississippi. Smith refused the request stating that it was physically impossible. He needed them to defend the territory they still held, and more importantly, that the men did not want to cross.[55] In one instance the Confederate army ordered the execution of Captain John Guynes of the 22nd Texas Infantry for encouraging his men to desert instead of crossing the Mississippi. Saddened by the death of the officer, Simmons angrily remarked, "That is what the orders to cross the Mississippi River have done."[56] Captain Manuel Yturri of the 3rd Texas Infantry also wrote of Guynes's execution and reinforced Simmons's comments when he wrote home that "I'll be very happy if we don't go to the other side of the Mississippi River because this order has caused more than two hundred desertions in the [Walker's] division from what I have been told, but they have captured more than a hundred. . . . But I do believe that if we're going to the other side [of the Mississippi] many more will desert."[57] Though the exact number of deserted Texans is unknown, overall from September 7, 1864, to January 31, 1865, 2,207 Confederates deserted their ranks and swore an oath of allegiance to the Union in the Nashville region. Weeks later the flood of deserters continued and many were taken to Nashville as prisoners of war, bringing the final report up to 4,045 men.[58]

Texans fought in more battles than any other group of men from other states. Though they and other Confederates overcame many challenges throughout the war, the horrific loses at Franklin and Nashville, combined with a general feeling of neglect from the Confederacy, demoralized the men who had the highest reputation to maintain. Texans entered the war with the most collective martial experience of any state and fought to protect their homes, particularly those they left behind east of the Mississippi. By the winter of 1865 Lone Star soldiers witnessed men from Cis-Mississippi units receive leave to visit their families while the Confederate government denied furloughs to Texans. Distraught by a perception the war could last for another four years with Lincoln's reelection, and participating in a disastrous campaign only to be punctuated by denial of permission to visit their families, Texans took matters into their own hands and deserted the army. Major William Marion Walton summed up the Texans' feelings: "The men commenced to deserting—and a great many went off without leave or license. It was not exactly desertion—they were going home to see their folks."[59]

Notes

1. The only occupied region of the Lone Star State in the later months of the war was the Brazos Islands off the southernmost coastline near Brownsville. Stephen A. Townsend, *The Yankee Invasion of Texas* (College Station: Texas A&M University Press, 2006), 146; Stephen A. Dupree, *Planting the Union Flag in Texas: The Campaigns of Major General Nathaniel P. Banks in the West* (College Station: Texas A&M University Press, 2008), xii, 157.

2. Walter L. Buenger, *Secession and the Union in Texas* (Austin: University of Texas Press, 1984), 62, 64, 66; Dale Baum, *The Shattering of Texas Unionism: Politics in the Lone Star State during the Civil War Era* (Baton Rouge: Louisiana State University Press, 1998), 52, 53.

3. Randolph B. Campbell, *Gone to Texas: A History of the Lone Star State* (New York: Oxford University Press, 2003), 207; Buenger, *Secession and the Union in Texas*, 13, 14; Baum, *The Shattering of Texas Unionism*, 84; Joseph C. G. Kennedy, *Population of the United States in 1860; Compiled Returns of the Eighth Census* (Washington, DC: Government Printing Office, 1864), iv, xiii, xvii, xxix, xxxiii, 616–19; Jerry Thompson, *Cortina: Defending the Mexican Name in Texas* (College Station: Texas A&M University Press, 2013).

4. Charles David Grear, *Why Texans Fought in the Civil* War (College Station: Texas A&M University Press, 2010), 118–22; H. P. Edwards to May, September 19, 1864, H. P. Edwards, Twentieth Texas Infantry File, Texas Heritage Museum, Hill College, Hillsboro, Texas (hereafter citied as THM).

5. Lucia Rutherford Douglas, ed., *Douglas's Texas Battery, CSA* (Waco, TX: Texian Press, 1966), 135.

6. Ibid., 137.

7. Ibid., 136–37.

8. Ibid., 140. Douglas wrote his wife on October 1, 1864, "The army [of Tennessee] is in much better spirits since the beginning of this movement."

9. November 17, 1864, Diary, William G. Young, 15th Texas Cavalry File, THM.

10. *Tri-Weekly Telegraph* (Houston), November 25, 1864. The Union army occupied most big cities with newspapers in the Trans-Mississippi, except for Texas. Texas newspapers represent most clearly the Confederate point of view since they were not controlled by pro-Northern editors.

11. John Baynes, *Morale: A Study of Men and Courage; The Second Scottish Rifles at the Battle of Neuve Chapelle 1915* (New York: Frederick A. Preager, 1967), 101; Steven E. Woodworth, *Decision in the Heartland: The Civil War in the West* (Westport, CT: Praeger, Publishers, 2008), 129–34; October 26, 1864, Diary, William G. Young, 15th Texas Cavalry File, THM.

12. November 9, 17, 20, 1864, Diary, William G. Young, 15th Texas Cavalry File, THM; Charles D. Spurlin, ed., *The Civil War Diary of Charles A. Leuscher* (Austin: Eakin Press, 2000), 49.

13. November 23, 1864, Diary, William G. Young, 15th Texas Cavalry File, THM.

14. Douglas Hale, *The Third Cavalry in the Civil War* (Norman: University of Oklahoma Press, 1993), 261.

15. October 2, 28, 1864, November 17, 24, 1864, Diary, William G. Young, 15th Texas Cavalry File, THM.

16. Martha L. Crabb, *All Afire to Fight: The Untold Tale of the Civil War's Ninth Texas Cavalry* (New York: Post Road Press, 2000), 271, 274–75.

17. September 19, 1864, H. P. Edwards, 20th Texas Infantry File, THM.

18. November 17, 1864, Diary, William G. Young, 15th Texas Cavalry File, THM.

19. Walter Kamphoefner and Wolfgang Helbich, eds., *Germans in the American Civil War: Letters from the Front and Farm, 1861–1865* (Chapel Hill: University of North Carolina Press, 2006), 443; B. P. Gallaway, *The Ragged Rebel: A Common Soldier in W. H. Parsons' Texas Cavalry, 1861–1865* (Austin: University of Texas Press, 1998), 128.

20. Dilliard to Sallie, December 2, 1864, T. J. Dilliard, 28th Texas Cavalry File, THM. W. A. Kirkpatrick of the 19th Texas Cavalry commented in his diary, "the reports here is that old Abe Lincoln is a baboon. The next 4 years and we will have to fight on." November 27, 1864, W. A. Kirkpatrick, 19th Texas Cavalry File, THM.

21. Douglas, *Douglas's Texas Battery, CSA*, 150.

22. Thomas W. Cutrer, ed., *Our Trust is in the God of Battles: The Civil War Letters of Robert Franklin Bunting, Chaplain, Terry's Texas Rangers, CSA* (Knoxville: University of Tennessee Press, 2006), 294.

23. Jim Turner, "Jim Turner Co. G, 6th Texas Infantry, C.S.A. From 1861 to 1865," *Texana* 12 (1974): 176–77.

24. W. U. Carre, "Lieutenant Linson Montgomery Keener, His Four Years with the Seventh Texas Infantry C.S.A. as Told by Him," Linson Montgomery Keener, 7th Texas Infantry File, THM, 133.

25. Douglas, *Douglas's Texas Battery, CSA*, 150.

26. Cutrer, *Our Trust is in the God of Battles*, 294.

27. Douglas, *Douglas's Texas Battery, CSA*, 152.

28. Douglas John Cater, *As It Was: Reminiscences of a Soldier of the Third Texas Cavalry and the Nineteenth Louisiana Infantry* (1981; repr. Abilene, TX: Statehouse Press, 2007), 195.

29. *Tri-Weekly Telegraph* (Houston), December 16, 18, 1864.

30. *Daily True Delta* (New Orleans), December 22, 23, 1864.

31. Ibid., December 30, 1864.

32. *Marshall* [Texas] *Republican*, January 27, 1865; repr. *Dallas* [Texas] *Herald*, February 23, 1865.

33. Hale, *The Third Cavalry in the Civil War*, 267; U.S. War Department, *The War of the Rebellion: A Compilation of the Official Records of the Union and Confederate Armies*, 128 vols. (Washington, DC: Government Printing Office, 1880–1901), ser. 1, vol. 45, pt. 1: 772.

34. "Memoir of E. A. Kellogg," Ebenezer Albert Kellogg, 27th Texas Cavalry File, THM.

35. Cater, *As It Was*, 205.

36. Douglas, *Douglas's Texas Battery, CSA*, 152–53.

37. Fogle to Miss Loo, March 12, 1865, Andrew J. Fogle, 9th Texas Cavalry File, THM.

38. Thomas W. Cutrer, ed., "'We are Stern and Resolved': The Civil War Letters of John Wesley Rabb, Terry's Texas Rangers," *Southwestern Historical Quarterly* 91, no. 2, (October 1987): 223.

39. Henry Orr to Sister, November 28, 1864, in John Q. Anderson, ed., *Campaigns with Parson's Texas Cavalry Brigade, CSA: The War Journals and Letters of the Four Orr Brothers, Twelfth Texas Cavalry Regiment* (Hillsboro, TX: Hill Junior College Press, 1967), 152; Gallaway, *The Ragged Rebel*, 128.

40. Similarly William G. Young of the 15th Texas Cavalry kept a diary throughout the war. All of his entries before the Battle of Franklin are long and detailed, but he simply ended his November 1864 entry with "our losses very heavy." The subsequent entries are short and he concludes December 1864 with "All quiet." It was not until April 1865 that he starts to record more about his experiences by describing their surrender and men celebrating the conclusion of the war by getting "dead drunk." Diary, November 17, 1864–April 20, 1865, William G. Young, 15th Texas Cavalry File, THM; Simmons to Companion (wife), December 4, 1864, April 3, 13, 1865, John Simmons, 22nd Texas Infantry File, THM; Bell I. Wiley, *The Life of Johnny Reb* (Indianapolis: Bobbs-Merrill Company, 1943), 136.

41. E. W. Winkler, ed., *Journal of the Secession Convention of Texas, 1861* (Austin: Texas Library and Historical Commission, 1912), 61–65.

42. Storey to Lou, Ma, and Boy, April 19, 1865, Lt. L. J. Storey, 26th Texas Cavalry File, THM.

43. W. L. Gamanage, *The Camp, the Bivouac, and the Battle Field* (Little Rock, AR: Southern Press, 1958), 97–98; Grear, *Why Texans Fought in the Civil War*, 117–18.

44. Wiley, *Life of Johnny Reb*, 138; Elvis E. Fleming, "Some Hard Fighting: Letters of Private Robert T. Wilson, 5th Texas Infantry, Hood's Brigade, 1862–1864," *Military History of Texas and the Southwest* 9, no. 4 (1971): 297; Wilson to Penelope A. Wilson, December 17, 1864, Robert Wilson, 4th Texas Infantry File, THM.

45. Hunter to Dulcenia Pain Harrison, December 17, 1864, James T. Hunter, 4th Texas Infantry File, THM; Felder to mother, December 18, 1864, Rufus King Felder, 5th Texas Infantry File, THM.

46. Dunn to friend, February 1, 1865, John C. Dunn, 25th Texas Cavalry File, THM; Crabb, *All Afire to Fight*, 254.

47. "Letter on Wrongs of Ross's Brigade, January 1865," *Daily Clarion*, (Meridian, Mississippi) January 28, 1865.

48. Bradley to Little Honey, March 6, 1865, Bradley (L.D.) Papers, 1859–87, Pearce Civil War Collection, Navarro College, Corsicana, TX.

49. April 26, 1865, *Galveston* [Texas] *Weekly News*.

50. Simmons to Companion (wife), February 19, 1865, John Simmons, 22nd Texas Infantry File, THM.

51. Simmons to Companion (wife), March 15, 1865, Ibid.

52. Crabb, *All Afire to Fight*, 288, 290; S. B. Barron, *The Lone Star Defenders: A Chronicle of the Third Texas Cavalry, Ross' Brigade* (New York: The Neale Publishing Company, 1908), 268–69.

53. Mark A. Weitz, *More Damning than Slaughter: Desertion in the Confederate Army* (Lincoln: University of Nebraska Press, 2005), 278; Cater, *As It Was*, 205.

54. Watson to H. C. L., February 1865, Samuel S. Watson, 1st Texas Infantry File, THM.

55. Dr. Thomas B. Greyson noted that

> The young men—by which I mean the unmarried—of this command have within the past few days become impressed with the belief that it is their duty to make an exertion to get on the other side of "the big river." They say and rightly too—"Nothing is doing nor likely to be done for some time to come on this side—that on the other side the service is active, and that the country needs all the aid that can be afforded on that side—and that they, having gone into the service for the benefit of their country and its cause, are desirous of going where they can do the most good, and hence they have applied for a transfer to the Cos. [Confederacy's] Mississippi Department."

Greyson to wife, March 9, 1865, Dr. Thomas B. Greyson, Waul's Texas Legion File, THM; L. D. Bradley made a similar comment about unmarried men, "Some 35 or 40 of our Regt. Including some of my company, some weeks since, made an application to be transferred across the River; they were all going, unmarried men and I, not only, approved of their going, but thought that all of that sort ought to go." Bradley to Little Honey, April 16, 1865, Bradley (L.D.) Papers, 1859–87, Pearce Civil War Collection, Navarro College, Corsicana, TX. William Geise, "Decline and Collapse, December 1864–June 1865," *Military History of Texas and the Southwest* 16, no. 2 (1980): 108; Jeffery S. Prushankin, *A Crisis in Command: Edmund Kirby Smith, Richard Taylor, and the Army of the Trans-Mississippi* (Baton Rouge: Louisiana State University Press, 2005), 203.

56. Simmons to companion (wife), October 17, 1864, John Simmons, 22nd Texas Infantry File, THM; Richard Lowe, *Walker's Texas Division C.S.A.: Greyhounds of the Trans-Mississippi* (Baton Rouge: Louisiana State University Press, 2004), 245.

57. There are many more examples of Texans refusing to cross the Mississippi River. Sergeant William W. Heartsill asked his men if they wanted to cross and the men voted no. J. D. Wilson of Terry's Texas Cavalry Regiment (not to confused with Terry's Texas Rangers) wrote to his sister from Austin County that "they think we will have to cross the Mississippi River but I do not know whether we will have to cross the river or not but I hope we will not have to cross." William W. White, "The Disintegration of an Army: Confederate Forces in Texas, April–June, 1865," *East Texas Historical Journal* 26, no. 2 (1988): 40; Wilson to sister, March 29, 1865, J. D. Wilson, Terry's Texas Cavalry File, THM. Jerry Thompson, ed., *Tejanos in Gray: Civil War Letters of Captains Joseph Rafael de la Garza and Manuel Yturri* (College Station: Texas A&M University Press, 2011), 75–76.

58. Weitz, *More Damning than Slaughter*, 259, 283.

59. William Martin Walton, *An Epitome of My Life: Civil War Reminiscences* (Austin: Waterloo Press, 1965), 90.

12

WHAT COULD HAVE BEEN

CIVIL WAR BATTLEFIELD PRESERVATION AT FRANKLIN

Timothy B. Smith

Renowned National Park Service chief historian emeritus Edwin C. Bearss was in a nostalgic mood that late November day at Franklin, Tennessee. He and several other preservation-oriented luminaries were in town for the sole purpose of symbolically tearing down a pizza restaurant. It seemed almost surreal. But the underlying details clarified that seemingly odd occurrence. It was November 30, 2005, the 141st anniversary of the Battle of Franklin, where thousands of Americans had died or were wounded in one of the most horrific battles of the Civil War. The pizza place sat in the middle of where some of the heaviest fighting had taken place, in fact very near if not on the spot where one of the most famous participants had died: Confederate general Patrick Cleburne, who despite his Irish birth and appeal to arm slaves during the war has become somewhat of a southern cult hero much like Nathan Bedford Forrest. In an effort to reclaim the battlefield and preserve it, several groups had come together to celebrate this unique success.[1]

Bearss made his feelings known: "What if we placed a Pizza Hut on Mount Suribachi where our Marines flew the flag at Iwo Jima?" He further compared Franklin's situation to putting a restaurant on Omaha Beach at Normandy. "I stand here today more as a veteran than a historian," Bearss confided, but his presence as a historian and preservationist was most important. Bearss was perhaps the most recognized, revered, and respected historian/preservationist there that day, and that he would come to celebrate Franklin's victory made it even more special. When he swung the sledgehammer to begin the destruction, he symbolically undid decades of futility at Franklin.[2]

That futility went back to the beginning of the battlefield preservation movement in America. In fact, Franklin serves as a remarkable case study of the vast majority of the war's battlefields, because unlike the most famous

Civil War fields such as Shiloh or Gettysburg, most battlefields of the Civil War have until recently received little or no major preservation work. Franklin serves as a microcosm of the Civil War battlefield preservation movement; its history can be viewed as an example of the greater history of the preservation process, although Franklin has at times been far ahead of the rest of the nation in its preservation mentality.

Civil War battlefield preservation has moved through several generations. There was little conservation effort in the decades immediately following the Civil War, except at Gettysburg, and the task fell mostly to national cemetery and other private cemetery builders to conserve anything on battlefields. Whatever was done, however, was local, limited, and partisan; this early generation of preservationists was just too close to the martial events to make objective and bipartisan decisions. Then in 1890 came the "Golden Age" of battlefield preservation, when the federal government stepped in and began to create national, bipartisan, and fitting parks out of some of the biggest fields of battle. Chickamauga and Chattanooga, Shiloh, Vicksburg, Antietam, and Gettysburg all became national parks during the reconciliation-rich 1890s.[3]

Due to cost and other issues, however, the federal government took a long sabbatical from its preservation efforts. It was not until the 1920s and 1930s that the process began again, in large part due to the influx of money from the New Deal programs in the 1930s. Parks such as Petersburg, Manassas, Richmond, Stones River, and Fort Donelson were all established during this period, but on much smaller scales because of limited funding, smaller portions of battlefields available to preserve due to urbanization, and the absence of Civil War veterans to pinpoint troop positions and localities. With the slowdown in federal preservation, in addition to arguments over what battles were significant enough to save and the massive appropriations on World War II, state and even some local governments began to step in to preserve many of the remaining battlefields. But not all were conserved in this fashion, and by World War II there were still several very big battles, including Franklin, that had received no major preservation effort.[4]

By the later decades of the twentieth century, despite the Civil War centennial, even the state and local governments were finding it difficult to preserve battlefields, so it fell to private individuals and corporate sponsors to take up the slack with fund-raising activities and local support. The ultimate net result was the establishment of the big, national preservation entities that collectively are now the Civil War Trust. The Trust today is doing the work first begun by the veterans, then picked up by the federal government, then handed off to the state and local entities, and eventually taken on by private citizens with ties to big money.[5]

That is exactly the process that has occurred at Franklin. Little was done in the decades after the war, but there was a major effort to create a national park during the golden age. Although unsuccessful, there were continued efforts even during the 1920s and 1930s. These too were unsuccessful. Finally, there was some state involvement, but it literally fell to the citizens in corporate groups to initiate Franklin's preservation in the 1950s and 1960s. Their work foreshadowed the major efforts of the modern entities in the 1990s and early 2000s. Franklin thus served as an efficient model for anyone who would take notice.

In the early twenty-first century, preservationists at Franklin are leading the way again in what is potentially the future of battlefield preservation. After 150 years, much, although not all, Civil War battlefield land has either been preserved or is spoiled by urbanization or development. To be sure, there are still many battlefield areas untouched, as evidenced by the forty-thousand-odd acres saved by the Civil War Trust to date, but that group estimates that many acres of battlefield land are being lost every day. Such has been and is the case at Franklin. But Franklin preservationists have hit on a new method to help save some of the historic areas, if not the actual pristine land. The effort to rehabilitate what was once battlefield land and turn it back into pastured battlefield parks is a major emphasis at Franklin. And it is potentially the way many other preservationists will go in the future.[6]

It is unfortunate that the site of such a horrendous battle as Franklin has not received the preservation attention it deserves. Historians have argued that it witnessed actually a larger assault than the famed Pickett's Charge at Gettysburg. As far as casualties in the time allotted to battle, it had to be one of the worst engagements of the war. The aura of all the Confederate generals killed is haunting. Historians James Lee McDonough and Thomas Connelly have termed the fighting simply "Five Tragic Hours."[7]

Yet, there was even immediately after the battle and continuing on for decades some tourism of the battle site at Franklin. One Confederate noted immediately after the fighting that "the unwise rambling of our men over the battlefield at Franklin" caused the morale of the army to sag because of the horrendous sights. But there was little or no attempt to commemorate or memorialize what had happened there.[8]

The closest thing to an early memorialization process at Franklin started with the burial of the bodies produced during the battle. Hastily buried bodies were regularly unearthed on many battlefields, one local attesting that after a rainstorm he saw "a line of human hands sticking up—some with fingers shut tight, some pointing, and all so ghastly that they were covered hurriedly." It was not uncommon to see the famous Carter family, who lived in a house that sat squarely amidst the fighting, out reburying the dead in the days and months immediately after the battle.[9]

Due to the ghastliness and health concerns, as well as patriotic duty, there were soon after the war major efforts to remove the dead from the battlefield. The federal government removed all the Union bodies it could and placed them in individual graves in the Stones River National Cemetery, starting in 1866 and continuing for several years. But there was no government to care for the Confederate dead. And worse, newspapers all across the South reported in the spring of 1866 that the battlefield at Franklin was "rented by the proprietor to freedmen, and is about to be given to the plow." Many southerners were trying to "secure means to remove the bodies before the traces of the graves are trampled out."[10]

The Confederate remains were thus gathered and reburied on the McGavock place, "a fine old plantation" recalled a returning veteran. In a quiet lot northwest of the plantation mansion, Carnton, John McGavock cut out two acres on which to rebury 1,481 Confederate dead. The graves were organized by state, and the nearly fifteen hundred Confederate dead were originally given wooden headboards, although only about half could be identified.[11]

Despite the establishment of the cemetery, several newspapers still accused the Freedmen's Bureau of allowing former slaves to work the battlefield land: "The ground is being plowed up, and the bodies of the dead inhumanely disinterred and abused." Even the *Buffalo* (New York) *Courier* called such acts "brutal vandalism." As late as 1884, there was even a viral rumor of Union remains being plowed up on the battlefield, but that was quickly quashed by a visit to the site by staff members of the Grand Army of the Republic (GAR). Moscow Carter, son of Fountain Branch Carter, who had built the famous house that bears the family name, had indeed dug up one body in building a foundation for a barn, but accounts of plowing up bodies were few and far between. One veteran involved in the removal of bodies admitted there may have been isolated incidents of missing the dead here and there at Franklin, but declared, "No Government on earth ever exercised such care and caution in the removal of her dead as this Government of ours." Because of the removal of most bodies to various cemeteries, Carter himself noted by 1882, "Now bones are uncommon sights and the plowman is not startled as at some wilder grounds which I have visited."[12]

Through the following years, little other commemorative effort was made, although visitors, especially veterans, frequently toured the site. One Union veteran described what he saw upon his return: "the old cotton gin has vanished; but the bullet-marked Carter House . . . is still extant." He also described the ground covered by the Confederate charge as "in about the same condition as during the battle." And if the visitors were fortunate, they could meet and perhaps get a tour of the area from Moscow Carter. One veteran noted, "Mr. Carter takes great pleasure in showing any one over the battlefield, and takes great interest in preserving every vestige of the terrible battle."[13]

One veteran received a special tour from a local black man who took him to the Carter House in the early 1880s. He noted that the house "shows many marks of Minie balls," as did outbuildings and even the trees surrounding the house. When the tourist saw Moscow Carter himself coming in from hunting, he willingly gave the veteran a short tour, describing the Confederate attack and other actions on the place. "Neither through love nor by money could I have found so good a guide," the veteran remembered, and showed his obvious emotion when he recounted how "this was the very ground of slaughter." He noted that the only earthworks left by that time was a three-hundred-yard line on the extreme Federal right near the river, still "much as it was left."[14]

Eventually, more and more veterans and their families came to commemorate Franklin, and one old soldier even requested a piece of wood from near where Cleburne fell. Someone sent him a board from the cotton gin prior to its removal, but in sawing it the blade hit "a dozen or more bullets." In addition to other larger gatherings through the years, a major Confederate reunion took place in September 1887, with speeches, a parade, and martial music. There was also some effort to mark historic places. One veteran mentioned "an attempt was made some years ago to mark the spot where Gen. 'Pat' Cleburne fell at the head of his men," but he did not elaborate on its success. He did mention, however, that "a small tablet tells where General [John] Adams died." So there was at least some early marking of the field.[15]

The only major monument dedication came on November 30, 1899, a month and a day prior to the twentieth century. On that day, the thirty-fifth anniversary of the battle, the local United Daughters of the Confederacy (UDC) chapter unveiled and dedicated a Confederate monument on the public square in Franklin. There was a short service, during which former Confederate general George W. Gordon, who had been wounded and captured there, attended, and Franklin resident J. H. Henderson gave a short address on the process of erecting the monument. Henderson told his hearers that the women raised much of the money by "ice cream suppers, cake walks, etc." He also noted the reconciliation of the times, remarking that the monument was dedicated in love: "the corner stone of this monument is love—every rock in its foundation is cemented in love; every stroke of the chisel that worked out its beautiful symmetry was made in love; love, pure and simple, welled up in grateful hearts, as a token by which we transmit this monument to posterity."[16]

The major effort to commemorate and preserve the Franklin battlefield came in March 1900, in the middle of the battlefield preservation craze sweeping the nation. Congressman Nicholas N. Cox added a bill to establish a "Franklin National Military Park." Cox was a native Tennessean who had lived in Texas as a child prior to returning to Tennessee to study law. He was a Confederate veteran, having led the 10th Tennessee Cavalry as colonel during the conflict. After the war, he lived in Franklin where he was a lawyer and farmer. He was first elected to the 52nd Congress that began in 1891, and his term ending in 1901 would be his last, as he planned to retire. Perhaps realizing his influence on the national stage was ending, Cox took the opportunity before he left Congress to offer a bill to establish the Franklin park.[17]

Several veterans' organizations as well as the local people of Franklin supported Cox. One newspaper reported both the UDC and the United Confederate Veterans (UCV) were making a "strong effort" to get the bill passed, and many GAR camps had offered their assistance as well. The local people had also met and formed a committee to push the project.[18]

Cox's bill was similar to the legislation that had established the other major parks. The focal point was to be "the lands embracing the grounds along the firing line of the two contending forces . . . and including the graves of the dead there buried," but it also included "such approaches and such other lands contiguous to the lands above described." But all in all, there would only be about 150 acres, much smaller than the other parks such as Shiloh and Chickamauga. Cox read the sign of the times and realized that the big parks established in the 1890s were a thing of the past. Concern over money matters had caused Congress to slow down their preservation efforts by the end of the 1890s. In fact, only a scaled down version of Vicksburg passed in 1899, and it took several long years of agitation to get that done. Neither Congress nor the War Department, which oversaw the battlefields, was very interested in creating any more huge parks.[19]

Although the size was much smaller, the proposed Franklin park would be much like the others in essence, with provisions in the bill to allow tenancy for those living on park grounds, condemnation if owners were unwilling to sell, a commission of three veterans to oversee the work, and the ability for states and organizations to erect monuments, tablets, and "such other artificial works as may from time to time be erected by proper authority." Other attributes included the hiring of a historian, the marking of lines of battle, and the opening of roads on the park. In all, it would take $100,000 to fund the project.[20]

Although the bill went to the Committee on Military Affairs, it was never acted upon; Cox retired from Congress without a park for his hometown. But others continued the fight. Lemuel P. Padgett of nearby Columbia, Tennessee, was elected to Cox's seat and continued the work, offering unsuccessfully a bill to establish the park for twelve straight years. Padgett was not a veteran of the war, having been born only in 1855, but he was a believer in the need for the park. In December 1901, he offered the same bill Cox had offered earlier, but it likewise failed to get much attention. At the same time, numerous other park bills were languishing as well. In fact, none of the bills then pending would become law.[21]

Over time, other congressmen also offered bills to create the Franklin park as well as other parks nearby. Tennesseans James B. Frazier and Robert L. Taylor in the U.S. Senate and Padgett in the House continually offered legislation. Taylor, in fact, was also interested in parks at Stones River and Nashville and offered bills that included those battle sites. Even Ohio congressman and Franklin veteran Isaac R. Sherwood offered several bills for the park over the years. Yet none of the efforts were successful, and the battlefield of Franklin continued to be privately owned.[22]

Realizing the lack of interest in Congress, there were periodic surges of enthusiasm from local people for protecting the battlefield. The local UDC group, chaired by Mrs. N. B. Dozier, took over the effort by 1909, establishing a "Franklin National Park Committee." Perhaps the residents of Franklin looked to the other battlefields that were now parks and realized that each one had been pushed successfully through Congress by an active local park committee or association. The women agitated faithfully for the park, and could have been the catalysts for Congressman Padgett to offer his bill year after year. They also encouraged veterans to write their congressmen and asked publishers to advocate for the park; one Ohioan wrote the *Confederate Veteran*: "It is a crying shame that nothing has been done for the field of Franklin. It deserves monuments upon which should be inscribed the deeds of the men who fought there, that coming generations visiting this spot could read the lines dedicated to American valor." The writers especially honed in on the fact that many Franklin veterans were dying by 1910 and the field needed to be preserved "before the last of the gallant men who fought there have passed over to rest 'under the shade of the trees.'" They obviously utilized the reconciliation of the era, citing the "kindly feeling that has grown up since the war by the blue and the gray."[23]

But there was one major change in the more recent effort. After a decade of defeat, the proposed park's size was scaled down even more from the 150-acre park envisioned in 1900. Dozier and her committee realized that the more economical the plan, the better chance it had of passing. She admitted, "at one time we desired to have included in this park a greater portion of the battlefield." Now, they concentrated their efforts strictly on a portion of land east of the Columbia Pike (where the pizza restaurant would eventually stand), the precise location of the cotton gin where generals Adams and Cleburne fell. West of the pike, they only wanted to preserve the Carter House, riddled with bullet holes, as a definite reminder of what had happened there. They also wanted to erect "a beautiful memorial arch" across the pike to connect the two points, "a monument to the soldiers of 1861–65." With reconciliation in mind, it was to be dedicated to "sons of both the North and the South."[24]

Even these scaled-down efforts were too expensive for Congress, however, and the UDC ladies were never successful. General George W. Gordon, now in Congress himself, wrote Mrs. Dozier that the military affairs committee was just "not favorably disposed" to spending any more money. Senator Frazier similarly wrote that "the Committee on Military Affairs in the House has determined that it will not pass any bill creating additional military parks," and went on that "President Taft would likely veto any bill for a military park if one was indeed passed by the Congress."[25]

There were a few successes during this time, however, including individual states sending money for upkeep of the Confederate cemetery. For example, the Mississippi legislature appropriated $200 in 1910 to help clean up the cemetery damaged by a storm the year before. (Of course, many Mississippians were buried in that cemetery.) The most notable achievement was a grand reunion at Franklin in November 1914, the fiftieth anniversary of the battle. A "United Survivors' Association of the Battle of Franklin" had by that time been established, and a large crowd gathered on the field on November 30 to commemorate and remember. Unlike the Confederate reunion in 1887, this one was for both sides. Reconciliation was in the air, even at the horrendous battlefield of Franklin.[26]

Over the ensuing years, little more commemoration of Franklin occurred. Even an attempt to create a movie with Franklin as its centerpiece never materialized, despite a massive reenactment that was filmed in 1923. Taking place on the actual battlefield, the movie personnel dug trenches and staged a huge mock battle, but the director who was the driving force behind the movie soon died and the effort went awry.[27]

Perhaps the best chance Franklin had to become a national park, or even to garner some support on the state level, was in the 1920s and 1930s when in a resurgence of preservation work, numerous other Civil War battlefields were established and preserved. But these New Deal–era parks were smaller and cheaper than those established previously. The "Antietam Plan," used most famously at its namesake battlefield, had been devised in the 1890s as an alternative to the big, fully preserved parks created during that decade. Unknowingly, the push for the Antietam Plan back then had actually had a more drastic result: the massive number of cheaper parks proposed pushed Congress to stop preservation work altogether instead of simply doing it on a smaller scale. No new parks were created until the mid-1920s. When a few of the new generation of parks came about, however, they were established along the lines of the Antietam Plan: smaller, more economical parks containing only the most important extant sites.[28]

Yet in all the ruckus of the New Deal–era preservation, Franklin garnered very little attention. Congress sponsored a study, to be made by the War Department, about which battlefields should be preserved. The War Department set up a classification system, with Class I being the most famous and important—places that were already national military parks such as Gettysburg and Vicksburg. The next class, interestingly named Class IIa, included battlefields of secondary importance that needed to have lines of battle marked, but were not fully made into national military parks. These were essentially the Antietam Plan parks, and they included sites such as Fredericksburg, Fort Donelson, Petersburg, and, interestingly, Nashville. The third and lowest class, termed Class IIb, would encompass battles of lesser importance that could be marked simply with an acre site and a monument. This group included Champion Hill, Kennesaw Mountain, Pea Ridge, Cedar Creek, and, inexplicably, Franklin. The War Department reported "that a single monument should suffice" for these.[29]

The department thus recommended that $40,000 be appropriated for the creation of the site at Franklin, and estimated that it would take only $250 annually for upkeep. But in the end, these recommendations, scant though they were, did not come to fruition either. With the economic downturn of the 1930s and the focus on huge public works programs and then the massive spending and attention paid to World War II, Franklin, it seemed, was destined to be left unpreserved. And this lack of preservation is even more perplexing because a native son, Joseph W. Byrns, was Speaker of the House in Washington in the mid-1930s.[30]

With little attention paid to Franklin by federal officials and with no better success on the state, county, or city level, Franklin locals, fearful of the obvious urbanization taking place, began the process of preserving their own assets. Starting in the late 1940s and continuing over the next couple of decades, Franklin residents decided that they would have to do it themselves. They began a grassroots effort to actually preserve, not to lobby. This private effort was far in advance of the same type of movement that would become the standard in later decades, so Franklin really led the way. But it was not easy.[31]

In 1948, a local UDC group first preserved a portion of Winstead Hill, the Confederate command area from which they had charged, and that group and several Sons of Confederate Veterans (SCV) chapters maintained the site. It was admittedly only a little less than ten acres and clearly pro-Confederate, but it was preservation nonetheless.[32]

The first major success came in 1951 when local residents and historians, led by famed author Stanley F. Horn, succeeded in convincing the state of Tennessee to buy the Carter House. Although the Carter family had not owned the house since 1896, it was the scene of some of the most vicious fighting at Franklin, and the house and its outbuildings were a natural place to commemorate the battle. Still extant in the 1950s (and today because of the preservation work) were numerous buildings pocked with bullet holes and other damage. Of all the Civil War sites in America, the Carter House is one of the best because visitors can actually see the devastation and allow the mind to roam back to what it must have been like that November day in 1864. While it is sometimes difficult to get a full grasp of what it must have been like at the tranquil Bloody Pond at modern-day Shiloh or the soothing tall grasses dancing in the fields at Gettysburg, it is much easier to conjure up the devastation of battle at Franklin's Carter House.[33]

The legislature appropriated $20,000 for the purchase of the house and six thousand for its restoration, but had to add additional monies periodically as the restoration went far over budget. The money went to the Tennessee Historical Commission, but the agreement was that the state would not run the site. That would be left up to a private corporation, the "Carter House Association," established in May 1951 by five local women: Volenia W. Hays, Lucile C. Henderson, Mary Nichol Britt, Annie Z. Walker, and Margaret H. Nolen. Their avowed purpose was "maintaining and preserving as a shrine and memorial to the Battle of Franklin the Carter House on Columbia Avenue in the Town of Franklin."[34]

After overseeing several renovations that returned the house to its original 1864 state and equipping it with period furnishings, the Carter House Association opened the doors in 1953, charging for membership in the association as well as for tours of the site, which they used for repair and upkeep. The general public now had a major site to visit and gain understanding about the Franklin battle. Through the years, the Carter House Association added several attending features such as a visitor center, museum, and parking lot. The site soon became the major Civil War attraction in Franklin.[35]

The work at the Carter House and elsewhere gained some attention, and a movement to get several portions of the Franklin battlefield recognized by the federal government succeeded. Franklin attained National Historic Landmark status in 1960, with four properties being listed as part of it: the Carter House, Carnton Mansion, Winstead Hill, and Fort Granger. The Heritage Foundation of Franklin and Williamson County, established in 1967, was an outgrowth of this success and promoted a vision for more preservation; they in fact succeeded in saving the Union headquarters office in town. Groups such as the UDC and the SCV also continued their work on Winstead Hill. They placed walkways and the Tennessee Historical Commission put up a relief map denoting the Confederate and Union positions on the battlefield. In a reversal of earlier sentiments, in 1975 the city of Franklin also took charge of some twenty acres at Fort Granger, a large extant earthwork across the Harpeth River from the battlefield.[36]

The same year the city acquired Fort Granger, however, a major setback occurred: a golf course opened on 110 acres near the Carnton plantation, forever obliterating a pristine section of the battlefield. Perhaps because of that defeat, two years later, in 1977, local Franklin preservationists led by Dr. Joseph L. Willoughby added another nearby site for visitors: the Carnton Mansion, where the many Confederate generals had been laid out on the porch and also the site of the massive Confederate cemetery. The McGavock family had owned the house until 1911, when they sold it. Having gone through several owners since then, Carnton was beginning to run down as the decades passed. But yet another corporation, the Carnton Association, emerged in the 1970s, and with the aid of the Heritage Foundation of Franklin and Williamson County, gained title to the house and ten acres in 1977. Carnton's owners, Dr. W. D. Sugg and his wife Ruth, donated the house and land on the condition that the association could prove they had the money to restore the dilapidated mansion. Sugg declared that he and his wife, both then living in Florida, had bought the house because of its architecture and history, but could not keep it up and wanted the people of Franklin to see to its "perpetual cherishing and care." He noted that "we feel that almost no where in America have people shown themselves so worthy of such a trust as you wonderful folks of Williamson County." The house and grounds opened in 1979.[37]

A few other successes occurred in the 1980s. In 1985, after Dr. Sugg had passed away, his widow Ruth sold an additional amount of land to the association. The association has since built several facilities, including a museum and bookstore. The city also continued its work, as in the case of some fifty-six acres added as a city park on Winstead Hill in 1985, after a measure to open an industrial park there was defeated. The next year, a "Historic Zoning Ordinance" went into effect in Franklin.[38]

The work done at Franklin from the 1950s through the 1980s came at a time when very little preservation work was being done elsewhere. The major accomplishments by private organizations at Franklin foreshadowed the advent of numerous private battlefield preservation societies, associations, and commissions in the 1990s and early 2000s. The effort would soon go national, with the establishment of several preservation groups that eventually morphed into today's Civil War Trust. But Franklin was ahead of the game.[39]

Although the Trust is active today at Franklin, the local people have not stopped their work. Franklin preservationists have recently stepped up even more and begun to preserve all they can. One of the major factors in getting the people moving was a *National Geographic* article that appeared in 2005, bringing attention to Franklin and other Civil War sites in need of preservation. It also did not hurt when a major local preservationist, Robert Hicks, wrote *The Widow of the South*, a *New York Times* best-selling novel about the subject. In the *National Geographic* article, Franklin was depicted as being "lost." In fact, one preservationist went so far as to admit the locals were for decades against any commemoration at Franklin. "The battle was viewed by many as an embarrassment," one of them noted. A 1920s-era resolution of the city leaders against a national park at Franklin, because it would alter housing, was plain enough. Commemoration at Franklin was also an issue with the African American community hesitant to back anything that might be viewed as Confederate focused, such as the SCV site on Winstead Hill.[40]

Such attitudes have changed in recent years. Many other preservation-minded entities such as the Save the Franklin Battlefield organization, the city of Franklin, and the Heritage Foundation of Franklin and Williamson County have performed significant work. Additional locations have recently been opened to the public such as the Lotz House, near the Carter House. Most significantly, the various preservation associations around Franklin are not competing against one another, but have joined together in an effort called "Franklin's Charge" to organize and combine resources for preservation. Together with the city of Franklin, Franklin's Charge has worked to obtain large amounts of money to purchase threatened land, most prominently $300,000 for the pizza restaurant and $5 million to buy the former 110 acres at the golf course near Carnton, which one local preservationist has termed "the unprecedented formation of a unique public/private partnership." It is scheduled to be returned to its original state and opened as the "Eastern Flank Battle Park."[41]

The result of all this activity is that much of Franklin's battlefield land is being purchased before housing can be built on it. Yet a new wave of preservation mentality is emerging as well on less pristine sites, that of taking somewhat disrupted land and rehabilitating it into a battlefield park. One local preservationist has called the golf course effort the "largest battlefield reclamation project in North American history." And that in itself is historic. Just as the Carter and Carnton associations predated and foreshadowed what was to come nationally in later decades, so possibly will Franklin's rehabilitation be the national wave of the future. Obviously aimed at commemoration of the battle but also looking at economic tourism as well as racial healing, these combined efforts have proven successful at Franklin and are an example to other locales of what can be done.[42]

The future is thus bright at Franklin, with plans to rebuild the famous cotton gin and other efforts to save additional historic lands underway. And most of these successes, at least the most modern phases, have been done without the aid of the U.S. Congress, the National Park Service, or even state resources. The preservation at Franklin is a testament to what local people can do. Moreover, these efforts have seemingly awakened the national authorities to the possibilities at Franklin and elsewhere. Written off by the Civil War Trust as too far gone to preserve, Franklin is now seeing renewed interest from that organization as well as from the federal government. In 2005, the U.S. Congress passed legislation to provide for a resource study at Franklin, and the National Park Service has finished the study. In addition, numerous federal and state grants have been awarded to the preservation organizations.[43]

Obviously, it would have been better if Franklin had been preserved in 1900. It would be very special for modern Americans to visit the site built by veterans, much like they do at Shiloh or Gettysburg, without dodging in and out of pizza restaurant parking lots. It would have been better if rehabilitation was not needed at Franklin. But that is the reality. The fight goes on. The cry of what could have been when Congressman Cox offered his bill for a national military park in 1900 has changed to a cry of success in 2015, just by a different (and futuristic) route than that taken by most battlefield preservationists in the past.

Notes

1. "Franklin, Tenn., Celebrates Demise of the Pizza Hut," *Civil War News*, January 2006.

2. Ibid.

3. For more detail on this age, see Timothy B. Smith, *The Golden Age of Battlefield Preservation: The Decade of the 1890s and the Establishment of America's First Five Military Parks* (Knoxville: University of Tennessee Press, 2008).

4. Ibid., 211–13.

5. Ibid., 219–21.

6. For more on the Civil War Trust, see their website: http://www.civilwar.org.

7. Stanley F. Horn, *The Army of Tennessee* (Indianapolis: Bobbs-Merrill Company, 1941), 402–3; James L. McDonough and Thomas L. Connelly, *Five Tragic Hours: The Battle of Franklin* (Knoxville: University of Tennessee Press, 1983). For more on the battle in addition to McDonough and Connelly, see Wiley Sword, *The Confederacy's Last Hurrah: Spring Hill, Franklin, and Nashville* (Lawrence: University Press of Kansas, 1992); James Lee McDonough, *Nashville: The Western Confederacy's Final Gamble* (Knoxville: University of Tennessee Press, 2004); Eric A. Jacobson, *For Cause and for Country: A Study of the Affair at Spring Hill and the Battle of Franklin* (Franklin: O'More Publishing, 2007).

8. "Western Battle-Fields," *National Tribune*, September 9, 1882; "The Grand Army," *National Tribune*, November 13, 1884.

9. "The Grand Army," *National Tribune*, November 13, 1884; "Western Battle-Fields," *National Tribune*, September 9, 1882.

10. Untitled Article, *Keowee Courier*, May 19, 1866; Untitled Article, *Columbia Daily Phoenix*, May 12, 1866; "The Battle of Franklin," *Western Kansas World*, May 29, 1886; "Western Battle-Fields," *National Tribune*, September 9, 1882; "The Grand Army," *National Tribune*, November 13, 1884.

11. "Western Battle-Fields," *National Tribune*, September 9, 1882; McDonough, *Nashville*, 137–38; Franklin Battlefield National Register of Historic Places Inventory—Nomination Form, November 5, 1982, NPS Archives; Virginia McDaniel Bowman, *Historic Williamson County: Old Homes and Sites* (Nashville: Blue and Grey Press, 1971), 60–61.

12. "Plowing up the Remains of the Confederate Dead," *Columbia Daily Phoenix*, June 14, 1866; "Western Battle-Fields," *National Tribune*, September 9, 1882; "The Grand Army," *National Tribune*, November 13, 1884; Dan M. Robison, "The Carter House, Focus of the Battle of Nashville," *Tennessee Historical Quarterly* 22, no. 1 (March 1963): 17.

13. "Make a National Park at Franklin," *Confederate Veteran* 17, no. 1 (January 1909): 15; "The Grand Army," *National Tribune*, November 13, 1884.

14. "Western Battle-Fields," *National Tribune*, September 9, 1882.

15. "Western Battle-Fields," *National Tribune*, September 9, 1882; "Make a National Park at Franklin," *Confederate Veteran* 17, no. 1 (January 1909): 15; McDonough and Connelly, *Five Tragic Hours*, 183–84; National Park Service, *Battle of Franklin Sites, Williamson County, Tennessee: Special Resource Study* (Washington, DC: National Park Service, undated), 71; Robison, "The Carter House, Focus of the Battle of Nashville," 17.

16. "Daughters at Franklin," *Confederate Veteran* 8, no. 4 (April 1900): 172–73.

17. "H.R. 9567," 56th Congress, 1st Session; *Biographical Directory of the United States Congress, 1774–2005* (Washington DC: Government Printing Office, 2005), 883–84.

18. "A National Park in Tennessee," *Washington Times*, February 27, 1900; "For a New Military Park," *St. Louis Republic*, November 18, 1900.

19. "H.R. 9567," 56th Congress, 1st Session, Law Library, Library of Congress.

20. Ibid.

21. "H.R. 4316," 57th Congress, 1st Session, Law Library, Library of Congress; *Biographical Directory of the United States Congress, 1774–2005*, 1692.

22. National Park Service, *Battle of Franklin Sites, Williamson County, Tennessee*, 74. See the various *Congressional Record* indexes through the years for Franklin bills offered in the various congresses.

23. "Make a National Park at Franklin," *Confederate Veteran* 17, no. 1 (January 1909): 15; "The Battlefield of Franklin," *Confederate Veteran* 16, no. 11 (November 1908): 555; "From 'The Other Side' at Franklin," *Confederate Veteran* 17, no. 1 (January 1909): 15; "Franklin Battlefield as National Park," *Confederate Veteran* 17, no. 8 (August 1909): 374.

24. "National Park at Franklin," Confederate Veteran 17, no. 3 (March 1909): 136.

25. McDonough and Connelly, *Five Tragic Hours*, 179; National Park Service, *Battle of Franklin Sites, Williamson County, Tennessee*, 74.

26. "U. D. C. Desire National Park at Franklin," *Confederate Veteran* 18, no. 5 (May 1910): 207; "Anniversary of the Battle of Franklin," *Confederate Veteran* 22, no. 11 (November 1914): 523.

27. McDonough and Connelly, *Five Tragic Hours*, 183–84.

28. Smith, *The Golden Age of Battlefield Preservation*, 212.

29. *House Reports*, 69th Congress, 1st Session, Report 1071, 1–10.

30. *Senate Reports*, 70th Congress, 2nd Session, Report 187, 1–10.

31. National Park Service, *Battle of Franklin Sites, Williamson County, Tennessee*, 76.

32. Ibid., 16–17.

33. Robison, "The Carter House, Focus of the Battle of Nashville," 17–18; Bowman, *Historic Williamson County*, 144–46.

34. "Charter of Incorporation," April 10, 1952, Carter House Archives; Robison, "The Carter House, Focus of the Battle of Nashville," 17–18.

35. Robison, "The Carter House, Focus of the Battle of Nashville," 18–20; National Park Service, *Battle of Franklin Sites, Williamson County, Tennessee*, 14.

36. Franklin Battlefield National Register of Historic Places Inventory—Nomination Form, November 5, 1982, NPS Archives; Bowman, *Historic Williamson County*, 111; Robison, "The Carter House, Focus of the Battle of Nashville," 20; National Park Service, *Battle of Franklin Sites, Williamson County, Tennessee*, 77.

37. Joseph L. Willouby to unknown, September 25, 1978, Carnton Archives; "Department of State Certificate," November 21, 1977, Carnton Archives; W. D. Sugg to Joe Willoughby, September 17, 1977, Carnton Archives; Carnton Deed, August 21, 1985, Carnton Archives; Warranty Deed, August 21, 1985, Carnton Archives; W. D. Sugg and wife to unknown, undated, Carnton Archives; National Park Service, *Battle of Franklin Sites, Williamson County, Tennessee*, 15, 77; Bowman, *Historic Williamson County*, 61–63.

38. Carnton Deed, August 21, 1985, Carnton Archives; Warranty Deed, August 21, 1985, Carnton Archives; National Park Service, *Battle of Franklin Sites, Williamson County, Tennessee*, 15–16, 19, 77, 79.

39. See the Civil War Trust website for more history on the organization: http://www.civilwar.org.

40. Adam Goodheart, "Civil War Battlefields: Saving the Landscape of America's Deadliest War," *National Geographic* (April 2005): 62–85; Robert Hicks, *The Widow of the South* (New York: Warner, 2005); National Park Service, *Battle of Franklin Sites, Williamson County, Tennessee*, 16–17, 75, 77–78.

41. Robert Hicks to attendees, undated, "Why Franklin Matters: Exploring the Preservation and Interpretation of Franklin's Civil War Story" and "Why Franklin Matters," in handbooks given out at the June 21–24, 2007, Conference, Franklin, Tennessee; Goodheart, "Civil War Battlefields," 74–75; National Park Service, *Battle of Franklin Sites, Williamson County, Tennessee*, 16, 19, 79. See the Franklin's Charge website (http://www.franklinscharge.com) for more detail on the effort. See also the website for Fort Granger (http://www.franklin-gov.com/index.aspx?page=160) and the Lotz House (http://www.lotzhouse.com).

42. Goodheart, "Civil War Battlefields," 75.

43. National Park Service, *Battle of Franklin Sites, Williamson County, Tennessee*, 80–82.

13

PRESERVING THE NASHVILLE BATTLEFIELD

THE SOUTH'S TRUE LOST CAUSE

Jennifer M. Murray

Captured by Union forces in February 1862, Nashville became the first Confederate state capital to surrender. Nearly three years later, Lieutenant General John Bell Hood initiated a campaign to recapture Middle Tennessee, resulting in one of the most decisive operations of the Civil War. On December 15 and 16, 1864, Hood's Army of Tennessee battled Union forces commanded by Major General George H. Thomas in rain, mud, and sleet. Hood moved in to Middle Tennessee with a force of approximately thirty-eight thousand. After a month of campaigning, including battles at Spring Hill on November 29, Franklin on November 30, and the two-day fight at Nashville, Hood sustained nearly twenty-four thousand casualties, almost two-thirds of his army. The shattered remnants of Hood's command crossed the Tennessee River near Florence, Alabama, on Christmas Day, then turned westward into Mississippi, finally ending their retreat in Tupelo. Reflective of the virtual destruction of his army, Hood resigned his command on January 23, 1865. That winter several thousand of Hood's remaining soldiers joined Confederate forces in the Carolinas in an attempt to forestall General William T. Sherman's advance. These efforts, like Hood's at Nashville, proved futile. General Robert E. Lee surrendered at Appomattox on April 9, 1865, and later that month, on April 26, General Joseph E. Johnston surrendered the Confederate forces in the Carolinas at Bennett Place, near Durham, North Carolina.[1]

In the ensuing years, northerners and southerners, veterans and civilians alike, joined together to preserve the Civil War's "hallowed ground." Commemorative activities and preservation efforts initially focused on five battles widely considered the critical ones of the war: Chickamauga and Chattanooga, Shiloh, and Vicksburg in the western theater, and Antietam and Gettysburg in the eastern theater. Years later additional battlefields gained federal recognition as national military parks. Beginning in the early twentieth century, local residents championed federal protection for Nashville as well, but ultimately Congress denied their proposals on two different occasions. Today, 150 years after the Battle of Nashville, little remains of the field over which Hood's and Thomas's men fought. Instead of becoming a preserved, memorialized, and interpreted national military park, the Nashville battlefield fell victim to neglect, urban sprawl, and inevitable development. Through the efforts of local preservation groups, notably the Battle of Nashville Preservation Society, six parcels of battlefield terrain are preserved, amounting to approximately 100 acres total. These fragmented parcels, situated amidst housing developments, are tangible reminders to the failure to protect the landscape of the Nashville battlefield. Efforts of local preservation groups notwithstanding, the preservation of Nashville stands as a genuine "Lost Cause."[2]

The roots of battlefield commemoration and preservation lay with Civil War veterans and local preservation-minded citizens who undertook efforts to honor the men who had given what President Abraham Lincoln termed the "last full measure of devotion." The final two decades of the nineteenth century ushered in what Timothy Smith defines as the "golden age of battlefield preservation." As Smith demonstrates, several critical factors collided in the 1880s and 1890s that provided for this unparalleled preservation movement. Reflective of heightened reconciliationist sentiments, Union and Confederate veterans strove to mark and commemorate the war's battlefields. Congress eagerly assisted these initiatives. The timing was opportune in Washington; in 1890, half of the congressmen were Civil War veterans. In the final decade of the nineteenth century, Congress authorized the establishment of five Civil War battlefields to be administered by the War Department: Chickamauga and Chattanooga (1890), Antietam (1890), Shiloh (1894), Gettysburg (1895), and Vicksburg (1899).[3]

By the turn of the century, however, fewer veterans remained in Congress and enthusiasm for battlefield preservation had waned. Vicksburg would be the last battlefield granted protection by the federal government for nearly a quarter of a century. Local preservation affiliates and state political officials, however, continued to introduce proposals for the creation of additional national military parks. Between 1901 and 1904, for example, members introduced thirty-four bills in Congress to establish other national military parks, including Bull Run, Appomattox, Franklin, Wilson's Creek, Stones River, and Perryville. Economic considerations, however, held sway and influenced subsequent preservation attempts. In 1902, Secretary of War Elihu Root reported that the maintenance of Chickamauga and Chattanooga, Shiloh, Vicksburg, and Gettysburg amounted to approximately $2 million. New parks would have more than doubled that expense.[4]

As the idea of battlefield preservation spread rapidly across the nation, Nashville residents too organized to protect the grounds associated with the December 1864 battle. Across the state of Tennessee preservation efforts had been underway for decades. Both the Chickamauga Memorial Association and the Shiloh Battlefield Association had successfully lobbied for federal status as a national military park for each. With a similar objective in mind, in 1909 Nashville citizens formed the Nashville Battlefield Association (NBA). Nashville advocates sought federal assistance in marking the battlefield and constructing a road network, which would create the needed infrastructure of a small national military park. The influential *Confederate Veteran*, published in Nashville, commonly ran pieces that raised awareness of the efforts to mark, memorialize, and preserve the battlefield. Columnists declared Nashville the "decisive battle" of the war. Acknowledging some aversion to memorializing a Confederate defeat, the NBA assured skeptics, "This is in no sense to celebrate defeat," but instead a means to commemorate "many feats of heroism."[5]

In 1910, the NBA and prominent local residents first petitioned Congress for federal recognition. Congressman Joseph W. Byrns introduced the bill and led the political movement. On April 7, 1910, the Committee on Military Affairs of the House of Representatives considered H.R. 6179, a bill to create a national military park at Nashville. Recognizing that the prevalent War Department sentiment now opposed additional federal sites, Byrns and the NBA approached House members with a conservative plan to mold Nashville into a military park. Proponents requested governmental assistance in locating and marking unit positions and constructing a series of roadways to facilitate visitor access to the determined points of historical interest. Park Marshall, a Franklin native, lawyer, and public servant who became the NBA's historian, maintained that federal assistance to mark the battlefield would provide the landscape "a dignity and credit" not maintained otherwise. Byrns requested $10,000 to complete the necessary work.[6]

H.R. 6179, in other words, reflected a conservative preservation philosophy. Nashville advocates declared that they did not want the government to acquire large amounts of land, but merely assistance in marking unit positions and securing land along the respective armies' battle lines. Marshall simultaneously championed a utilitarian landscape, noting that extensive land acquisition would "not be really desirable" because the property was more "desirable and valuable for building sites and farming." Yet Marshall's testimony reflects some degree of inconsistency when he lamented modern developments and encroachments on the historic grounds. By 1910, for instance, fertilizer buildings stood where on December 15, 1864, Major General

James Steedman's forces assaulted the right flank of the Army of Tennessee, held by Lieutenant General Benjamin Franklin Cheatham's troops. Articles in *Confederate Veteran* promoting the protection of Nashville likewise echoed the undesirability of creating a large national park, noting the battlefield ground was "far too valuable for an extended park." Instead, the NBA recommended the federal government secure some "central or otherwise important part of the field," of approximately fifty to one hundred acres.[7]

During the April 1910 hearings, congressmen heard testimony from Marshall, S. A. Cunningham, editor of the *Confederate Veteran* and vice president of the NBA, Michigan congressman Washington Gardner, and W. V. Cox, the son of a Confederate veteran of the battle. Congressman Gardner offered a patriotic plea befitting of reconciliation rhetoric. "There is in this proposition no South, no North," he declared. "There is no Confederate, no Union, but Americans and fellow countrymen all." He also implored the representatives to mark the fields while the veterans were still alive and capable.[8]

True to the prevalent aversion of funding for additional national military parks, Congress denied assistance to mark the Nashville battlefield. Though defeated in their effort to gain federal recognition, local residents began to mark and protect portions of the grounds and erect commemorative markers. Two years after the defeat of the national military park bill, in 1912 the Nashville Industrial Bureau, in cooperation with the NBA, sponsored and erected twenty markers to identify various points of interest on the battlefield. These tablets primarily marked the unit locations for the first day's battle, December 15. In addition to marking twenty key points, the Nashville Industrial Bureau produced a small touring booklet that offered directions to selected points, accompanied by a short narrative of its historical significance. The Nashville trolley lines provided access to the points of interest, thereby establishing the first tour route, albeit primitive and rudimentary.[9]

The post–World War I years ushered in a new era of battlefield preservation. Hypersensitivity to American patriotism as a result of the war engendered additional commemorative efforts in Nashville. On November 11, 1927, residents gathered for the dedication of the Battle of Nashville Monument, erected on Franklin Road. May Winston Caldwell, wife of James E. Caldwell, a Nashville banker and capitalist, championed the concept and realization of the monument. With Caldwell's guidance, women's organizations, including the United Daughters of the Confederacy, donated funds toward the monument and sponsored events to raise the $30,000 for its construction. In the wake of World War I and six decades removed from the Civil War, the monument depicted a decidedly reconciliationist and patriotic narrative. Two horses representing the North and South are joined together by a young man, symbolizing a reunited nation. The word "unity" is inscribed on the banner the man holds to entwine the horses.[10]

Meanwhile, in the 1920s, Congress granted national military park status to three additional Civil War battlefields—Petersburg, Fredericksburg and Spotsylvania (to include Chancellorsville and the Wilderness), and Stones River. Hoping to capitalize on this resurgence of aid, in 1928 Nashville advocates tried once more to gain federal recognition for the battlefield. And once more Congressman Byrns, the force behind the 1910 proposal, led the fight. He introduced H.R. 10291, which sought to create a national military park at Fort Negley, a bastion of the federal defenses at Nashville. In 1862, Captain James St. Clair Morton oversaw the fort's construction, just south of Nashville. Named for Union general James Negley, the fort was built by free blacks and conscripted slaves. When completed, Negley stood as the largest inland masonry fort constructed during the war. After Tennessee rejoined the Union in July 1866, Federal forces abandoned the fort in September. During the tenuous social strife of the postwar years, Fort Negley stood as a physical testament to Union victory and a symbol to the war's racial implications. The Ku Klux Klan, for instance, used the fort as a meeting location until 1869.[11]

Byrns's bill differed from the 1910 initiative; he sought not to preserve multiple areas associated with the Battle of Nashville, but proposed only to purchase Fort Negley and twenty-five acres of surrounding land. Byrns estimated the cost to purchase the fort at $25,000 and an additional $100,000 for its restoration. Testimony, however, reflected the rhetoric that preservation advocates championed nearly two decades earlier. Mrs. Flora Myers Gillentine, Nashville resident and the vice president of the Daughters of the American Revolution, testified in favor of preserving Fort Negley. Though the window of sectional reconciliation had long since closed, Gillentine presented the case for the preservation of Fort Negley as a "gesture toward solidarity." Echoing the recurring case for Nashville as one of the decisive battles of the war, Gillentine also noted that this effort merited special consideration because southern women sought to preserve and restore a Union fort. The Committee on Military Affairs, however, remained unconvinced of its value. Offering a practical assessment of the effort to preserve forts and posts across the nation, Congressman Lister Hill of Alabama reminded listeners, "there is a limit to which we can go."[12]

Indeed, overwhelmed with bills proposing the creation of national military parks, in the years shortly after World War I, Congress passed legislation to establish parameters to historic preservation by classifying battlefields based on their historical significance. Evaluating the merits of a national military park at Fort Negley based on the battlefield classification system and the affiliated costs of a federal presence at the fort, Congress once again denied the proposal to preserve the Nashville battlefield.[13] The failed 1928 effort represented Nashville's last significant preservation movement for nearly seven decades.

Enthusiasm for the Civil War centennial regenerated interest in the Civil War and renewed preservation initiatives. In Tennessee, the Tennessee Civil War Centennial Commission took the lead in preparing the state's centennial activities. Established in 1959, the commission worked to coordinate events with county and local governments. Stanley Horn, Davidson County native and noted historian, chaired the commission. In one of its most significant accomplishments, the commission erected eighty-five historical highway markers across the state. Yet visitors interested in driving around Nashville to visit key battle sites lacked comprehensive markers identifying the armies' position or narrating the fighting, excepting the twenty Nashville Industrial Bureau markers erected in 1912. During the centennial, the Tennessee Historical Commission placed twenty-five additional markers on the battlefield, representing the first systematic attempt to mark and interpret the two-day battle.[14]

In 1964, the Davidson County Civil War Centennial Committee sponsored and coordinated the battle's centennial activities, held on December 11–13. A small battle reenactment at Percy Warner Park, with roughly a thousand reenactors participating, highlighted the events. The activities concluded with a rededication of the Battle of Nashville Monument, a memorial service for the Confederate dead at Mount Olivet Cemetery, a memorial service for Union dead at the National Cemetery, and a memorial service on Shy's Hill. In an attempt to increase visitation to the battle's sites, the Davidson County Civil War Centennial Committee and the Nashville Chamber of Commerce each produced and distributed a touring brochure for the occasion. Although the Civil War centennial renewed enthusiasm for the war across the nation, interpretive and preservation interests in Nashville remained incomplete.[15]

The reemergence of the preservation movement found its roots in the plight of Fort Negley. After the failed preservation effort in 1928, the city of Nashville acquired the fort. Yet, for more than seven decades Fort Negley lay abandoned and neglected. New Deal funding during the 1930s marked the first occasion of federal involvement in protecting parcels of the battlefield. Between 1936 and 1937 laborers from the Works Projects Administration (WPA) restored the fort to its Civil War appearance. In 1938, after an investment of $84,000, Fort Negley opened to the public. Unfortunately before the fort gained momentum as a historic attraction, World War II consumed

Americans' attention and economic resources. In the years after the war, Fort Negley again fell into a state of disrepair; locals used the grounds as a garbage dump and the fort became a popular site for vandalism and petty crime. Consequently, in the 1960s, Metro Parks, the site's administrator, closed it.[16] Ultimately the city of Nashville found the grounds around the Union fort to be more valuable as a recreational center than as a historical site. The city authorized the construction of a minor league baseball stadium, Hershel Greer Stadium, home to the Nashville Sounds, and the Cumberland Science Museum on grounds immediately adjacent to Fort Negley.

To be sure, Fort Negley, its associated symbolism, and multiple layers of history divided area residents, which helped to explain in part the prevalent neglect of the site. A portion of the city's residents accepted the fort as a recreational site and promoted the development of additional recreational opportunities. The more contentious camps divided along the historical implications of the fort. African Americans championed the restoration of Fort Negley and its interpretation as a means to recount the role of blacks in the Civil War and to present a broader sociocultural narrative. Some of Nashville's black residents felt the fort's neglect was a deliberate attempt to ignore the racial context of the Civil War. In a letter to the editor in the *Tennessean*, one resident commented on this perceived slight: "One wonders if a Confederate fort would receive the same treatment, or rather, lack of treatment."[17]

Local interest in improving and interpreting Fort Negley resurfaced only in the 1980s and gained momentum in the early 1990s. Nashville, or Metro Parks, had done little to interpret or preserve the fort. In 1988, a visitor from Ohio wrote a letter to the editor commenting on the deplorable shape of Fort Negley. He lamented, "It speaks ill of your local and state governments that the condition of Negley is beyond pathetic." After decades of neglect, on December 16, 1993, the 128th anniversary of the battle, Nashville mayor Phil Bredesen confronted the plight of the fort. Bredesen appointed a fourteen-person commission to oversee its restoration and development. Ultimately the city of Nashville appropriated approximately $2 million for the fort's restoration, representing the largest expenditure of city funds for the preservation of a Civil War site. A decade later, on December 11, 2004, the restored Fort Negley opened to the public. Reenactors representing the 13th U.S. Colored Troops (USCT), the unit that garrisoned Negley during the war, participated in the opening celebrations. The four-acre fort sits on approximately fifteen acres of park ground complemented with walking paths, interpretive waysides, observation platforms, and viewing scopes. Meanwhile, construction on the interpretive center continued. Three years later, on December 15, 2007, the Fort Negley Visitor Center opened. At a cost of approximately $1 million, the visitor center offers a small collection of exhibits and an introductory film, "The Fall of Nashville."[18]

The restoration of Fort Negley and the opening of the visitor center is the most significant and sizable accomplishment of the Nashville Civil War preservation movement. Unfortunately, most of the key terrain over which Union and Confederate soldiers battled in December 1864 is lost. Denied federal status as a national military park on two different occasions, the battlefield had remained unprotected and vulnerable to the inevitable developments and commercial intrusions of a metropolitan area. Hood's and Thomas's men fought over approximately twenty thousand acres; today an estimated 100 acres of historic terrain are protected. Certainly the sheer size of Nashville, at approximately 545,000 in 2000 and a metropolitan population of 1.2 million, compound modern preservation challenges. Once historic terrain is now littered with commercial and residential developments, while modern roadways bisect once contested battlegrounds. Without federal stewardship, the preservation agenda fell to proactive historical organizations capable of only saving small, fragmented parcels of battlefield terrain.[19] In addition to Nashville's Metro Parks, other groups involved with battlefield preservation include the Tennessee Historical Society, the General Joseph Johnston Camp of the Sons of Confederate Veterans (SCV), the Land Trust for Tennessee, and the Battle of Nashville Preservation Society (BONPS). Collectively these organizations have preserved or maintain responsibility for six parcels of historic terrain: Fort Negley, Kelley's Battery, the Glen Leven Estate, the Battle of Nashville Monument, Shy's Hill, and Redoubt No. 1.

In addition to managing Fort Negley, Metro Parks also administers Kelley's Battery. Located nine miles west of Nashville, along Bell's Bend on the Cumberland River, Kelley's Battery marks the location where for two weeks prior to the battle, Confederate artillery, commanded by Colonel David Campbell Kelley, engaged and harassed the Union Navy. For nearly six years, advocates urged the preservation of the site from impending development. Fortunately, Metro Parks secured the site, consisting of six acres, and developed it as part of the city's "greenway program," opening the area in 2003.[20]

The General Joseph E. Johnston Camp of the Sons of Confederate Veterans, meanwhile, maintains a section of the Nashville battlefield. On December 15, 1864, Major General Benjamin Franklin Cheatham's corps held the right flank of the Confederate battle line. The fortified position, which the troops named Granbury's Lunette in honor of their brigade commander who fell mortally wounded at Franklin, consisted of four artillery pieces. The Confederate flank held after a strong attack by Union general James Steedman's troops. Today only remnants remain of Granbury's Lunette and the historic railroad cut into which Union troops inadvertently veered during their offensive. Members of the Johnston Camp own the salvaged section of Granbury's Lunette. The largest parcel of battlefield terrain is acreage of the Glen Leven Estate, maintained by the Land Trust for Tennessee. Located south of Nashville, along the Franklin Pike and used as a field hospital during the battle, the estate consists of sixty-five acres. Susan West, the estate's last owner, bequeathed the property to the Land Trust for Tennessee. To date, however, minimal interpretation is done with the property.[21]

The history of the Battle of Nashville Monument also represents modern-day challenges and triumphs in preservation. In the 1940s the Tennessee Historical Commission acquired the monument and its acreage and continued to maintain the property as a memorial park. Unfortunately, in 1974 a tornado destroyed the shaft marker and the angelic figure on top. The subsequent construction of a nearby interstate interchange in the 1980s left the disfigured monument isolated from public view. In 1988, *Tennessean* reporter Renee Elder wrote a series of articles drawing attention to the disgraceful status of the monument. Responding to the increased awareness to the neglect of the Battle of Nashville Monument, the Tennessee Historical Commission initiated a movement to relocate and repair it. The commission selected a small tract of approximately three acres, at the intersection of Granny White Pike and Battlefield Drive, as the new location. With interest in the monument renewed, the commission received donations and grants from Nashville songwriters, the city of Nashville, the Tennessee Department of Transportation, the state of Tennessee, and assorted individuals. After years of fundraising, the Tennessee Historical Commission rededicated the Battle of Nashville Monument on June 16, 1999.[22]

The Battle of Nashville Preservation Society currently leads the fight to save portions of the Nashville battlefield and to interpret the battle. Formed in 1992, the society took its roots from the local chapter of the Sons of Confederate Veterans and residents interested in the battle and protecting key sites of the engagement. Shortly after its establishment, the society advocated the preservation and enhancement of Kelley's Battery, and worked with Metro Parks to make the protection of the site a reality. Early preservation efforts, and the organization's most significant accomplishments, were made possible by generous donations from BONPS founding member and Nashville lawyer, William "Wes" Shofner.[23]

The newly created BONPS selected Redoubt No. 1 as its first preservation project. Built by Confederate forces along the south side of Nashville, between the Hillsboro Pike and the Granny White Pike, Union troops captured the redoubt on December 15, 1864. Typical of most of the battle landscape, the area surrounding the redoubt had been partitioned as a housing development. Shofner purchased a small parcel of undeveloped land, approximately one-half acre, at Redoubt No.1 for $75,000. On December 2003, the BONPS dedicated an interpretive sign at the redoubt to narrate the battle action along the Confederate army's left flank. Wanting the society to take ownership to the accomplishment, members of the organization raised or donated money to retire the debt on Redoubt No. 1. Now the association maintains the redoubt, the wayside exhibit, and a replica artillery piece.[24]

One of the most critical pieces of terrain on the battlefield was Compton's Hill, also located along the left flank of the Confederate battle line, just west of the Granny White Pike. The Union assault on December 16 broke the Confederate line and routed the southern forces. The hill was later named for Confederate colonel William Shy, commander of the 20th Tennessee Volunteer Infantry, who fell mortally wounded on the hill. Shy's Hill remained relatively undisturbed by modern intrusions until the mid-1950s, when a local developer acquired the tract for the construction of a residential development. The developer, C. B. Kelly, deeded the summit of the hill, amounting to approximately two acres, to the Tennessee Historical Society. Encouraged by the success in saving a small tract of battlefield land at Redoubt No. 1, Shofner and the BONPS sought to enlarge the protected area of Shy's Hill. As with Redoubt No. 1, Shofner purchased a small parcel of land, approximately 1.3 acres, to hold for the Battle of Nashville Preservation Society. On April 11, 2006, the BONPS, through fund-raising and donations, celebrated the debt retirement for the tract of land.[25]

In the early 1990s, the federal government evaluated its preservation practices at the nation's Civil War battlefields. Congress established the Civil War Sites Advisory Commission (CWSAC) in 1991; its purpose to identify significant Civil War sites and access preservation threats. The commission's report, issued in 1993, prioritized the sites according to their historical significance, as well as preservation status and potential. Preservation priorities ranged from Priority I, sites most threatened, to Priority IV, sites lost to development. The commission identified Nashville as a lost battlefield, Priority IV. Though the advisory report classified Nashville as a bottom-tiered preservation priority, committee members did acknowledge that fragments of the battlefield, namely Fort Negley and Shy's Hill, offered opportunities to develop interpretive programming. Nonetheless, as a result of Nashville's Priority IV classification the federal government devotes minimal attention to the site's preservation or interpretation challenges.[26]

The CWSAC classification of Nashville as a "lost" battlefield dictates any preservation assistance. The efforts of the Battle of Nashville Preservation

Society and the plight of the battlefield did gain national attention in the early twenty-first century. In 2003, the Civil War Preservation Trust (CWPT) ranked Nashville as one of the nation's top ten endangered battlefields. A year later, in the summer of 2004, the trust's magazine, *Hallowed Ground*, made Redoubt No. 1 its feature story. In April the CWPT held its annual conference in Nashville and recognized Mayor Bill Purcell for his commitment to protecting and interpreting Fort Negley. These events aside, the CWPT has not taken any significant active, or economic, involvement in saving parcels of the Nashville battlefield. On the other hand, the trust has worked to preserve the battlefield of Franklin, fought just two weeks before Nashville and approximately twenty miles south. Subjected to urban development, the CWSAC classified the Franklin battlefield as "fragmented," a priority above Nashville. In 2004 the CWPT ranked Franklin as one of the nation's top ten endangered battlefields, and in cooperation with local preservation associations, namely Franklin's Charge, the trust is working to reclaim historic terrain and to promote heritage tourism in Williamson County.[27]

Virginia holds the nation's most Civil War battlefield sites at 123. Tennessee ranks second with thirty-eight key Civil War battles, campaigns, and engagements. Believing that the preservation and interpretation of these would "make an important contribution to the understanding of the heritage of the United States," Congress authorized the Tennessee Civil War Heritage Area in November 1996. This heritage area had four objectives: to preserve and interpret the legacy of the Civil War in Tennessee; to interpret key Civil War events and sites within the state; to recognize and promote the effect of the war and Reconstruction on the state's residents; and to create preservation partnerships between federal, state, and local entities. The following year, the state of Tennessee established the Tennessee Civil War Preservation Association, a nonprofit organization, with a mission to "protect, interpret and make accessible Tennessee's surviving Civil War battlefields and contributing landscapes for the benefit of present and future generations."[28]

Stating its mission quite simply to save what was not destroyed, the Battle of Nashville Preservation Society remains Nashville's leading steward. The BONPS owns two critical pieces of the battlefield: Redoubt No. 1 and Shy's Hill, which amount to no more than three acres. Tentative future projects include the acquisition of Peach Orchard Hill, a one-acre parcel of undeveloped land and the scene of fierce fighting between the Confederates and the USCT soldiers. Notwithstanding the irrevocable alteration to the historic landscape, minimal support for preservation, limited recognition, and constrained economic factors also limit their capabilities. The association recorded approximately seventy-five paying members for the 2011 year. Thus, something seemingly as simple as erecting historical markers represents a significant economic investment at approximately $2,200 per marker.[29]

The 150-year history of the Nashville battlefield closely mirrors the narrative of the battlefield preservation movement and also reflects the wavering popularity of protecting Civil War sites. Unfortunately for the fate of Nashville, by the time legislation had been introduced in Congress to mark and preserve the battlefield in 1910, the "golden age" of the preservation movement had passed. The modern preservation effort, relying on collaborative efforts of various organizations, has been the most successful in protecting the remaining tracts of land and also in interpreting the battlefield to visitors. For one of the truly decisive battles of the Civil War, little remains of the ground over which Thomas's and Hood's men battled. At a mere 100 acres, the preservation and interpretation of the Nashville battle stands as one of the South's true "Lost Causes."

Notes

1. James McPherson, *Battle Cry of Freedom: The Civil War Era* (New York: Oxford University Press, 1988), 828; James Lee McDonough, *Nashville: The Western Confederacy's Final Gamble* (Knoxville: University of Tennessee Press, 2004), 273–74. For additional reading on the Battle of Nashville and the Army of Tennessee see Wiley Sword, *Embrace an Angry Wind: The Confederacy's Last Hurrah, Spring Hill, Franklin, and Nashville* (New York: HarperCollins Publishers, 1992).

2. The defining work on Civil War memory is David Blight, *Race and Reunion: The Civil War in American Memory* (Cambridge: Harvard University Press, 2001). For additional reading on the process of preserving battlefields see Timothy Smith, *The Golden Age of Battlefield Preservation: The Decade of the 1890s and the Establishment of America's First Five Military Parks* (Knoxville: University of Tennessee Press, 2008); Timothy Smith, "Civil War Battlefield Preservation in Tennessee; A Nashville National Military Park Case Study," *Tennessee Historical Quarterly* 64, no. 3 (2005): 236–47; Jennifer M. Murray, *"On A Great Battlefield": The Making, Management, and Memory of Gettysburg National Military Park, 1933–2013* (Knoxville: University of Tennessee Press, 2014).

3. Smith, *The Golden Age of Battlefield Preservation*, 241.

4. Ronald F. Lee, *The Origin and Evolution of the National Military Park Idea*, section IV, "Later Evolution of the National Military Park Idea, 1900–1933" (Washington, DC: Office of Historic Preservation, National Park Service, 1973), accessed November 2011, http://www.cr.nps.gov/history/online_books/history_military/index.htm. The online version was consulted for this essay and will be cited by sections.

5. "Nashville Battlefield Association," *Confederate Veteran* 17, no. 1 (February 1909): 53.

6. Hearing Before the Committee on Military Affairs, House of Representatives, on H.R. 6179, April 7, 1910 (Washington: Government Printing Office, 1910), Tennessee State Library and Archives (TSLA), Nashville, Tennessee [hereinafter cited as H.R. 6179, TSLA]; "Marking Battlefield of Nashville," *Confederate Veteran* 17 (June 1910): 281; "Nashville Battlefield Association," 14–15.

7. H.R. 6179, TSLA; "Nashville Battlefield Association," 53; Park Marshall, "Nashville Battlefield Merits Attention," *Confederate Veteran* 17, no. 1 (May 1909): 221.

8. H.R. 6179, TSLA; "Nashville Battlefield Association," 53; Marshall, "Nashville Battlefield Merits Attention," 221.

9. W. E. Beard, *The Battle of Nashville* (Nashville: Nashville Industrial Bureau, 1913), Tennessee State Library and Archives, Nashville, Tennessee. The marker at Granbury's Lunette is one of the original 1912 markers.

10. "The Rededication of the Battle of Nashville Monument," June 26, 1999, sponsored by the Tennessee Historical Commission, Civil War Monuments folder, Battle of Nashville (Peace Monument), Metro Library, Nashville, TN; "Mrs. Caldwell Succumbs Here," unidentified newspaper, December 15, 1939, May Winston Caldwell folder, Metro Library, Nashville, TN; "Majestic Longview Begun in the 1840s," *Nashville Banner*, October 4, 1989, James E. Caldwell folder, Metro Library, Nashville, TN.

11. Lee, section IV, "Later Evolution of the National Military Park Idea, 1900–1933"; Hearing before the Committee on Military Affairs, House of Representatives, 70th Congress, 1st Sess., on H.R. 10291, February 2, 1928 (Washington, DC: Government Printing Office, 1928) [hereinafter cited as H.R. 10291].

12. H.R. 10291.

13. Lee, Section IV, "Later Evolution of the National Military Park Idea, 1900–1933." Congress did create a national military park at Fort Donelson in March 1928. In total, between 1926 and 1933, Congress added fourteen battlefield sites to the national military park system, including the Civil War sites of Brices Cross Roads, Monocacy, and Appomattox.

14. James B. Williams, *The Tennessee Civil War Centennial Commission: Looking to the Past as Tennessee Plans for the Future* (Nashville: Tennessee Civil War Heritage Area Publications, undated); "Battle of Nashville, 1864–1964, Centennial Commemorative Program," Civil War Commemorations, Hood's Campaign, 1864 folder, Wars and Military Ephemera files, Metro Library, Nashville, TN.

15. "Proposed Commemoration, The Battle of Nashville, 1864–1964," reel 1 (box 1, folder 1 to box 6, folder 4), TSLA, Nashville, TN; "Battle of Nashville, 1864–1964, Centennial Commemorative Program"; Ed Huddleston, "Concert Will Open Civil War Program," *Nashville Tennessean*, December 10, 1964, vertical files: Battle of Nashville, TSLA, Nashville, TN; "The Decisive Battle of Nashville" touring brochure, distributed by the Nashville Chamber of Commerce, Civil War, Battle of Nashville files, Metro Library, Nashville, TN. The Tennessee Historical Society and the Metropolitan Historical Commission produced a self-guided driving tour in the 1980s, "The Civil War Battle of Nashville: A Self-Guided Driving Tour," published by Tennessee Historical Society and the Metropolitan Historical Commission, 1983, Civil War, Battle of Nashville files, Metro Library, Nashville, TN.

16. Davidson County Deeds, Metro Library, Nashville, TN; "Searching For Truth about Fort," *Nashville Tennessean*, October 20, 1992.

17. N. Z. Becher, letter to the editor, *Nashville Tennessean*, February 12, 1986; Renee Elder, "City Divided Over the Future of Fort Negley," *Nashville Tennessean*, February 18, 1994.

18. David Chollet, letter to the editor, *Nashville Banner*, March 16, 1988, Fort Negley file, Metro Library, Nashville, TN; "Mayor Moves to Save Negley," *Nashville Banner*, December 16, 1993. Bredesen served as Nashville's sixty-sixth mayor from 1991 until 1999;

Judith R. Tackett, "Fort Finally Opened 60 Years Later," *City Paper*, November 23, 2004; Michael Cass, "Center Tells Fort Negley's Story," *Nashville Tennessean*, December 14, 2007; "History Comes Alive with Fort Negley's Reopening," *Nashville Tennessean*, December 11, 2004, Fort Negley file, Metro Library, Nashville, TN. The visitor center is about 4,600 square feet; Fort Negley brochure, produced by Metro Parks. Admission to Fort Negley is free. In 2010, the site recorded approximately 10,500 visitors.

19. American Battlefield Protection Program Application, 2006, Shy's Hill, BONPS files, James Kay, Jr. Law Office, 222 Second Avenue North, Nashville, Tennessee (all notes hereinafter from Kay's Law Office, will be cited as Kay Office, Nashville, TN. Mr. Kay served as the president of the BONPS from 2009 to 2010 and his law office holds the majority of the organization's archival and contemporary records); Bill Ditenhafer, "The Forgotten Battle: Has Nashville Lost Its (Potentially Lucrative) Civil War Heritage?" *Nashville Scene*, October 17, 2002, Wars and Military Ephemera subject files, Civil War Battle of Nashville folder, Metro Library, Nashville, TN.

20. "Kelley's Point Now Complete: Battlefield Now Incorporated into Greenway," undated press release, BONPS Press Releases folder, BONPS files, Kay Office, Nashville, TN.

21. See *The Land Trust for Tennessee: Glen Leven Farm*, http://www.landtrusttn.org/glenleven/.

22. "The Rededication of the Battle of Nashville Monument," June 26, 1999. Sponsored by the Tennessee Historical Commission. Folder: Civil War Monuments, Battle of Nashville (Peace Monument, 1997–99), Metro Library, Nashville, TN; "The Battle of Nashville Monument and Related Memorial Movements: A Brief History." Folder: Civil War Monuments, Battle of Nashville (Peace Monument, 1998).

23. Oral interview with Wes Shofner and Ross Massey, November 10, 2011, Nashville, TN; oral interview with James Kay Jr., November 9, 2011, Nashville, TN; Articles of Incorporation of the Nashville Battlefield Preservation Society, Inc., signed March 19, 1992; By Laws of the Battle of Nashville Preservation Society, By Laws folder, BONPS files, Kay Office, Nashville, TN.

24. Ross Massey to Mike Gavan, October 4, 2003, Redoubt No. 1 folder, BONPS files, Kay Office, Nashville, TN; "Interpretive Sign Dedication Ceremony at Redoubt No. 1," press release, BONPS Press Releases folder, BONPS files, Kay Office, Nashville, TN; Redoubt No. 1 Monument file, Philip Duer's Law Office, 530 Church Street, Nashville, TN (all notes hereinafter from Duer's Law Office, will be cited as Duer Office, Nashville, TN. Mr. Duer served as president of the BONPS from 2011 to 2012).

25. Shy's Hill Debt Retirement Ceremony Brochure, April 15, 2006, Shy's Hill folder, BONPS files, Kay Office, Nashville, TN.

26. "Civil War Sites Advisory Report on the Nation's Civil War Battlefields, 1993," Civil War Sites Advisory Commission Report on the Nation's Battlefields, prepared for the Committee on Energy and Natural Resources, U.S. Senate Committee on Natural Resources, U.S. House of Representatives (Washington, DC: National Park Service, 1993).

27. "America's Most Endangered Battlefields," Civil War Preservation Trust, February 2003; "National Battlefield Preservation Group Hosts Annual Conference in Nashville," CWPT press release, April 15, 2004; "Civil War Sites Advisory Report, 1993," Civil War Sites Advisory Commission. For additional information on Franklin's Charge, visit their website at: http://www.franklinscharge.com/home.

28. Public Law 104–333, November 12, 1966, "Tennessee Civil War Heritage Area"; brochure, Tennessee Civil War Preservation Association, Wars and Military Ephemera subject files, Civil War Monuments, Battle of Nashville folder (Peace Monument, 1998), Metro Library, Nashville, TN; Tennessee Civil War Preservation Association website, available at: http://www.tcwpa.org. The TCWPA was formed as part of the Tennessee War's Commission to interpret and protect the state's Civil War battlefields and sites; "History in Peril: A Proposal for a Civil War Protection Plan for Davidson County, Tennessee," November 6, 1998, Civil War, Preservation 1998 folder, Metro Library, Nashville, TN.

29. The society also advances educational initiatives, lectures, and seminars. In 2004, the society produced *Guide to Civil War Nashville,* a complete tour booklet. See Mark Zimmerman, *Guide to Civil War Nashville* (Nashville: Battle of Nashville Preservation Society, 2004).

CONTRIBUTORS

INDEX

CONTRIBUTORS

Stewart Bennett is the department chair of social and behavioral sciences and teaches history at Blue Mountain College in Blue Mountain, Mississippi. He authored *The Battle of Brice's Crossroads* (2012) and is the coeditor of *The Struggle for the Life of the Republic: A Civil War Narrative by Brevet Major Charles Dana Miller, 76th Ohio Volunteer Infantry* (2004).

Andrew S. Bledsoe teaches history at Lee University. His work on American Civil War soldiers and officers has appeared in a number of books and journals. He is the author of *Citizen-Officers: The Union and Confederate Volunteer Junior Officer Corps in the American Civil War* (2015).

John J. Gaines teaches for American Public University. Social aspects of the Civil War are the primary topics of his published works, including *An Evening with Venus: Prostitution during the American Civil War* (2014).

Charles D. Grear is a professor of history and the online manager for history and geography at Central Texas College. He has written extensively on the involvement of Texas in the Civil War, including *Why Texans Fought in the Civil War* (2010), and has edited several books, among them *The Chattanooga Campaign* (with Steven E. Woodworth, 2012).

John R. Lundberg teaches at Tarrant County College. He is the author of *The Finishing Stroke: Texans in the 1864 Tennessee Campaign* (2002) and *Granbury's Texas Brigade: Diehard Western Confederates* (2012), as well as numerous articles on Texas and Civil War history.

Jennifer M. Murray teaches history at the University of Virginia's College at Wise. She is the author of *"On a Great Battlefield": The Making, Management, and Memory of Gettysburg National Military Park, 1933–2013* (2014) and *The Civil War Begins, 1861* (2012). She also worked for the National Park Service at Gettysburg National Military Park.

Paul L. Schmelzer taught American history at Colorado State University at Pueblo and teaches military history at Fort Carson. He is currently working on a biography of U. S. Grant.

Brooks D. Simpson is the ASU Foundation Professor of History at Arizona State University. Among his books are *America's Civil War* (1996), *The Reconstruction Presidents* (1998, 2009) and *Ulysses S. Grant: Triumph over Adversity* (2000).

Timothy B. Smith, a veteran of the National Park Service, teaches history at the University of Tennessee at Martin. He is the author or editor of fourteen books on the Civil War, among them *Champion Hill: Decisive Battle for Vicksburg* (2004), *Corinth 1862: Siege, Battle, Occupation* (2012), and *Shiloh: Conquer or Perish* (2014). He is currently working on a volume covering Forts Henry and Donelson.

Scott L. Stabler, PhD, teaches history at Grand Valley State University, Allendale, Michigan. His published works include "Nuanced History: Westward Expansion in the Context of the Civil War and After," with Abilyn Janke, a comprehensive contextual multipart lesson plan for the *Journal of the West* (2012), and "Atlantic Slavery: Lost in Trans-lation," with Mary Owusu, in the *African Journal of Teacher Education* (2013).

Jonathan M. Steplyk earned his PhD at Texas Christian University, writing his dissertation on Civil War soldiers' attitudes toward killing in combat. He has also worked in the National Park Service at Harpers Ferry National Historical Park and Cedar Creek and Belle Grove National Historical Park.

D. L. Turner is an independent historian and author. She currently teaches U.S. and oral history at Chandler-Gilbert Community College at Chandler, Arizona.

William Lee White is a historian and park ranger at Chickamauga-Chattanooga National Battlefield Park and has worked for the National Park Service since 2000. His published works include a chapter in *A Meteor Shining Brightly: Essays on Major General Patrick R. Cleburne* (2000) and *Great Things Are Expected of Us: The Letters of Colonel C. Irvine Walker, 10th South Carolina, C.S.A.* (2009), coedited with Charles Denny Runion.

Steven E. Woodworth teaches at Texas Christian University and has authored, coauthored, or edited thirty-one books on the Civil War era, among them *Nothing but Victory: The Army of the Tennessee, 1861–1865* (2006) and *Jefferson Davis and His Generals: The Failure of Confederate Command in the West* (1990).

INDEX

Italicized page numbers indicate figures and maps.

CIVIL WAR CAMPAIGNS IN THE HEARTLAND

The area west of the Appalachian Mountains, known in Civil War parlance as "the West," has always stood in the shadow of the more famous events on the other side of the mountains, the eastern theater, where even today hundreds of thousands visit the storied Virginia battlefields. Nevertheless, a growing number of Civil War historians believe that the outcome of the war was actually decided in the region east of the Mississippi River and west of the watershed between the Atlantic and the Gulf of Mexico.

Modern historians began to rediscover the decisive western theater in the 1960s through the work of the late Thomas Lawrence Connelly, particularly his 1969 book *Army of the Heartland,* in which he analyzed the early years of the Confederacy's largest army in the West. Many able scholars have subsequently contributed to a growing historiography of the war in the West. Despite recent attention to the western theater, less is understood about the truly decisive campaigns of the war than is the case with the dramatic but ultimately indecisive clashes on the east coast.

Several years ago, three of Steven E. Woodworth's graduate students pointed out that the western theater possessed no series of detailed multi-author campaign studies comparable to the excellent and highly acclaimed series Gary W. Gallagher has edited on the campaigns of the eastern theater. Charles D. Grear, Jason M. Frawley, and David Slay joined together in suggesting that Woodworth ought to take the lead in filling the gap. The result is this series, its title a nod of appreciation to Professor Connelly. Its goals are to shed more light on the western campaigns and to spark new scholarship on the western theater.

CIVIL WAR CAMPAIGNS IN THE HEARTLAND SERIES

Published

The Shiloh Campaign

The Chickamauga Campaign

The Chattanooga Campaign

The Vicksburg Campaign, March 29–May 18, 1863

The Tennessee Campaign of 1864

To Be Published

The Vicksburg Assaults

Vicksburg Besieged

Forts Henry and Donelson

The Kentucky Campaign of 1862

Vicksburg: To Chickasaw Bayou

The Atlanta Campaign from Rocky Face Ridge to the Oostenaula: The Battle of Resaca

Vicksburg: Grant's Winter Endeavors

The Atlanta Campaign from the Oostenaula to the Etowa: Dallas, New Hope Church, and Pickett's Mill

The Atlanta Campaign from the Etowa to the Chattahoochee: The Battle of Kennesaw Mountain

Iuka and Corinth

Peachtree Creek

The Battle of Atlanta, July 22, 1864